Understanding Relations Between Scripts

Understanding Relations Between Scripts

The Aegean Writing Systems

edited by

Philippa M. Steele

OXBOW | books
Oxford & Philadelphia

First published in the United Kingdom in 2017. Reprinted in 2020 by
OXBOW BOOKS
The Old Music Hall, 106–108 Cowley Road, Oxford OX4 1JE

and in the United States by
OXBOW BOOKS
1950 Lawrence Road, Havertown, PA 19083

Paperback Edition: ISBN 978-1-78570-644-8
Digital Edition: ISBN 978-1-78570-645-5 (epub)

A CIP record for this book is available from the British Library

Library of Congress Cataloging-in-Publication Data

Names: Steele, Philippa M., editor.
Title: Understanding relations between scripts : the Aegean writing systems / edited by Philippa M. Steele.
Description: Oxford ; Philadelphia : Oxbow Books, 2017. | Includes bibliographical references.
Identifiers: LCCN 2017015744 (print) | LCCN 2017019903 (ebook) | ISBN 9781785706455 (epub) | ISBN 9781785706462 (mobi) | ISBN 9781785706479 (pdf) | ISBN 9781785706448 (pb)
Subjects: LCSH: Inscriptions, Linear B. | Inscriptions, Cypro-Minoan. | Inscriptions, Linear A. | Writing--Aegean Sea Region.
Classification: LCC P1035 (ebook) | LCC P1035 .U53 2017 (print) | DDC 487/.1--dc23
LC record available at https://lccn.loc.gov/2017015744

For a complete list of Oxbow titles, please contact:

UNITED KINGDOM
Oxbow Books
Telephone (01865) 241249, Fax (01865) 794449
Email: oxbow@oxbowbooks.com
www.oxbowbooks.com

UNITED STATES OF AMERICA
Oxbow Books
Telephone (800) 791-9354, Fax (610) 853-9146
Email: queries@casemateacademic.com
www.casemateacademic.com/oxbow

Oxbow Books is part of the Casemate Group

Front cover image: Linear B tablet. Photograph courtesy of Silvia Ferrara.
Back cover: Cypro-Minoan tablet. Photograph courtesy of Silvia Ferrara.

To the memory of our dear friend, Anna Morpurgo Davies

The conference attendants, taken at the dinner in the Parlour Room, Magdalene College. Photo by James Bowe.

Cake depicting the early Cypro-Minoan inscription ##001 ENKO Atab 001, made by Anna Judson. Photo by Anna Judson.

Contents

List of figures

Preface

This book is the outcome of a conference held in Cambridge on 20–21 March 2015 in the Faculty of Classics of the University of Cambridge. Following a partial solar eclipse on the morning of the 20th (sadly obscured by cloud in Cambridge), nine papers were delivered by this volume's contributors over the course of the two days, culminating in a delightful (and delicious) conference dinner hosted by Magdalene College.

Many thanks are owed to all involved in the conference. My first thanks go to the speakers/contributors themselves, for being so generous with their time and ideas, as well as to everyone who attended the conference, for making it such a success. I know that the conversations and discussions that went on during the event added a great deal to this ensuing publication. Over the two days, everything was set up for us beautifully by the Faculty's custodian, Tony Brinkman, and there were several people who volunteered to help out with running the event: above all my partner, James Bowe, who was working wonders behind the scenes throughout, along with my colleagues Ester Salgarella, Matthew Scarborough, Sarah Finlayson, Moreed Arbabzadah and even two of the speakers themselves, Anna Judson and Roeland Decorte. The conference would not have been able to take place without the generous contributions of the British Academy and the John Chadwick Fund of the Faculty of Classics.

Further thanks are owed to everyone who had a hand in shaping this edited volume. Giorgios Douros's freely available Aegean, Cretan and Cypro-Minoan fonts were indispensable in the preparation of most chapters, where special characters were essential to illustrate our arguments. The editors at Oxbow have been very helpful at every turn, and I would like to express my gratitude in particular to Clare Litt, Julie Gardiner, Mette Bundgaard, Katie Allen, Becca Watson and Hannah McAdams for all their hard work and attention to detail at every stage of the book's production. I am also grateful to everyone who played a role in the peer review process in the early stages of manuscript preparation, and to the contributors for dealing attentively with queries and edits. My Mother, Anne, deserves special mention for the immeasurable help she has given me throughout my editorial activities on this book. The final stages of the publication process were completed during my tenure of a European Research Council grant (no. 677758), as Principal Investigator of the project *Contexts of and Relations between Early Writing Systems* (CREWS), also held at the Faculty of Classics in Cambridge.

My final words are devoted to a dear colleague and friend, who is sadly no longer with us: Anna Morpurgo Davies. It is impossible to express in a few words just how great a debt is owed to Anna by all of us who work in ancient linguistics and epigraphy, not only for her insights and intellect but above all for her generosity and kindness. I will always be grateful for the support she gave me when I was researching for my doctorate and forging the beginnings of an academic career, for writing references and giving advice, for her incisive comments on my work, and above all for her warmth and good humour. This volume is dedicated to her memory.

Abbreviations

CDE	Chantraine, P. (1968) *Dictionnaire étymologique de la langue grecque: Histoire des Mots*, Paris.
CHIC	Olivier, J. P. and Godart, L. (1996) *Corpus Hieroglyphicarum Inscriptionum Cretae, Études Crétoises* 31, Paris.
CM I	Ferrara, S. (2012) *Cypro-Minoan Inscriptions. Volume I: Analysis*, Oxford.
CM II	Ferrara, S. (2013) *Cypro-Minoan Inscriptions. Volume II: Corpus*, Oxford.
CMS	*Corpus of Minoan and Mycenaean Seals*, Heidelberg.
CMS II.6	Platon, N., Müller, W. and Pini, I. with contributions of other authors (1999) *Iraklion, Archäologisches Museum. Teil 6. Die Siegelabdrücke von Aj. Triada und anderen zentral- und ostkretischen Fundorten, unter Einbeziehung von Funden aus anderen Museen.* Corpus der minoischen und mykenischen Siegel II:6. Berlin, Mann.
CMS V S3	Pini, I. with contributions of numerous other authors (2004) *Kleinere Griechische Sammlungen. Supplementum 3. Neufunde aus Griechenland und der Westlichen Türkei.* Corpus der minoischen und mykenischen Siegel V Supplement 3: 1–2. Berlin, Mann.
COMIK	Chadwick, J., Godart, L., Killen, J.T., Olivier, J.-P., Sacconi, A. and Sakellarakis, I.A. (1986–1998) *Corpus of Mycenaean Inscriptions from Knossos, vols 1–4. Istituto per gli Studi Micenei ed Egeo-Anatolici: Incunabula Graeca LXXXVIII*, Cambridge/Roma.
DMic	Aura Jorro, F. (1985–1993) *Diccionario micénico, vols I–II. Diccionario griego-español.* Madrid, Instituto de Filología.
Docs[1]	Ventris, M. G. F. and Chadwick, J. (1956) *Documents in Mycenaean Greek*, Cambridge.
Docs[2]	Ventris, M. G. F. and Chadwick, J. (1973) *Documents in Mycenaean Greek*, 2nd edition, Cambridge.
GORILA	Godart, L. and Olivier, J.-P. (1976–1985) *Recueil des Inscriptions en Linéaire A*, vols I–V, Études Crétoises 21: 1–5, Paris.
HoChyMin	Olivier, J.-P. (with the collaboration of F. Vandenabeele) (2007) *Édition holistique des textes chypro-minoens*, Pisa/Rome.
ICS[2]	Masson, O. (1983) *Les inscriptions chypriotes syllabiques: recueil critique et commentée*, 2nd edition, Réimpression augmentée, Paris.
Kouklia	Masson. O and Mitford, T. B. (1986) *The Syllabic Inscriptions of Kouklia*, Constanz.
LGPN IIIA	Fraser, P.M. and Matthews, E. (1997) *A Lexicon of Greek Personal Names*, vol. IIIA, *Peloponnese, Western Greece, Sicily, Magna Graecia*, Oxford.

LIV Rix, H., Kümmel, M., Zehnder, T., Lipp, R. and Schirmer, B. (2001) *Lexikon der indogermanischen Verben. Die Wurzeln und ihre Primärstammbildungen*, 2nd edition, Wiesbaden.

LSJ Liddell, H.G., Scott, R., Jones, H.S., McKenzie, R. and Glare, P.G.W. (1996) *A Greek-English Lexicon*, 9th edition, with a revised supplement, Oxford.

Μεθώνη 2012 M. Besios, Tsiphopoulos, G. and Kotsonas, A. (eds 2012), Μεθώνη Πιερίας ι: Επιγραφές, χαράγματα και εμπορικά σύμβολα στη γεωμετρική και αρχαϊκή κεραμική από το 'Υπόγειο' της Μεθώνης Πιερίας στη Μακεδονία, Thessaloniki.

NIL Wodtko, D. S., Irslinger, B. and Schneider, C. (2008) *Nomina im indogermanischen Lexikon*, Heidelberg.

PMK1 Evans, A. (1921) *The Palace of Minos at Knossos*, vol. I.

PMK4 Evans, A. (1935) *The Palace of Minos at Knossos*, vol. IV.

Rantidi Mitford, T. B. and Masson. O (1983) *The Syllabic Inscriptions of Rantidi-Paphos*, Constanz.

SM1 Evans, A. J. (1909) *Scripta Minoa, The Written Documents of Minoan Crete with Special Reference to the Archives of Knossos*, Volume I, Oxford.

SM2 Evans, A. J. (1952) *Scripta Minoa II, The Written Documents of Minoan Crete with Special Reference to Archives of Knossos* (ed. Myres, J.), Oxford.

Chapter 1

Introduction: The Aegean writing systems

Philippa M. Steele

1. Introduction

Many writing systems were in use across the ancient world, and while a few of them began as primary inventions (i.e. created *ex nihilo*, without influence from any other writing system), the majority bear some relationship with other known scripts. Since the first attested examples of writing systems in the 4th and 3rd millennia BC, we know of numerous instances when writing was passed on from one group of people to another, with each process of adoption usually accompanied by one of adaptation. The results of such processes are writing systems that we classify as separate entities, sharing some properties with each other while in other aspects they differ or innovate. While individual ancient writing systems have not themselves been neglected in scholarship, there has been quite limited and indirect treatment of the ways in which we can study relationships between them, based on the evidence that has survived. This is where the *Understanding Relations Between Scripts* (URBS) series aims to redress some of the overlooked or underrepresented questions regarding script adaptations and how we understand them, beginning with this first volume focused on the syllabic writing systems of the ancient Aegean.

There are many questions that we might ask about how different writing systems are connected to each other, from both epigraphic and contextual points of view. How do we tell one script from another? What are the indicators that tell us how different scripts are related to each other? How does the process of adapting an old script to create a new one work? What are the motivations behind adapting the new script? How do the adaptors communicate with the original possessors of the script they are borrowing? What is the socio-cultural background to these communications and processes? The conclusions we draw and the assumptions we make about the participants in, and the contexts of, script adaptations will necessarily play an important role in our understanding of the propagation of writing. An attempt to answer some of these questions, and an investigation into the methodology we might be able to use to answer them, therefore has the potential to change our view not only of the technology of writing itself, but also of the linguistic and cultural contexts in which writing was used and developed.

This volume concentrates on one particular set of related scripts, which have been termed in the book's title 'the Aegean writing systems'. These are writing systems of the Middle and Late Bronze Age Aegean, attested mainly on Crete and the Greek mainland, as well as some related systems of Late Bronze Age and Iron Age Cyprus. Each of the volume's contributors deals with one or more of these scripts, looking at issues of adaptation and context in order to develop our understanding of how and why writing was passed on. This introduction will begin with a brief overview of the scripts under consideration, aimed at non-specialists or at those who might be more familiar with one of the scripts than with the others, followed by a description of the book's chapters and their themes.

2. The Aegean writing systems

Writing first appeared on Crete in the Early Minoan III or Middle Minoan I period, around the beginning of the 2nd millennium BC. Although it has been suggested that the concept of writing was borrowed from elsewhere in the Mediterranean, with Egypt as the most cited candidate, it is impossible to be certain what prompted the initial impetus to begin using writing. Some of the very earliest inscriptions have often been classed as belonging to the 'Archanes script', consisting of a small number of undeciphered inscribed seal stones that are sometimes (but not always) considered to be written in a separate script, otherwise unattested. However, they are perhaps better included with the main body of material belonging to the first of the well attested writing systems, Cretan Hieroglyphic.

Cretan Hieroglyphic survives in about 300 inscriptions, many of which are on seal stones although there are also numerous clay documents and other objects, dating between the beginning of the 2nd millennium and about 1600 BC (up to the end of the Middle Minoan III period). Like the names for most other scripts of the Aegean group, the term 'Cretan Hieroglyphic' was coined by the archaeologist Arthur Evans, who famously excavated Knossos and published the first treatments of Aegean writing systems in the early 20th century in the first volume of *Scripta Minoa*. The basis for labelling it 'hieroglyphic' was that its signs are relatively pictorial in nature and often have the appearance of real-world referents such as people, animals and objects. However, the script is not a 'pictographic' one (i.e. one where most signs represent whole words or concepts) and is in type quite different from the Egyptian Hieroglyphic script that inspired its name. Although it is considered undeciphered,[1]

[1] The term 'undeciphered', however, should be treated with some caution. We can in fact be reasonably certain of the values of a number of Cretan Hieroglyphic signs, just as we can to an even greater degree for the next of the Aegean scripts, Linear A (the chapter by Steele and Meißner, this volume, is concerned with just this issue). The languages underlying these two writing systems remain mysterious, but that

it appears to be a script of a type closely related to those of the other Aegean scripts, namely one consisting of a core of syllabic signs (where each sign represents a vowel or a consonant + vowel combination) that also features an ideographic component (a group of signs representing whole words or concepts employed alongside the syllabic signs that were used to spell words out).

The next script was termed Linear A by Evans, in reference to the less pictorial and more abstract-looking nature of many of its signs. Linear A makes its first appearance not long after Cretan Hieroglyphic, *c.* 1900 or 1800 BC (Middle Minoan IB–II) and co-exists with it for some hundreds of years. As far as we know from surviving inscriptions, Linear A continued in use for 100 years or more after the last attested Cretan Hieroglyphic inscriptions, making its final appearances around the Late Minoan IA period or even slightly later (*c.* 1500–1450 BC). Its inscriptions come from both administrative and private contexts, ranging from clay tablets and sealings to votive inscriptions and texts on luxury items including jewellery, and are found mainly in Crete but also in the Greek islands and even on the mainland. Since it is better attested than Cretan Hieroglyphic with around 1,500 surviving inscriptions, our resources for studying Linear A enable a finer appreciation of the structure and use of the script. Like Cretan Hieroglyphic and the other related scripts, it is a syllabic system, with a supplementary set of ideographic signs used to represent quantities and commodities whose use is best attested in the administrative documents originating from Cretan sites such as Knossos, Hagia Triada and Phaistos. The content of the Linear A inscriptions cannot be understood in any detail, however, because the language in which they are written (often referred to as 'Minoan'[2]) remains unidentified.

The Linear B script was adapted from Linear A, presumably around or before the period of its first attestations in Late Minoan II–IIIA1 (*c.* 1450–1400 BC); in scholarship this period is now referred to as 'Mycenaean', continuing until the final destruction of the Mycenaean palaces on the Greek mainland *c.* 1200 BC (the end of Late Helladic IIIB). The best attested of all the Aegean scripts, Linear B was deciphered[3] in the mid-20th century by Michael Ventris, who collaborated with John Chadwick and built on the earlier work of scholars including Alice Kober and Emmett L. Bennett. The decipherment was undoubtedly aided by the serendipitous fact that what was written in this script was an early form of a language well understood and surviving

---

does not mean that we cannot 'read' sequences written in them to some extent. A script can be partially deciphered without achieving the ultimate aim of understanding fully the content of its inscriptions as well as the values of its signs.

[2] Whether Cretan Hieroglyphic and Linear A were used to write the same language or different ones similarly remains an open question.

[3] Again the term 'deciphered' can be considered problematic: while we know the values of the majority of its signs and understand its underlying language reasonably well, there remain some unknown factors concerning the signs of Linear B and the interpretation of many words written in it.

up to the modern day, namely Greek. For this reason, the study of Linear B is able to reach a level of refinement far surpassing anything that can be done with Cretan Hieroglyphic or Linear A: we have a good understanding of the repertoire of the script's signs, the spelling rules employed by its users (necessary because each sign represents an open syllable, which presents a challenge when trying to write the consonant-clusters and final consonants that are common in Greek), the immediate and wider administrative context of its use and the content of the documents written in it. Although there remain some uncertainties, overall the corpus of Linear B material, with *c.* 6,000 documents, provides an invaluable record of the early Greek language and the workings of the Mycenaean palaces, allowing historical as well as linguistic, epigraphic and archaeological analysis.

The writing tradition of the Bronze Age Aegean was at some point carried eastwards. In the Late Cypriot I period (the 16th or early 15th century BC), the technology of writing began to appear on the eastern Mediterranean island of Cyprus in a form that was clearly related to the writing systems of Crete and the Aegean, labelled by Evans as 'Cypro-Minoan' to highlight its connection to the other scripts. Too early to have been adapted directly from Linear B, it is likely that it was adapted from the earlier script Linear A, although this is difficult to confirm beyond doubt because the repertoire of signs appears somewhat different and must have undergone some changes in the new script's creation. With only *c.* 250 inscriptions of very disparate types, most of them very short, it is even difficult to tell whether only one or multiple writing systems existed in Cyprus during the Late Bronze Age, and, as with Cretan Hieroglyphic and Linear A, we cannot understand the content of the texts.

Finally, by the 8th century BC a new script had been adapted from Cypro-Minoan on Cyprus. This is usually labelled the Cypriot Syllabic script, although some different names for it persist in scholarship, including the Classical Cypriot Syllabary and, more recently, the Cypro-Greek Syllabary (by analogy with the term Cypro-Minoan). The new script again has advantages over the earlier Cypriot one(s) in terms of our ability to understand it, not only in the larger number of surviving inscriptions (*c.* 1,500) but also in the fact that, like Linear B, it was used to record the Greek language. Alongside one or more other languages that are now poorly understood (the best attested of which is usually termed 'Eteocypriot'), the Cypriot Greek dialect stands out as the only form of Greek used during the 1st millennium BC that was written in a syllabic script, while the rest of the Greek-speaking world was using the Greek alphabet (itself derived from the Phoenician script in or by the 8th century BC). The last of the surviving Cypriot Syllabic inscriptions date from well into the Hellenistic period, probably the 3rd or 2nd century BC. The script was deciphered in the 19th century, largely by the Assyriologist George Smith, with the aid of a bilingual text in Phoenician and Greek. Because we can read many of the inscriptions written in it, we know that the script was composed of a core of signs representing open syllables, just as in Linear B, although it lacked any ideographic component beyond basic numerals. As the first of the Aegean scripts to be deciphered, it has long aided our understanding of the type and composition of the other writing systems.

3. The contents and structure of this volume

Following this introduction, the first two chapters deal with the emergence of writing in the Aegean and the question of how the impetus for literacy arose around the end of the Early Minoan period. Chapter 2 (Silvia Ferrara) introduces the problem of how and why writing systems are acquired, emphasising the degree of creativity that is essential in the adaptation of a new script, and looking at not only the beginnings of writing in Crete and Cyprus but also at other areas such as Anatolia and Ugarit. In assessing these factors she shows the importance of considering both the linguistic features that to some extent dictated the type and composition of a new script and the social and cultural context in which writing was perceived as a necessary or desirable technology to develop. The following Chapter 3 (Roeland Decorte) focuses on the earliest of the Aegean scripts, Cretan Hieroglyphic, and the problematic and arguably false division that has often been drawn between early writing and decorative or artistic elements. In a writing system whose very pictorial nature affected scholarly perceptions of it from the start, this has had a significant effect on the analysis of its sign repertoire: challenging previous assumptions about what constitutes a script sign, and in particular what does not, has the potential to open up a wealth of new evidence for this writing system.

The next two papers turn to the question of how the administrative context of much surviving writing from early Crete affected the development of Cretan scripts and the documents written in them. Chapter 4 (Helena Tomas) considers where, when, why and how Linear B was adapted and demonstrates the importance of separating the development of the script itself from the contexts and inscription types in which it was used. While the Linear B script was clearly developed directly from Linear A, the administrative system in which its texts existed appears to have been influenced at least in part also by the types and usage of Cretan Hieroglyphic documents. Chapter 5 (Vassilis Petrakis) also concerns the development of Linear B document types, and the links between Cretan Hieroglyphic, Linear A and Linear B administrative systems. Taking a different approach, he argues for the appropriation of existing bureaucratic practices alongside new innovative developments as the Mycenaean administration came to dominate in north-central Crete. This also has repercussions for our understanding of the preceding administrative system, in which the co-existence of Cretan Hieroglyphic and Linear A has never satisfactorily been explained.

The following two papers shift the emphasis from the context of writing to the composition of the writing systems themselves, with two chapters focusing on the adaptation of Linear B from Linear A. Chapter 6 (Philippa Steele and Torsten Meißner) looks at the sign values of both scripts and shows that even though Linear A has traditionally been labelled an 'undeciphered' script, we can be reasonably confident that we know the values of most of its signs. The existence of sign sequences shared by both Linear A and Linear B, along with the remarkable stability of sign values in related scripts across the Aegean and Cyprus and several other features, points conclusively towards an adaptation process in which the values of Linear A signs were borrowed along with the signs themselves in the creation of Linear B. Chapter 7 (Anna Judson) focuses on a subsection of the Linear B syllabary, a set of 'extra' signs that provided optional variant spellings used by Mycenaean scribes. Through an analysis of the use and palaeography of these signs, she demonstrates that they are not useful indicators of the structure or underlying linguistic features of Minoan Linear A, as has often been assumed, while conversely they offer a valuable insight into the adaptation and early development of Linear B.

The final three papers focus on the related writing systems found on Cyprus, including their relationship with the other Aegean scripts and their separate development on the island. Chapter 8 (Miguel Valério) takes a palaeographical approach to the connections between Linear A and Cypro-Minoan, looking in detail at the ways in which individual signs developed in the adaptation of Cypriot writing. The combination of script comparison with an internal analysis of the signs as they appear in inscriptions allows a greater degree of certainty in the reconstruction of Cypro-Minoan sign values. This is followed by Chapter 9 (Yves Duhoux), in which the long-hypothesised internal divisions in the Cypro-Minoan repertoire are considered via a statistical analysis. By comparing the signs attested within particular groups of Cypro-Minoan inscriptions, he shows that Cypro-Minoan writing at Ugarit (labelled 'CM3') appears to have different characteristics from the samples originating from the mainland, and suggests that a different Cypro-Minoan writing tradition was in use at this site. Finally, Chapter 10 (Markus Egetmeyer) focuses on the inscriptions of the Cypriot Geometric period, sparked by the recent discovery of two new inscriptions. His discussion of the epigraphic material shows the importance of considering not only developments in script signs and their shapes, but also the cultural background of script use, in an attempt to understand the development of the new Cypro-Greek Syllabary from earlier Cypro-Minoan.

Chapter 2

Another beginning's end: Secondary script formation in the Aegean and the Eastern Mediterranean[1]

Silvia Ferrara

> 'Hegel seems to be always wanting to say that things which look different are really the same. Whereas my interest is in showing that things which look the same are really different'.
> Wittgenstein

> 'Every new beginning comes from some other beginning's end'.
> Semisonic, *Closing Time*

> 'That was their genius, and that made a heap of difference'.
> Weingarten (2005, 765)

1. Re-thinking early writing in the Eastern Mediterranean

Recent contributions on literacy have focused on analysing writing as a mode of communication, rather than a technology, and as an entity that is socially learned, shaped, or transmitted (Houston 2004a, 2012; Baines *et al.* 2008), rather than a tool for language notation. This approach is embedded in a model whose focus is to integrate literacy into social practices, attaching an ideological significance to writing (Basso 1974; Street 1984, 1993). From this perspective, writing becomes a subject worthy of ethnographic attention, to be analysed as the product of practices within the specificity of a cultural setting. Recent anthropological narratives also mark the

[1] I am most grateful to Philippa Steele for having organised such a stimulating and entertaining conference and for having invited me to take part, and to the other participants for their lively and thought-provoking contributions. I am also grateful to John Bennet and Orazio Cappello for having read previous drafts of the manuscript. The final draft was written at the Institute of Classical Studies, School of Advanced Studies, during a Visiting Fellowship. I thank the Director, Greg Woolf, for his support.

connections of scripts to the social and political needs of power structures within society, constructing them as artefacts of culture, beyond language notation (Cardona 1981; Keller-Cohen 1994; Gaur 2000).

The important contributions in the publications mentioned above consider general and particular aspects related to the creation, development and disappearance of writing systems in a multitude of areas for which a literate culture is attested. Scholars specialising in the scripts of Egypt, Mesoamerica, Mesopotamia, China, India, and Japan have developed a comprehensive explanation of the phenomenon of writing on a global scale. With exceptions (Bennet 2008), the Aegean features very little, and the broader Mediterranean basin is treated in a few articles with a regional focus (Hawkins 2008, for Anatolia; Lomas 2008, for Italy). A more in-depth, wide-ranging investigation is needed. The focus should be on origins (script creation and adaptation in the many cultures of the Mediterranean) seeking to investigate developments (the regional trajectories in which forms of writing are used) and to assess transmissions (the choices that are made when a template is adapted into local contexts at the hands of local groups). This perspective goes beyond the scope of linguistics or archaeology, as it seeks to investigate the contextual variables that influence the phenomenon of writing in general, without any particular overarching slant. What follows, therefore, intends to address all the issues mentioned above, which centre on the contexts in which the formative stages of secondary scripts occurred in the Aegean and the wider Eastern Mediterranean.

We shall consider four case studies that appear to be of specific socio-cultural importance, scattered at the cardinal points of the Mediterranean basin: Crete, Cyprus, Anatolia, and Syria. The perspective adopted here will focus on the beginnings of literacy in regional contexts during different phases of the 2nd millennium BC, spanning from the earliest attestations of writing on Crete (Cretan Hieroglyphic), the re-shaping of Cretan models on Cyprus (Cypro-Minoan), the re-engineering of a pictographic template in the Anatolian peninsula (Anatolian Hieroglyphic), and the formation of an alphabetic system at Ugarit, towards the end of the millennium (Ugaritic alphabet).

On a general level, when creating secondary scripts, modifications of the template source can vary a great deal. As items of inherited practice, structure, and content, model scripts can be tinkered with by vigorous reaction, or can equally be left almost unchanged by cultural inertia (Houston and Rojas 2015, forthcoming). In between, a whole gamut of manoeuvring is possible. For the Eastern Mediterranean, together with attending to the fundamental question of how this spectrum of possibilities can be understood, we need to broaden the scope of semiotic significance of secondary scripts, and explain their genesis for the particular cases mentioned above. These cases are paradigmatic of a period in which pre-existing literate cultures pave the way for a number of new reinventions, during centuries in which intercultural communication and contacts and exchanges of an ideological nature are thriving. The difficulty lies in offering valid parameters that can explain different processes of literacy acquisition.

These issues have already been considered in more general terms, by establishing models that attempt to explain secondary script formation (Daniels 2000, 2003, 2006, 2007; Salomon 2012). In these, the fundamental prompt for any new script invention pivots on language change. For instance, Daniels maintains that language change can trigger script variation through the alteration, addition, and reshuffling of signs. He proposes a classification of possible transfers, which are based on different levels of phonological understanding of the source by the adapters. Daniels thus envisions a gentle adaptation ('adaptive reuse') in which changes are minimal, to a shift in which adapters apply more radical changes, calibrating their intervention on variable knowledge of the template, from sophisticated ('scholarly input model') to unsophisticated ('misunderstanding model') (Daniels 2006, 2007). Salomon, conversely, takes a more systemic and general view of modifications engendered by unrelated language shifts (Salomon 2012).

Recently, a perspective that consciously excludes language as a determining factor in script transfers has focused on the materiality of script as a cultural symbol of expression, and as a self-contained device significant beyond language recording (Houston and Rojas 2015 forthcoming). Drawing on a modified version of the three-category scheme developed by Daniels, Houston and Rojas offer an alternative scheme to describe three kinds of secondary invention. The first, defined as 'accommodation', describes a slow and long-term adjustment of a writing system within a single stream of broader tradition. The second, termed 'contrast', takes place rapidly and involves more radical changes. The third is 'rupture' and represents the most radical and rapid change of all, in which form is pervasively modified. The three models are charted in Table 2.1.

While all contributions acknowledge that changes in script transfers may be multifaceted, their position in relation to the role played by language varies fundamentally. Thus, it may be instructive to probe into this different approach: how much importance should be attributed to language change when scripts are transferred from a source to a receiver? Script and language constitute very separate entities, whose existence and purpose may at times intersect, but may also follow independent and autonomous trajectories (Morpurgo Davies 1986; Morpurgo Davies and Olivier 2012). There are many examples of writing systems that are replaced or remoulded, regardless of the intention to mark significant phonological differentiation. This means that deliberated choices may be made when a new script is created that

Table 2.1: Chart of the models explaining script transfers

1	P. Daniels (2000, 2007)	Adaptive reuse Scholarly input model Misunderstanding model
2	R. Salomon (2012)	Superficial/Systemic change
3	S. D. Houston and F. Rojas (2015)	Accommodation Contrast Rupture

forsake a distinctive intention to stress linguistic, or even dialectal, differentiation. As pointed out by Houston and Rojas, 'a writing system is not only about recording sound: it also figures into assertions of identity, of wanting to be like those using the source or craving a distinct or opposed identity' (2015).

In any case, the significance of writing as identity marker and as technological vehicle for language unveils a very complex interface. This has been explored in depth at a theoretical level, but predominantly in terms of alphabetic literacy. Explanations have ranged from Enlightenment-inspired universalist views that emphasise the ground-breaking impact of the alphabet as a democratising instrument of progress (Diringer 1948; Goody and Watt 1963; Havelock 1982), to Romantic theories that assign writing to a uniform cultural package that comprises other features such as language, land or ethnicity (Herder 1985; Bauman and Briggs 2003; Dietrich and Loretz 1988, for the cuneiform alphabets; Sanders 2009, for a general critique).

It seems that no theoretical framework that either reduces writing to a technology or confines it to an ethnic cauldron has proven satisfactory. Scripts are fluid components of material culture that need to be explained without recurring to any modelling that falls short of viewing their semiotic complexity. As Sanders claims, 'the linkages that ancient writers made between language, script and culture are important, but they were the result of deliberate creative effort, not a natural uniform, or spontaneous phenomenon' (Sanders 2009, 42). So their flexible, (often) changing shape and meaning can only be understood if particular attention is paid to the social circumstances in which adopters operate, to the cultural significance they may (or may not) attach to writing, to the degree of awareness of its potential value, and to the intentions projected when a specific graphic template is chosen. At the same time, scripts are not genetic organisms that spring off or evolve biologically from a parent, but rather entities that reflect historical conditions, human input and deliberate intention (Houston 2004b, 279).

Any special link that may tie script and language is context-orientated and, as such, the result of intervention, modulation, mediation. If ever language plays a role in script adaptations, it plays a minor one. This is true in a great number of cases (to quote just a few, the Turkish alphabetic reform, Lewis 1999, the Italic alphabets, Lomas 2007, 2008, Anatolian Hieroglyphic, Payne 2008, the epichoric Greek alphabets, Luraghi 2010). In light of this, what follows below will consciously concentrate on the pragmatics of script creation in the Eastern Mediterranean of the 2nd millennium BC from a social and cultural perspective. The overall aim is to investigate the choices, objectives and perceptions projected by its makers and users.

2. Laying the foundations: primary inventions

Before turning to the earliest case of secondary script creation in the Mediterranean, it is worth casting an eye on several features observable in first inventions and then compare them. They will be useful to explain several idiosyncrasies in the Cretan

Table 2.2: Structural and functional characteristics of primary systems of writing

	Primary Systems
Structure	Pronounced iconicity (Logo)syllabary Under-grammaticalisation (Phonic opacity, limited semantic categories, limited syntax)
Function	Limited application

and Anatolian hieroglyphs. Primary inventions of scripts are of limited occurrence. They took place probably four times in the entire history of writing, broadly in Eurasia and South America (Sumer, Egypt, China, and Mesoamerica) at different periods of time, from the end of the 4th millennium, to the beginning of the 1st BC (Michalowski 1994; Baines 2004; Houston 2004a; Boltz 1986, 2001). All other ancient writing systems represent secondary derivations of these four inventions, whether directly or indirectly.

It is a relatively recent suggestion that there were multiple attestations of pristine creations. For decades, a monogenetic view remained prevalent, that considered writing as a single original invention of the Sumerians, who devised the cuneiform system that became template for all other scripts (Gelb 1963). Now that discrete acts of script invention, separate and independent, can be reconstructed, further probing can be made into identifying similarities in first writing. Naturally, not all primary systems are identical, but, despite being relatively separated in time and place, they tend to share a set of structural and functional features that need to be explained before we can discuss secondary creations.

These common features are summarised schematically in Table 2.2, where a distinction is made between structural patterns (namely those related to the organisation of the sign repertoire in terms of shape, sound and meaning) and functional patterns (namely in the application and use of the systems). In what follows, each feature is treated separately.

2.1. Iconicity

In terms of structure, all first writing begins with pronounced graphic iconicity, expressed through a set of pictorially recognisable signs that have a correspondence with referents present in the natural world or as objects of specific material culture. These are expressed by different degrees of sign-shape stylisation and abstraction (Justeson and Mathews 1990). Houston notes that such elements, for instance in early Olmec, essentially constitute emblems (see also the Chinese 'clan name' inscriptions discussed by Boltz 1986, 421), open to being recognised by different groups who can interpret their meaning beyond the specificity of any one language (Houston 2004b, 284). Order, coherence and repetition of iconographic elements progressively pave the way for language notation. This may not apply indiscriminately, however. If it appears to be true for the Mesoamerican context and for other pristine inventions in Mesopotamia (Cooper 2004, 84; Woods 2010) and Egypt (Baines 2004), the earliest examples for Shang writing in China do not seem to resort to a representational set as foundation for the sign repertoire, nor do they seem to evolve from pictorial to more abstract in a linear fashion (Bagley 2004, 207–8, 227, and 246, n. 74).

Pictorial signs in emergent writing systems, therefore, do not work in the same way, nor can they be taken as uniform entities. The relationship between the written sign and its object can be classified, as suggested by Peirce, by a tripartite system of iconic, indexical and symbolic representation (Robertson 2004, with direct references to Peirce's work, Peirce 1931–58). Icons tend to work like pictograms, representing by similarity or analogy pictures of the object signified; indexes point to a less direct image of what the sign signifies, semantically indicating it by metonym or synecdoche; and symbols indicate an arbitrary or habitual relationship to what the sign signifies. In the spectrum between iconic pictographs and symbolic ideograms, imagistic representation decreases progressively from icon to symbol. The unwritten law is that at the beginning of writing, a logograph will change from icon to symbol, but not the reverse (Robertson 2004, 26).

Primary writing systems may retain or lose iconicity in time and with incremental use, but no trajectory is the same. Even in cases where iconicity is pronounced all along, the sign-repertoire is never entirely pictographic, as schematic signs form part of it from the beginning. Realistic iconism can thus be a primary characteristic, but it always co-exists side-by-side with a number of abstract, symbolic signs. In the case of cuneiform, for instance, signs that originally had a pictographic relationship with their referents gradually lost this iconic quality, and the script assumed its cuneiform appearance relatively soon, by the time of the Uruk III period, at the end of the 4th millennium BC (Cooper 2004; Woods 2010, 37). The same applies to Chinese (Boltz 1986, 4). In Maya and Egyptian, iconicity was retained for the duration of their use, no doubt for the aesthetic impact the script had on monumental engravings.

2.2. Syllable

The second structural aspect of primary scripts is that they are organised around the basic phonotactical principle of syllabic recording. According to Daniels, all pristine scripts happen to record monosyllabic languages, and therefore the most salient element of speech coincides with the most salient constituent of grammar (Daniels 1992, see also Harbsmeier 1988). This aspect, however, may be more 'biological' than constrained by language structure. Recent cases of script invention such as the systems devised for the Bamum (Cameroon), Cherokee (North American), Woleian (Caroline Islands), Njduka (Surinam) languages – scripts that are not, of course, invented *ex nihilo*, but are created for languages to be recorded for the first time – testify that syllables seem to be a natural go-to choice as structural units for new scripts.

Language or linguistic awareness may play a marginal role *vis à vis* that played by cognitive development.[2] Proto-syllables may have constituted the primitive cognitive units of phonic utterance in hominids, where each syllable embodied a holistic vocal gesture (MacNeilage and Davis 2000). This should hardly surprise. The syllable is a much more natural element of articulation than the phoneme (Jackendoff 2002), and the rhythmic organisation of language (be it stress or timing) effortlessly revolves around it in articulating the close-open-close cycles of the mouth. Indeed, this is how children normally organise their phonetic gesture from the beginning (Levelt 1994), and this tendency to segment syllables more readily than phonemes continues to improve with age (Liberman *et al.* 1974). If, in turn, the syllable plays such an important role in language perception and production, it will follow that it should play an equally crucial role in translating speech to writing. The only diversion is Egyptian Hieroglyphic, which is logoconsonantal, but its status as primary invention is *sub judice* (Ray 1986, 309; Postgate *et al.* 1995, 463; Trigger 2004, 52, 61). If Sumerian cuneiform influenced its creation more than hitherto assumed, the working syllabic principle of Sumerian could have undergone a thorough and conscious reorganisation into consonantal structure.

2.3. Syntax development

A third structural aspect charts the accuracy with which pristine scripts record language at the phonic, semantic, morphological, and syntactical level. In the early stages, grammaticalisation, i.e. the process by which a lexical item or a sequence of items become grammatical morphemes, is always underdeveloped. This implies that, semantically, few categories (which constitute the basis of lexical lists, for instance) are recorded. Syntax is underspecified. But if early scripts are characterised by incompleteness, they are also defined by imprecise phonetic coding. In fact, the incipient stages defined as proto-writing (for proto-cuneiform see Englund 1998; Damerow 1999), are not constrained by the specificity of speech. In some cases, as for early Egyptian, the language recorded cannot even be identified (Baines 2004). Substantial oral explanation was, and is, the only avenue for understanding meaning. This, for instance, applies to the earliest attestations of Egyptian. In the Maya system too, sequential speech recording came at a relatively late stage, after a step-by-step series of adjustments and reshuffling of semantic principles for its glyphs.

If sequential recording of speech is underspecified, the application of early scripts also was, in all instances, restricted to defined contexts for specific activities (Trigger 2004, 48; Cooper 2004, 80). Function was inherently limited. Its later expansion to

[2] The suggestion that pre-existing familiarity with literate cultures can affect typology when a new syllabary is created (a process defined by Daniels as 'grammatogeny'), with abugidas being the result of sophisticated knowledge, while syllabaries are the result of the opposite (Daniels 2000), is schematic, as the outcome of script creation cannot be over-systematised into structurally determined trajectories that underplay creative input.

different genres and subtleties may well have exceeded the expectations of the first inventors (Houston 2004c), but it lay already dormant in the potential expressed in the earliest attestations. Despite this potential, incipient writing was not meant to be used extensively or to fulfil every function (Houston 2004c): restricted application may have influenced its structure and semantics (Damerow 1999). Form, in a way, may have followed function.

3. As good as new: Cretan

The excursus on early writing outlined above is particularly important when introducing secondary writing in the Aegean. It is claimed that secondary inventions offer a striking contrast to primary ones. They tend to display limited iconicity, a broader range of functions, and a high degree of expressive potential (Houston and Rojas 2015, forthcoming). This is generally true, but not without exception. The hieroglyphic systems of derivative origin, in all regions and periods, offer a departure from this rule. The first and, in historical terms, earliest of the examples that will be considered, the Cretan Hieroglyphic script (CH), is a case in point.

Attested on the island of Crete from the beginning of the 2nd millennium BC, (in Minoan chronology, Early Minoan III period to the Middle Minoan IA period), its introduction coincides with the critical phase of transition that led to the emergence of the first palaces. Scholarship is divided on the date of such introduction. Whether to assign a pre-palatial or proto-palatial dating to the earliest attestation of writing (Macdonald and Knappett 2007, 137 and n. 51; Webb and Weingarten 2012, 94 and n. 72; Younger 1998, 380–1 and n. 6; but see Schoep 1999, 2006, 45) is significant: was the script invented independently from a central authority (Weingarten 2000; Schoep 2006, 2007) or was it part of the bureaucratic machine of the early palaces? On such uncertainty partly hinges the idea that writing is a necessary tool to manage a complex economy, as advocated largely by theories developed by Childe (1957) and Lévi-Strauss (1955), and discussed in depth by Goody (1986), Larsen (1988), and more recently Postgate *et al.* (1995), now evaluated in more nuanced terms (Harbsmeier 1988; Houston 2004c; Kelly 2006). For Crete, the suggestion that palace administrators may not be central to the invention of writing is gaining more and more momentum (Schoep 2006; Bennet 2013; Flouda 2013).

Whatever the exact moment of inception, the transition to phoneticism on Crete is a tantalisingly ineffable phenomenon for a number of reasons, which have to do with sampling problems (few inscriptions are present), interpretation (the script is undeciphered), origin (where does the script come from?), and point of departure (how does the script transition from pictographic to phonographic?). Let us survey the evidence, attempting to address the issues that are relevant to our discussion.

First: quantities and decipherment status. The corpus that comprises the earliest attestations of writing is very limited. Termed 'Archanes script' (Yule 1980) after the necropolis of Archanes-Phourni where some (but not all) of the inscriptions were uncovered (Sakellarakis and Sapouna-Sakellaraki 1997, 326–30), the earliest writing, dating to the Early Minoan III–Middle Minoan IA period, consists of a handful of inscriptions attested on sealstones: the precise number oscillates between four (*CHIC*) and seven (Sakellarakis and Sapouna-Sakellaraki 1997).[3] This script was singled out from the CH of later date because of a perceived homogeneity in terms of style and text: the sealstones have the same type of decoration, defined 'Border/Leaf Complex' (Yule 1980, 209-10) and bear the same formula.[4] But whether we can call it a self-contained group is, all the same, doubtful and may be an artificial construction (Olivier 1986). The formula on the earliest sealstones from Archanes proper fits well with the palaeography of the other CH script on sealstones of a slightly later period that bear the same text and come from other parts of the island, such as Knossos (*CHIC* #134, #179, #203), Samothrace (#135–137) Crete (?, *CHIC* #201 and #205), Gouves (*CHIC* #292) and Moni Odigitria (*CHIC* #313), and perhaps even with the later votive formula inscribed in Linear A (Godart 1999a).

In any case, boundaries can at times be very fluid between the two scripts of Protopalatial Crete (*CHIC*, 18; Tomas 2010, 350) and separating Archanes from the rest bears a heavier burden of proof than accepting it as part of the same tradition that ties CH to Linear A. CH was both employed in the palatial administration on clay documents, and was also engraved on sealstones during the whole duration of its use, in the Middle Minoan II–III period. The totality of the inscribed objects is very small (fewer than 500 short inscriptions altogether), which explains why it remains to this day undeciphered (Olivier 1989).

Second: origins. It is significant that the earliest attestations of the script, at the transition from Prepalatial to Protopalatial, are, to the best of our knowledge, manifest only on sealstones. Sealing practices tend to antedate the inception of writing (Palaima 1990; Pittman 1994; Rothman 1994; and Cagni 2000; Mander 2000; Topçuoğlu 2010; Woods 2010), and this aspect provides a profitable (and fresh) avenue for explaining the transition to phoneticism on Crete, because seal designs can define a possible substratum for the inception of writing. This is a perspective that should receive more attention, as the relationship between script and the pictorial tradition on Cretan seals is not only a complicated subject (Palaima 1994, 334), but also a very understudied one (Decorte this volume).[5]

---

[3] Olivier and Godart (*CHIC* #202, #251, #252 and #315) exclude three inscriptions that the Sakellarakis include (Sakellarakis and Sapouna-Sakellaraki 1997, 329, figs 288–90) because they are single isolated signs or because they come from burial buildings within Archanes that have not been published in detail (Burial Buildings 3 and 7).

[4] Incidentally, such formula is almost identical to the votive formula that is later attested in Linear A (Schoep 2006, 45). The Archanes formula reads A-SA-SA-RA-NE, whereas the Linear A A-SA-SA-RA-ME. This has led Godart to claim that the former is but a variety of the latter (Godart 1999a). To be noted is that the reading is altogether tenuous, as it relies on the backward application of phonetic values drawn from Linear B.

[5] A suggestion that all CH on sealstones represents ornamental writing, rather than writing *stricto sensu*, has been proposed (Olivier 1981, 1989, 2000), emphasising the possibility that the hieroglyphic signs

When classifying CH as a separate script from Linear A and Linear B, Evans suggested a derivation from Egyptian Hieroglyphic (in *SM1*). Now that study on the script has been refined further, we can be certain that the relation between the two systems is non-existent on a graphic level, as there are no sign-correspondences whatsoever (Olivier 1986, 1989, 1996; *CHIC*; Powell 2009). This does not disprove that exposure to Egyptian inscriptions may have taken place, as the material record testifies. Already in the Prepalatial phase (by the Middle Minoan IA period), Egyptian scarab-amulets and scaraboids made their way to the island (Pini 2000; Weingarten 2005, 760, Aruz 2008, 54ff.) and some of them were also found in burials at Archanes-Fourni (Sakellarakis and Sapouna-Sakellaraki 1997, 357, fig. 328). If a number of the Egyptian seals are genuine imports (but it is very difficult to tell), others are very refined local imitations that mimic Egyptian types,[6] styles, and significantly, bear pseudo or *bona fide* Egyptian writing.[7] So, even though it is plausible that contact with Egyptian literacy may have inspired the creation of CH, the hieroglyphs surely did not offer a precise graphic template that the Cretans adopted.

Despite acquaintance with foreign traditions, the creators of CH may have drawn inspiration more from their surroundings than from elsewhere. A thorough study of the pre- and proto-literate glyptic designs on Crete is needed, since they show a remarkable thematic variety upon which the script may have been conceived. Socio-politically, the formative time leading up to the first palaces was a period of political instability among different groups. In this uncertainty, seals tend to acquire a social role, increasingly working as emblems that score social position and strengthen a specific sense of group affiliation (Rothman 1994; Weingarten 2005; Wengrow 2008). Symbols of status and icons drawn from far-away exotic realms, such as the Parading Lions on seals for instance, showcase this mechanism of social tension, and one wonders if the inception of writing would not fit comfortably in such interstices of group competition.

Thus, rather than drawing inspiration from a specific script template, the origins of CH could be more imbued in local flavours than derivative, lying at the cornerstone that separates indigenous art and incipient language recording. This idea finds a corroborating parallel in the development of Mesopotamian writing (Michalowski 1990; Ferioli *et al.* 1994). The earliest Uruk seals employ symbols that bridge the boundary between iconography and writing, and a number of the graphs of the cuneiform writing system have their origins in the protoliterate visual arts (Woods 2010). Both writing and visual narration appear to have been invented in the same

can be both decorative and communicative. On the contrary, the fact that stiktograms mark reading direction, diagrammatical signs denote punctuation, and several morphemic correspondences are found both on CH seals and on CH documents inscribed on clay (Younger 1990) points rather in the direction of phoneticism right from the Archanes script onwards.

[6] Cretan imitations try to reproduce the burnt steatite or talk of Egyptian scarabs: these are the so-called 'white pieces' (Weingarten 2005, 760; Pini 2000; Karetsou 2000, 302–34).

[7] Karetsou 2000, cat. nos 301 (CMS II.1 180), 311 (pseudo?), 314 (CMS II.2 34), 317, 318, 322, 324.

crucible (Pittman 1994, 192), with some design elements acting iconically through resemblance, others working as logograms, through abstract symbols representing morphemes, and others functioning as determinatives, inserted and slotted into a 'narrative' scheme. And while there is no secure way to set a sharp division between phonological writing and more symbolic modes of communication, between art and writing, the similarity between some signs and some design elements used in glyptic is undeniable. Woods claims that 'pristine writing systems in general appear to occupy the ambiguous grey area between [art and writing]' (Woods 2010, 45).

The same seems to apply to the initial stages of CH. So, how 'pristine' is it? In its iconicity CH occupies the same interstice, but it has never been considered a pristine invention like Sumerian, Chinese or Mesoamerican. Indeed, regular and increasing contacts with literate cultures may have paved the way for inspiration. Cretan seal-cutters may have started to first mimic writing first, and then record language, in a way that worked in similar fashion to the Egyptian custom. However, if we look closely at the internal structure of CH, and its initial stages of development and use, the script looks and behaves in a strikingly original, influence-free, fashion.

First, it retains its iconic appearance not just on the sealstones but also on the archival clay documents, which betray a more stylised and cursive *ductus*, but do not relinquish iconicity altogether. Second, in its internal structure, it is essentially logosyllabic, with a limited logographic set (*CHIC*, 17). And while we cannot ascertain whether the local Cretan language was essentially monosyllabic, like Sumerian, Chinese and Maya, to be efficiently recorded in syllabic phonotactics, it remains a tantalising suggestion that the Cretans may have consciously chosen to put the first sounds of recorded speech into syllables, recognising them as the basic cognitive unit of phonetic reality. This happened in the context of what we may define as a semi-illiterate environment, in a way that is strikingly similar to syllabaries that were newly devised in recent times, such as those created by Sejong the Great for Korean Hangul, by Njoga for Cameroonian Bamum, or by Sequoyah for Cherokee. The cognitive process seems to be the same in all instances, despite a specific graphic template being available (Chinese for Hangul, the Roman alphabet for Cherokee), or not (Bamum, CH). Thirdly, as for the level of grammaticalisation, the texts on the CH seals are dramatically short, the syntactical extension very limited. Cretan seals are especially minute in size, and unwieldy vehicles for any elaborate amount of information. In this aspect, they resemble the earliest attestations of Anatolian Hieroglyphs (Mora 1991; Yakubovich 2008), or, albeit on a different medium, the earliest hieroglyphs on the bone tags from Abydos in Egypt (Dreyer 1998; Baines 2004). Matters of reading and interpretation are problematic in all early writing (and apply also to the two examples just mentioned), but for CH the situation is further complicated by the difficulty in recognising semantic categories such as pictograms, logograms and phonograms. Recent research has suggested that a number of signs on the seals appear to take the function of logograms and of determinatives in certain contexts (Jasink 2009; Decorte this volume), but this is a topic that deserves further study.

Therefore, in structure and early function, CH behaves in the same way as pristine script inventions do. Any inductive reasoning, such as the duck test ('if it looks like a duck, swims like a duck, and quacks like a duck, then it probably is a duck') would be too narrow to explain the creation of this script. Instead, the adverb *probably* should caution us and state quite the opposite: the CH system is *probably* not a pristine invention, but it shows all the structural ingredients of one.

4. The imitation game: Anatolian

In general, systems that are radically implicated with images, like all hieroglyphic scripts, challenge the definition of writing itself (Bennet 2013), because their relation to language and its representation may be loose. Semasiographic writing, like music, mathematical notation or dry-cleaning instructions, transcends the specificity of language, but also requires conventionality and a great deal of context to be understood. This implies reliance on speech (Sampson 1985; Hill Boone 2004; Powell 2009). As already mentioned, iconicity in early writing may progressively wane with increased use, but in certain cases it is retained. This is interesting, because it reveals a departure from the progressive stylisation and abstraction that we can see in the linear or cuneiform traditions. Sustained resilience in iconicity is idiosyncratic, and common to some, but not all hieroglyphic systems (Ferrara 2014). Systems that retain it all along are the Mayan, or the Egyptian Hieroglyphs. Another is the Anatolian Hieroglyphic (AH), to which I shall now turn.

The historical and linguistic circumstances that led to the creation of this script have received plentiful attention (Güterbock 1956; Mora 1991; Neumann 1992; Melchert 1996; Hawkins 1986, 2003; Payne 2008, 2012; Yakubovich 2008), but its source is still uncertain. Attested from the 18th–17th century BC (although the date is still debated, as the texts from this period may not be more than pictograms, Mora 1991) and continuing to be used during the Neo-Hittite states of the 1st millennium BC, the script took its first steps, much like the earliest CH, on seals (Laroche 1956; Morpurgo Davies and Hawkins 1978; Hawkins 1986). The earliest specimens show few logographic signs, unconnected to any language (Marazzi 1990; Melchert 1996; Weeden 2014). Progressively used to record names, titles and good-luck symbols, it is only during the 15th–14th centuries that fully formed texts, mostly represented on monumental inscriptions on rock reliefs or stone, are attested.[8] But on what model did the script draw initial inspiration for its sign-repertoire?

The AH script, in its late, full-fledged shape, has a logosyllabic structure (with open syllables of the consonant-vowel type), completed by a category of determinatives. Sometimes logograms, just like in the cuneiform or Maya systems, are accompanied by a phonetic complement that can be represented by a single syllable, or by a full

[8] There is ongoing debate as to the date of the earliest, properly phonetic, texts. The famous seal of Isputaḫsu, king of Kizzuwatna, one of the earliest datable uses of hieroglyphic writing, is dated to the 16th–15th century (Carruba 1976; Morpurgo Davies and Hawkins 1978, 774).

syllabic spelling of the word expressed by the logogram. The basic syllabic structure is thus composed of consonant-vowel series, much in the same way as all Aegean scripts from the early CH to Linear B. By virtue of this similarity, Hawkins proposes that the AH modelled itself on the Aegean tradition, ultimately deriving, he argues, from the Egyptian (Hawkins 1986). Thus the place of origin lay in the western Anatolian kingdom of Arzawa, the area closest to the Aegean, home to a Luwian-speaking population, a language similar to Hittite, which was the main language of the cuneiform archives of the Hittite capital Hattusa.

An explicit connection to the Luwian language had already informed the proposition that AH must have been a creation of Luwians to record their own language in their own land (Güterbock 1956, 518). However, as is now apparent (Yakubovich 2008, 10, with further bibliography), the sociolinguistic context was far more fluid, discernible in a pronounced interference between the two linguistic branches. Luwian as a language was not marked by a distinct geographic boundary, and AH as a script was used for other languages than Luwian, such as Hurrian and, later, Urartian (Morpurgo Davies and Hawkins 1978, 756). The two intersected in the mixed, bilingual environment of the Hittite capital.

Starting from this premise, it would be fruitful to explore this setting further. Crucially, this can be done not from a linguistic point of view, but from a wider perspective taking into account an exposure to pre-existing literate cultures and the already established use in Anatolia of the cuneiform syllabary for writing Hittite.[9] These two aspects are interlinked, and offer significant clues that may help to explain the origin of AH.

Regarding origin, let us go back to the internal structure. The argument for an Aegean indirect derivation, based on typology and the consonant-vowel series, presumably deriving from the CH repertoire, is weak (Mora 1991). Graphically, the signs of the two scripts are similar only at first sight, as the same vague resemblance can be traced to Mesopotamian and Egyptian sources (Yakubovich 2008). Just as in the CH case, a direct transmission from a specific source cannot be reconstructed; for AH, however, the significant difference lies in the environment that made its formation possible.

The cultural milieu where AH was formed rubbed shoulders with the cuneiform tradition. In the words of Yakubovich, 'it is only logical to assume that the use of the Mesopotamian cuneiform by the Hittites facilitated the creation of hieroglyphic syllabograms' (Yakubovich 2008, 13). But to what extent was exposure to cuneiform decisive? To be sure, the elements that constitute the fully formed typology of AH as a script, namely the categories of syllable, logogram (significantly, often tied to a phonetic component), and determinative, are shared by cuneiform, which may in all

[9] At the beginning of the Old Kingdom, in the middle of the 17th century, under Hattusili I, the Hittites adopted the cuneiform writing system and started (gradually, but speedily) to adapt it to their own language, until, by the ascension of Tudhaliya I to the throne in 1420, a professional chancellery had emerged in the capital Hattusa (van den Hout 2010).

likelihood have influenced the structure of the new script. Its syllabic core immediately distances it from Egyptian Hieroglyphic, which is consonantal, but even this may be but an accident: after all, syllables, as we have seen, are the natural units around which new scripts are constructed.

But at the same time, the choice of a syllabic structure may not have been automatic and unmarked (as may have been arguably the case for CH). What militates against this is the co-habitation of AH with cuneiform: a script that had a long tradition in the Anatolian environment, especially at Hattusa. And it is precisely in the way in which AH diverges typologically from cuneiform that we can explain its genesis. On the one hand, AH avoids vowel-consonant or consonant-vowel-consonant signs (heavily present, instead, in the cuneiform repertoire), and on the other, it forsakes the rampant polyphony of its neighbour. This could show that the process of creation may have been a more deliberate, linear and streamlined process than the gradual evolution of cuneiform in Mesopotamia. Even so, it is less probable that this was instantaneous. More likely, it may have started progressively from the 16th–15th centuries, finalising the phonetic system alongside the logographic by the time of the Early New Kingdom in the early 14th century.

This excursus on the internal structure of AH corroborates the suggestion that the script, at least as far as its phonetic component, was developed in Hattusa in a mixed Hittite and Luwian environment (Yakubovich 2008). Scribal schools were established when cuneiform writing was introduced to record Hittite (Bryce 2002, 57), but there is plentiful evidence for the presence of many Luwians among the scribes in Hattusa, and for Luwian interference in the Hittite language from the 14th century onwards (van den Hout 2007). Such language convergence of two ethnic groups resulted from the direct proximity in which they lived over an extended period of time. In this bilingual backdrop, we could place the origin of AH, where the overwhelming majority of seals and impressions originated. This environment was not just multilingual, it was also the hub of highly specialised scribal practices, where an educated class of professionals, already versed for generations in the art of cuneiform literacy, would, with what we can presume entailed little cognitive effort, transpose the structural features of cuneiform onto a new script. In Daniels' model this script formation was sophisticated grammatogeny, born out of scholarly input, implying that the script adapters had a refined linguistic knowledge of the source script. If the technical mechanism may suggest this, there is also reason to believe that this creation had a much more significant implication in socio-cultural terms, and was intended to produce an intensely contrastive effect.

If cuneiform provided the fundamental basis for fashioning the structure of AH, the trigger for its creation may have received input from somewhere else. AH came to be employed for monumental purposes, self-consciously used for writing Anatolian names and titles on durable objects such as seals, and displayed on rock inscriptions. The choice of an iconic script, marked visually by referents, cannot have been accidental. The literate societies that used iconicity as a means of communication, with the intention of projecting power, were not Mesopotamia, where cuneiform had become stylised and abstracted, or the Aegean, where CH was long dead. The contrast that the Anatolians perhaps wished to mark was with the broad shadow cast by the imperial power of Egypt and its hieroglyphs. A comparison with Egypt, or 'at least with other peoples who had invented scripts' has been suggested (Payne 2012, 13), but this proposition, if seen from a historical and cultural perspective, could be more specific and point directly to Egypt.

The birth of AH goes hand in hand with the genesis of a nascent state. Only in the later period of the Hittite Empire, from 1400 until 1200 BC, did the kingship of the Hittites become centralised and powerful. In the formative centuries preceding this, the act of creating a new script may have worked towards forging an identity of a people whose unity was in the making, and in doing so, worked to indicate a unified self-representation. This endeavor was precisely what Payne has called 'a way of presenting oneself' (Payne 2012, 13), even to illiterate members of the population. Indeed, language differentiation may have not been a particular concern, or a specific prompt. It is in the iconic literacy of the new script (Messaris and Moriarty 2005; Perego 2013), not in its linguistic connotation, that its significance lay, in opposition to, and in competition with, a pre-existing well-known model that lay further south, across the Mediterranean. Quite differently from the Greeks who, centuries later, borrowed the Phoenician abjad, 'thrown back on the only writing system which they were familiar with [...]: [that] of the Phoenicians, in opposition with whom they were engaged in defining their own identity' (Sherratt 2003, 233–4), the Anatolians were deliberate in their contrast.

Nevertheless, the impetus to create an Anatolian script does not undermine the indigenous trajectory of its creation. There is evidence to suggest that AH arose out of an indigenous set of symbols and pictograms, representing figures, body parts, plants, animals, and objects, in the course of the 2nd millennium BC. Probably this took place alongside increasing contacts with Egypt (Carruba 1976). The process was gradual, and in the crucial period after the formation of the Hittite kingdom in about 1650 BC, individual symbols were combined with each other for the purpose of rendering simple messages (Yakubovich 2011). This transition happened through the systematic application of the acrophony principle (whereby a sign is used to represent only the initial sound of the original value of the sign), which goes to show again that cuneiform rules may have dictated the strategy to build the AH core syllabic set. In the succeeding centuries, to which we can date the earliest *bona fide* inscriptions, when state institutions were emerging, certain attestations such as the *ankh* or the triangle (in its value 'good') were particularly resonant of the Egyptian prototype (Carruba 1976, 297).

Therefore, rather than being a parcelled attempt to demarcate language distinction (which in the early stages is absent), the creation of AH was an endeavour to bring together a pan-Anatolian spirit embodied in a script that drew inspiration from everyday local life, that made writing animate through the manipulation of indigenous rather than derivative symbols. In doing so, this writing system was reserved for the maximal monumental display on public buildings and the mini-monuments of power embodied by the royal seals, and came to represent a determining element in the unifying process of a people in the process of expanding into a centralised entity. Indeed, what Yakubovich calls 'nationalistic sentiments' (Yakubovich 2010) may well have been alive and kicking, but it is the competitive tension played out in the bigger arena that included and (perhaps consciously targeted) Egypt, against which the Anatolians were measuring their literate strength.

5. Hieroglyphs around the Mediterranean

The CH and AH systems have little in common in their overall graphic appearance. What makes them similar is the syllabographic structure, and the iconic shape of their signs. Both elements arguably point to independent creations, devoid of a heavy-handed influence from abroad. Moreover, both scripts follow local dynamics of development and ordered representation through icons and symbols extracted from daily life. In both cases these are culture-specific and likely used as metaphors. Their fundamentally autonomous routes to creation need to be explained according to the models developed for secondary scripts, as illustrated above.

A desire to distinguish themselves by creating a new script may have worked for elite groups (CH), or nascent states (AH), that were trying to experiment their role in relation to a competitive power (Egypt?). In this way, the creation of a new script is a reactive response to an established literate tradition and a contrastive answer to the presence of a precursor. This is clearly the case for AH, which was used to measure Anatolia's incipient strength as an organised political entity. It may be less the case for CH, which was used in a more nuanced way, which, all the same, worked to highlight status and control by incipient, competitive elite groups. In both instances pronounced boundaries are marked against literate neighbours: both systems worked alongside others used locally, Linear A and Hittite cuneiform. As such, CH and AH may have been created by reactive contrast to Egyptian, but the impact of such contrast involved traditions that were run alongside them, and in close, or very close, proximity.

In such way, a double effect was produced: on the one hand, it triggered a conscious departure from a precursor, and on the other, through the manipulation of local symbols, it constructed a visual, local literacy, accessible to society at large, in contrast to less accessible systems. So it is possible to envisage a scenario whereby Cretan individuals, projected towards a nascent palace economy, decided to depart drastically from their source and, at the same time, played out a conscious distinction from a co-inhabiting writing system, Linear A, by wilfully maintaining an iconic script. On the other side, the central Anatolian scribal class, embedded in a trajectory of political unification, contrived an iconic, monumental script for display purposes. Both instances ran parallel, but predated, the emergence of institutionalised social complexity. If the effects of such creations may be similar, the cultural roots are very different. The introduction of AH broke into the Hittite cuneiform tradition, and made Anatolia a fully biscriptal environment. The dominant system of writing still carried 'normal' communication, and the new script functioned as foil, and a deliberate reaction.

6. Vague beginnings: Cypro-Minoan

Our third case brings us to the island of Cyprus, where a syllabic script was developed in the middle of the 2nd millennium BC. The script was christened Cypro-Minoan (CM), due to a perceived similarity with Minoan Linear A (see *SM1*). However, its origins are particularly complicated: like CH, the script is undeciphered, thus tracing possible sign-correspondences with other scripts is feasible only to an extent.

Reconstructing the context is also fraught with other problems. The earliest contacts the archaeological record can trace between the islands of Crete and Cyprus date to the middle centuries of the 2nd millennium BC, a period of burgeoning advancement in the smelting of copper on Cyprus and in its trading networks both east and west. The preceding phase, the Middle Cypriot III period, may have witnessed cross-island exchanges, but the material record showcasing this is stunningly poor (Catling 1979; Masson 1979a; Portugali and Knapp 1985; Merrillees 1993; Sherratt 2013). It is during these decades (starting from *c.* 1700 BC) that the earliest evidence of metalworking is attested from an urban site on the island, Enkomi (Dikaios 1969–1971). A century and a half later, within the greatest concentration of metal workshops in the north section of the site, the earliest Cypro-Minoan inscription was found (Dikaios 1963, 1969–1971; Godart and Sacconi 1979).

Was the emergence of writing on Cyprus the result of a direct influence from Minoan Crete, and was its inception a consequence of a burgeoning phase of inter-island trading in copper? Moreover, was writing developed on Cyprus as a direct trigger of such contacts, and linked to booming copper production? More specifically, to what extent can we define it as derivative of the Minoan script? Given the poor context, answering these questions is particularly problematic. Sherratt's detailed archaeological work frees us to discuss more theoretical concerns (Sherratt 2013). The idea that Minoan Crete exerted any kind of socio-political influence on the creation of CM, as a result of the intensification of its power abroad, is untenable. Minoanisation is an ill-applied concept, as it is, more generally, a heuristically improper term. This counts for Cyprus as much as for the wider Aegean (Broodbank 2004): no Minoan package of cultural substance invested the creation of writing on Cyprus by emulation.

Also, for Cyprus, the bias is further emphasised by the intellectual influence exercised by Evans' assuredness in pronouncing a direct Minoan derivation for CM. Thus, the coin 'CM' still exerts a subliminal power in explaining where the script came from (Sherratt 2013), even though it is difficult to reconstruct a possible historical context to explain this, beyond arguing that the script was the result of an apparent reverberation of Minoan thalassocracy (Morpurgo Davies and Olivier 2012, 105).

Sherratt's suggestion that we should look to less trodden paths for possible sources, such as the Anatolian and Levantine literacy and the long-established Cypriot marking systems, rather than a single, uncertain template (Sherratt 2013) refreshes the picture and goes some way to explain the creation of the script without reference to ingrained assumptions.

An 'Aegean' flavour in graphic appearance of Cypro-Minoan signs is undeniable (Palaima 1989; Hirschfeld 2014). However, the similarity is only skin-deep, and a direct root in a Minoan template still needs to be demonstrated rather than be taken as fact (Palaima 1989, but see Bombardieri and Jasink 2010, and Sherratt 2013 for doubts in sign matches across the two scripts). This is significant, because it is precisely the vagueness of the resemblance that can help us to understand the context of transmission better. The earliest attestation of CM (a tablet fragment, ##001 in *HoChyMin* and *CM II*) may be linked directly to copper production, but even so, it does not appear to be connected to monitoring the administrative or industrial activity, as the tablet bears no numerical notations or logograms. Being considerably different in its graphic look and layout, this tablet was divorced from the other inscriptions (branded CM0 in *HoChyMin*), whose date is considerably later. This separation can have two possible explanations: either this specimen represents a dead branch of Cypro-Minoan with no epigraphic continuation (but why? – see *HoChyMin*, 61; Duhoux 2009a; Valério this volume), or it exemplifies an experiment with a new script. Either account has implications of a temporal nature for the borrowing process: if we accept the former, the date of transmission should be likely pushed as far as the 17th century BC to allow for a mini-obsolescence. Conversely, if we accept the latter, we should assume a more circumscribed, almost synchronic window for the borrowing.

Already at the start of its life, and progressively more in its later stages, CM departs from both Aegean and Near Eastern templates. Contacts with neighbouring literate environments must have been regular occurrences, presumably creating awareness in the Cypriots of how other systems of writing worked. Despite such relative exposure, and whatever the original template for CM – as a working hypothesis I should assume that any coeval script could be a candidate – CM is, from the start, a very original script, not just graphically, but also typologically. CM is characterised by a very streamlined signary, with a core syllabografic set, a numerical system (of the Aegean type), and, crucially, very few logograms. Thus, the heavy logography of the supposed source, Linear A (or of cuneiform Akkadian, for that matter) was virtually overlooked by the adapters of CM.[10] With that, the plethora of structural 'complications' of Linear A, such as ligatures, monograms, and fractions, was equally rejected. While it appears more and more probable that some level of logography is present in CM after all, in the form of isolated signs identical to syllabograms acting as logograms (Ferrara 2015), before

[10] There seems to be little evidence for logograms in CM (notably on ##093, a clay ostrakon with two signs, each followed by numerals). For a discussion of these attestations, see Sherratt 2013, 82, n. 6.

a decipherment is accepted, we can only speculate. But simplification is evident, and points to a deliberate, heavy-handed intervention, which may have taken place at the moment of transmission. Let us go back to this point. What were the Cypriot adapters trying to do, eluding the logographic sets of their neighbouring writing traditions? CM is inscribed on a wide variety of objects and, with the exception of a number of clay balls bearing short inscriptions (possibly used to indicate names linked to production processes), the supports range from metal bowls, miniature ingots, ivory objects, to ceramics and stone and clay cylinders. On most of these items, marking property or social position with personal names seems to have been a primary concern. Precious, prestige artefacts, and utilitarian objects alike, were used as vehicles for ownership statements across the whole island. Archival, economic records are largely absent, and an administrative use of writing almost non-existent.

More importantly perhaps, the Cypriot epigraphic tradition presents a unique feature in not having developed sealing practices of any sort. In this aspect, it distances itself from all other cultures in the Mediterranean of the latter half of the 2nd millennium BC. Cypriot settlements did not establish a heavy bureaucratic machine that required writing to run internal activities, or else they did not elect to employ writing to manage it, at least not by using clay as a medium. While we cannot discount the possibility that accounting records were written on perishable organic material, the total absence of inventory tablets, pervasive both in the Aegean and in the Near East, militates against this. The argument, admittedly, could fall easy prey to circularity: if durable materials were not used for the economy, then all epigraphic data that remains does not function as economic. But the poverty of numerical notations attested and the (by and large) lack of logograms, tied with the absence of sealings, all raise the prospect that in fact the Cypriots did not perceive writing as an instrument of bureaucracy. As Younger has recently stated: 'the script was obviously not recording incoming taxes and outgoing disbursements. It was recording something else. CM scholars need to deal with that fact' (Younger 2015).

Indeed, it seems that the Cypriot adapters made an assertive U-turn over what was perceived (by the Minoans, predominantly) to be the 'normal' purpose of writing and they manipulated it for other ends. They intentionally attributed a different value to what literacy meant for other cultures, and converted the power of such value from a predominantly administrative to a predominantly 'symbolic' one. It is worth stating again that the use of parchment or papyrus for administrative purposes may create a disclaimer, but all the same, statistically, the evidence is overwhelming. CM was used as a marker of local, social status on prestige items, to mark possession and to emphasise social position. This statement could be taken a step further: is there a possibility that this script was in fact not just used, but also *created* for such ends?

If CM was created for the elites only, it was created to mark a strong contrast not just *vis à vis* its template (Linear A if we accept it as source), but also to exert reactive force in the face of practices adopted in the Near Eastern milieu, where writing was employed as channel for long narratives, epic cycles, local literature, as well as administrative documents. This custom was different from the Linear A and Linear B in the Aegean, where central inventories were the scribes' main concern. We could argue that the Near Eastern tradition was more extensive, the scribal classes of longer and larger standing in palace establishments, literacy less stunted socially than in (any other) Aegean tradition, and that the Aegean ultimately represents a veritable exception. But the fact that Cyprus may have done the opposite, and given preference to recording things other than accounts should not be overlooked. The practice of inscribing longer texts, observable on four CM tablet fragments from Enkomi (two of which are joined, see *HoChyMin* ##207–209, but see *CM I* and Younger 2015 for the invalidity of the join), indicates a practice borrowed from the Near East (applied, perhaps, to record native genres?). Conversely, the texts of Neopalatial Crete and the palace economies of mainland Greece gave no incentive to Cyprus to establish an administrative tradition of its own.

So can we claim that CM is derivative of Minoan Linear A? The answer is yes and no. Leaving palaeography and matches in sign-shapes aside (Palaima 1989; Duhoux 2009a; Bombardieri and Jasink 2010; Sherratt 2013; Valério in prep.), let us ponder over one final consideration, of contextual importance. If we were able to access further texts in CM dating to the Late Cypriot I period or slightly before, when the transmission from Linear A may have taken place, we would perhaps be forced to recognise a complete departure from the Aegean template. This is of course to be proved rather than assumed as fact, but in creating a virtually new script, the Cypriots may have been eager to emphasise contrast and express distinction from their source. This could have been the case from the very beginning of their literacy, rather than an afterthought or a later development.

In the succeeding centuries, use, function, epigraphic preferences, and, crucially, sign-shapes of CM, all bear the marks of such distinction to a high degree, despite the varied manners in which CM was applied on its supports. Therefore, I would speculate (with the due caveats imposed by arguments that are, to an extent, from silence) that CM was since its beginning a very new system of writing. New scripts may not change the typology of the source, and thus preserve their syllabic or alphabetic structures, but they can revolutionise perceptions of what being literate means. In the hands of the Cypriots, literacy became a tool for the elites, who employed it to mark their prized possessions and show off their status. In such a way, they controlled production, possession, and their own position in society.

7. Revolutions? The Ugaritic alphabet

The last case under consideration is the Ugaritic alphabet,[11] attested from Ugarit-Ras Shamra in Syria in the last two centuries of the Late Bronze Age. The script created at

[11] The Ugaritic alphabet is technically an augmented abjad, a system where consonants are represented, together with vowels after the glottal stop.

Ugarit adapts the cuneiform tradition (by impressing wedges with a stylus on clay), which was normally used to write logosyllabaries, to an alphabetic system. Contrary to what is often stated, this does not represent an invention, since the alphabetic principle was known from centuries earlier, although precise dates are uncertain (Sass 2004–2005). Examples of linear alphabet are attested from the beginning of the 2nd millennium BC in the Sinai (Proto-Sinaitic), in Canaan (Proto-Canaanite), and in the western desert of Egypt – the recently discovered Wadi el-Hôl inscriptions (Pardee 1997a, 1997b; Darnell 2003, respectively).

The linear alphabetic inscriptions from first millennium Syria-Palestine, which show the same conventional order of signs as various abecedaries from Ugarit, directly descend from those alphabets: this is where the alphabetic form developed at Ugarit comes from. Indeed, Pardee suggests that the cuneiform alphabet may have imitated a linear prototype used in the region, adapted to the cuneiform principle (Pardee 2007; Bordreuil and Pardee 2009). Evidence for such a prototype is absent. Whatever the case, the type of system created by the scribes of Ugarit is neither new, nor revolutionary: it represents a re-adaptation (accommodation, or adaptive reuse, according to the models in Table 2.1) of a known structure (alphabet) into a well-established graphic format (cuneiform). However, if we look closely at the context, the picture changes: in socio-linguistic terms, the introduction of this alphabet marks something much more radical. Its impact is very similar to the one described for Cyprus, with the introduction of the CM script: the re-engineering of an existing model, invested with a completely new perception of its social value.

For 2000 years, the kingdoms of the Near East used the cuneiform syllabic system that dominated the scene as vehicle for a number of unrelated languages, Indo-European (Hittite and Indo-Iranian), Semitic (Babylonian, Amorite and Canaanite), Hurrian, Sumerian, Elamite and Kassite. Side-by-side with this monolithic, cosmopolitan expression, attempts at creating alphabetic writing had already taken place in sections of the southern basin of the Mediterranean during the second millennium, but had never been regulated. The case of Ugarit is different. Eighteen abecedaries are attested in Ugarit (Hawley 2008), bearing evidence for three different alphabetic systems, whose variants are, at least in part, linked to linguistic differentiation or scribal tradition (Pardee 2007; Lehmann 2012).[12]

In fact, despite their divergences, the Ugaritic alphabets are but the result of one single process, that of standardising a new script. The reasons behind these efforts have nothing to do with simplification: a phonemic alphabet could be seen as a

[12] The long alphabet, developed specifically for the North West Semitic Ugaritic language, is the most widely used. It differentiates itself over the short one (with 27 signs) by the presence of three additional *alephs* used to record other languages than Ugaritic, where syllables beginning with a vowel (Hurrian, Akkadian) are possible, a feature not shared by Ugaritic. The third version of the alphabet follows the so-called *halaḥam* tradition (RS 88.2215), because it follows a different letter order (h, l, ḥ, m), which is later found in the South Arabian peninsula; another attestation of this alphabet comes from Beth-Shemesh (Bordreuil and Pardee 2001).

normal choice for the consonantal structure of a Semitic dialect. Their significance lies in the idea that a local system could be put to use to record local expressions, such as native works (local mythical poems, ritual texts, etc.), as well as internal affairs. The alphabet became 'a literal emblem of the Ugaritic city-state's attempt to inscribe its own distinctive place in a larger world' (Sanders 2009, 54). This is why the scribes produced abecedaries and school texts, not only to make their local vernacular accessible to a greater number of people, but also to 'challenge' the conventional system that they were trained in. Ugarit was the only literate environment of the 2nd millennium BC where a script was actively associated with the particulars of its own culture, and this will remain the case at least until Cypro-Minoan is deciphered.

Contemporary, if not later, uses of alphabetic writing in the Levantine coast were largely detached from a standardised format, and not absorbed by demands of bureaucracy or scope for literature. The Lachish ewer, the inscriptions from 'Izbet Ṣarṭah and Gezer, and the arrowheads from 'El Kaḏr, dating from the 13th century onwards (Cross 1989), show free 'style' in their epigraphic conventions, such as reading direction or sign shapes. This independence also involves the application of the alphabet, which is often personal, experimental, individualising, rather than linked to a collective voice or institution. The final centuries of the 2nd millennium mark the end of long period during which the alphabet was never embraced, with the exception of the Ugarit case, as the instrument of a state, in a centralised, regulated, 'industrial' manner. Its incipient stages, in the inscriptions from Serabit el Khadim and at Wadi el Hôl show the (short-lived?) initiative of Semitic groups (soldiers, merchants, traders) living in literate Egyptian society, who imitated the script of the empire, but never crystallised its use. They simply used writing in an improvised fashion, for what appear to be practical and almost intimate purposes.[13]

This, however, does not necessarily imply that the Proto-alphabet adapters were on the margins of cultural activity, because they operated in desolate, out of the way places. The fact that they took independent initiative does not imply that the earliest alphabetic inscriptions were unsophisticated graffiti, or 'relatively crude' specimens created 'on the desert fringe' (Sanders 2009, 40). In fact, the opposite seems to be the case. Darnell himself claims that the authors of the inscriptions of Wadi el-Hôl were experts who learned Egyptian directly from professional military scribes (Darnell *et al.* 2005, 90), a view echoed by Rollston (2010). As it happens, their intervention shows sophisticated handling of the Egyptian script, and even more significantly, a cognitive awareness of linguistic complexity. After all, they applied the principle of acrophony to their Semitic dialect. This seems more a case of refined experimentation than rough adlibbing.

Unlike these early experiments with older (or even coeval) shapes of the alphabet, the multilingual environment of Ugarit produced a different kind of alphabet that

[13] This remains a hypothesis before the inscriptions from Wadi el Hôl become clearer.

became standardised for the first time, the official instrument of a regulating centre. However, the creation of the Ugaritic script was not tied simply to notating the local language for the first time. In fact, if such were the case, the addition of supplemental signs attached to the basic alphabet (see note 11), created for sounds that were not phonetically at home in the local dialect, would make no sense. The prompt must have been another, of a more universal nature. It perhaps hinged on making accessible a whole plethora of characteristically 'Ugaritian' features to the widest number of people possible: Ugarit's own native literature, internal affairs, history, practices, and rituals. The specificity of language was less important than the specificity of culture. As such, the alphabet was, to be sure, a particularising endeavour to record a vernacular (Sanders 2009), but its impact went beyond language: it was meant to produce a cultural dent in the monolithic and official cuneiform canvas.

8. Old forms, new meanings

CM and the Ugaritic alphabet are in structure and substance two very different scripts. CM is syllabic, and in this respect it follows in the footsteps of the Aegean tradition, but it breaks new ground by simplifying the repertoire of its source and by radically changing the graphic appearance. It also modifies the view of a largely bureaucratic application of writing and adds a strong symbolic flavour to it, largely relinquishing the administrative function. In other words, despite a strong Aegean lineage, the script becomes, in time, fully Cypriot, and used by the Cypriots in a strongly re-elaborated (I could even say 'Cypriot', but the risk is that such term be heuristically void) way.[14] And so, while the concept of ethnoscript (Houston 2004c, 229) is a less than palatable definition for any writing system, the fact remains that CM worked as a material consolidator of a specific identity. All through its life, it embodied a strong cultural manifestation that reflected specific elites and the image they wished to project. Ugaritic had a double inspiration: a structural one, drawn from the cursive alphabet, and an epigraphic one, that came from the cuneiform school. At the end of this two-pronged path, it breaks into the syllabic structure of all cuneiform writing then known and enters with an operational principle drawn from elsewhere.

Despite being so different, the use and the value attached to both scripts by their creators are very similar. They are situated in socio-cultural contexts that have one feature in common: they favour self-differentiation. Whatever their constituent characteristics, be they syllabic or alphabetic, linear or cuneiform, CM and Ugaritic both project a new idea of writing, and a new perception of that idea, onto an old

[14] Some of the few (eight in total) CM inscriptions found at Ugarit represent a departure from this conclusion. There is reason to believe that at least two specimens of tablets were written as experiments with CM performed in situ by Ugaritian scribes, rather than letters sent from the island (Ferrara 2016).

script, that gets to be re-engineered *ad libitum* and systemically, to signify something completely different from what was chosen as inspiration. Both worked as material reflections of specific cultures that needed to be visibly different from all others, proximal or more distant.

In attaching a new value to scripts, however, Cypriots and Ugaritians behaved, again, differently. Contrast (in Houston and Rojas' sense) is less tangible in the CM case, because, at least on the island, the script was not used in direct coexistence with any other. Competition was not played out externally. The life of CM was, for the most part, an insular, intramural affair (if we exclude the plethora of potmarks found abroad, whose relation with formal writing is complex, Hirschfeld 1999). This means that the tension was internal, and writing became a powerful tool in the hands of the elites that made their position felt through the added value they attached to writing. Competition was therefore perceived at the core of the Cypriot pyramid and cast its effect on the relations among individuals that manipulated writing (whether they understood it or not) and groups who could not access it directly.

Ugaritic produced, instead, a real rupture. Its impact received more emphasis in the face of its very cohabitation with a dominant system. The Ugarit setting is of highly unequal internal relations, with the use of syllabic cuneiform largely preponderant. So, it may not be a coincidence that the structure of the script itself was radically changed to stress distance once again, as modern cases of ruptures testify: the already mentioned Bamum and Cherokee are cases in point, syllabic scripts derived from alphabets. Ugaritic went the opposite way but, all the same, its core structure underwent changes. The break was not complete, however: a gravitational pull was felt insofar as the system to which Ugarit scribes were more exposed, cuneiform, was adopted, instead of another, or instead of creating new signs. This is normal in radical transformations, the shadow of the 'dominant' script still cast on a new creation. But (just like in CM) the repertoire and its structural components were, at the same time, radically simplified: the logograms and determinatives of syllabic cuneiform forsaken, the phonograms redrawn and kept to a minimum. This made the new scripts vastly more accessible, simpler systems, perfectly suited to record complex narratives on the art, custom, and life of their people.

But does any creation need a purpose? If it is true that the act of inventing a script cannot be disconnected from its uses and applications, we need to explore the difficulties inherent in reconstructing this aspect. On the one hand, empirical evidence is always partial, slanted, or limited, and on the other, the real intentions of the creators are always largely unknown, dependent on the available data, subjective for interpreters. With these two problems in mind, we can argue that, *at least* on the basis of what remains, those who wrote in CM did so for reasons that went beyond keeping track of bureaucracy, and certainly deployed writing to enhance their prestige and status. The creators of Ugaritic built a scribal institution, complete with schools and practice texts, geared to promoting all aspects of their local life. Use and significance of these two scripts may have been different, the one more limited (in scope and quantity), the other more extensive, but they both appear to function to promulgate a new idea of writing, original in shape, but also in meaning.

9. New beginnings, in local settings

Sweeping general assumptions are often made when thinking about writing. As we have seen, at least for the vast and complex region considered here, the practical and symbolic effects that new writing produced (be it new and pristine writing, or secondary and derivative) are invariably contextual, situational, and unpredictable. Romantic models that tie writing to ethnicity and view its many forms as the expression of a uniform typifying mass (where equally elusive concepts such as language, state, land, and people coexist), fail to grasp the wide range of meaning that a newly introduced script can assume. Similarly deficient are universalist models that treat writing as a technology of progress, portending that the introduction of an accessible system of data-transfer (such as the alphabet) can change human and collective consciousness. Neither model works for what we have seen to be the case with newly introduced scripts in the Mediterranean during the 2nd millennium.

If the goal of understanding the effect, impact and significance of new scripts needs to be freed from models that appear too narrow, the goal of understanding the triggers underlying secondary script formation may equally need to be disengaged from the feeble concept of 'stimulus diffusion'. In this respect, the theoretical models developed by Houston and Rojas and Daniels are helpful. To their contribution, I would like to add that each secondary script needs a constant check-up of the archaeological, historical, epigraphic and anthropological contexts that make its creation possible. The factors at play are endless, each requiring a detailed, often difficult, reconstruction. One of the factors may be language change, but the preponderant role attributed to it should be downgraded. The cases described in this contribution should reinforce this view.

So what are the actual triggers for script change? One example, drawn from the Aegean, should help to challenge traditional belief that writing is born for one reason only and that its introduction will produce predictable effects. Early writing in the Aegean is classified as predominantly administrative, and this is certainly not untrue. Yet, the earliest occurrences visible to us come from seals. Seals are hybrid creatures, because they operate simultaneously across bureaucracy and as signifiers of product identity, symbol of personal aesthetic codes, and tools of regulation. Functions are intertwined, the relationship with language minimal. In a way, they work as early brands (Wengrow 2008). Therefore, the realms of administration and display, along which the function of early writing has been sharply divided (Postgate *et al.* 1995), are an artificial dichotomy, whose boundaries should perhaps begin to fade instead of sharpening, in favour of gaining more nuances.

It has been said that necessity is the mother of invention. Inventions arise when a society has a need to fulfil. A number of inventions do conform to this practical view, but many inventions were, and still are, driven by curiosity, tinkering, experiment.

Some 'things', invented to serve one purpose, can find their use for another, unforeseen purpose. Therefore, at times invention is the mother of necessity, and not *vice versa*. It could be argued that writing in some parts of the Aegean and the Eastern Mediterranean at least, was *not* a case of *vice versa*. Scripts are semiotic systems that stem from deliberate creative efforts, rather than from potent dictates imposed from the top, or from ethnic tags that need to be expressed one way or another, or from an agent-free evolution outside human control (Smith 2013).[15] Monocausal arguments put forth for the origins of writing are not useful in describing its kaleidoscopic and multi-stranded socio-cultural significance, as witnessed in the examples described above, but also in general, and in the countless modulations that a scheme will never be able to classify.

To end, one must go back to the beginning. No sentence is complete without a subject. The third citation on page 7 is an extrapolated phrase where the grammatical subject is omitted. What, and whose, was the genius mentioned? The citation refers to the Minoans specifically, but it can be extended to all cultures that invented scripts of their own: the genius was in breaking (and in keeping) with tradition, in modulating shape, function, significance and value, and in making possible all things we can (and cannot) understand about a new writing system. That genius goes beyond being technical, or ideological, natural or necessary; that genius has only one possible subject, and that subject is creativity.

[15] Smith proposes that writing may have emerged from a gradual reflex of neural processing and unconscious impulses linked to archaeological variables such as the intensification of production of sign-bearing objects, and the formation of communities of increasingly full-time specialists.

Chapter 3

Cretan 'Hieroglyphic' and the nature of script[1]

Roeland P-J.E. Decorte

This paper deals with a problem that has been haunting the study of Cretan 'Hieroglyphic' for over a century, ever since the first publication of Cretan 'picture-writing' by Evans (1894a, 1894b, 1895). It is an issue that was purportedly solved by the publication, two decades ago, of the script's corpus (Olivier 1989),[2] but which in reality remains highly relevant and ill-defined today. The problem is that of defining 'script' in relation to 'decoration' ('writing' in relation to 'art'), and the definitions we supply directly determine what we consider to constitute the 'Cretan Hieroglyphic' script.

Since the publication of *Corpus Hieroglyphicarum Inscriptionum Cretae* (*CHIC*) by Olivier and Godart, reviews have criticised the omission of script signs in individual instances (Younger 1998; Karnava 1997; and Palaima 1998), while Jasink (2009)[3] – though still 'following, as much as possible, the suggested criteria of *CHIC*' – has proposed the reinstatement to the syllabary of as many as 30 signs, maintaining even more elements as 'decorative'. It is testament to the tremendous influence of *CHIC*, however, and the strength of its arguments – first published as a series of articles by Olivier (1981, 1989, 1990, 1995, 2000, 2010) – that scholarly response has limited itself

---

[1] This paper was first presented in March 2015, and a final version was sent to the editor in April 2015. Thanks go out to Philippa Steele for the invitation to speak on Cretan Hieroglyphic at the URBS conference on Aegean scripts, leading to the publication of this volume. Further thanks go out to Cyprian Broodbank, my supervisor. Silvia Ferrara peer-reviewed the paper in September 2015 and provided useful comments. I subsequently became aware of the development of a broadly parallel analysis as published in Ferrara, Weingarten and Cadogan 2016.

This work arises from a PhD thesis on Minoan iconography and the relationship between early writing and art, in preparation at the University of Cambridge (Christ's College). I am grateful to the UK Arts and Humanities Research Council for funding this work. Abbreviations are listed at the top of the bibliography. *CHIC* conventions are used when referencing documents (preceded by #) and individual signs (001–309).

[2] While preparing *CHIC* for publication, Olivier (1989, 48) argued that deciding which signs to understand as script, and which not, was 'not an easy decision to make (...) but it is now a resolved problem.' Olivier (2010, 287) more recently stated that 'en une trentaine d'années, on en est arrivé, *grosso modo*, à un certain consensus.'

[3] Building upon groundwork already laid in this direction by Karnava (2000, unpublished PhD).

to refining the corpus' approach: not a single serious redefinition of the interpretative framework for understanding Cretan Hieroglyphic has been suggested since its publication. It is exactly such a conflicting approach that will be developed here.

Cretan Hieroglyphic, in active use on Crete between Middle Minoan I and the end of Middle Minoan III (roughly 2000–1600 BC),[4] is unique among the writing systems of the Bronze Age Aegean in that roughly half of the script's surviving attestations – next to more typical appearances on clay and ceramic surfaces – are found engraved on seal-stones. In comparison, Linear A, roughly contemporary, can be identified on two or three seals (*CMS* II.2, 213b, cf. *CHIC* p. 12, n. 17; Younger 1998; *CMS* XII, 96, cf. Raison-Pope 1994, 242–3; Perna 2014; Anastasiadou 2016; *CMS* VII, 31) and one signet (*CMS* II.3, 38), while Linear B produces a single seal (*CMS* V, 415). Though much less well attested (its signs were estimated by Olivier in 1989 to constitute only 2% of the whole corpus of Myceno-Minoan scripts),[5] Cretan Hieroglyphic appears on more than 280 seals and sealings,[6] as well as, as will be argued below, potentially many more. It is exactly on these seals and sealings that we find the complex renditions of the script that, together with the supposed 'naturalistic' form of its signs,[7] have led many scholars to argue for the 'ornamental' nature of the writing system.

1. Past approaches

As early as 1901, before even the appearance of *Scripta Minoa*, doubts about the nature of the script were expressed. It was argued by the German scholar Zahn, on the basis of Evans' initial announcements, that the writing system was nothing more than a sequence of religious symbols (Zahn 1901, 23; cf. *SM* 1, 21). Evans himself, however, maintained a firm belief in the 'pictographic' nature of the script, hypothesising the existence of phonographic elements for those cases where sequences made no clear pictographic sense (*SM* 1, 12; 134; 245; 247). Following then-popular notions of the supposed 'universality of early writing', Evans interpreted elements such as 038 'gate' as 'keeper', and 005 'eye' as 'overseer', with the well-known formula 044-005 'trowel-eye' representing an 'overseer of builders' (*SM* 1, 3 for ideas of 'universal writing'; *SM* 1, 245–7 and 267–8 for sign values).

An extreme of this approach, often ridiculed (laughing away the very real problem of the rarely addressed relationship between sign and image), is Evans' interpretation

[4] In this paper I follow traditional low dates established on ceramic and other material synchronisms with Egypt and Mesopotamia, awaiting the resolution of the current stand-off in radiocarbon dating for our period (the result of a noted oscillation in the calibration curve and questions as to quality of data and results: see Wiener *et al.* 2009).

[5] Olivier (1989) estimated that, at the time, surviving attestations of Cretan Hieroglyphic totalled roughly 1,500 signs, compared to 7,500 for Linear A and 65,000 for Linear B (30,000 at the time of Ventris' decipherment).

[6] The numbers here used are conservative estimates based upon *CHIC*, Karnava (2000) and Jasink (2009).

[7] See e.g. Branigan (1965, 1966) for early attempts to identify the real-world objects behind these 'naturalistic' signs.

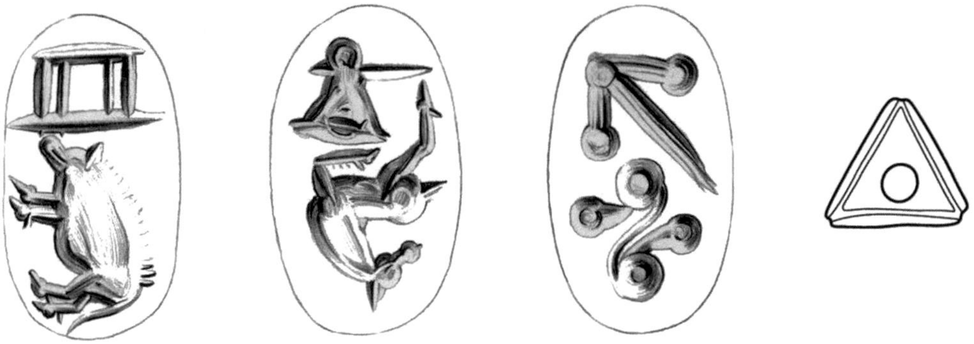

Fig. 3.1: CHIC #256/CMS VI,95a-c. Evans' 'keeper of the swine'. Images after CMS VI, courtesy of the CMS Heidelberg, recoloured by author.

of 'keeper of the swine' (Fig. 3.1). Crucially for us, Evans was the first to systematically argue for some signs as pictographic 'badges' (*SM* 1, 264) and others as mere 'decoration', both classes fully detached from the actual script. The 'decorative' signs were a result, he argued, of the Minoan artist's supposed '*horror vacui*' (*SM* 1, 229–231).[8]

In 1951, reacting against the tendency to explain away the script's idiosyncrasies as due to its 'decorative' nature, Chapouthier reinstated the suggestion that the repetition of signs in Cretan Hieroglyphic might be meaningful, perhaps indicating plurals and duals as in Egyptian Hieroglyphic. Though this had previously been denied for want of tripled signs representing the more common plural, Chapouthier provided exactly such an example, arguing that we could now exclude 'toute intention décorative' (Chapouthier 1951, 73). Observing the appearance of 053 on actual ceramic material, he furthermore suggested an ideographic function for certain signs as '*déterminants*' (see also *SM* 1, 247), a concept we will come back to later in this paper.

In 1963, Grumach published the now famous seal #262 (Fig. 3.2), in which the reduplication of middle signs seemed to disprove Chapouthier's thesis. To Grumach, reduplication was instead reminiscent of the flanking elements in the 'mistress of animals' motif, well known from Late Bronze Age art. The script was once more to be understood ideographically: words or sounds may not, he argued, be redoubled at will (Grumach 1963a, 12–3: '*in jedem Fall können Zeichen, die entgegen der 'normalen' Schreibung der Gruppen verdoppelt und nach ästhetischen Prinzipien angeordnet werden können, nicht phonetische Zeichen sein*').

Maurice Pope at the first Congress of Mycenology argued, conversely, for a syllabic interpretation of the script, pointing out that 'the script has often been vaguely called "ideographic", [yet] I do not know of any consistent theory of how [this] would work' (Pope 1968, 438–9). Cautioning, however, against interpreting every inscription as

[8] Evans thus started the long tradition, continued to this day, of identifying the idiosyncrasies of Minoan art and iconography as a direct consequence of such a perceived '*horror vacui*'. For perhaps the earliest mention of this, see Evans' (1894a) very first article on Mycenaean/Minoan writing in *Athenaeum*, p. 812.

Fig. 3.2: CHIC #262/CMS XII,117. Face a-b with supposed formulae 036-092-031 and 038-010-031 . Images courtesy of the CMS Heidelberg.

meaningful, Pope drew attention to two problematic instances: a seal (#294) showing heavy repetition seemingly uncharacteristic for syllabic texts, and a clay document (#43a) showing what he considered 'arms and legs gathered together' (007-010-006,). Arguing that most such instances of 'dubious writing' appear on seals, Pope famously stated that 'we cannot tell whether the seal inscriptions communicated awe, prestige, or pleasure, but they are unlikely to have conveyed serious information' (Pope 1968, 446).[9]

At the same congress, John Reich once more posited the opposite view. Stressing the need to look at all sides of the seal, Reich argued that accompanying figural and pictorial scenes are 'no less significant [than] hieroglyphic signs': such naturalistic scenes and signs were not, he stressed, 'merely decorative in purpose; on the contrary, their function as particularizing elements for the hieroglyphic signs (...) appears to be among the most important features of the script' (Reich 1968, 456 and 461). Reich's application of these ideas to the material evidence, however, led him to interpret scenes in a straightforward, pictorial way, arguing seals displaying animals alongside tools to be related to the hunt, and even suggesting different vessel-signs as indicative of 'local variations in methods of cooking' (Reich 1968, 457).

[9] Using Mackay's (1965) formula, Pope assured himself that the Cretan Hieroglyphic found on clay documents was, indeed, true writing. In the failure of the formula to prove pertinent for the script on seals, however, Pope saw a final confirmation of their detachment from 'true script'. It is my belief that these calculations underlie the current tendency in scholarship to omit supposed 'decorative' elements completely from our analyses of the script, without the apparent need for further justification. If this is indeed so, it is never explicitly stated. There are, however, some serious problems in regarding Mackay's formula as a certain predictor of what is script and what is not: not only was the formula devised for a different purpose altogether (the estimation of the number of signs in a syllabary/alphabet), it is impossible for it to have any use when there is still debate as to what to identify as the 'signs' of a script, as the selection of input data is, in itself, necessarily biased. Such objections were already made by Reich (1968) as a comment to Pope (1968). Especially problematic to my mind is Pope's stated omission of single 'isolated' signs from his calculations, an issue further addressed below. A similar inability to define a syllabary without fully grasping the nature of a script, may be recognised in Cypro-Minoan (see Ferrara 2012, 220–1), where the problem of palaeographic 'variants' (cf. the chapter by Valério, this volume) creates, I would argue, issues of carrying forward bias from the selection of individual signs put into the formula (cf. the chapter by Duhoux, this volume) to our investigation of the typology of the script(s).

It is in reaction to the latter kind of imaginative approach that the currently accepted framework for understanding Cretan Hieroglyphic was formed. In 1978, Olivier reiterated the problem of defining writing, taking a first crucial step towards a more consistent approach by offering his own clear definition of the term: '*une technique graphique permettant à un individu de transmettre à un ou à plusieurs autres individus, aussi bien dans l'espace que dans le temps, un message bien précis et univoque*' (Olivier 1981, 106; an updated, slightly modified, but semantically identical version is given in *CHIC*, p. 12).

At the time, Olivier agreed with Pope that writing on seals was wholly ornamental (Olivier 1981, 113–5).[10] Elsewhere, he argued that any serious study of Cretan Hieroglyphic should start from 'real inscriptions, that means the archival inscriptions' (Olivier 1989, 43–4). In 1990, however, Olivier admitted that certain seals *could* be read, even if they were not necessarily *meant to be*, stressing that he was nonetheless 'more convinced than ever that the script on the seals is a *decorative* one' (Olivier 1990, 13). Based mainly on #256 (see Fig. 3.1 above), displaying all its supposed 'non-script' signs on a lower level, Olivier also contended that in some cases only half a seal contained script, and thus only half would be impressed (Olivier 1995, 175). The 'non-script' signs were once more identified as 'badges', without any further elaboration on the supposed function or workings of such 'badges'.

It is clear, as Pope already alleged in 1968, that 'no consistent theory' for tackling the relationship between 'script' and 'decoration' has as of yet been developed. Though Olivier's system has progressed the furthest – providing its own definition of writing – the interpretation of some features as 'decorative' and therefore somehow meaningless, and others as 'badges' (in some instances 'talking badges') remains highly ill-defined. It is furthermore highly revealing that despite the definitions of writing offered over the past few decades specifically for the study of Cretan Hieroglyphic, not a single definition of 'art' has ever been brought forward in the context of the script.

My argument in this paper is thus divided into two parts: first, I identify and problematize each category of the so-called 'decorative' signs lost in the normalised transcriptions of *CHIC*. Secondly, I propose a theoretical framework for the interpretation of each of these signs as an integral part of the script, building upon concepts borrowed from the typologies of other early writing systems. However, we first need to address the problem identified above of defining 'art' and 'writing' in the context of Cretan Hieroglyphic: though necessarily and unavoidably subjective, scholars' unstated understandings of these have formed the basis for every approach to the script, past or present.

[10] In response to a question by Van Effenterre, Olivier (1981) further argued that there are no clear associations between sign-combinations and 'decorative' motifs in Cretan Hieroglyphic, an observation here considered to be incorrect.

Let us start by adopting Olivier's definition of writing, seen above. Though to my mind highly restrictive (favouring only the most traditional forms of writing), for the purpose of this paper – and at this comparatively early point in the discipline – it is deemed best to start from a consensus, which may then be made more precise as we uncover more of the complexities presented by the script. My objections, however, may be briefly summarised as follows: even if classic examples of sematographic writing,[11] such as musical notation or numerals (Sampson 1985; Bennett 1963, 98 in the context of Aegean scripts), can still be argued to fit under this definition, more unconventional examples, such as Pre-Columbian Mesoamerican map-writing (see e.g. Boone and Mignolo 1994), cannot. Indeed, some forms of 'writing' depend, it seems to me, exactly on exploring that boundary between the graphic universality of art and Olivier's specificity of script. Forcing such complex scripts into the framework of more recognisable writing systems, or disregarding them as a forms of writing altogether, seems wholly unjustifiable.

For the definition of 'art', as already pointed out, there is no scholarly tradition to build on in the context of the script. Any definition offered here will, like that of writing, be inherently controversial and, no doubt, strongly contested. However, the virtue of offering such definitions lies exactly in the clear exposition of the interpretative structures involved in our analyses, bringing these to the fore, rather than burying them in unstated and implicit assumptions (cf. Morgan 1985, in the context of iconographic analysis). It is clear that a definition of art in the context of Cretan Hieroglyphic must pay special attention to framing hermeneutic interpretation, specifically the scope and limits of signification. As we have seen, and as we will consider more extensively below, recent implicit definitions of art in the context of the script have been highly restrictive, side-lining the signifying value of elements by dismissing them as 'decorative' and thus somehow meaningless. For the purpose of opening up and deepening the narrative, I thus here propose a radically inclusive synthesis of definitions developed by art-historian Gombrich and art-critic Danto: 'art is any manipulation of the human environment of which the material result (i) is about something, and (ii) embodies its meaning' (Gombrich 1950; Danto 1997, 195).[12]

Let us now start our analysis of the so-called 'decorative' signs lost in the normalisations of *CHIC*. As the scope of this paper does not allow for a comprehensive list of all signs omitted in *CHIC* or elsewhere, discussion in part one will limit itself to some token examples of each category.

[11] For a definition of the term, see below.

[12] The opening sentence of Gombrich's (1950) seminal volume *The Story of Art* famously reads '[t]here really is no such thing as Art, only artists'. Asked to clarify his position fifty years later, Gombrich professed that he went 'back deliberately to the old meaning of the term "art", when art was identified with skill or mastery, the art of war, the art of love, or whatever else. Art is something with a skill. There is no disembodied skill as such' (Carrier 1996, 279).

2. Identifying the problem

First, let us address the *omission of otherwise accepted 'syllabic' signs*. Often omitted because their absence transforms the sequence into well-known formulae, the 'decorative' nature of such signs was first proposed by Pope (1968). Let us, by way of illustration, consider all instances on seals or sealings of the two most common formulae in Cretan Hieroglyphic: 044-005 and 044-049.[13] Of 37 instances of 044-005 attested in the index of *CHIC* as solely present on a single epigraphic surface, three may be immediately dismissed: one (#259) requires reading across different seal-faces, one hypothesises signs on an illegible surface (#311), and another is formed by arbitrarily adding a non-existent trowel to a suspicious-looking eye (#314). Of the 34 seal faces left, only *seven* present us with just the formula on a single seal-face, while *18* show us the formula plus an omitted syllabic sign.[14] A further nine show the formula in combination with 'decorative' signs that Jasink (2009) has argued to be part of the script.

Thus, of all the seal-faces identified as showing the formula – and nothing else – in the index of *CHIC*, only 19% actually do. Even if we would accept Olivier and Godart in disregarding Jasink's (2009) signs, just over half of the instances identified in the index remain 'false' attestations. It is furthermore highly revealing that the omitted signs found in combination with 044-005 sometimes recur, such as 013 in the case of #140 and #264 (see Fig. 3.3). Such signs may even appear more than once in the same position: 065 is considered to appear in the middle of the formula on both #158 and #174 (Fig. 3.3).[15] It is worth noting that *CHIC* considers 065 to appear in the same medial position with the formula 044-049 (see #278), though there too the sign is omitted from the index.

Let us now consider 044-049: of the 63 attestations in *CHIC*'s index of just the formula on seals or sealings, we can dismiss four (#235, #259, #285, #311) for the same reasons as with 044-005 above,[16] leaving us with 59 possible instances. Twenty-four of these show only the formula (as well as 'decorative elements' associated with 044 discussed below), 18 show the formula with additional syllabic signs, and 17 show the formula with Jasink (2009) script signs. Only 38% can therefore be conclusively said to just show the formula (see Fig. 3.4).

It is thus extremely common for syllabic signs to disappear in the normalisations of *CHIC*, and to be subsequently disregarded by scholars in their study of the script. From the basis of our definitions (including *CHIC*'s own definition of writing), however,

[13] The formula 044-005 only appears twice on the clay documents (#18 and #59).

[14] Three of which admittedly show the additional sign in a smaller font, with another three showing variations on the combined formulae 044-005/044-049.

[15] Though the middle sign in #158 is transcribed as 065 in *CHIC*, 062 is to my mind equally possible here. A sign cognate to 065 and 062 might also be seen in the same position in #247c in Figure 3.6 below.

[16] #235 is too badly broken to be read with any degree of confidence; #259 reads across multiple seal faces (and includes a dubious version of 049); #285 is severely damaged, with only 044 clearly attested; #311 is weathered to the point that individual signs cannot be identified with any certainty.

	CHIC transcription	*CHIC* index
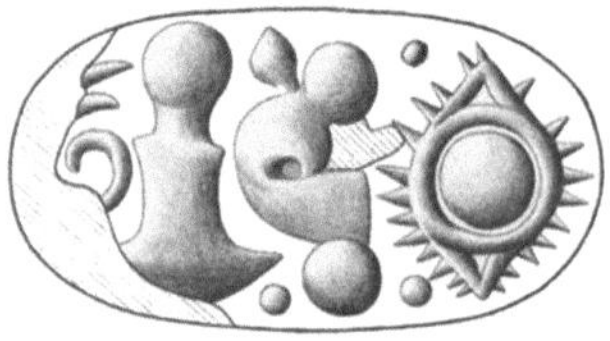 *CHIC* #140/*CMS* II.8,64		
 *CHIC* #264/*CMS* VI,92b		
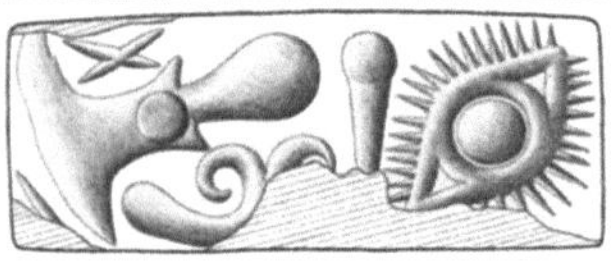 *CHIC* #158/*CMS* II.8,65	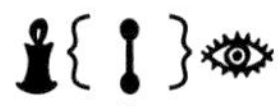	
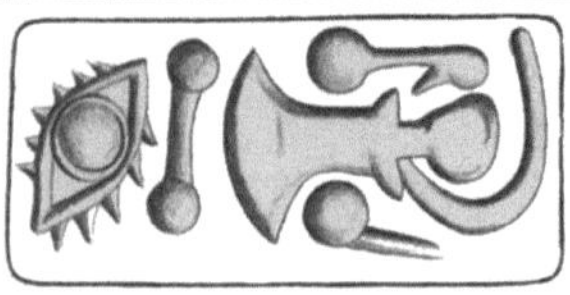 *CHIC* #174/*CMS* II.6,245		

Fig. 3.3: Instances of 044-005 with recurring CHIC signs. Adapted from images courtesy of the CMS Heidelberg.

there is little justification for such an approach: we are still entirely uncertain about the meaning of the formulae, and as such we cannot with any certainty argue that the omitted signs do not contain '*un message bien précis et univoque*'.

In the case of the recurring instances of syllabic signs in the middle of our formulae, e.g. 065 seen in Figure 3.3 above, there is no reason not to accept the combinations as sequences in their own right. Nor are hapax sequences in any way problematic in a corpus as limited as ours: none of the sign-groups found in the recently excavated archive at Petras, for instance, had previously been attested in the corpus (Tsipopoulou and Hallager 2010, 176) – a highly revealing, though in scholarship as of yet rarely mentioned, fact which we need to keep in mind at all times. For recurring signs associated with the formulae in varyingly initial, medial and final positions, e.g. 013

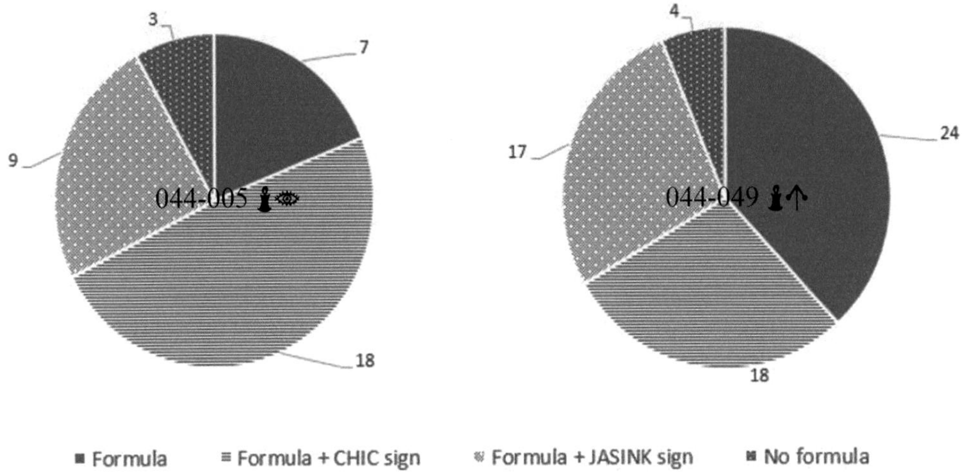

Fig. 3.4: Instances of just 044-005 and 044-049 on a single seal-face according to CHIC.

in Figure 3.3 above, though perhaps hapaxes, a more complex approach may need to be developed. We will do so below. It is important to note here, however, that such omission of 'syllabic signs' is equally well attested outside our token investigation, often on the basis of their size and supposed 'ornamental' position.[17]

Another category of otherwise accepted script-signs omitted in the corpus is that of isolated single signs. It was once more Pope who first suggested not allowing instances of less than two signs into the study of the script, to facilitate statistical discussion.[18] Similar ideas of 'dressing the material for statistical analysis' (Olivier 1989, 53) are perhaps at the basis of *CHIC*'s omission of these signs.[19] Once more, such signs cannot, however, be argued with any certainty not to conform to Olivier's own definition of 'writing': in *CHIC*, isolated signs interpreted as 'logograms' are accepted as part of the writing system. Furthermore, in one document (#56, see Fig. 3.5) a clear relationship between numbers associated with 044-049 and numbers associated with a variable longer sign-group – a relationship best characterised as (x) to (x/~10) – seemingly proves the existence of single-sign abbreviation in Cretan Hieroglyphic.[20] This is made even more

[17] An example of such omissions not associated with formulae in *CHIC* can be seen in the omission of 028 and 026 on #300c in Figure 3.7 below. Another token example of a much larger corpus of such omissions is #309g (Figure 3.19, below), where possible instances of 025 and 081 are omitted.

[18] See above, n. 9. See Olivier (1981, 108) for his justification in leaving out single signs.

[19] At the end of his survey of possible methods of decipherment, Olivier (1989, 52) concluded that 'finally, the statistical methods will probably be the most satisfactory.' This 1989 article is, I would argue, crucial to understanding the methods of selection employed in *CHIC*, written at a time when computer analysis acquired far-reaching fame in deciphering complex signaries, a result of the successes and excitement of post-World War II and Cold War computerised cryptography.

[20] This relationship was already described by Younger (1998, 390–1); for a different deconstruction of the document, see his Appendix H. Extremely interesting from a linguistic point of view are the variations

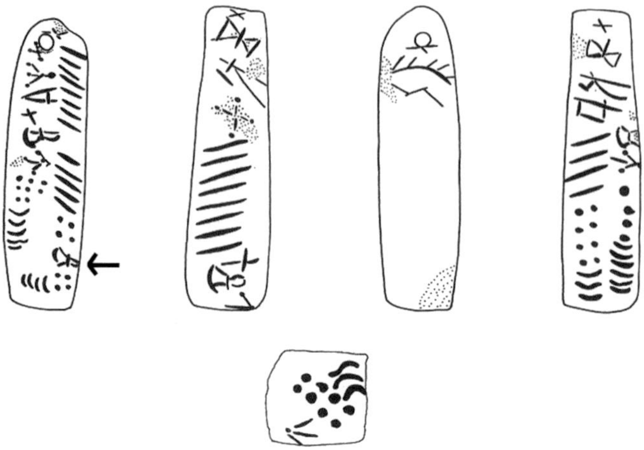

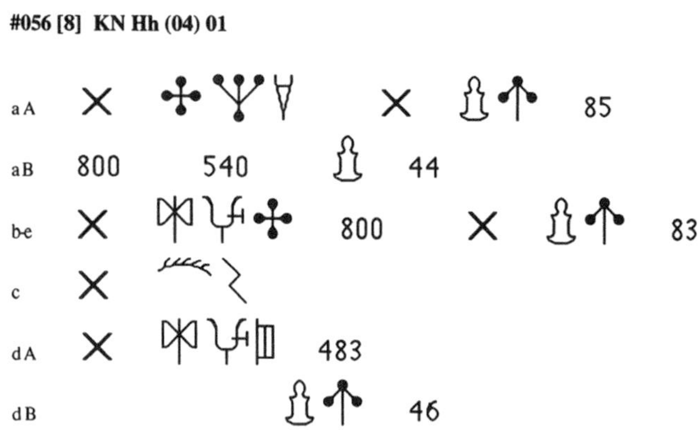

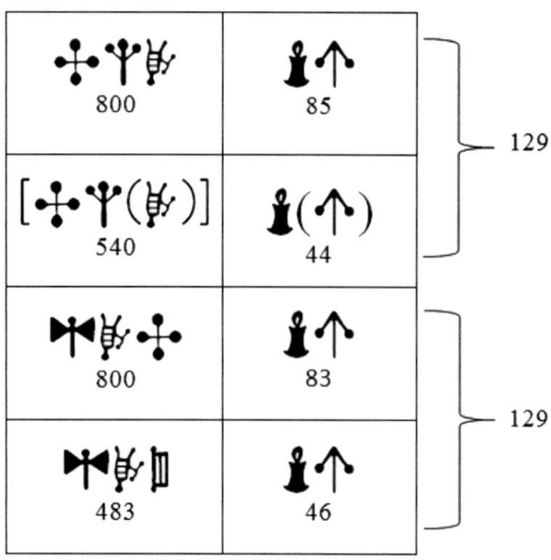

Fig. 3.5: CHIC #56, drawings and transcription courtesy of J.-P. Olivier and L. Godart; an arrow highlights the possible abbreviation 044(-049) (sign). Deconstruction (table) by author.

clear by the fact that the numerals accompanying 044-049 on face aA, when added to those accompanying the abbreviation 044 on face aB, come to the exact same sum, namely 129, as the two sets of numerals accompanying the two instances of 044-049 further in the document. Olivier, however, dismisses the instance as a mistake: '*il ne s'agit pas d'une abréviation, mais d'un oubli du second signe*' (Olivier 2000, n. 34).

Regardless of what one thinks of this particular document, there is the extremely telling instance of two signs (042 and 089), both on the same document (#65), forcibly incorporated into *CHIC*'s lists as 'adjuncts' due to their peculiar placement in front of 'logograms', the only two of their kind supposedly attested. The latter signs once more prove the acceptance in *CHIC*, at least to some extent, of single signs being able to contain '*un message bien précis et univoque*.' Furthermore, *CHIC* allows for the identification of single signs on seal-faces when these are thought to form a well-known formula across those faces (e.g. #256 and #259).[21] In conclusion, it is clear that we have unjustifiably excluded what may be up to multiple hundreds of single-sign inscriptions from a script which is currently thought to possess only a few hundred inscriptions overall. How we can envisage such isolated signs as part of our script, however, will once more be discussed in the theoretical exposition below.

Let us now, as our second category, consider the *omitted large 'ornamental' signs*, recently exhaustively surveyed by Jasink (2009). These are either ignored completely in *CHIC*, or variously marked with {!} or { }, though all such signs are omitted from the index. Some of these signs could already be seen interacting with the formulae above. The most frequent to appear with, for example, 044-005 were the 'spiral' , (#165, #261, #266, #309), Jasink's 'scroll' / (#145, #158 in Fig. 3.3, #246, #254) and the famous 'cat-mask' or full-bodied cat / (#247, #295; #309 in Fig. 3.8 below).[22] Some examples are given in Figure 3.6. All of these signs alternate in position with regards to the formula, and all of them behave in identical ways to the first category of the 'omitted syllabic signs associated with formulae' discussed above. More generally, large 'decorative' signs also very often form part of simple script-sequences (e.g. #154, #288, #304, #310, etc.) in which, as already argued by Jasink (2009), there is little justification for their omission.

There is a further category to be discussed here: large ornamental signs seemingly connected with specific syllabic signs. Let us once more undertake a token investigation, this time of two signs which maintain a consistent relationship with

in endings of the sign-group on faces b and dA: I hypothesised a similar situation for the potentially omitted sequence associated with the abbreviated formula on side aB (see deconstruction in Figure 3.5).

[21] It should furthermore be noted that single-sign inscriptions are abundant in GORILA (*Études Crétoises* 21: Godart and Olivier, *Recueil des Inscriptions en Linéaire A*), the five-volume corpus of Linear A, which was compiled by the same authors.

[22] See Krzyszkowska (2015, 105) for the 'cat-mask' and full-bodied cat in relation to the formulae 044-005 and 044-049 . The paper in question offers a holistic investigation of cat iconography in MM II glyptic. See also Krzyszkowska (2012, 152-3; forthcoming) for the standing female as a potential hieroglyphic sign.

	CHIC transcription	*CHIC* index
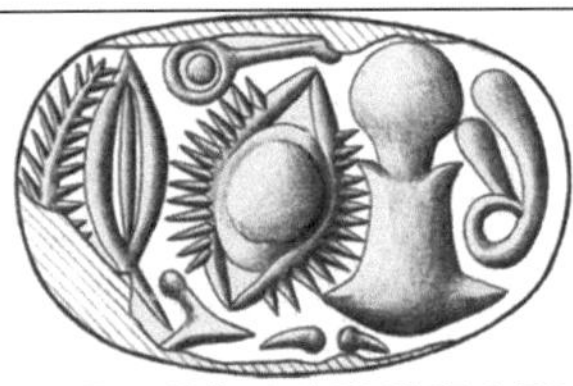 *CHIC* #145/*CMS* II.8,78	{ }	
 *CHIC* #246/*CMS* VI,27a		
 *CHIC* #247c/*CMS* IV,156b	{!}×	
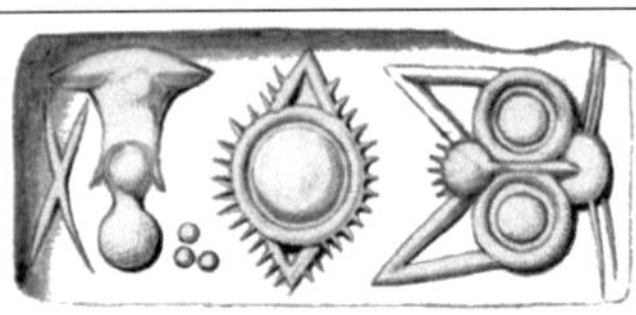 *CHIC* # 295/*CMS* II.2,316d	× {!}	

Fig. 3.6: Selected instances of 044-005 with recurring Jasink signs. Adapted from images courtesy of the CMS Heidelberg.

omitted 'decorative elements': 036 and 044 . The addition of 'decorative elements' to 036 seems to make 'aesthetic sense' if we accept Evans' idea of the '*horror vacui*' of Minoan artists; in the case of 044 , however, this is less clear.

Let us first have a look at 036 : of 25 instances of the sign in our corpus of seals, 21(!) embrace another sign, ten such instances recognised by *CHIC*. Of the remaining 11, where the extra signs have been omitted from transcriptions/index, six of the omitted signs are accepted elsewhere by *CHIC* as syllabic, while five are Jasink (2009) signs. Particularly puzzling is the omission of 031 in #131 (Fig. 3.7.2), as it is part

Fig. 3.7.1: CHIC #300c/CMS X,52c. 3.7.2: CHIC #131/CMS II.6,179. Drawings courtesy of J.-P. Olivier and L. Godart.

Fig. 3.8: CHIC #309a. Drawing courtesy of J.-P. Olivier and L. Godart.

of a common formula, and Younger (1990, 91–2) has already described the tendency of the formula 036-092-031 to form a 'cartouche' around its final sign (see e.g. *CHIC* #272b/*CMS* IX,D21c). Combined with the omission of 028 (and possibly 026) in #300c, it is clear that this decision has been made purely on the basis of size (Fig. 3.7.1).

Let us now move to 044 . In the whole of *CHIC* I counted 109 clear instances of the sign on seals, of which 51 seemingly carry no 'attached' decoration, and 58 instances do. Of the latter, 22 showed a single or double version of the 'spiral' (seven single, and 15 double: for an example of the latter, see Fig. 3.8), nine instances had Jasink's 'scroll' / attached or nearby (e.g. #140 and #158 in Fig. 3.3), and nineteen instances showed varying numbers of crescents or dots surrounding 044 (most often four, symmetrically arranged). Of the remaining eight, five were associated with small versions of *CHIC* syllabic signs, and three with Jasink (2009) script signs.

Interestingly, 044 flanked by double 'spirals' and 044 flanked by crescents does not appear anywhere in the corpus except with our two previously discussed formulae. However, as most instances of 044 in *CHIC* are part of these formulae, this may simply be coincidence. The minute size of some of these elements, sometimes less than a millimetre (thus properly belonging to a separate category of small 'ornamental' signs discussed below), makes them hard to chalk up to the traditional '*horror vacui*'. A good example of such intricacies are the minute flanking elements in #308 (see Fig. 3.9).

I would suggest that we can perhaps even recognize such elements flanking 044 in our clay archives, where peculiar dots sometimes appear in or next to 044 (Fig. 3.10). A common argument against considering some of these elements as part of the script is that they are occasionally found attached to each other in seemingly decorative ways (e.g. #295); however, we may find 'proper' signs behaving in the same way elsewhere (e.g. #242).

Fig. 3.9: Impressions and drawings of #308g-d in CHIC. Images courtesy of J.-P. Olivier and L. Godart.

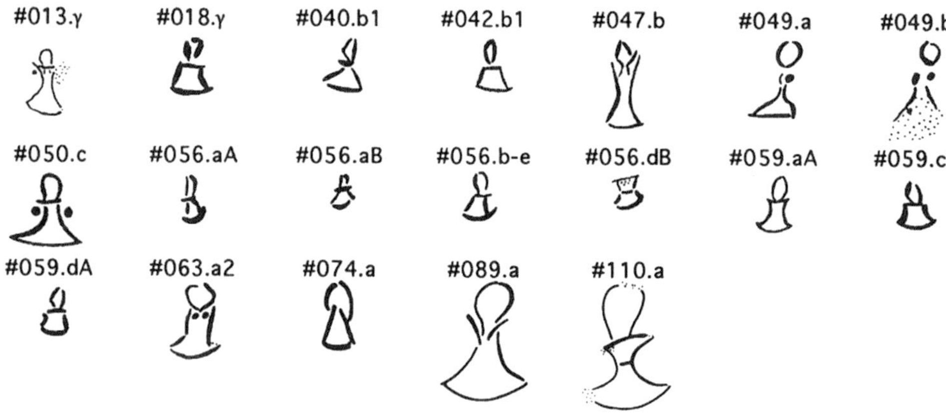

Fig. 3.10: All instances of 044 on clay documents in CHIC. Image courtesy of J.-P. Olivier and L. Godart.

Having presented some token examples, let us now move on to the *omitted small 'ornamental' signs and 'decoration'*, already briefly touched upon in the context of 044 above. Such minute signs consist, among others, of dots (see e.g. #262b in Fig. 3.2; #140, #264 in Fig. 3.3; #295 in Fig. 3.6), 'crocuses', *fleurs-de-lis*, and crescents. The so-called 'initial x' stiktogram is not discussed here, as its participation in the script is well accepted.

A first observation that ought to caution us against the long tradition of neglecting these 'background elements', is that some of them closely mirror – or are indeed identical to – accepted script signs, as we have already seen earlier in this paper when we encountered small versions of 062, 063 and 065 (see e.g. Fig. 3.9). Equally revealing is 154, found on the clay documents, perhaps a visual abbreviation of 023; the latter, quite common on the clay documents, is accepted as a sign on seals by *CHIC* in some instances (e.g. #243g), ignored as part of our *omitted large ornamental signs* in others (e.g. #301g). Indeed, 154 bears quite a resemblance to the 'ornamental' crocuses (e.g. top left #124; bottom right #212; #214; #262b in Fig. 3.2) mentioned above. Similarly, the '*fleur-de-lis*' variously appears same-size next to accepted script signs (e.g. #283b; #293a; #301d; #268c; CMS II.8,74), or in a smaller size elsewhere on the glyptic field (e.g. #295a–g; #155; #160-1; #254a). Crescents occur in the script as numerals, but it would be a step too far to consider them as such here, even if their symmetrical arrangement in certain instances (such as with 044 discussed above) reminds us of their archival counterparts.

Most of these elements are, once more, generally considered as completely detached from the script. Various approaches have, however, argued them to be differentiating in nature, allowing for the identification of individuals: Weingarten, for example, has likened the use of 'decorative fillers' on Cretan Hieroglyphic seals to modern PIN numbers (Weingarten 1995, 307). Though this suggestion may carry some truth, the constant reappearance of only a small number of physically identical signs (some identical to syllabic signs), as well as the association of these signs with specific patterns, seems to defeat such a purpose.

Finally, what I term 'true artistic motifs' such as cross hatching (see Fig. 3.19 below), 'decorative frames' (e.g. #257) and parallel lines (e.g. #273 or #274g), also appear on some of our seals. To my knowledge no scholar in the discipline has ever considered these as part of the Cretan Hieroglyphic script. I will, however, attempt to link even these into my interpretative framework. Having thus surveyed all categories of so-called 'ornamental' signs, let us now build the long promised theoretical framework to accommodate each of these instances as part of the script.

3. Theoretical framework

Let us first address the 'syllabic' and 'ornamental' *signs, whether large or minute, that appear either in isolation, or interjected in varying positions among well-known formulae* and other seemingly closed sign-groups.

From the administrative documents (e.g. #56 and #59) we know that the 044-005 and 044-049 formulae discussed above are occasionally followed by numerals. We have already considered the case where a direct relationship seems implied (#56, see Fig. 3.5 above). One observation, which I think ought to be stressed, is that in each attestation of these two formulae accompanied by numbers, another sign group is present, whether as header of the document as a whole, or of a section: the formulae seemingly need to be qualified by other sign groups. This fits well with the two possible readings currently offered in scholarship of the formulae as either transactional terms or administrative entities:[23] though both groups could conceivably

[23] See Olivier (1990) for the initial hypothesis that they represent administrative institutions; for elaborations on Olivier's thesis, see Weingarten (1995, 303) and Poursat (2000), the latter stressing the various hierarchies of administration that the formulae represent. See Meriggi (1973), Brice (1991) and Younger (1998) for the interpretation of the formulae as transactional terms. Cf. http://www.people.

stand on their own when directly inscribed onto objects qualifying the sign group (as demonstrated by their impression on ceramic materials),[24] neither would normally be expected to appear isolated on administrative documents. If we subsequently consider the nature of some of our so-called 'interjected' signs, identified elsewhere in *CHIC* as 'logograms' (e.g. 152, 153, 177), the relation between formula and single 'erratic' sign(-group) may become somewhat clearer.

Rather than following the typical path of vague 'ideographic' interpretation, as criticised by Pope, let us use these examples to establish part of our interpretative framework. In 1963, Emmett Bennett – writing in the context of Aegean scripts – proposed to divide all writing systems into lexigraphic and sematographic elements, 'writing representing speech, implying that the signs have a linear order directly corresponding to that speech,' on the one hand, and 'writing not representing speech, implying that signs may have any conventional order or arrangement' on the other (Bennett 1963, 109–10; see 119 for an overview of Bennett's definitions of various categories of writing). Bennett further proposed to subdivide lexigraphy into 'logography' and 'phonography' (representing words and representing non-significant segments of speech respectively), and remarked that any lexigraphic part, when 'ordered on sematographic principles' can become sematographic in nature (Bennett 1963, 110). This is the nature of the so-called 'logogram', which presents the marriage of lexigraphic meaning and sematographic presentation.

The sematographic elements of writing systems generally, and the ideogram specifically, have come under serious attack over the last half century, most famously by Gelb (1952) in his *Study of Writing*. Though Gelbian ideas on the evolution of writing no longer hold sway, many scholars and grammatologists have supported his rejection of the 'ideogram', and within our field specifically, Olivier has stated his support for the complete removal of the term from our corpora (Thompson 2010, 545): a stance arguably at the basis of many of the omissions in *CHIC*. As already discussed in this paper in the context of Cretan Hieroglyphic, the rejection of the ideogram came as a reaction to past approaches focussing on the magical, mythological or 'universal' nature of early writing, giving sematography, to quote Thompson (2010, 546), 'a certain lunatic air'.

As argued by Thompson, however, the presence of ideographic elements in our scripts is undeniable and their presence in the Bronze Age Aegean scripts demonstrable: think only of numerals. The practice of 'double-writing' and the behaviour of monograms – retained across scripts and ordered not according to lexigraphic, but aesthetic principles – hint at such sematographic structures. The most convincing examples in Linear B are the famous 'sexing' signs, which, as shown by Killen (1964, 10), do not straightforwardly signify gender, but more complex ideas of 'breeding age females' and 'all animals', changing in meaning only when contrasted to each other (Thompson 2010, 558).

ku.edu/~jyounger/Hiero (interestingly, Younger there suggests 026 to be a possible logogram or determinative; for the latter of which, see below).

[24] See e.g. #150/*CMS* II.6,189, where the 044-049 formula is impressed on an amphora handle.

Let us now look at some parallels further away from home. Phonetic complementation, repeating phonetic elements for semantic reasons (a practice perhaps not entirely unlike the so-called 'double-writing' identified in Linear B), can be found in, to give only some examples, Egyptian (Ritner 1996), Akkadian (Caplice 2002, 5–7), Anatolian Hieroglyphic (Morpurgo Davies and Hawkins 1978; Melchert 2004), and Mayan Hieroglyphic (Bricker 2008, 168–73; Grube 2010; Grube 2012, 849; Kettunen and Helmke 2014, 19/151),[25] see Figure 3.11 and Figure 3.12. In the latter it was likely initially used to differentiate logograms with several variant readings, and later extended to unambiguous logograms (Bricker 2008, 169; Grube 2010, 27). We may theorise similar functions for some of the above identified elements in Cretan Hieroglyphic.

Similarly, signs commonly recognised as semantic determinatives or classifiers, disambiguating interpretation and indicating semantic categories, appear, amongst others, in the Chinese, Mayan, Egyptian and Bronze Age Mesopotamian scripts. Examples of such determinatives include the cuneiform sign '*dingir*' (Akkadian '*ilu*'), a star-like symbol used in both art and writing to denote divinity (see Fig. 3.13), as well as minute elements used to differentiate animal types and human body parts in Mayan glyphs (Fig. 3.14; Hopkins 1994; Hopkins and Josserand 1999; Mora-Marín 2008, 200–1: 'if these authors are correct, semantic classifiers are so pervasive in the script that epigraphers have taken them for granted'). Punctuation – in Cretan Hieroglyphic referred to as 'stiktogrammatic' – and diacritic markers are equally common in early scripts (Fig. 3.14 shows an example of the remarkable 'syllabic doubling sign' in Mayan, which consists of two small dots in the margin indicating that the phonetic value of the adjacent sign should be repeated: Stuart and Houston 1994, 46, 50; Kettunen and Helmke 2014, 20/151) .

I would thus suggest approaching the supposedly erratic signs in Cretan Hieroglyphic as potential sematograms, within a framework of either: (i) semantically meaningful phonetic complementation, (ii) semantic classifiers or determinatives, (iii) stiktogrammatic or diacritic markers, (iv) abbreviations or adjuncts, or (v) simple or complex ideograms – distinct in that they can appear on their own.

That such possible sematograms are seemingly scarce on the clay documents may be indicative of different writing practices, perhaps due to the static nature of the visual information encoded on seals, and the more dynamic nature of contemporary archives. Yet they are certainly not absent: the signs identified by *CHIC* as adjuncts, the logograms, as well as individual instances such as the abbreviation on #56, or

[25] The problem of defining writing and its complex relationship with art has been extensively explored in the context of Mesoamerican scripts: see e.g. Boone and Mignolo (1994). As such, theoretical approaches developed in these disciplines may be used to inform directly upon the study of Cretan Hieroglyphic, and as comparative evidence to improve our general understanding of early scripts and their relation to other modes of visual communication. The gradual decipherment of the Mayan script was already cited with excitement in the 1980s and 90s in scholarship on Bronze Age Aegean writing systems (see e.g. Duhoux *et al.* 1997, 7).

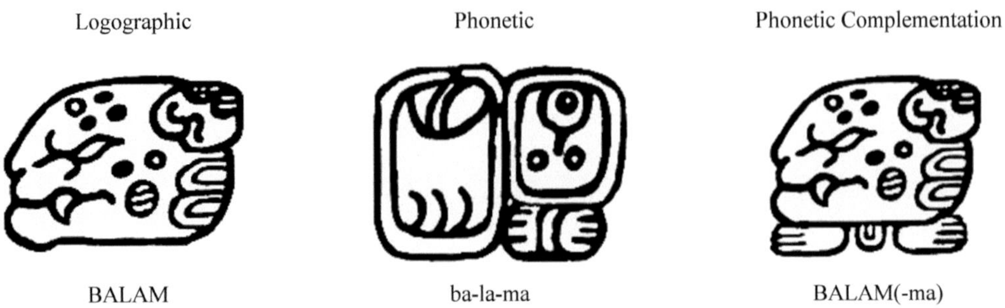

Fig. 3.11: Phonetic complementation in Mayan: 'jaguar' in logographic, phonetic and phonetically complemented logographic form. Drawings by author after Harris and Stearns 1997. Though in the latter work (and many other reference works), (ba-)BALAM is also depicted, such a glyph is not actually attested in the epigraphic record (Grube 2010, 28). BALAM(-la-ma), on the other hand, does seem to exist: Kettunen and Helmke 2014, 80/151.

Fig. 3.12: First row: the royal name Yaxun Balam or 'Bird-Jaguar' on Yaxchilan lintel 43 and lintel 30 respectively, with preposed, and then pre- as well as postposed phonetic complementation. Drawings by author after Kettunen and Helmke 2014, 18/151. Second and third row: further examples of preposed, postposed and full phonetic complementation in iterations of the word WAY 'spirit/co-essence', and MUYAL 'cloud'. Second row drawings courtesy of Stephen Houston (Stuart and Houston 1989), third row drawings by author after Stuart and Houston (1994).

Fig. 3.13: Left: opening lines of the famous law code of Hammurabi, with 'dingir' *as a logogram for the god Anum in the header, and as a determinative next to Anunnaki (all gods) on the second line, and Enlil (a deity) on the third line. Drawing after normalisation by Harper (1904). Right:* 'dingir' *in art, accompanying a ewe suckling a lamb on a 13th century BC cylinder from Ashur (Harper* et al. *1995, 73), drawing by author.*

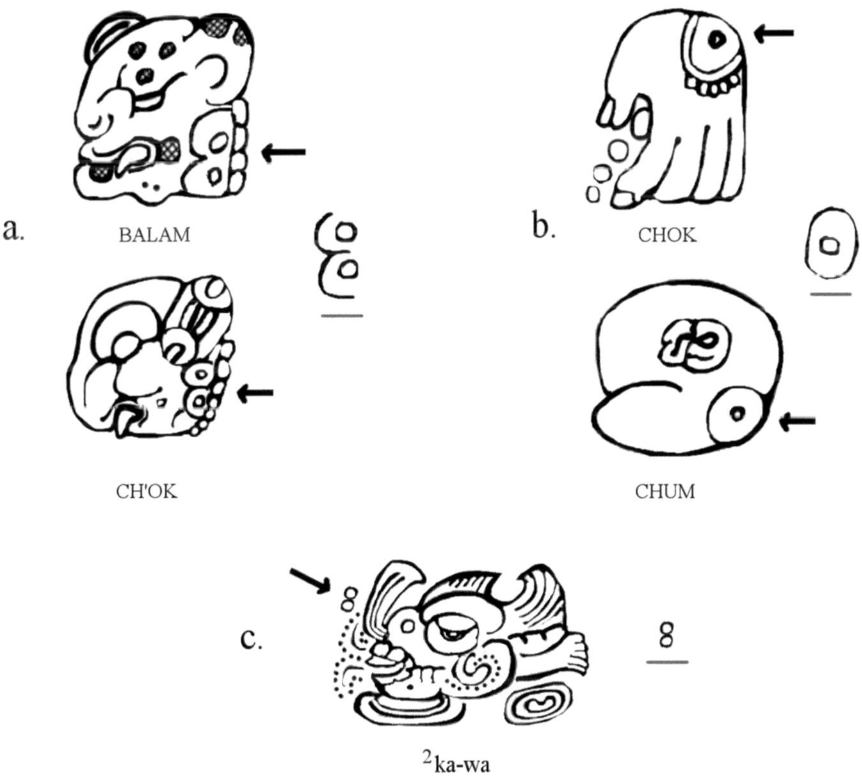

Fig. 3.14: Double bracket elements signifying 'night animals' (Stephen Houston, pers. comm.; Stone and Zender 2011), dotted circle elements signifying human body parts, and the 'syllabic doubling sign' accompanying the word 'ka-wa' – to be read as 'kakaw' or cacao/chocolate – in Mayan. Drawings by author after glyphs from Kettunen and Helmke (2014).

perhaps even the possibly meaningful dots accompanying instances of 044, all point to a complex sematographic system being in place.

A final example here brings together both engraved and inscribed material, in the form of the inscriptions accompanied by seal-impressions on the crescent nodules from the Knossos Hieroglyphic deposit. Though divorced from each other in *CHIC* (supposed non-Hieroglyphic seal impressions even omitted altogether), I consider these elements to constitute one document, and contend that they should be interpreted as such. Weingarten has already argued for a meaningful relationship between the text on sealings and that on sealed documents, based on repeated instances of sequences and individual signs in the Hieroglyphic deposit from Mallia (Weingarten 1995, 292).[26] The Knossos crescents have so far only been published as a single unit in schematic form by Weingarten, and currently cannot be consulted in full anywhere.[27]

The specific example I want to pick out here, however, is that of #18. This particular crescent nodule is traditionally argued to show the formula 044-005 repeated three times: once incised, twice impressed. A closer look at the sealings (#140 and #158 in Fig. 3.3), however, reveals that each contains two 'omitted' signs, both times one from the *CHIC* syllabary and one from Jasink's (2009) list. Though the document has been used in the past as 'proof' for the redundant nature of script on seals when used sphragistically, I would here argue the exact opposite: namely that this document presents us with one of the most convincing indications of the semantic relevance of the omitted signs. For, if we want each part of the document – in its essence a utilitarian tool – to be meaningful, an appreciation of the three instances of the formula as somehow different is almost inescapable.[28]

[26] Four noduli – Weingarten's (1986) class of nodules that seemingly did not seal anything – were found as part of the same assemblage as 12 medallions in room III 3b of Building A in Mallia, Quartier Mu. Each nodulus contained Cretan Hieroglyphic sealings, all depicting 'one or more animal heads', while 'similar signs were written (...) on six of the twelve medallions' (Weingarten 1995, 292). One nodulus contained a sealing displaying but a single sign (016): in the context of this 'animal head' archive, this single sign seems to strongly support our contention that isolated signs ought to be viewed as inscriptions in their own right, not as a separate class of 'figurative' or 'decorative' art. In her article, Weingarten identifies and discusses this issue, arguing that 'other seemingly naturalistic seals [may], in fact, [be] lurking hieroglyphs' (Weingarten 1995, 304–5).

[27] The schematic nature of the drawings Weingarten (1995) had to work with bear testament to just how much the study of Cretan Hieroglyphic owes to *CHIC* (as well as the continued publications of the *CMS*).

[28] I say 'almost', as a counterargument could be made by likening the crescents to the so-called 'roundels' (Hallager 1990), where the number of seal-impressions on each nodulus, rather than their content, has been argued to be of importance (Hallager 1990, 126–7). However, the apparent relationships between sign-sequences inscribed on the clay and the glyptic material, as already noted in this paper (and by Weingarten 1995, 292; cf. n. 26), as well as the fact that the Knossos crescent nodules display a maximum of up to three sealings at any time (while roundels carry up to 15), caution against interpreting the nodules in this way.

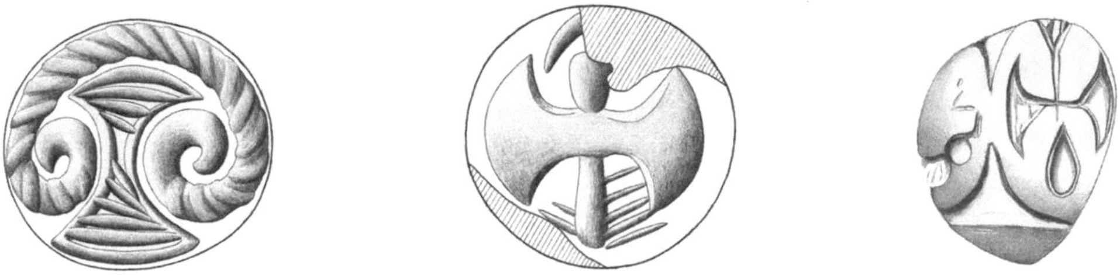

042-049 ? 042-025 ? 042-019 ?

Fig. 3.15: Possible ligatures in sealings found on the Knossos crescent nodules. Left: CMS II.8, 49; for instances of 049 in a similar form, see CHIC p. 407 (e.g. #219, #208, #209 and #312). Middle: CMS II.8, 55. Right: CMS II.8,124. Images courtesy of the CMS Heidelberg.

A holistic analysis of the crescents yields 40 sealings from 33 unique seals, of which 18 are hieroglyphic according to *CHIC*, and 15 are supposedly 'non-hieroglyphic'. Of the 15 supposed 'non-hieroglyphic' seals, however, all but four display single *CHIC* signs, the remaining four displaying Jasink (2009) signs. Despite the prevalence of figure scenes in the corpus of Middle Minoan seals, only one such scene is attested on all of the 40 sealings impressed (see Fig. 3.16). Some of the isolated signs omitted from *CHIC* may, I would suggest, further elucidate the script's sematographic structures. Indeed, it is possible to identify some of the supposed single signs as potential ligatures (see Fig. 3.15), Cretan Hieroglyphic being the only Aegean writing system to include ligatures in its syllabary.

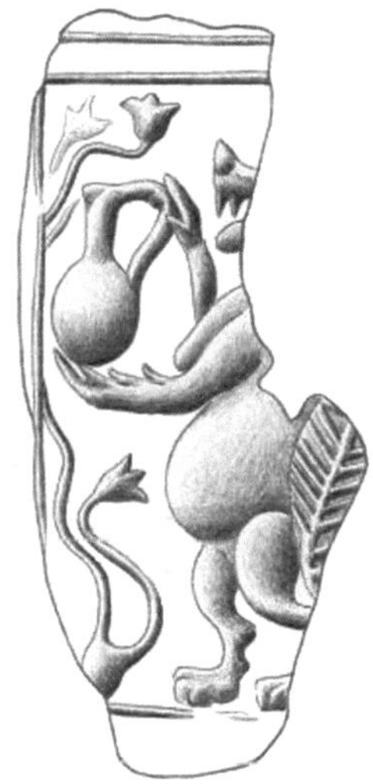

053 and 023 ?

Fig. 3.16: Tentative identification of script values in figurative sealing CMS II.8,195. Image courtesy of the CMS Heidelberg.

It is even tempting, though a different matter entirely, to interpret the one figurative scene as part of the same sematographic network, whether as incorporating known script signs (e.g. 053 and 023), or as an image with a semantic significance strongly related to that of ideographs.

It is here, at the end of our paper, that our definition of art finally proves its use, helping us to address *the most convincingly 'decorative' elements in the script*. If we accept that all art (i) is about something, and (ii) embodies its meaning, then we cannot simply dismiss any element as 'decorative' or 'ornamental' and be done with it. Though various degrees of meaning are obviously encoded in the various elements found on our seals, scenes such as the one displayed above encode a complex set of interpretative structures, as does their relationship with the script signs on the same object. Both categories, 'image' and 'sign', are, after all, elements of the same visual language, even if the modes of viewing can differ.

Figs. 3.17 and 3.18: CHIC #207b/CMS II.1,420b and CHIC#274a/CMS XII,105a respectively. Images courtesy of the CMS Heidelberg.

The fact that Cretan Hieroglyphic stands at the earliest diverging point of 'art' and 'script' in our region, cautions against viewing them too differently.[29] In many ways, the assertion, often encountered in scholarship, that Cretan Hieroglyphic seals ought to be 'viewed' not 'read', thus becomes meaningless.

One example of this may be demonstrated by #207b (Fig. 3.17): the formula 044-049 is here combined with a scene generally interpreted as a figure stomping grapes. That this scene might have had the same effect as our isolated signs appearing alongside known formulae may be suggested by the fact that on another seal (#274a, Fig. 3.18) we find 044-049 accompanied by the logogram for wine, 156 . Similarly, a version of the formula with an extra sign can be found on a sealing on crescent #007 from Knossos, which has 156 inscribed. If the figural scene indeed represents wine-making, a function of the figurative scene similar to the logogram 156 seems here very likely.

A final token investigation of what we called a 'true artistic motif' above, namely cross-hatching, may elucidate another aspect of the nature of this relationship between 'art' and 'writing'. Of the 12 instances of cross-hatching on hieroglyphic seals, nine remarkably lack the extremely common × stiktogram indicating direction of reading. A clue for such omissions can be found in #298d (see Fig. 3.19), where the formulae 044-005 and 044-049 are combined on a single field, a feature already discussed above (cf. n. 14). It seems clear that attention is drawn here to

[29] The prevalent tendency to present and transcribe Cretan Hieroglyphic in a way that is purposefully identical to its later linear counterparts is therefore, I would argue, highly problematic. Indeed, attempts at a standardised approach to all writing systems of the Bronze Age Aegean arguably underlie many of the problems faced in the study of Cretan Hieroglyphic today. Conformance to the principles set in the Mycenological conventions of Gif-sur-Yvette (1956), Wingspread (1961) and the first Congress of Mycenology (1967) has come at the cost of compromising – at times even ignoring – the idiosyncrasies of our script. The authors of *CHIC* ought to be commended for rejecting the original suggestion made at Ohrid (1985; Ilievski and Crepajac 1987) of compiling all signs of the Cretan Hieroglyphic, Linear A and Linear B scripts into a single numerical list (see Karnava 1997; Palaima 1998), as this would have further integrated – and presented as a virtually consistent system – three scripts which are, in most of their attestations, highly individualised and fundamentally independent.

Fig. 3.19: Row 1: CHIC #298d/CMS XI,14b; CHIC #298b/CMS XI,14d; CHIC #147/CMS II.8,88. Row 2: CHIC #268a/ CMS III,229a; CHIC #309b; CHIC #309g. Row 3: CHIC #268b/CMS III,229b; CHIC #161/CMS II.8,83. Images 1, 2, 8 courtesy of the CMS Heidelberg. Images 3–7 courtesy of J.-P. Olivier and L. Godart.

044 as the initial sign of two different sign-sequences, differentiated from 005 and 049 by vertical lines as well as our cross-hatching motif, indicating opposing reading directions. Cross-hatching may also be tentatively identified as dividing two sign groups on another side of the same seal (#298g), and as stressing what are most likely initial signs (as many display common sign groups) on others (#147, #268a and #309g in Fig. 3.19). The fact that the motif only appears in instances where additional signs are added to our formulae, supports such suggestions. Furthermore, only in the company of same-size 'extra' signs does cross-hatching engulf a different initial than that which we have come to expect (#268b, #161 in Fig. 3.19), arguably indicating the validity of these as independent sign-sequences (something anticipated above).[30]

4. Conclusion

The 'decorative elements' of the Cretan Hieroglyphic script, most of which have been detached from scholarly investigations since the very beginning of the discipline, have here been shown to possess all necessary qualities to form an integral part of the writing system. This indicates that there is no justification for the overly

[30] Interestingly, such a potential stiktogrammatic use of cross-hatching seems to be attested on rectangular or flat oval seal-faces only: round faces (e.g. #176, #181, #193 and #195) display a much more complex use of cross-hatching in the glyptic field.

syllabocentric view employed in the study of Cretan Hieroglyphic today. Indeed, through the rejection of possible sematographic elements, we have limited an already extremely limited corpus, excluding perhaps as many instances as we currently possess. A more careful approach for understanding the relationship between 'art' and 'writing' needs to be adopted in our study of the script, taking into account the nature of script as necessarily intertwined with, and part of, other modes of visual communication.

In conclusion, these elements of our script can no longer be dismissed without justification: to ensure that we can accommodate all probable paths of interpretation, nothing but a *complete turnaround* in the way we approach and define Cretan Hieroglyphic is needed.

Chapter 4

Linear B script and Linear B administrative system – different patterns in their development[1]

Helena Tomas

1. Main questions concerning the origin and development of Linear B

After 115 years since its discovery, the issue of the origin of Linear B is still unresolved. The scholarship of the past century considered questions of *where* and *when* Linear B was created as the most pressing ones, whereas less attention was paid to the question of *how* that was done – something that was meticulously dealt with by Thomas Palaima (1988a).

Opinions about the place of the creation of Linear B are divided into two main groups: those who believe that Linear B originated on Crete after the Mycenaean arrival to the island (e.g Pugliese Carratelli 1945, 463; Pope 1961–1962, 312; Sacconi 1976, 65; Olivier 1979, 46; Heubeck 1982, 201–2; Driessen 1990, 130; Palaima 1990, 99), and those who favour the Mainland, and who consequently argue that the script was created prior to the Mycenaean arrival to Crete (e.g. Chadwick 1976, 106–7; Godart 1979, 35–6; more recently Hallager 2011, 326–7). Other candidates have also been proposed: the Cyclades as a mediator in transferring the script from Crete to the Mainland Greeks (Palaima 1982, 18), or Miletus at the west Anatolian coast, which was settled by Minoans and later by Mycenaeans (Melena 2014, 7).

The answer to the question of *when* the script was created partly depends on other, still unresolved chronological intricacies, such as the date of Linear B deposits at Knossos,[2] or the date of the Mycenaean arrival to Crete (assuming that the script

---

[1] I would like to thank Pippa Steele for inviting me to this stimulating symposium, and all the participants for their observations and discussions that improved some of my thoughts expressed here. I would also like to thank Vassilis Petrakis who read the draft of this paper and reacted to it with helpful and insightful comments. Naturally, all omissions are solely my responsibility.

[2] In this paper and elsewhere I accept Driessen's argument that tablets from the Room of the Chariot Tablets (RCT) are chronologically earlier than the rest of the Knossian tablets and that they should be dated to LM II or early LM IIIA1 (Driessen 1990, 130, 1997, 2011, 71–2). I believe that results of my own research support such a view (Tomas 2003), as does the research of some other scholars, for example

was created on the island).[3] In brief, the dates proposed for the creation of Linear B span over several centuries, starting from the Middle Helladic III period, which would assume that the script was created on the Mainland prior to the Mycenaean arrival to Crete (Godart 1999b, 42–3, 2003, 234).[4] Although some other scholars have also argued for an early date of the creation of Linear B (for example, Pope 1961–1962, 312, 1964, 6; Hallager 2011, 326–7), the majority, starting from Arthur Evans, has settled for either LM I or LM II periods, or the transition between those two periods (Evans 1902–1903, 53; *SM1*, 38; *PMK1*, 646; Olivier 1979, 45; Heubeck 1982, 201; Duhoux 1985, 30–4; Rehak and Younger 2000, 288–93).

The question *why* Linear B was created is probably the least debatable question concerning the origin of Linear B and most scholars will agree with the answer that it was an adaptation of Linear A for the purposes of recording a new language.[5] And if we want to tackle the issue of why the new language needed to be recorded, we will come across several suggestions. The most prevalent one is that Linear B was introduced for the purpose of facilitating economic transactions of developing Mycenaean centres (some of the economic motives behind the creation of Linear B are listed in Palaima 1988a, 277). Pope argued that keeping the palace accounts was the only purpose of Linear B – when that purpose vanished with the destruction of the palaces, there was no longer any reason for the existence of the script (Pope 1961–1962, 311). Hooker, on the other hand, suggests that the script could also have been created for the writing of continuous texts, perhaps those of a literary character (1979, 38–9), but for now there is absolutely no evidence in favour of this option (except, perhaps, those few flat-based nodules from the RCT that may have been used for sealing documents on perishable material, see below). Quite a different view was more recently expressed by Driessen who thought that the creation of Linear B was one of the means of imposing political domination over Crete and of enhancing social stratification. Linear B was thus employed as a mechanism of control by the political elite (Driessen 1998–1999, 99; Driessen and Langohr 2007, 187–8).

Firth's work on find-places of tablets (1996–1997, 75, 2000–2001, 188–9), or Landenius Enegren's prosopographical study (2008, 30–6). While most scholars accept this earlier dating of the RCT, others disagree with it (see, for instance, Warren 1992; Popham 1993, 177; Pini 2002, 8–9; Hallager 2005a, 250–1, 2011, 327, n. 14).

[3] For various proposals on the date of the Mycenaean arrival to Crete, see Driessen and Farnoux 1997; Driessen and Macdonald 1997; Haskell 1997; Alberti 2004; Preston 1999, 2004, 2008, 314–6; D'Agata and Moody 2005.

[4] Godart uses the Kafkania pebble, presumably inscribed in Linear B and dated to the end of MH III, as an argument for such an early date for the beginnings of the script (Godart 1999b, 2003; Maniatis *et al.* 2010). Here, however, the pebble is not taken as conclusive for the date of the origin of Linear B since no agreement has been reached amongst scholars about its significance (see, for example, Palaima 2002–2003, 2010, 359).

[5] Mind, however, that some differences between the two scripts suggest a more complex scenario, as has recently been discussed by Petrakis who pointed out the significance of changes in the non-phonographic repertoire and commodity sematograms in Linear B (Petrakis forthcoming).

The final question that remains to be addressed is the question of *how* was Linear B created. This question, however, encompasses a range of sub-questions, such as: 1) what was the source for the creation of Linear B, i.e. according to which prototype it was modelled; 2) who were the executors of this process; 3) was this creation a sudden act which followed a resolution of a ruling body; or was it a gradual process, that was a result of a spontaneous development rather than an articulated decision?

As for the first of these sub-questions, most scholars are confident that Linear B was developed from Linear A (see for example Duhoux 1985, 19; Palaima 1988a, 272; Steele and Meißner in this volume). A minority of scholars, however, have allowed for the possibility that Linear B was developed from a script other than Linear A, perhaps a common predecessor to both Linear A and Linear B (Evans *PMK4*, 683; Sacconi 1976, 63; Hooker 1979, 31–2). This idea is supported by the shape of some Linear B signs, which look more cursive and ornate than the most advanced Linear A signs from Haghia Triada.[6] Due to a lack of evidence for the existence of some other script, Cretan Hieroglyphic has been proposed to have played the role of this common predecessor, although, as we will see below, the number of matching signs remains unsatisfactorily low. Petrakis (2014, this volume) assumes a completely fresh view: that we should in the case of north-central Crete avoid strict divisions between Cretan Hieroglyphic and Linear A writing systems. Instead, there may have been a 'fusion' of elements, elsewhere classified either as Cretan Hieroglyphic or as Linear A, which may have shaped the conditions that produced the features of what he calls, 'Third Palace period bureaucracies'.

When it comes to the second sub-question, historical circumstances favour one of the options: that it was the Mycenaeans who created the script in order to accommodate their language. A small number of scholars accepted a possibility that the Minoans executed this task, i.e. transformed their own script to satisfy the needs of a foreign language (Peruzzi 1960, 38, 48–9; Chadwick 1976a, 106–7; Hooker 1979, 71–3; cautiously explored in Driessen and Macdonald 1997, 117). The compromise solution is that this was a collaborative effort (Begg 1987, 184; Driessen 1990, 130).

Along with the first two sub-questions concerning how Linear B was created, the third sub-question will have to be explored on some other occasion. For now it suffices to summarise the two main streams of thoughts on how abrupt the creation of Linear B was: one sees it as a carefully planned and sudden act (Heubeck 1982, 2000; Palaima 1988a, 341; Driessen and Schoep 1999, 392), and the other as a result of a gradual process (Hooker 1979, 41).

[6] Another reason for the elaborateness of Linear B signs has been proposed: that the script was formed to be written primarily on material other than clay – perhaps papyrus – that was susceptible to a more cursive style (Hooker 1979, 33, 71).

2. Distinguishing the development of the Linear B script and the development of the Linear B administrative system

A more systematic study of the last set of questions (how was Linear B created?) is, I believe, crucial for better understanding of the origin and development of Linear B. However, any further analysis in this direction will demonstrate that a search for the origin of the script is intertwined with a study of the main purpose for which the script was created. Thus, the administrative system behind the script plays an important role in understanding the origin of Linear B. This is where the whole issue becomes more complex because it is easy to fall into a trap of assuming that the two originated from the same source. Further sections of this paper focus on showing that it is difficult to maintain a self-assuming notion that both Linear B script and the administrative system were modelled after a single prototype, and that the origin of Linear B becomes clearer if analysed from two different points: the origin of the script and the origin of the administrative system. Since Linear B is a name used to designate both, scholars typically conflate these two aspects. A notable exception is Bennet who has suggested that:

> '... the structure of a writing system is distinct from the broader set of practices embodied in an administrative system as reflected in sealings. It is worth at least entertaining the possibility that the adaptation of the Linear A script to record the Greek language – the script we call Linear B – is a different, or parallel, process from development of a new sealing system.' (Bennet 2005, 270)

It is precisely the differences in the sealing system that has convinced me that Linear B could not have taken Linear A administration for its model (as elaborated in detail in Tomas 2003). Although Linear A remains the most convincing predecessor for the Linear B script, when it comes to the administrative system Linear A does not provide convincing parallels. Some of these parallels are, surprisingly, found in the Cretan Hieroglyphic administration (Hallager 2011; Tomas 2012b), which, on the other hand, is not a plausible scriptual predecessor. Thus it is indeed wrong to assume, at least on the basis of current evidence, that Linear B in its origin and development relied on a single source. I would still partly agree with the general consensus that it was an offspring of Linear A. I do not think, however, that this means that Linear B was *exclusively* developed from Linear A, and here follow my arguments in brief.

3. Linear B script

3.1. Similarities and differences in the signaries

Due to a very limited choice, there has not been much speculation about the source for the creation of Linear B. For now, there are only three options: 1) that Linear B was created from Linear A, as supported by most scholars on the basis of numerous common signs; 2) that it was created from Cretan Hieroglyphic, as suggested on the basis of some more embellished forms of signs, and the fact that some Linear B signs can be traced back to Cretan Hieroglyphic; and 3) that Linear A and Linear B were created from another script, yet un-evidenced 'Linear X', as a common predecessor to both. Early studies proposed that in fact Cretan Hieroglyphic may have played the role of the common predecessor. This was partly due to a lack of any other candidates, and partly due to a belief that Cretan Hieroglyphic was the earliest of the three scripts (Evans *SM1*, 18, 38; *PMK1*, 612–3; *PMK4*, 683; Myres in Evans *SM2*, 1–2, 74; Pugliese Carratelli 1945, 461–2). Subsequent discoveries of documents, however, revealed that for now it is not possible to show that Cretan Hieroglyphic preceded Linear A, unless EM III–MM IA inscribed seals from Archanes are considered as early examples of Cretan Hieroglyphic (as is done in *CHIC*), and not as a separate script (for the summary of chronology of Cretan Hieroglyphic and Linear A inscriptions and the question of the Archanes script, see Tomas 2010, 341–3). To sum up: the main argument for Linear A as a predecessor to Linear B are the numerous similarities between the two scripts (such as a large number of shared signs, or the shape of signs), whereas the main reason for regarding Cretan Hieroglyphic or some third script as a common predecessor to both are certain differences between Linear A and Linear B (more recently the issue has been taken up by Hallager 2011; see also the relevant discussion by Petrakis 2014 and in this volume).

The reason why the majority of scholars readily accepted that Linear A was a persuasive prototype for the Linear B script is the large number of matching syllabograms, giving almost 80% of all Linear B syllabograms (*GORILA* V, XXII; Melena 2014, 8, fig. 17.1). The correspondence between some logograms is still present (Palmer 1995), yet many new logograms were introduced to Linear B (Petrakis forthcoming). As for other types of signs, Linear B abandoned, with a few exceptions, the rich repertoire of Linear A monograms and ligatures, but increased the number of adjuncts. The Linear A system of aliquot fractions was replaced by a new metrical system. The system of numbers, however, remained the same. One further link with Linear A is evident: the manner in which transactions were presented, namely in sequences of sign-groups + logograms + numbers (explored by Hooker 1979, 39; note that Cretan Hieroglyphic tablets display a similar pattern).

If the number of common signs is the main criterion for establishing a predecessor, then Linear B relates to Linear A better than to Cretan Hieroglyphic. This is not to deny that some Linear B signs resemble those in Cretan Hieroglyphic, since ca. 25% of Linear B syllabograms can be traced to Cretan Hieroglyphic (see tables of corresponding signs in Evans *PMK1*, 643; *Docs*[2], 33; Hooker 1979, 75; *CHIC* 19; Duhoux (1998, 5) argues that only a dozen Linear B signs have parallels in the Cretan Hieroglyphic script), but these are in most cases the same signs that also show a connection between Linear A and Cretan Hieroglyphic. According to the comparative list in *CHIC*, a very small number of signs shows a link between Cretan Hieroglyphic and Linear B without a Linear A intermediary (*CHIC* 19). In saying that the Linear B script was developed from Linear A rather than Cretan Hieroglyphic the latter is thus not completely excluded, since some signs, as said, are common to Linear A and Cretan Hieroglyphic. However, when an immediate influence is sought, more numerous similarities indicate that Linear B scribes looked primarily at Linear A texts, rather than those in Cretan Hieroglyphic, and probably consulted Linear A scribes.

The scenario that Linear B was adapted from Linear A for the purposes of a new language was established immediately after the decipherment, and this became the crucial explanation for the changes in the syllabary from Linear A to Linear B (*Docs*[1], 39). If we discount the above mentioned differences in logograms and in the metrical system, which may have been caused by reasons other than the unsuitability of the script to a new language (for example, different economic interests, different levels of administration reflected in preserved records, different trade-contacts, a different political structure, cultural differences, etc.), and concentrate on syllabograms, then the differences in the two scripts are minor.[7] The number of common signs, however, is not the only criterion to be considered while discussing the development of the Linear B script. Two other categories of similarities and differences are important: phonetic values of the syllabic signs (the phonetic aspect), and the shape of matching signs (the palaeographic aspect).

3.2. The phonetic aspect of the signary

This aspect of the similarities and differences between Linear A and Linear B is very difficult to assess. What we are interested in is how many Linear A syllabic signs were suitable for expressing Greek, i.e. how many adjustments the devisers of Linear B had to undertake to render it suitable for the new language? The large number of common signs indicates that these adjustments were not immense. However, two points need to be taken into consideration before concluding that the phonetic systems of the two languages are therefore similar.

The first point is that it is not clear that we can indeed read Linear A by applying Linear B values. Although most signs were transmitted from one script to the other, we have no conclusive evidence that the same was done with their phonetic values. Nevertheless, if we examine more recent and better documented adaptations of a script for the purpose of recording a new language – for example, the replacement of Arabic script with the Latin alphabet for the purpose of recording Turkish, or the transformation of the Greek alphabet into the Cyrillic script for recording Slavic languages – we see that the phonetic values of signs were adopted wherever possible.[8] Additional signs were introduced only in those cases where the phonetic peculiarities of the new language could not be expressed by already existing signs in the adopted script. This is not an argument about the inadequacy of the new script-users, but an

[7] Which undermines a change of language as a convincing motive for the system reform that led to the creation of Linear B (see Petrakis forthcoming).

[8] However, there is one exception to such a process: the Carian adoption of the Greek alphabet (see Steele and Meißner in this volume).

argument of efficacy. Why alter the values if the model script mostly worked? The same, I believe, goes for Linear A and Linear B. We should furthermore keep in mind that this was, as far as we know, the first time that the Greeks adapted a script to record their language. Accordingly, they probably would not have taken the radical step of completely altering the phonetic values of the adopted signs, but would have sought to make the process as uncomplicated as possible. However, until the language of Linear A is identified, we cannot be entirely certain that this was the case. Thus, although most scholars accept the application of Linear B phonetic values to matching Linear A signs (and the present study does not differ from this consensus), some reservation should always be kept in mind.

The second point is that even if we were fully certain that Linear B phonetic values can be applied to Linear A signs, this would not necessarily tell us much about the phonetic system of the Minoan language. Various conventions were used when writing Greek in the form of Linear B and one sign may stand for different spoken syllabic combinations.[9] The same may have been the case with the Minoan language(s) and Linear A, but we cannot be certain, since both Minoan phonology and the spelling rules of Linear A are for now entirely based on assumptions.

Yet, if the two scripts are taken as reliable manifestations of phonetic combinations represented in the two languages, we may conclude that the differences between Linear A and B were not overwhelming – at least when the earliest stages of Linear B are considered – since such a large proportion of Linear A signs were retained in Linear B. It appears that Greeks found it largely suitable to record their language in the Linear A syllabary. This is not an argument for the similarity of the two languages (although some scholars have argued that the Minoan language(s) may not have been drastically different from Mycenaean Greek, e.g. Duhoux 1998, 26), but for the similarity of methods by which these languages were written down. Since mostly common signs were employed, this aspect of the analysis leads me to believe that Linear B script was indeed created from Linear A script.

3.3. *The palaeographic aspect of the signary*

Some Linear B signs are more elaborate or embellished than the latest Linear A signs, especially than those from Haghia Triada, which some scholars consider the most likely substrate for the creation of Linear B. Two solutions have been offered as a response to this problem. The first is that the parent-script was not Linear A, but Cretan Hieroglyphic script, some of whose signs resemble Linear B better than Haghia Triada signs do (Evans *SM1*, 38; *PMK1*, 645; *PMK4*, 683; Pope 1961–1962, 310; *contra* Palaima 1988a, 318–9). The second solution is that the parent-script was Linear A, but not that from Haghia Triada and the rest of the LM IB corpus, but rather MM III

[9] For example, *a-ko* may stand for the following words: ἄγω, ἄκος, ἄλγος, ἀργός, ἄρχων, ἀσκός, etc. (example taken from Palmer 1980, 31).

Linear A, evidenced by the two cups from Knossos with painted inscriptions (KN Zc 6 and 7) and some libation tables (Pope 1961–1962).

Both solutions can easily be dismissed. The first fails because of the low correspondence in the signaries of the Cretan Hieroglyphic script and Linear B, especially compared with the obvious correspondence between the Linear A and Linear B signaries (see above). The second solution fails because the ornate nature of the signs on clay cups and libation tables does not have any chronological repercussions, but can be explained in other ways: for example, since the inscriptions on such objects had a decorative value as well, scribes may have been more careful in making the signs resemble archetypal forms; the tablets, on the other hand, reflect a daily routine where no such embellishment would be expected (Palaima 1988a, 319).

Driessen has similarly claimed that the signs from the Minoan 'monumental' testimonia – inscriptions on stone and metal – show better graphic parallels with the signs from the Room of the Chariot Tablets than those from the LM IB administrative documents. According to him, the former should be regarded as predecessors to the RCT signary (Driessen 2000, 109, 147). Palaima, however, argues that newly invented Linear B signs are more embellished because they did not undergo simplification through use; thus, they would be closer to archetypal forms (Palaima 1988b, 166).

We conclude that the elaborateness of signs is not a good criterion to establish Cretan Hieroglyphic or monumental inscriptions in Linear A as the parent-signary, since so many other factors may account for the elaborateness of certain Linear B signs.

3.4. What was then the source for the creation of Linear B script?

Although my premise has been that – due to a high proportion of common signs – Linear B signs were modelled after Linear A, I did not want *a priori* to dismiss a proposed Cretan Hieroglyphic influence on the nascent Linear B signary. To test this possibility in my dissertation (Tomas 2003) I compared the Cretan Hieroglyphic signary to the signs from the chronologically closest Linear B deposit, i.e. the Room of the Chariot Tablets, and then contrasted them to the Linear A counterparts. Due to the word limit, the results cannot be elaborated here in detail. In brief they led me to conclude that the possibility of the Cretan Hieroglyphic script serving as a prototype for Linear B script remains very weak. It is mentioned above that only about a quarter of syllabograms match (and some of the proposed Cretan Hieroglyphic matches have a very low number of occurrences on tablets, so such matches are difficult to prove). Of these, a majority of signs have a Linear A intermediary. The overall conclusion therefore is that Linear A and not Cretan Hieroglyphic must have served as a source for the creation of the Linear B script (*contra* Hallager 2011, 323–6; for a different approach by which a system displaying a seeming fusion of Cretan Hieroglyphic and Linear A may have been a source for Linear B, see Petrakis in this volume).

4. Linear B administrative system

4.1 Similarities and differences in types of documents

Whereas the numerous similarities in the signaries of Linear A and Linear B reveal them as a parent-script and its offspring, the administrative systems behind the two scripts were not likewise related. Both Linear A and Linear B administrative systems consisted of many different types of clay documents used for running administrative business. They can be divided into three groups: those that were only written, those that were only sealed, and those that were both written and sealed. When analysing a particular administrative system, however, it is not only the types of documents that are relevant, but also the mutual correlation of those documents, methods of organising information on them, and so on. Again, due to the word limit they cannot all be discussed and compared here in detail, for the purpose of the overall argument of the paper more attention is paid to the typology of documents.

The clay tablet is the most prominent document-type exclusively serving as a script-carrier in both Linear A and Linear B administrations, but clay tablets display significant differences in the two systems. Whereas Linear B makes use of both page-shaped and elongated (palmleaf-shaped) tablets, only the former is employed during the latest stages of Linear A. We do find several elongated tablets inscribed in Linear A, but they are dated to MM II–III periods and no elongated tablets with Linear A were found amongst the latest (LM IB) documents. Furthermore, page-shaped tablets also differ in the two systems. I have compared them from the pinacological (size, crowdedness of incised signs, cutting, clay texture, preservation, palm- and finger-prints) and epigraphical (opisthography, ruled lines, line-spacing and blanks insertions and squeezing, majuscules and minuscule, palimpsest and erasures) points of view, as well as their contents and roles in the administrative cycle, and striking differences are visible almost everywhere which made me conclude that clay tablets were, despite their identical name, fairly different types of document in the two administrative systems (presented in detail in Tomas 2011, 2012a, 2013, 2014).

Apart from tablets, the following types of documents were used in Linear A during its latest phase, LM IB (around 1450 BC) that led to a transition to Linear B (and these are presented in the descending order of the total number of documents): the single-hole hanging nodule (about 960), the flat-based nodule (about 670), the roundel (about 150), the nodulus (about 100) and the two-hole hanging nodule (70 exmples) (for the most detailed study of all these types, see Hallager 1996). There is another Linear A sealing type I would like to mention, although it was not employed during the latest stage of Linear A administration. This is the direct object sealing, probably the simplest type of an administrative document. This is a lump of clay placed directly onto objects and was meant to prevent unauthorised access to the sealed container or room; thus, it had a twofold function: control of movable goods and control of centralised storage. Direct sealings were generally a Middle Bronze Age feature, and nearly disappeared thereafter, only to reappear in Linear B administration (Weingarten 1988, 6–7).

When we move to Linear B, we find, surprisingly, that only two document-types continued from the latest Linear A: the page-shaped tablet and a variety of the two-hole hanging nodule. Occasional noduli are found as well, but with a total of only nineteen examples (Weingarten 1990, 17; Pini 1997, 52), we cannot claim that the nodulus was a widely employed Linear B document. The three most represented Linear A types of sealings were abandoned in Linear B: the single-hole hanging nodule, the roundel and the flat-based nodule; of this last one we only find a few examples in the earliest known Linear B deposit – the Room of the Chariot tablets at Knossos (Weingarten 1988, 10–11; Driessen 1990, 64; Hallager 2000, 105, 2005a, 252). Since this deposit is considered by a number of scholars, including myself, to represent the transitional stage in the development of Linear B (as proposed by Driessen 1990), I may regard its flat-based nodules as a short-lived legacy from Linear A.[10]

As for the documents that are supposedly common to Linear A and Linear B, any meticulous study will show that noticeable differences are present. The similarities between those 'common' types are often only superficial and the same name is sometimes applied to fairly distinct types of documents in these two systems. This problem has been stressed by Erik Hallager on a number of occasions, particularly in the case of the two-hole hanging nodule, typical of Linear A administration. Its name was readily applied to similar-looking Linear B sealings, although in their nature and function they were quite different, which is why Hallager introduced a new name for these Linear B documents: regular string nodules (Hallager 2005a, 253–8). They, in fact, find a more convincing predecessor in a certain Cretan Hieroglyphic document – crescent – rather than in the Linear A two-hole hanging nodule (see Petrakis this volume).

This example indicates that we must be more careful in equating the types of documents in the two administrative systems. And, as we saw earlier, the other supposedly common document type – the page-shaped tablet – is in fact another case where use of the same name may lead us to believe that the two groups of documents played the same role in the two administrative systems. Linear A and Linear B page-shaped tablets appear to be similar only in their shape. The types of information found on them do not suggest that they had similar purposes. Whereas Linear B page-shaped tablets served as summaries of the primary information from sealings and elongated tablets, this cannot be established in Linear A, where we find no evidence that the information from sealings was thereafter transferred onto tablets (as has been pointed

[10] Yet, Hallager has shown that RCT flat-based nodules and Minoan flat-based nodules display certain differences: RCT flat-based nodules are more simple and crude, and have a much thicker string (Hallager 2005a, 252).

out in a number of independent studies, see for example Hallager 1996, vol. I, 225; Schoep 1999, 213, 2001, 2002, 197; for a single possible exception see Palaima 1994, 317; Hallager 2002). Furthermore, pinacological and epigraphical features briefly mentioned above also reveal significant differences. Indeed, the dissimilarities are so notable that page-shaped tablets from the two administrative systems have little more than their shape and name in common. This last observation leaves us without a single type of document common to chronologically neighbouring Linear A and Linear B.

Now, Linear B introduced – or reintroduced, as we will see – several other types of documents, which cannot be traced to the latest Linear A. These are: the already mentioned elongated tablet and the string nodule, then a type of label pressed against wicker baskets in which tablets were transported, a type of direct object sealing, which, as was stated above, prevented unauthorised access to various types of containers, and the so-called combination nodule, which was a hybrid of a string nodule and a direct object sealing. None of these document-types can be found in the latest Linear A deposits, and some are not found at all in Linear A. So, were these types invented by Linear B officials, or were they adopted from some other source?

The clay label is unique, probably a result of an advanced archiving system (Palaima and Wright 1985, 260-1). The other three document types, however, are not novel; they all existed in Cretan Hieroglyphic administration. Direct object sealings were in general widely used during the Middle Bronze Age on Crete, both in Cretan Hieroglyphic and Linear A administration (Fiandra 1968; 1975; Militello 2000; Godart *et al.* 2000). As already said, elongated tablets were not found amongst the latest Linear A documents, but a few are known from MM II–III contexts. Cretan Hieroglyphic has so far produced only five tablets, and they are all elongated (Tomas forthcoming). As for the combination nodules and string nodules, none is attested in Linear A (Weingarten 1988, 6–7). The recently discovered Cretan Hieroglyphic deposit at Petras, however, has yielded several examples (Tsipopoulou & Hallager 1996; Hallager 2005a, 253; Tsipopoulou and Hallager 2010, 93–101, 185–6).

Thus we see that some of the Linear B document-types which were obviously not inherited from the chronologically closest Late Minoan Linear A existed during the Middle Bronze Age period of Minoan administration, two of them, surprisingly, only amongst the Cretan Hieroglyphic documents. This is what led me to believe that Cretan Hieroglyphic administrative practice in some way influenced the development of Linear B administrative practice (as already elaborated in Tomas 2012b).

4.2. What was then the source for the creation of Linear B administrative system?

When searching for the source for the creation of the Linear B administrative system, it is not only the fact that more Linear B documents can be traced to Cretan Hieroglyphic rather than to Linear A that is particularly telling, but also the fact that the chronologically closest phase of Linear A, LM IB, failed to impose its typical types of documents on the developing Linear B. I wonder if the reason for this phenomenon could be that the nascent Linear B administration, especially its sealing practice, did not look into the latest Linear A as the model for their documents, but rather into another source. As already said, I believe that this other source may be found in Cretan Hieroglyphic (as also suggested in Godart *et al.* 1996, 597–8; Hallager 2011).

The main problem connected to the idea of Cretan Hieroglyphic influencing the developing Linear B is of chronological nature. A significant gap exists between the latest Cretan Hieroglyphic documents and the earliest Linear B. Most Cretan Hieroglyphic documents are of MM II–III date. As mentioned at the beginning of this paper, the date of the Knossian Linear B documents is still debated, whereas most of the Mainland ones are of LH IIIB date, with some being of the LH IIIA2 date (such as recently discovered tablets from Ayios Vasileios in Laconia, Vasilogamvrou forthcoming). The RCT documents, as argued by Driessen, should be dated to LM II–IIIA (see above). If the Hieroglyphic Deposit at Knossos can be dated slightly later than the rest of Cretan Hieroglyphic documents, i.e. to MM III–LM IA, as suggested by Pini (2002, 6–7), this gap would be reduced significantly, but would still be present.

5. Conclusion

In conclusion, I would like to stress again that I am not proposing that Linear B as a script was developed from the Cretan Hieroglyphic script, rather than Linear A, since the similarities with the latter are far more persuasive. However, I do not think that we should limit ourselves to one single source for the creation of Linear B. I believe that our understanding of the origin of Linear B is improved if approached from two different angles: the origin of the script itself and the origin of the administrative practice rendered by the script. In consideration of the latter point, I hope that this paper has succeeded in showing that some link between Cretan Hieroglyphic and Linear B administration should be acknowledged. This link can consequently shed light on one of the crucial questions mentioned at the beginning of the paper: the place where Linear B was created. Evidence of the Cretan Hieroglyphic influence leads me to conclude that Linear B did after all originate on Crete where Cretan Hieroglyphic influence could be felt, and not on the Greek Mainland.

Chapter 5

Reconstructing the matrix of the 'Mycenaean' literate administrations*

Vassilis Petrakis

During the Third Palace period, spanning from the end of the Second Palace period administrations at the close of the Late Minoan (hereafter LM) IB phase to the end of the Late Bronze Age (hereafter LBA) IIIB phases, literate administrative activity has been identified in a considerable number of southern Aegean sites from coastal Thessaly to Crete. Even a cursory survey of the material reveals three developments that were without precedents in the Aegean: the almost exclusive restriction of writing to administrative use, its considerable expansion in regions that had never been truly literate before (the Greek Mainland) and an astonishing level of uniformity, observed in the typology of the documents used, the uniform spelling rules of the shared writing system (Linear B, hereafter LB), as well as in text-formatting techniques, specific palaeographic traits and even technical vocabulary, offices and titles. This is the general picture, painted in the broadest possible strokes. This paper is concerned

* This paper is a slightly modified version of the oral presentation delivered at the symposium. It reflects a further development of ideas first put forward during a Mycenaean Seminar given on 16 January 2013 (Petrakis 2014) that will hopefully be dealt with in a much longer format in the future. I should like to thank Pippa Steele for her kind invitation and arrangement for accommodation during the excellent and stimulating occasion she put together, as well as for her editorial patience. Helena Tomas is also thanked for her review of the final draft of this chapter. For feedback and stimulating discussion of these ideas at Cambridge I am also grateful to Yves Duhoux, Silvia Ferrara, Anna Judson and Torsten Meißner. I am grateful to Oliver Dickinson, Georgia Flouda, Erik Hallager, Walter Gauss, Artemis Karnava, Olga Krzyskowska, Tom Palaima, Diamantis Panagiotopoulos, Ingo Pini, Todd Whitelaw, Jörg Weilhartner and Judith Weingarten for discussions pertaining to arguments included herein on other occasions, and again Tom Palaima for the opportunity to present some of these ideas to a broader audience during my visit to PASP in the spring of 2016. I wish to thank Artemis Karnava and Kevin Pluta for permission to cite their unpublished doctoral theses; Diamantis Panagiotopoulos for an early draft of his study of Third Palace period sealing practices; Jean-Pierre Olivier and Louis Godart for the use of images for the figures that accompany this paper; Adamantia Vasilogamvrou for permission to refer to still unpublished material from her excavations at Ayios Vasileios in Laconia; and Alexandra Salichou for constructive criticism and everything else. It is my honour and pleasure to acknowledge that an early stage of this research was supported by the Michael Ventris Memorial Award for 2011.

with the reconstruction of the conditions in which it came into being; it is in this sense that the 'matrix' in my title is intended.

Any attempt to reconstruct the conditions in which the Third Palace period (or 'Mycenaean'[1]) literate administrations could have taken shape must necessarily be composed of certain seamlessly intertwined questions concerning the place, date and socio-political context of the system's emergence, its degree of reliance on the earlier Cretan systems and the reasons behind those features that we consider as innovations. Here I focus on the relationship of these Third Palace period administrations to systems (literate or not) that had been used earlier in the Aegean and stress its probable implications for any reconstruction of the 'matrix' of these administrations. In order to assess this relationship, I propose to begin by focusing primarily on the administrative document types associated with the LB writing system and their ancestries, although other epigraphic features will also be brought into the discussion.

1. The systemic unity of the Third Palace period administrations

A typological survey of these different document types readily reveals that these function in two distinct yet overlapping and complementary 'modes' (i.e. ways of conveying significant information): one literate (involving the employment of writing on various tablet formats, nodules and labels) and one that I have chosen to call *para-literate* or *ad-literate* (involving the action and effect of sealing on a variety of documents). Table 5.1 shows the distribution of the various document types employed by these administrations in the southern Aegean of the time (for a map showing the distribution of the different types of sealings see Panagiotopoulos 2014, 5, fig. 1). At first sight, it might be arguable that the development of the document types could have followed a trajectory different from that of the LB script itself. This position has been indeed entertained by Bennet (2005, 270) and Tomas (2012b; this volume). However, there are some strong indications favouring the *systemic unity* between script and administrative document types, as well as between the two aforementioned administrative 'modes'.

First, we need to carefully consider that frequently cited fact, namely that LB is only known to have been used for administrative purposes, and especially on those documents whose distribution is shown on Table 5.1.[2] Although some restricted (but

[1] Throughout the paper, a deliberate attempt has been made to suppress the term 'Mycenaean' and the pseudo-ethnic connotations it may carry (cf. also Bennet 2005, 270–1). The chronological term 'Third Palace period' (coined by Dickinson 1994, 13, fig. 1.2) is favoured here as a convenient reference to the LBA II–IIIB southern Aegean, nicely underscoring a degree of continuity from the preceding First and Second Palace periods, which in Dickinson's scheme correspond to the Protopalatial and Neopalatial respectively. As they efficiently emphasise diachronic associations in Aegean administrations, Dickinson's terms are used throughout this paper.

[2] This statement invites some comment on two categories of administrative documents that have been excluded from Table 5.1, namely inscribed stirrup jars and the clay stoppers that secured their spouts. This is no special pleading: scientific analyses of both have demonstrated that they *moved* in a scale

Table 5.1: Distribution chart of the various types of administrative documents in the Third Palace period Aegean

Type	*RCT*	*KN#*	*PY*	*IK*	*TH#*	*MY#*	*TI#*	*MI#*	*KH#*	*SI*	*MA#*	*VOL*	*HV*	*Kolonna*
regular string nodules	×*	×*	×*	–	×*	×*	–	×*	–	–	×	–	×*	–
irregular string nodules	×	×	×	–	×	×	–	–	?	–	–	–	–	–
'fold-over' nodules	–	×	–	–	–	–	–	–	×	–	–	–	–	–
inscribed unsealed string-nodule	×*	×*	×*	–	–	–	–	–	–	–	–	–	–	–
direct-object sealings	–	×	×	–	?	–	–	–	–	–	–	–	–	?
combination nodules	×?	×	×	–	?	×	–	–	–	–	–	–	–	–
dome-noduli	–	×*	×	–	–	×	–	–	–	–	–	–	–	–
flat-based nodules	×	–	–	–	–	–	–	–	×	–	–	–	–	–
single-hole hanging nodules	–	?	–	–	–	?	–	–	–	–	–	–	–	–
tablets (various formats)	×*	×*	×*	×*	×*	×*	×*	–	×*	–	–	×*	×*	–
labels	–	×*	×*	–	–	–	–	–	–	×*?	–	–	×*	–

Clay stoppers are excluded; inscribed stirrup jars are noted only when concurring with other document types. × : occurrence (number of occurrences is not marked); ? : probable occurrence of type (identification not certain); ×* : occurrence of *inscribed* administrative documents (Types with inscribed examples are in **bold**); – : absence; # : occurrence of inscribed transport stirrup jar (number of occurrences is not marked).

RCT: 'Room of the Chariot Tablets' (Knossos: West Wing); KN: Knossos (deposits other than the RCT); PY: Ano Englianos/Pylos (western Messenia); IK: Iklaina (western Messenia); TH: Thebes (Boeotia); MY: Mycenae (Argolid); TI: Tiryns (Argolid); MI: Midea (Argolid); KH: Khania (west Crete); SI: Sissi (north-central Crete); MA: Malia (north-central Crete); VOL: Volos *Kastro-Palaia* (coastal Thessaly); HV: Hagios Vasileios (Lakonia).

Attributions of sealings to the RCT follow *CMS* II.8 with additions by Hallager 2005a, 252, n. 21. Note that the assignment of the combination nodule HMs (= Herakleion Museum sealing inv. no.) 1546 = *CMS* II.8, no. 691 adds a new type to this deposit. For the identification of the Sissi document as a label see Driessen 2012, 24, fig. 1.5. A supposed 'label' from Petsas house at Mycenae, originally classified as **MY Wq 4**, has now been reclassified as a **Ui** tablet fragment (Iakovidis *et al.* 2012, 51). *Probable* (but not certain) hapax occurrences of single-hole hanging nodules have been noticed at Knossos and Mycenae (cf. Panagiotopoulos 2014, 117 with references). 'Fold-over' nodules are a newly-identified variant of irregular string nodules (Hallager 2005b). Although judgment may be suspended in the case of the fragmentary Kolonna sealing (Gauss 2007, 165–7, fig. 6), the find is tentatively included here for the sake of completion.

admittedly controversial) evidence does exist for some *possible* non-administrative uses of the script (most recent overview in Pluta 2011, 95–118), the patchiness of this material (whose interpretation is in any case far from straightforward) suggests that such usage was indeed non-canonical. This is a major obstacle in any attempt to draw a distinction between the script and its contemporary administrative *instrumenta*: minor aberrations aside, it might be fair – albeit bold – to say that the LB writing system did not properly exist outside the realm of administrative activity.

Such exclusivity is obvious in the case of tablets and labels, whose *raison d'être* is to carry the script. However, one might wish to argue that the sealings, functioning in a different 'mode', could be viewed as a separate sub-system (cf. Bennet 2005, 270), as sealing administrations can theoretically function in non-literate contexts. However, the distribution of Aegean documents makes such a position difficult: our extant data reveal that sites that have yielded sealings (inscribed *or not*) during this period, have yielded evidence of literate administrative activity as well,[3] in the form of tablets or inscribed regular string-nodules[4] (Table 5.1). This pattern suggests a degree of overlap between the *literate* and the *para-literate* 'modes' that is meaningful and intense, further and best exemplified in the regular concurrence of writing and sealing on the same documents, namely the regular string-nodules. Beyond accidents of discovery or recovery, such close correspondence cements the case for what has been described as the 'quasi-complementary, quasi-supplementary and quasi-independent' partnership (Palaima 1990, 83) between writing and sealing in the Third Palace period Aegean.

These observations indicate a mutually inclusive relationship between writing and sealing administration during the Third Palace period: on the one hand, with few

quite alien to the rest of the extant administrative apparatus, even between regions that constituted different administrative *polities* during the Third Palace period, such as West Crete and the Argolid or Boeotia (Haskell *et al.* 2011); treating these categories separately from the rest of the document types is therefore justifiable. We have no evidence that tablets themselves were transported in any considerable distance; although this would not have been physically impossible (Hallager forthcoming), whether this was actually practised is a different issue. The mobility of nodules is a far more complicated and debatable issue; however, even if these could have been produced at peripheral sites (yet still within the same region), there is no positive indication at all of a Third Palace period nodule that was produced outside the administrative catchment of the site where it was eventually deposited.

[3] This statement needs two additional comments: (*i*) one string-nodule has been found in Quartier Nu at Malia (Panagiotopoulos 2014, 103, fig. 34), and, although Malia has not yielded archival LB documents, fragments of inscribed stirrup jars have been found in Quartier Nu, suggesting at least some level of literacy during the period concerned; (*ii*) the fragmentary Kolonna sealing (Gauss 2007, 166–7, fig. 6) from a LH IIIA context and a site that has yielded no further evidence for administrative activity (literate or not) seems, at first sight, to shake the consistent association between sealings and literacy. However, its typological affinities are not certain (E. Hallager pers. comm.); in Table 5.1 it is classified tentatively as a direct-object sealing and this identification, if confirmed, would demonstrate that, during the Third Palace period, direct-object sealings could also work in non-literate contexts, as in the First Palace period (Monastiraki).

[4] Regular string nodules constitute the inscribed sealing type *par excellence* during the Third Palace period. This term refers to the gable-shaped, two-hole nodules that are found mostly intact in literate Third Palace period sites and probably had a labelling function (Hallager 2005a, 253–4; Panagiotopoulos 2010, 301–3, 2014, 108). On document typology, I generally follow Hallager's nomenclature with slight modifications.

debatable exceptions, LB, the writing system employed by these administrations was seemingly used for administrative purposes only; on the other hand, there is extreme difficulty in identifying contemporary administrative contexts that functioned without literacy. Although the structure of a writing system and the structure of an administrative system are conceptually unrelated, one can strongly argue, on the basis of the distribution and use of the LB documents, that, during this era, the two were at least *functionally* interdependent.

Admittedly, we cannot easily assume that synchronic unity can be used to safely infer unity throughout the system's development: convergences are indeed far from impossible. Still, we must admit that no hint at such a convergence process is apparent from our available evidence. Rather, despite certain oddities apparent in some (probably early) deposits (e.g. the flat-based nodules from the Room of the Chariot Tablets at Knossos), Third Palace period bureaucracies seem to have been fully developed already by the beginning of the LH IIIB period, as the perfectly 'canonical' document typology from the ongoing excavations at Ayios Vasileios in Laconia shows (Vasilogamvrou forthcoming; data included in Table 5.1).

Accepting the unity of the LB writing system and the administrative system in which this script was almost exclusively employed might have a considerable consequence for our study: it suggests that we should arrive at a plausible hypothesis that has the potential to explain *all* aspects and features of the system.

2. The ancestries of the Third Palace period administrative document types

Returning to my stated intention to focus on Third Palace period administrative document typology, I should readily observe that wonderful overviews of the various document types and their development and association with earlier Aegean administrations have already been performed by Erik Hallager and Helena Tomas (Hallager 2011; 2015; Tomas 2008; 2011; 2012b; this volume). The method employed has been to compare the form and function of the documents associated with the LB administrations with the range of document types associated with administrations using the Linear A (hereafter LA) and the so-called 'Cretan Hieroglyphic' (hereafter CH) scripts, observing continuities and discontinuities, as well as possible correspondences among the different systems. Before I embark upon a more detailed discussion of the picture that they have managed to draw so effectively, I would like to comment on the rationale and objectives behind such valuable exercises in document type comparison.

A seeming inconsistency has generated a considerable puzzle: although most of the LB phonographic signary may be a further development or adaptation of the LA one (as many as 68 out of 87 or *c.* 80% of the LB syllabograms have certain or probable LA correspondences[5]), this is not reflected in the considerable changes observed in

[5] For the most recent overview see Melena 2014, 8, 12, figs 17.1–17.2. However, the figures of LA correspondences are considerably lower in the non-phonographic component of the LB system (Petrakis forthcoming).

the types and functions of the administrative documents used to carry the LB script. Important documents associated with LA, such as the roundel and the varieties of hanging string-nodules seem to fall entirely out of use during the Third Palace period (Hallager 2005, 245–9, figs 1–2; Hallager 2011; Tomas 2012b), while the inscribed LB document *par excellence*, the tablet, also seems to differ considerably in form, format and function from its LA counterpart (Tomas 2011, this volume).

It is important to be aware of the assumptions that form the background of these comparisons. *Comparanda* to the LB document types have been predominantly sought in the latest known horizon of the administrative use of LA, with significant assemblages yielding evidence for both the *literate* and the *para-literate* administrative modes, associated with LM IB destruction horizons from Ayia Triada in south central Crete, Kato Zakros in far eastern Crete and Khania in west Crete. Implicit in such comparisons is the assumption that these administrations were typical of their era, the phase that might have immediately preceded the genesis of the LB system (both writing and administrative). The reluctance to extend the range of *comparanda* to include documents predating the LM IB period may be understandable. But the crucial question of how representative of the overall administrative 'landscape' the LM IB material is has seldom been raised, despite the generally acknowledged differences between the assemblages that already hinted at significant regional diversity. However, well-known facts, such as the overwhelming dominance of standing flat-based nodules at Kato Zakros versus the popularity of single-hole hanging nodules at Ayia Triada (Hallager 1996 I, 236; Krzyskowska 2005, 184, 192; Panagiotopoulos 2014, 51), do suggest that using the extant assemblages to reconstruct *the* typical LM IB administrative assemblage may be based on the false axiom of uniformity, as well as representativeness. The latter may be particularly significant, since we lack LM IB deposits from the largest Cretan centre at the time, Knossos itself. Given the evidence for considerable regionalism in Second Palace period sealing practices, we must not light-heartedly assume that the Knossian *lacuna* can be easily filled by referring to material from other sites.

In 2010, the full publication of a seemingly unrelated assemblage, the Middle Minoan (hereafter MM) IIB 'Archive' recovered in 1996 at Petras near Siteia (Tsipopoulou and Hallager 2010), revealed that a lot of what seemed unprecedented in the Third Palace period administrations now could be traced to a much earlier system employing not LA, but the CH script. By inviting the CH evidence into the picture, the differences between the LM IB and Third Palace period document typologies were put in a new perspective, although the chronological distance between CH assemblages and Third Palace period ones remained a concern (Hallager 2011, 326; Tomas 2012b, 38, 44). We shall review the problem of this chronological gap later on; for the time being, let us focus on the forms and functions of the documents themselves.

The initially surprising CH 'correspondences' of Third Palace period documents are particularly apparent on certain sealing types, as well as tablet formats. Table 5.2 shows the basic associations of the LB document types with those associated with

Table 5.2: The administrative document types associated with the LB script and their correspondences with types of documents inscribed in the LA and CH scripts

LB document type	*LA*	*CH*
portrait 'page-shaped' tablet	× (different function from LB?)	Ø
landscape 'page-shaped' tablet	Ø (but HT 10, HT 133 are almost square)	× (KN HD; PH; *dubitanda* that could be LA: Table 5.3)
elongated ('palm-leaf') tablet	× (PH; KN; all evidence is pre-LM IB)	× (MA; cf. also *CHIC* #108; 'lames'; four-sided bars)
Label	Ø	Ø
inscribed unsealed string-nodule	Ø	Ø (but cf. inscribed unsealed crescents at KN HD)
regular string nodule (occas. inscribed)	Ø (cf. two-hole hanging nodules, see discussion in text)	Ø (but cf. inscribed crescents, see discussion in text)
irregular string nodule	× (KN ETR)	× (KN HD; PE?)
'fold-over' nodule (KN, KH only?)	Ø	? (cf. PE 'lumps' L9-10?)
direct-object sealing (*various sub-types*)	×	×
combination nodule	Ø	× (PE; perhaps KN: *CMS* II.8, 13 of unknown context)
dome-nodulus (inscribed only at KN)	× (rarely inscribed)	× (uninscribed)
flat-based nodule (KN RCT, KH? uninscribed)	× (rarely inscribed)	× (KN HD; MA DH)

KN: Knossos; ETR: East Temple Repository (Knossos); PH: Phaistos; MA: Malia; DH '*Dépôt Hiéroglyphique*' (Malia); HD: Hieroglyphic Deposit (Knossos); PE: Petras

The difference between the so-called 'portrait' and 'landscape' formats of the page-shaped tablet refer to whether the text (usually of more than three lines) follows alongside the short or the long side of the roughly rectangular writing surface. On the possibility of the Petras 'lumps' being 'fold-over' nodules see Hallager 2005b, 108–9, figs 6–7. Types whose association with Third Palace period administrations is still open to doubt (e.g. 'irregular flat-based nodules', see Hallager 1996 I, 202–3) have not been included. Other references: *CMS* II.8; Hallager 1996, 2011; Panagiotopoulos 2010, 2014; Petrakis 2014; Tomas 2011, 2012; Tsipopoulou and Hallager 2010.

the other two writing systems that were put in administrative use in earlier periods, namely the CH and the LA scripts. The emerging picture is already complex enough, but it must be supplemented with a few important additions. It must be stressed from the outset that *ex silentio argumenta* need to be formulated with extreme caution: absence of evidence is not evidence of absence and one should be careful in assessing such 'absences', even when the quantity and quality of the evidence suggests that they are meaningful. Nonetheless, we cannot refrain from considering the picture as it is.

The overall picture presented in Table 5.2 is already discussed to some extent by Hallager and Tomas (Tomas this volume, with references). Hallager has justifiably stressed that correspondences between LB- and CH-associated types are more numerous and better, emphasising that those types shared between LA and LB (i.e.

various tablet formats, stoppers, direct-object sealings, *noduli* and flat-based nodules) are not exclusive, since they also occur in association with CH (Hallager 2011, 322).

It is necessary to refer to the strong affinity between the Third Palace period gable-shaped regular string-nodule (the LB-inscribed sealing type *par excellence*) and the very similar so-called crescents associated with CH administrations and very often inscribed in the CH script. 'Mycenaean' regular string-nodules are closer to crescents than to Second Palace period two-hole hanging nodules, which are relatively scarce, very rarely inscribed and morphologically rather diverse (as opposed to the gable-shaped variant which is remarkably uniform across the Third Palace period southern Aegean, cf. Hallager 2005a, 254). Such correspondence between the Third Palace period regular string-nodules and CH crescents becomes even more compelling when one considers the similarity between the LB document type named here the *inscribed unsealed string-nodule* (classified as **Wo** at Pylos and as **Wm** at Knossos), which has no parallel at all in the Second Palace period administrations associated with LA[6], and the CH *inscribed unsealed 'crescents'* (Hallager 2011, 322). The inscribed unsealed crescent is so far only known from three examples from the 'Hieroglyphic Deposit' at Knossos,[7] an assemblage located at the North End of the Long Corridor in the West Wing of the palace, that will be of critical importance in our discussion, although its chronology and coherence should invite some comments (see *infra*).

Closer study of some probably early LB assemblages reveals a few more features on documents *other than sealings* that are paralleled in the so-called CH administrations, but not attested in relationship to LA. Although what we can associate is a sporadic feature in one system with what is far more common and canonical in the other, these parallelisms deserve to be considered here, since they can be placed within a broader framework of interconnections among the three categories:

i. The practice of cutting elongated tablets to form separate shorter mini-documents, very popular in the Room of the Chariot Tablets (hereafter RCT)[8] also at Knossos and extremely rare anywhere else (Driessen 2000, 48–9; Duhoux 2012a; Tomas

[6] Besides tablets, the only inscribed documents without sealing impressions are those sporadic instances tentatively named as 'irregular *noduli*' or 'labels', which are not a homogeneous category (Hallager 1996 I, 203–4).

[7] **KN Ha(01) 01-03** = *CHIC* #001-#003.

[8] I here accept the view that the Linear B documents from the RCT may be dated to a comparatively earlier stage of the development of the Third Palace period administrative system, quite plausibly within the LM II–IIIA1 range (see Driessen 2000 for a thorough analysis of the deposit). A crucial feature is the occurrence of a few examples of a variant of the flat-based nodule, a type of clear Second Palace period descent (associated chiefly with LA but also with CH) that probably sealed 'packages' of leather documents; these flat-based nodules are found with LB documents nowhere else except in the RCT. As Hallager (2005a, 252) has emphasised, the RCT flat-based nodules are somewhat different from the usual Second Palace period varieties (e.g. those found at LM IB Kato Zakros). So far, the best typological parallel for the RCT nodules is a flat-based nodule found in a LM IIIA1 context in Khania (Hallager 2005a, 252–3; *CMS* V S3, no. 103). Still, parallelism is not exact, since the Khania nodule bears the impression of thick twisted cord (E. Hallager, pers. comm.), instead of the (leather?) straps on the RCT nodules (*CMS* II.8, 43, fig. 11).

2013), is unknown in LA, but has been identified in two CH four-sided bars from Knossos (**KN Hh(04) 02** and **Hh(04) 03**[9]) that were originally cut from a longer document (Olivier 1994–1995).

ii. The unusual tall dividers evident in the Knossos **Vd** tablets, again from the RCT (see also Duhoux 2012a, 216–18), resemble the CH vertical dividers (< **|** >) that occur chiefly on archival documents (*CHIC*, 446–7), but are so far unknown from LA administrative documents.[10]

iii. An interesting correspondence in format exists between two four-sided bars inscribed in CH from the so-called 'Dépôt Hiéroglyphique'[11] at Malia (probably on **MA/P Hh(07)** *01* face a; more confidently on **MA/P Hh(07)** *02* face cA-cB[12]) and a very popular arrangement on LB elongated tablets: what I will call here the 'half-way ruling': a horizontal ruling line does not divide into two registers the entire length of the elongated writing surface, but a part of it is reserved without horizontal ruling and written with larger signs.[13]

A couple of possible morphological correspondences that seem to link the LB and CH phonographies directly (i.e. without any extant LA correspondences) might also be mentioned: (*i*) between B 33 <*ra*$_3$> < > (so far exclusively Helladic in its phonographic use and exclusively Knossian in its non-phonographic or sematographic use) and CH sign 023 < >; (*ii*) between B 62 <*pte*> < > (of more general distribution) or perhaps untransliterated B 63 < > (so far exclusively Helladic) and CH sign 036 < > (*CHIC*, 19). Other instances noted as possible by Olivier and Godart may also be considered (e.g. between CH sign 008 < > and B 52 <*no*> < > in *CHIC*, 19, but AB 28 < > can also be considered). However, I hasten to note that any such similarity (and I also note these are not absolutely compelling matches) needs to be treated with great caution, because their significance principally rests on negative evidence, namely the uncertainty or absence of corresponding LA forms. The case of AB 48 <*nwa*> < >, once considered as a direct and exclusive link between the CH and LB phonographic signaries (e.g. Hallager 2011, 324), is very didactic as to the dangers involved in such assessments: the sign was, in the meantime, identified on **SY Za 4**, a so-called 'libation table' from Kato Symi inscribed in LA (Muhly and Olivier 2008, 207–8, 216).

We might here add an example of a non-phonographic LB sign that does show an intriguing affinity to CH. A non-canonical variant of **159* < > TELA ('cloth') is found

[9] *CHIC* #057 and #058 respectively.

[10] Tall vertical marks that resemble dividers appear in Linear A graffiti on stucco from Ayia Triada (**HT Zd 155-157**, see *GORILA* 4, 130-135), but are lacking from archival documents. The CH vertical dividers occur also – albeit somewhat questionably – on a few inscribed seals (*CHIC* #206, #283, #291, #292, #297 and #305 that, interestingly, also include a few questionable occurrences of 'klasmatograms' 308 and 309).

[11] The French term is retained here throughout in order to avoid confusion with the Knossos 'Hieroglyphic Deposit'.

[12] *CHIC* #112 and #113 respectively.

[13] The registers thus formulated are transcribed through uppercase Latin characters (.A, .B, etc) in LB editions and a similar practice is followed in *CHIC*, 165 for the four-sided bar **MA/P Hh(07) 02** face c.

on tablets from the 'Megaron' (Room 6) of the Main Building of the 'Palace of Nestor' at Pylos (**PY La 623** *verso*; **626** *verso*; **630**). There, besides the ubiquitous (and therefore 'canonical') fringes commonly found in the bottom part of the main rectangular element of the sign, fringes also appear on the top (Nosch 2012, 306–7, fig. 3, 326, fig. 10 *bottom*); this specific feature, unknown in the examples of its LA homographs, is paralleled in the CH sematogram **163* <  > known from a clay medallion from the Malia 'Dépôt Hiéroglyphique' (**MA/P He(07) 01** face b[14]). It is interesting, in this perspective, that Melena has advanced a persuasive argument favouring the earlier (pre-LH IIIB, probably LH IIIA) date of the these 'Megaron' tablets (Melena 2000–2001, 367; Skelton 2009).

Of course, none of them may be considered unequivocal evidence for 'direct' links between the LB and CH signaries: just as the case had been with <*nwa*> until the publication of the Symi inscription, their significance rests on the absence of such features or variants from the extant LA material. We cannot afford to underestimate the complexity of palaeographic interrelationships within the Aegean and the sheer number of unknowns that lurk behind the enormous gaps among the patches of our evidence, not just about 'early' LB, but almost all Aegean epigraphic material predating the 13th century BC.

Having raised these cautionary warnings, I must note that the ancestry of LB signs must be approached with an open mind: no *exclusive* affinity with LA should be axiomatically accepted for those LB graphemes that have reliable homographs in both CH and LA scripts. Besides a careful comparative reassessment of their palaeographic variants, the regional and chronological distribution – as well as patterns of use of these signs – need to be taken into account. Unfortunately, such an analysis could not be undertaken in the present context (but see comments in Tomas, this volume).

Let us now consider all the three separate 'groupings' of evidence suggesting the association between the LB and CH administrations. We have so far considered the considerable correspondences in document types (Table 5.2 with references), the aforementioned epigraphic traits, and the very questionable – albeit not entirely impossible – correspondences in a few graphemes. Overall, it is the accumulation rather than the individual definitiveness of the aforementioned associations that prove them collectively significant. It is of considerable importance that such 'links' actually transcend what was previously argued to be an artificial (even if heuristically useful) division between the literate and the para-literate administrative 'modes'.

However, we cannot lose sight of the fact that, impressive as their concentration might seem, those CH features so far considered cannot possibly stand alone as an explanation of the formation of the Third Palace period assemblages. Quite the contrary: they should be considered *alongside* those features that can *also* (or even perhaps *exclusively*) be understood as a further development of the LA system, most notably a considerable part of the LB phonographic signary. We should also carefully consider those features or elements that are found in association with all three writing

[14] *CHIC* #103.

systems: such shared links actually obscure any positive assignment of their Third Palace period correspondences, making any inference about the development and ancestry of these common types a matter of speculation.[15]

This baffling condition has generated a variety of responses. Hallager, rejecting any plausible genetic link between the LB system and the LM IB administrations using the LA script, chose to overemphasize the CH links, thereby suggesting that

> 'the Linear B administration did not derive directly from Linear A, but also and basically from the Cretan hieroglyphs'. (Hallager 2011, 326)

Other scholars have been willing to consider the possibility that the Third Palace period system had multiple origins, as suggested by the different patterns observable in the development of the various aspects or components of the system. Tomas has advocated such a position, carefully suggesting that

> 'the origin of Linear B was *not limited to a single source* [...] whereas Linear A remains the main source for the script, the administrative system appears to have derived *partly* from the Cretan Hieroglyphic administrative system'. (Tomas 2012b, 44, emphasis added)

A somewhat similar thesis is also tentatively put forward by Diamantis Panagiotopoulos who has referred to the

> '*Möglichkeit eines hieroglyphischen "Substrats" in der mykenischen Siegelpraxis [...] Es wäre durchaus möglich, dass im mykenischen Verwaltungssystem Elemente aus beiden kretischen administrativen Traditionen (Hieroglyphen und Linear A) fortlebten*'. (Panagiotopoulos 2014, 56)

These views may well offer possible interpretations of the picture we have so far encountered. Especially the hypothesis of multiple origins is an elegant one (Tomas 2012b; this volume). However, there are serious obstacles created by the strong – almost exclusive – association between writing and administration during the Third Palace period, as well as the consistency and uniformity of the LB system. These patterns make it difficult to accept any explanatory framework that isolates specific components, aspects or features of the system in order to advance *ad hoc* interpretations of one independently of the others.

My working hypothesis here is as follows: if, in order to explain *the full range* of the features attested in Third Palace period administrations, we find ourselves needing to refer both to elements *hitherto* associated with LA *as well as* elements *hitherto* associated with CH, this may suggest that the context of the emergence of this new system somehow included a co-existence of both categories. It might even be necessary to carefully reconsider the degree to which these had so far been considered as mutually exclusive entities.

[15] For instance, Hallager uses the typological correspondences to argue that the CH administrative system could have been the common ancestor of the sealing systems associated with LA and LB (Hallager 2011, 323 with fig. 4). Much of the same evidence is interpreted by Tomas (2012b; this volume) as indicative that the LB administrative system developed out of *both* CH and LA components.

Further exploration of this line of argument invites consideration of a phenomenon not previously associated with the genesis of the Third Palace period bureaucracies, but which now emerges as directly and fundamentally relevant: what has often been described as the 'co-existence' of the CH and LA writing systems.

3. Paradox or unrecognized norm? The interplay between CH and LA in Bronze Age Crete

The co-existence of features that are considered as 'canonically' associated with CH and LA, once considered an oddity of the Malia so-called '*Dépôt Hiéroglyphique*' (originally published in Chapouthier 1930), can now be documented in at least two more sites, a fact which strongly suggests the need for a change in perspective (cf. Meriggi 1973, 172, n. 1; Olivier 1996, 108; also Karnava 2007 on First Palace period evidence). In what follows I wish to place the emphasis on two significant aspects of the problem: (i) the existence of *dubitanda*, documents which our modern *etic* scholarly perspective may classify as either CH or LA and (ii) the remarkable interplay between CH and LA features, especially in the Knossos 'Hieroglyphic Deposit' and the Malia '*Dépôt Hiéroglyphique*'.

As the editors of *CHIC* have noted, a number of documents they eventually chose to classify as CH could, with varying degrees of certainty, be understood as actually being inscribed in LA (*CHIC*, 18). I have also *tentatively* added to this list three more documents whose affinities are, for the moment, unclear: (a) **KN Wc 23**, a roundel from the 'East Temple Repository' (hereafter ETR) located in the West Wing of the Knossos palace, which was excluded from the LA corpus since it bears a mark that had not been considered a writing sign proper (*GORILA* 2, lvi), and has not been accepted as a CH inscription either; (b) a small four-sided bar from Palaikastro, published by Brice as bearing a LA inscription (Evans and Bosanquet 1923, 146, fig. 128, pl. xxxiiib; Brice 1961, 21, pl. xxvii: no. iv 6); (c) *CHIC* #110 = **MA/P Hf (06) 02**, a probable '*lame à deux faces*' or tablet fragment from the Malia '*Dépôt Hiéroglyphique*'. Although this has been included as an unproblematic CH document in *CHIC*, it was originally published as bearing a CH inscription [H.19] on one side and a LA inscription [L.3] on the other (Chapouthier 1930, 23, 56, pl. ii [H.19]; Brice 1961, 19, pl. xxvi, no. iii 11). One might excuse Chapouthier's original identification, by considering the overall context of the 'Dépôt Hiéroglyphique' (where a 'co-existence' of CH and LA would justify the presence of a document written in both scripts), but the identification of the only legible sign on side *b* (Chapouthier's 'LA' side), CH sign 085 <  > is only found on this document and on *CHIC* #041 = **KN He (06) 02**, a clay medallion from the Knossos 'Hieroglyphic' Deposit'. The significance of this limited distribution will be discussed *infra*.

Besides these three examples (two of which are currently absent from all extant *corpora*), extant *dubitanda* documents (Table 5.3) include three crescents, two tablets and one three-sided bar. Out of seven documents, it may be highly significant that five *dubitanda* come from the Knossos 'Hieroglyphic Deposit' (the other two being

Table 5.3: Dubitanda: Inscribed documents that might be identified either as written in the CH or in the LA writing system

CHIC # no.	*Document*	*Museum inv.*	*Type*	*Provenance*	*Reference*
010	**KN Ha (02) 07**	HMs 190	crescent	Knossos 'Hieroglyphic Deposit'	*CHIC*, 18, 72–73
014	**KN Ha (02) 11**	HMs 249	crescent	Knossos 'Hieroglyphic Deposit'	*CHIC*, 18, 74–75
019	**KN Ha (03) 04**	HMs 189	crescent	Knossos 'Hieroglyphic Deposit'	*CHIC*, 18, 78–79
048	**KN Hg 01**	HM 1303	three-sided bar	Knossos 'Hieroglyphic Deposit'	*CHIC*, 18, 98–99
068	**KN Hi 01**	HM 1268	tablet	Knossos 'Hieroglyphic Deposit'	*CHIC*, 18, 122–123
122	**PH Hi 01**	HM 1	tablet	Phaistos (unknown context)	*CHIC*, 18, 182–183
not included	**KN Wc 23**	HMs 342	roundel	Knossos 'East Temple Repository'	*GORILA* 2, lvi; Hallager 1996 II, 160
not included	**IV 6** [Brice]		'four-sided bar'	Palaikastro	Brice 1961, 21, pl.xxvii: no. iv 6
110	**MA/P Hf (06) 02**	HM 1384	*lame à deux faces or tablet?*	Malia *'Dépôt Hiéroglyphique'*	*CHIC*, 158–159

Their concentration at Knossos in notable, especially in the so-called 'Hieroglyphic Deposit'. Note also the concentration of klasmatograms shared between CH and LA in the Knossos 'Hieroglyphic Deposit' (see text for discussion). HM = Herakleion Museum no.; HMs = Herakleion Museum sealing inv. no.

the ETR roundel – but still Knossian – and the Phaistos tablet **PH Hi 01** of unknown context). The situation is highly intricate. *If* we allow these *dubitanda* to be actually identified as inscribed in LA (an admissible option), then the Knossos 'Hieroglyphic Deposit' would feature the very same 'oddity' as the Malia *'Dépôt Hiéroglyphique'*: a seeming co-existence of CH and LA documents (cf. Olivier 1996, 108).

Still, to term this as mere 'co-existence' is an understatement of the highly complex situation revealed when these *dubitanda* come to focus. Most intriguing is the Knossos three-sided bar (**KN Hg 01** = *CHIC* #048). Olivier and Godart recorded their doubts (*CHIC*, 18), but eventually decided to include the Knossos three-sided bar in the CH corpus, while Artemis Karnava, on the other hand, has chosen not to consider it, identifying it as a LA document (Karnava 2000, 19). The only typological parallel for **KN Hg 01** is the three-sided bar **MA 2** from the *'Dépôt Hiéroglyphique'*, which, however, has been commonly classified as a LA document (Fig. 5.1). But the Maliote LA associations of **KN Hg 01** do not end here: it features signs **164* < > and **165* < >, which are unparalleled in the CH corpus (*CHIC*, 426), but bear a remarkable resemblance to sign AB 180 < > that appears (in simple or ligatured forms) on two of the Malia elongated tablets recognised as inscribed in LA, again from the Malia 'Dépôt Hiéroglyphique'

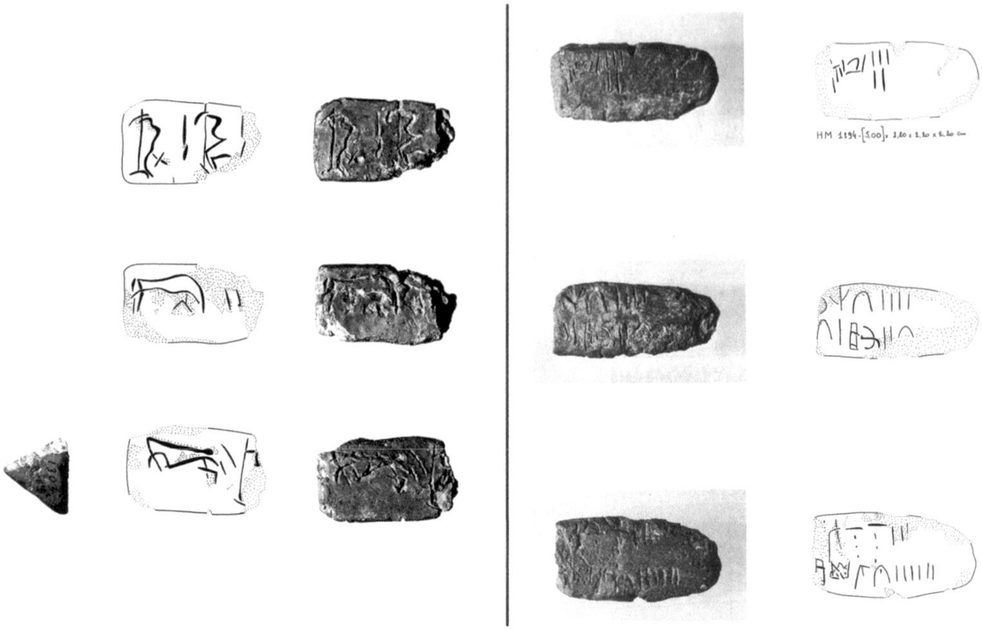

Fig. 5.1: Left: The three-sided bar from the Knossos 'Hieroglyphic Deposit' **KN Hg 01** = CHIC *#048; Right: the three-sided bar* **MA 2** *from the Malia* 'Dépôt Hiéroglyphique'. *Images after* CHIC, *98 and* GORILA *1, 270. Courtesy of Professors Louis Godart and Jean-Pierre Olivier.*

(**MA 4**; **MA 6**) (Fig. 5.2). On the other hand, if one follows Karnava in identifying **KN Hg 01** as inscribed in LA, just like the Malia three-sided bar, another point can be raised: the shape of the inscribed artefact itself recalls that of the three-sided prism, the commonest shape among *CH* seals (76 out of 148 examples as counted in Karnava 2000, 165, Table 32).

We are faced with nothing less than a true conundrum: we have a document type whose shape is clearly associated with the seal shape best represented in the CH corpus. But the clay document itself *may* never be inscribed in CH; both examples *might* be inscribed in LA; still, in both its occurrences, it is found in close association with inscriptions identified as 'canonical' CH in the Knossos and Malia deposits.

At this point, it is imperative that I add one observation on the signary used on documents from the 'Hieroglyphic Deposit': klasmatograms (signs representing fractional amounts) from this assemblage are almost all paralleled in LA (*CHIC*, 17, 19, 429–31) (Fig. 5.3). Their distribution elsewhere in the CH corpus is extremely limited: they do not occur in the First Palace period assemblages from Malia (Quartier Mu) or Petras. Their densest concentration is on three four-sided bars (bearing commodity signs and classified as **Hh(08)** = *CHIC* #065-#067) and the *dubitandum* tablet **KN Hi 01** = *CHIC* #068 from the Knossos 'Hieroglyphic Deposit'; besides three CH seals (*CHIC* #206,

*Fig. 5.2: Left: CH commodity signs *164–*165 on the three-sided bar from the Knossos 'Hieroglyphic Deposit' KN Hg 01 (sides a-c) =* CHIC *#048. Right: LA commodity sign AB 180 (plain and ligatured forms) on tablets* **MA 4** *(top) and* **MA 6** *(bottom) from the Malia 'Dépôt Hiéroglyphique'. Only sufficiently preserved occurrences of the sign are highlighted within rectangle frames. Images after* CHIC*, 98 and* GORILA *1, 272, 274, 276, rearranged and annotated by the author. Courtesy of Professors Louis Godart and Jean-Pierre Olivier.*

#291-#292),[16] non-Knossian attestations are on documents that either could be LA (the *dubitandum* Phaistos tablet **PH Hi 01** = *CHIC* #122), or 'co-existed' with documents classified as LA (the four-sided bar **MA/P Hh(08) 01** = *CHIC* #118 from the Malia '*Dépôt Hiéroglyphique*'). The distribution of these signs and their ligatures forms an additional intricate nexus between the Knossos and Malia assemblages.[17] The concentration of

[16] Jasink (2005) has argued that these signs, when they appear on seals, function as logograms or phonograms. Her analysis is persuasive, but we should observe that these 'odd' occurrences are on seals that feature other 'odd' features, such as the presence of vertical 'dividers' (admittedly, the 'cross' or X-shaped stiktogram occurs more widely on seals).

[17] Klasmatograms that hitherto exclusively occur on the **Hh(08)** bars and/or tablet **KN Hi 01** from the Knossos 'Hieroglyphic Deposit' (*CHIC* #065-#068) are: 303 Θ < ȶ >, 305 Ξ < Y >, 306 Π < ʃ >, as well

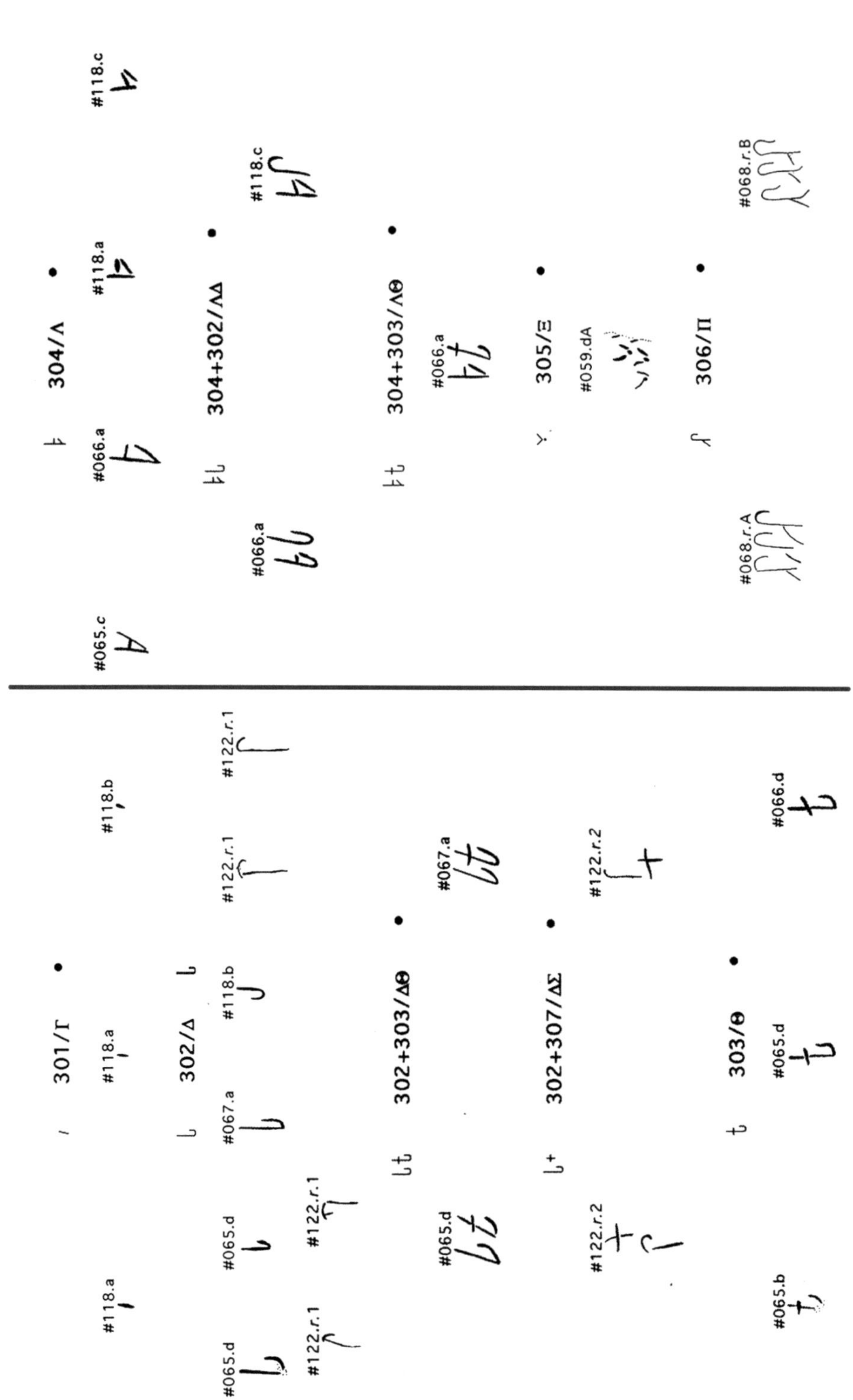

Fig. 5.3: Klasmatograms (fractional signs) used on CH clay documents. Numbers refer to CHIC documents. Images after CHIC, 429-430, rearranged by the author. Courtesy of Professors Louis Godart and Jean-Pierre Olivier.

klasmatograms on *dubitanda* and other documents from the Knossos 'Deposit' and the Malia 'Dépôt' suggest that their employment there might constitute a feature (or symptom) of the aforementioned CH-LA 'co-existence'.

It must have been clear by now how complicated the situation is in the Knossos 'Hieroglyphic Deposit' and how many and diverse links and parallelisms can be found with the Malia '*Dépôt Hiéroglyphique*'. This situation adds significance to the existence of signs (presumably phonograms) that are only shared between these two 'Deposits', such as the aforementioned CH sign 085 < ⩚ > between the clay medallion **KN He (06) 02** = *CHIC* #041, and the *possible* 'dubitandum' *lame* or tablet fragment **MA/P Hf (06) 02** = *CHIC* #110.[18] The least we can do is admit an intense interplay between the CH and LA categories in at least these two cases. However, to do so is actually to dance around the crucial question: what was really going on at the Knossos and Malia administrations represented by these assemblages? What kind of system (or systems) do they represent?

Directly relevant to any attempt to answer this is what stems from a comparison of the two assemblages. The types of inscribed documents attested in each 'deposit' are shown on Table 5.4. We must note that *if* the question-marks are removed from the Knossian *dubitanda*, we have a no less than impressive typological correspondence: both the Knossos and the Malia assemblages will then be featuring almost the same types of inscribed documents, distributed almost in the same way among the two scripts.[19] This surely cannot be accidental. The only exceptions seem to be the *lames à deux faces* and the roundels, two types which are present at Malia, but are absent from the Knossos 'Hieroglyphic Deposit'. However, we must observe that, on the one hand, the appearance of the *lames* at Malia can be explained as a local traditional feature, since such *lames* (class **Hf** in *CHIC*) occur almost exclusively at Malia Quartier Mu at the end of MM II (*CHIC* #085-#094[20]), while on the other hand Knossos has yielded

as klasmatogram ligatures 302 + 303 ΔΘ < ⌊t > and 304 + 303 ΛΘ < ⊬t > . Of these, all have reliable LA homographs, except the *hapax* 305 Ξ. 302 Δ < ⌊ >, 304 Λ < ⊦ > and ligature 304 + 302 ΛΔ < ⊬⌊ > (all three with LA homographs too) occur at the Knossos 'Deposit' as well as on a **MA/P Hh(08) 01** from the Malia 'Dépôt' (302 Λ < ⌊ > also occurs on **PH Hi 01**); ligature 302 + 307 ΔΣ < ⌊+ > occurs only on **PH Hi 01** and 301 Γ < ı > only on **MA/P Hh(08) 01**. 308 ♀ < ▙ > and 309 ⋋ < 8 > seem to appear on seals, but their identification there as 'klasmatograms' can be questioned (Jasink 2005). Nonetheless, 308 ♀ < ▙ > also occurs on a *lame* or bar from Symi (**SY Hf 01**, see *infra* n. 20), while 309 ⋋ < 8 > might occur on roundel **KN Wc 23** from the Knossos ETR, see *infra*). 307 Σ < + > appears on seals, but occurs also on **PH Hi 01** and has good klasmatographic homographs in both LA (A 702 or B) and LB (where, even as a metrogram, it is transcribed as AB 02 <*RO*>).

[18] It is acknowledged that a thorough palaeographic re-examination of these assemblages is demanded and is scheduled by the author for the near future.

[19] It is noteworthy that they also share one type of uninscribed document, the flat-based nodule. There may be reasons to sustain belief that the bulk of the material is chronologically and contextually homogeneous (see *infra* for comments on the 'integrity' of the 'Hieroglyphic Deposit' and the Malia 'Dépôt Hiéroglyphique').

[20] A seeming exception might be the fragment from the Kato Symi sactuary in the Viannos region (south-central Crete), identified as a *lame à deux faces* (**SY Hf 01**) (Lebessi *et al.* 1995). Since the diagnostic part

Table 5.4: Typological composition of inscribed documents from the Knossos 'Hieroglyphic Deposit' and the Malia 'Dépôt Hiéroglyphique'

Script	*Document type*	*Knossos 'Hieroglyphic Deposit'*	*Malia 'Dépôt Hiéroglyphique'*
CH	crescent	×	×
	lame à deux faces	–	×
	four-sided bar	×	×
	medallion	×	×
	tablet	×	×
LA	four-sided bar	–	×
	three-sided bar	–	×
	tablet	–	×
	roundel	–	×
Dubitanda	three-sided bar	×	–
	crescent	×	–
	tablet	×	–

× occurrence; – absence.
References: Hallager 1996 I, 57–60; *CHIC*; *GORILA* 1. Dubitandum *CHIC* #110 from the Malia '*Dépôt*' is formally published as a *lame à deux faces*, but could also be the fragment of a tablet.

roundels in the adjacent ETR assemblage, probably dated to the mature LM IA phase (see immediately *infra*).

In any case, the similarities between these two assemblages positively show that these must somehow reflect similar administrative realities. This suggestion, supported strongly by the impressive correspondence in their typological composition, invites a careful reconsideration of two much debated issues: their integrity and chronology.

First, the integrity of both assemblages has been called into question. Despite the many open questions surrounding the character of the Malia '*Dépôt Hiéroglyphique*', Pelon has given fairly conclusive evidence that the assemblage is coherent and dates to the close of the MM IIIB period (Pelon 1983, 701–3). Regarding the Knossos 'Hieroglyphic Deposit', while it seems clear from some of Evans' notes that documents recovered on other locations were also integrated to the 'Deposit', we should not be carried away by too much suspicion. One positive piece of evidence exists to suggest some degree of homogeneity in this assemblage (Hallager 1996 I, 36, n. 33; Krzyszkowska 2005, 115–16): the fact that two sealings of different types (the crescent

with a suspension hole is not preserved, however, it is possible to hypothesize that this document was the fragment of an elongated tablet (class **Hi** in *CHIC*), a suggestion compatible with its dimensions. One might note that the Syme document, if a *lame*, it would be the only one bearing a klasmatogram (308 ♀); otherwise, CH klasmatograms occur only on tablets or four-sided bars with commodity signs.

HMs 185 and the flat-based nodule HMs 195) were impressed with the same seal (*CMS* II.8, no. 79).[21] At the end, it might be fair to say that, despite any rightfully suspected false assignments by Evans that sadly transform most arguments into 'matters of faith' (Krzyszkowska 2005, 116), it can be argued that the correspondence in the typological make-up between the Knossos and Malia assemblages (Table 5.4) is extremely difficult to explain, unless both assemblages were more or less coherent.[22]

Regarding chronology, we must consider Ingo Pini's suggestion that certain impressions assigned to the Knossos 'Hieroglyphic Deposit' were made with seals that can be stylistically dated to the MM III/ LM I period (*CMS* II.8, 6–8[23]). Although this depends on the still problematic coherence of the assemblage, Pini's analysis clearly suggests the MM III/ LM I transition as a *terminus post quem* for the 'Deposit'. Such a late date may indeed cause 'consternation' to some scholars, as Krzyszkowska (2005, 116) notes; however, it enables things to fall neatly into place, since it establishes the 'Hieroglyphic Deposit' as almost contemporary to (perhaps even slightly later than) the Malia '*Dépôt Hiéroglyphique*' (see above), in the later part of the Second Palace period.

Under the circumstances described, and *for the specific contexts in question* (especially the Knossos 'Hieroglyphic Deposit'), maintaining any rigid distinction between CH and LA seems to become less meaningful, even misleading, an idea already voiced by Meriggi (1973, 172, n. 1). But, if so, how can the situation reflected in the Knossos

---

[21] Inspection of possible fingerprints could also be employed to test the coherence of the 'Hieroglyphic Deposit', but this investigation must be promised for the near future.

[22] Unfortunately, a full discussion of the coherence and chronology of the 'Hieroglyphic Deposit' could not be accommodated here and must be postponed. However, on the strength of the observed similarity between Knossos and Malia 'Hieroglyphic Deposits', we may bring into the discussion **KN 22**, the fragment of an elongated non-ruled LA tablet (also described as a two-sided bar) without proper context identified in the 1950s by Emmett Bennett at the Herakleion Museum (Bennett 1958, pl. 4 then numbered **Kn 5800**). Bennett classified this fragment as 'indeterminate script' noting that '[t]he shape of the tablet is not far from those of Linear A' (Bennett 1958, 36, 49). Despite the lack of any information as to its context, the similarity of **KN 22** in typology and layout to LA and CH tablets from the Malia '*Dépôt Hiéroglyphique*' (**MA 1; MA/P Hi 01-02** = *CHIC* #119–#120; also perhaps **MA/P Hf(05) 01** = *CHIC* #108), as well as CH tablets (**KN Hi 02** = *CHIC* #069) and bars (**KN Hh(06) 01** = *CHIC* #063) from the Knossos 'Hieroglyphic Deposit', should be nonetheless noted.

[23] HMs 189 = **KN Ha(03) 04** (a *dubitandum* crescent, see Table 5.3) is impressed with *CMS* II.8, nos 124 and 702, which are of MM III–LM I date; the same holds for HMs 140 (an irregular string-nodule) impressed with *CMS* II.8, no. 286. Other documents of MM III–LM I date (based on the style of the seal impressions) include single-hole hanging nodule HMs 128 impressed with *CMS* II.8, no. 157, the odd crescent HMs 132 impressed – amongst five different seals – with *CMS* II.8, no. 353 and three flat-based nodules (HMs 126 and OAM 1938.982 impressed with *CMS* II.8, no. 376; HMs 144 impressed with *CMS* II.8, no. 375). Moreover, three uninscribed crescents (HMs 176 impressed with *CMS* II.8, no. 55; HMs 179 impressed with *CMS* II.8, no. 40; HMs 202 impressed with *CMS* II.8, no. 195) and three flat-based nodules (HMs 180 impressed with *CMS* II.8, nos 41–2; HMs 197 impressed with *CMS* II.8, no. 97; and HMs 203 impressed with *CMS* II.8, no. 98) are of MM III date. One should stress again that these dates are based on the style of the seals, and are therefore *termini post quos*. Although the 'Hieroglyphic Deposit' includes documents with impressions of MM II seals, this does not necessarily indicate an earlier date for the documents themselves.

and Malia assemblages be positively assessed? And what are the implications of such a conclusion for the genesis of the Third Palace period bureaucracies?

I hope that the above discussion has done something to advance our understanding of the character of this 'co-existence' of the CH and LA scripts in the Second Palace period.[24] Certainly we can no longer speak of a paradox, an oddity or an anomaly (cf. also the thoughtful exposure by Olivier 1996, 108). The way these assemblages are shaped, and the intertwined associations between CH and LA elements within them, suggest that we may no longer label this as 'digraphia' or mere co-existence or symbiosis of scripts or systems that are otherwise well-defined. Proper description and interpretation of this phenomenon may call for a thorough revision of our conceptual and classificatory arsenal. I think just enough momentum has been gathered to make a rather provocative suggestion: that what the Knossos and Malia assemblages actually represent is neither CH nor LA, but a hitherto unrecognised entity: a 'North Central Cretan Second Palace period administrative system'[25] *defined* by the fusion of the CH and LA categories that modern scholarship, in other cases, had so far defined as distinct and mutually exclusive.

I feel obliged to deal in advance with a potential problem with the line of argument I am pursuing here. Besides the 'Hieroglyphic Deposit', Knossos has yielded one more significant Second Palace period administrative deposit, found in the East Temple Repository (ETR), again in the West Wing of the palace complex. The coherence of this assemblage is not questioned, its chronology is reasonably settled (mature LM IA) and the documents found in it have been commonly considered as LA. It is also true that the one tablet certainly assigned to this assemblage, **KN 1**, can be confidently assigned to LA.[26] Certain elements from the ETR are especially intriguing, however, as they seem to occur in no other 'canonical' LA administrative assemblage.

i. The inscribed sign or signs (two mirrored S-spirals: < SƧ >) that appear on one roundel from the ETR (HMs 342 = **KN Wc 23**) are so far unique among such documents inscribed in LA; therefore, the document had been excluded from *GORILA* on the argument that its inscribed signs do not represent writing at all (*GORILA* 2, lvi; cf. Hallager 1996 II, 160). However, discussion on these marks should also take into account their similarity to LA klasmatogram 703 (D), shaped as an inverted S, a virtual homograph to AB 75 < Ƨ > (LB value <*we*>) or, just as likely, a variant of the metrogram **116* or P or Linear A klasmatogram 703. In fact, the mirrored (i.e. S-shaped) variant of Linear A klasmatogram 703 occurs on a roundel from Kea (**KE Wc 2**); within the CH corpus, a sign similar to LA klasmatogram

[24] For the co-existence of scripts in First Palace period contexts see Karnava 2007. Cf. also recently Perna 2014.

[25] This somewhat cumbersome label is preferred here as it is plainly descriptive.

[26] Although it can be argued that it seems palaeographically removed from the LM IB LA of Ayia Triada, I must readily admit that a thorough study of LA palaeography still remains to be done; no assessment of palaeographic affinities or divergences can be presently made with accuracy and reliability.

703 has been identified as a klasmatogram (309 ⋋), although it occurs only on inscribed seals, where Jasink (2005, 23–9) has argued that it functions rather as a commodity sign or phonogram. Moreover, the much similar 8-spiral is a common motif on CH seals, although it is consistently not transcribed in *CHIC* (Hallager 1996 I, 106, fig. 39; Jasink 2005, 23–9). Given the above, and considering the occurrence of klasmatograms on roundels inscribed in the LA script, we should not light-heartedly reject **KN Wc 23** from the inscribed roundel corpus. The possibility that these marks could be accommodated within the LA *or* the CH signary must remain open.[27]

ii. Sphragistic practice associates the ETR with the Knossos 'Hieroglyphic Deposit' and the Malia '*Dépôt Hiéroglyphique*': although CH seals are properly absent from the ETR, roundels from there (**KN Wc 3**, **30** and **41**) do display repeated stamping (from the same or different seals), which is paralleled in the 'Hieroglyphic Deposit',[28] as well as on **MA Wc 13** and **14**, assigned to the '*Dépôt Hiéroglyphique*' (Hallager 1996 I, 59–60, n. 181, 108).[29]

iii. The ETR included a type of sealing so far not found in any other Second Palace period deposit, until recently known only from Third Palace period administrative contexts (see Table 5.1), as well as the Knossos 'Hieroglyphic Deposit' (HMs 140), but recently identified also in the MM IIB CH 'archive' at Petras (see Table 5.2): the irregular string-nodules that were used to secure, rather than merely label, as the twisted string-marks ('*Wickelbänder*' in the *CMS* terminology) and the regularly broken status of such objects suggest.[30]

We should be careful not to read too much into fragmentary and disparate evidence, but the existence of such non-canonical (and arguably CH-associated) elements in the ETR deserves our fullest attention. Seen alongside the mature Second Palace period dates of the Knossos 'Hieroglyphic Deposit' and the Malia 'Dépôt Hiéroglyphique', the unique marks on the ETR roundel **KN Wc 23** and the irregular string nodules associated with it in the broadly contemporary ETR lend strong support to the hypothesis that Knossos, and arguably north-central Crete in general, had undergone developments unparalleled elsewhere on the island during this period. This 'difference' of north-central Crete may be also hinted at by evidence from other sites in the region, such as

[27] Cf. also Hallager 1996 I, 106–7. The type of document does not preclude the CH identification: although roundels were until recently associated exclusively with administrations employing the LA script, a roundel (**PE Hc 002**) has been securely identified in the Petras CH 'archive' of MM II date (Tsipopoulou and Hallager 2010, 157, 182).

[28] HMs 132 (a unique document) bears impressions from as many as five different seals.

[29] However, it must be noted that the practice of multiple impression occurs elsewhere too on roundels (**PYR Wc 4**; **SA Wc 1-2**), as well as on other documents of more controversial typological identity, such as the Khania 'irregular flat-based nodules' (Hallager 1996 I, 202–3).

[30] On the type see Hallager 2005a, 254–8; 2010, 209–10; for impressions of '*Wickelbänder*' that secure the identification of irregular string-nodules in the ETR see Hallager 2010, 208, fig. 1 *middle row* (HMs 385, 391, 397, 1240).

the peculiarities found in at least one LA tablet from Tylissos (**TY 2**), as well as Olivier and Godart's observation that the rather 'archaising' LA from Archanes, located only 15 km south of Knossos, seems closer to LB forms than the better known Ayia Triada signary (Lembessi *et al.* 1974, 165).

4. The genesis of the Third Palace period bureaucracies

The hypothesis of a regional north-central Cretan system in the late Second Palace period is directly relevant to the problems posed earlier in this paper: I argue here that the aforementioned 'fusion' of CH and LA features has some kind of *genetic* association with the analogous 'fusion' of CH and LA elements discerned in the Third Palace period systems. 'Fusion', of course, only describes our *etic* understanding of what can be argued to have been a regional system, where these categories – arguably 'separable' in other contexts – may have naturally co-existed. I would strongly suggest that the system represented by the Knossos 'Hieroglyphic Deposit', the Knossos ETR and the Malia '*Dépôt Hiéroglyphique*' represents the closest we can get to the plausible typological and praxeological matrix, the 'womb' where the LB administrations took shape.

Accepting this line of reasoning has important implications for the *place* and *date* of the emergence of the Third Palace period bureaucracies. The fusion is not a pan-Cretan phenomenon; it is firmly located, as far as we can tell, in north-central Crete, and the hypothesis advanced here raises once more the question of the role of Knossos in the emergence of the administrations we have come to commonly label as 'Mycenaean'. Now, perhaps more intensely than ever, the burden of proof is with those who would wish to argue that the system could have been developed outside Crete.

Similarly, the dates of the Knossos 'Hieroglyphic Deposit' and the Malia '*Dépôt Hiéroglyphique*' give us a *terminus post quem* at the beginning of the LM I period, which is compatible with the powerful *terminus post quem* provided by the abrupt disuse of LA *as an administrative script* at the end of LM IB. As John Bennet has eloquently phrased it, LA 'did not simply disappear; rather, it was killed', at least in this realm of use (Bennet 2008, 22), even if the crudely painted LA inscription on the torso of the LM IIIA1 terracotta figurine from Poros (**PO Zg 1**) indicates the sporadic survival of the script in other (perhaps peripheral cultic) uses (Dimopoulou *et al.* 1993).

The disuse of the CH script is considerably more difficult to understand, and the phenomenon is much complicated by the uncertainty over the survival of CH literacy as potentially reflected in the preservation of CH seals (admittedly, not necessarily 'legible' at the time of their final deposition). However, a so far uniquely late *archival* document, the CH medallion (**PE He 001**) found on a floor with LM IB destruction debris in the North Magazines of the Second Palace period complex of Petras, without any further indication of disturbance in this particular locus, suggests that this script could have remained in use (and probably *alongside* the use of LA documents, such as tablets **PE 1-2**) until the very end of the Second Palace period (Tsipopoulou and

Hallager 1996, 39–42, fig. 16). If the 'co-existence' of CH and LA features in LM IB Petras is confirmed, we may have a third such case on the north coast of Crete, although as far east as Sitia, and as late as the very end of the Second Palace period.[31] Bennet's observation on the abrupt abandonment of LA may be applied to the CH script as well: it was not merely LA, but actually the administrative uses of all previously extant Cretan writing systems that were 'killed' at the very end of the LM IB period, to be effectively replaced by the unprecedentedly uniform Third Palace period system employing the LB script.

The approach advocated herein should open the way for a thorough reappraisal of the administrative landscape of Second Palace period Crete. Great caution will be necessary, and any progress must be based on assessments that are sensitive to the potentially meaningful differences on both diachronic and synchronic (i.e. local or regional) scales.

For instance, it can be argued that evidence for any 'co-existence' of CH and LA features is limited to the period *preceding* the final LM IB phase. Although such a conclusion would seem to downplay (i) the existence of the Petras CH medallion and (ii) the lack of uniformity observed across so-called 'canonical' LM IB assemblages, it does underscore the fact that, apart from Petras, LM IB Cretan administrations do not display features attributable to CH. Could this imply that the CH-LA 'fusion' had become obsolete by LM IB times?

The answer to this may lie in the aforementioned Knossos lacuna, what Olga Krzyskowska called 'a notorious black hole' administratively (Krzyskowska 2005, 189). The lack of *any* document from this phase at Knossos must be associated with the absence of closed LM IB deposits from the palace complex, which is in turn a reflection of the special 'fate' of this super-site and its subsequent LM II–IIIA1 take-off that I shall be returning to in a moment. A single hint at Knossos being functional during this period might be this site's participation in the nexus of the famous 'matching impressions' from finger-rings found across central Cretan sites and also Akrotiri on Thera (Krzyskowska 2005, 188–91): a combat or battle scene (presumably from a gold signet-ring) had impressed two single-hole hanging nodules from Knossos (*CMS* II.8, no. 279 on HMs 369 and HMs 1275), as well as five flat based nodules from LM IB Ayia Triada (*CMS* II.6, no. 15 on HMs 526/1–3, 595–6).

The hypothesis advanced here, in awareness of the complexities and problems it may present, is that LM IB Knossos may have employed an administrative system that displayed the forerunners of the full administrative apparatus of Third Palace period bureaucracies and whose earlier stage may be reflected – however patchily – in the Knossos 'Hieroglyphic Deposit' and Malia '*Dépôt Hiéroglyphique*',[32] as well as probably in those 'idiosyncratic' features of the ETR assemblage. The gaps in our knowledge of the

[31] One is also reminded of the 'dubitandum' from Palaikastro, also located in East Crete (Brice 1961, 21, pl. xxvii: no. iv 6), included here in Table 5.3.

[32] As well as possibly associated documents, such as **KN 22** (see above, n. 22).

administration of Second and Third Palace period Knossos are still quite formidable. What we are still almost completely missing is evidence for the development of the signaries in use at Knossos during the LM IB-LM II phases. But even if 'we are unlikely to get a second chance' (Krzyskowska 2005, 116) at filling information that has been lost from this exceptional site, efforts to reconstruct critical points in the administrative history of the Kephala should be nonetheless attempted.

Within post-LM I north central Crete, LM II–IIIA1 Knossos once more reappears as the most plausible accommodator of the system reform that the formation of the Third Palace period system clearly represents. This is the phase when Knossos, arguably the only functional administrative centre known so far in the contemporary Aegean, shows all the symptoms of what may be termed 'formative period anxiety' or 'early post-reform stress': an exploding monumentality and a degree of experimentation in art forms, imagery and mortuary investment that had no predecessor and would see no follow-up either on the Kephala hill (cf. Driessen and Langohr 2007; Preston 2008 for a general introduction to Third Palace period Crete). The genesis of the Third Palace period bureaucracies brought regionalism in administrative practice to an abrupt end. Their emergence was, in terms of administrative history, a true watershed, sweeping away to oblivion regional systems that had existed before it.

In the apparent attempt of the new Knossian elite groups to balance between the all-important associations with the Second Palace period past, a necessary resource of power legitimation, and a desperate need to exploit new power resources and strategies prone to concentrative manipulation, the genesis of the Third Palace period system had to stand on a balance point. It responded to novel needs and aspirations, but was also inevitably forged in the 'matrix' of pre-existing structures and practices. These latter I made here a preliminary, tentative, and admittedly bold attempt to reconstruct. I hope this might feed further discussion and re-examination of the problems pertaining to this system reform in some new perspective.

Chapter 6

From Linear B to Linear A: The problem of the backward projection of sound values

Philippa M. Steele[1] *and Torsten Meißner*

1. Introduction

This paper addresses the apparently simple question of whether, and if so to what extent, it is legitimate to use the sound values of Linear B in order to read the texts written in Linear A. This is hardly a new topic; already shortly after the decipherment of Linear B scholars were using its sound values to identify names in Linear A, most notably Furumark (1956, 28), Pugliese Carratelli (1957) and Palmer (1958), without, however, necessarily reflecting in depth on the methodology and the implications of doing so. It was Hooker (1975) and Olivier (1975) who first looked at the problem in detail, and subsequently a number of scholars, in particular Pope and Raison (1978, 38ff.), Godart (1984) and Duhoux (1989), have put forward good reasons why it is legitimate, at least in part, to apply Linear B sound values to the earlier Linear A. Still, it does remain a relevant issue as doubts about the legitimacy of this approach can still be seen and found in print. For example, one author recently writes:

> '... taking into account that the discussed words are attested in a very poor and unreliable way, the fact of finding the above mentioned connections between them does not seem to be an incontrovertible proof confirming the validity of the substitution of phonetic values of Linear B to Linear A.'[2]

In what follows, we try to provide arguments that it is legitimate *in principle and as an approximation* to read Linear A with the sound values of Linear B. To this end, we shall look at the problem in detail and, at the same time, take a broader approach. In principle, of course, reservations are quite in order from a methodological point of view. A great amount of time and effort has been spent elucidating the development

---

[1] This paper was written during Philippa Steele's tenure of British Academy funding for a Postdoctoral Fellowship.

[2] Zadka 2010, 183.

from Linear A to Linear B in all of its aspects, and with impressive results.[3] Although difficult in detail, this is at least methodologically straightforward, as the method of the archaeologists, historians and epigraphists is correct: the explanation of a later state of affairs on the basis of an earlier one. Anyone currently attempting to read Linear A, however, does exactly the opposite: by taking the sound values of Linear B and applying them to Linear A, one tries to explain and, crucially, interpret something earlier on the basis of a later state of affairs, and that is, of course, highly questionable from a methodological point of view, especially given that we have very little check on the results. For if we apply the sound values of Linear B to Linear A the result is a language of which we understand neither the grammatical structure nor, with a few minor exceptions, the content. *A priori* it is difficult to decide whether this is so because the underlying language is so different to the Greek that we see in Linear B, or because we are incorrectly inferring the sound values, or both.

Of course, even if, as we shall argue, it is entirely legitimate *in principle* to 'read' Linear A with Linear B sound values, this must be qualified immediately. Whatever the nature and structure of the Minoan language may be, it can be taken as certain that the Minoan language underlying Linear A, which we assume to represent a single language at least in the context of the administrative documents,[4] did not have the same phonological inventory as the Mycenaean Greek encoded in Linear B, meaning that an at present incalculable degree of phonological adaptation and realignment must have taken place in the process of creating Linear B from Linear A. A close phonetic interpretation, however, is not necessary. A reinterpretation or adaptation must from our vantage point be regarded as unproblematic if it is both plausible in phonetic terms and systematic. It is evident, then, that in the absence of secure phonetic correspondences and linguistic reconstruction typology, provides an important, though of course not fool-proof, check on the linguistic interpretation.

2. Linear B as a descendant of Linear A

A good first argument supporting the view that a backward projection of sound values is legitimate comes from our evolving view of the scripts themselves.

It is a trivial fact that the two scripts are extremely close, indeed arguably closer than any of the other Bronze Age scripts of the Aegean and Eastern Mediterranean are to one another. Indeed, sometimes the relationship is so close that in short or fragmentary texts it is very difficult to decide, on the basis of the sign shapes alone, whether we are dealing with a Linear A or Linear B document.[5] The view used to be

[3] See, for example, Palaima and Sikkenga 1999, Tomas 2003, 2011, 2012a.

[4] See in this sense also Davis 2014, 179ff.

[5] E.g. KN Ze 16 (see *GORILA*[4]: 138) which, assuming the dating to LM II is correct, is either an unusually late example of Linear A or an early example of Linear B on an unusual support.

common that there was a Proto-Linear ancestor out of which Linear A and Linear B developed independently.[6] The main reason for arguing this position was that overall the correspondences between Linear A and Linear B were not as numerous as one would expect for two scripts of which one evolved out of the other.

However, this was difficult from the beginning, as such a hypothesis fails to account for the stark discrepancy in the chronology of the attestation of the scripts. Put differently, if a Proto-Linear script had existed out of which Linear A and Linear B were developed independently as sister scripts, we would be at a complete loss to explain why Linear A was attested hundreds of years earlier, with no trace of Linear B all that time, and why Linear A falls out of use soon after Linear B enters the stage.

Such a view can be put to rest now, and it is abundantly clear that *essentially* Linear B was adapted out of Linear A and nothing else, meaning that the core part of the Linear B script, i.e. its syllabograms, go back, except for those that are Linear B innovations, directly to Linear A.[7] This is not just borne out by the chronology, the striking similarity of the scripts and their use, the likely historical context and the administrative set-up. Even though we are far from a complete understanding of the Bronze Age scripts from this area, there is, quite simply, no room for any other script out of which Linear B could have developed.[8] Crucially, the further we go back in time within Linear B itself, the greater the similarities with Linear A become.[9] Steady progress has been made both in the archaeological and historical understanding of the relationship between the Minoan and Mycenaean societies and administration, and in the epigraphy. The table in *Docs*[2] (p. 33) identifies 53 out of 89 signs as shared between Linear A and Linear B, a 60% identity. By now, due to new finds and better epigraphic study, this figure has risen to about 64 out of 89, giving a figure of 72%. So,

[6] Still found, for example, in Coulmas (1996, 96): 'During the Middle Minoan period (about 1700–1550 BCE) the proto-linear signs developed into two scripts known as Linear A and Linear B'.

[7] This is not to be taken to mean that the relationship between the two scripts is entirely straightforward, and almost every treatment of the subject begins by stressing how complex this relationship actually is. Thus, Melena (2014, 6) stresses the difference between Linear A and Linear B when it comes to measuring smaller quantities. This is undoubtedly true and could point to another source of input for the administrative reform that took place at the time of adaptation though Melena's suggestion that Miletus may have been the place of adaptation (Melena 2014, 7) is speculative and, as he himself admits, does not sit comfortably with the archaeological data currently available; for the administrative reform that led to certain changes in the overall use and structure of the script, cf. the papers by Tomas and Petrakis in this volume. Whatever the case regarding the place of adaptation, this issue has no bearing on the use of the syllabograms. A finely balanced view is expressed in Palaima and Sikkenga (1999, 606) who see Linear B as the product of 'certain features of Linear A' on the one hand and a 'considerable understanding of the phonemic and morphological structure of the Greek language' on the other, thus accounting for the new signs in Linear B and, at least in part, the loss of certain Linear A characters.

[8] There is little to be gained from Hooker's assumption (1979, 33) that Linear B which he characterises as 'more cursive and florid' partially owes its existence to a different – but unattested – form of Late Minoan writing on Crete and was not 'developed expressly for writing on clay'.

[9] See Driessen 2000, 224–8; Bennet 2008, 20.

Table 6.1: The Old Italic alphabet in relation to the standard Roman alphabet

𐌀	𐌁	𐌂	𐌃	𐌄	𐌅	-	𐌆	𐌇	𐌈	𐌉	𐌊	𐌋	𐌌	𐌍	𐌏	𐌐	𐌑	𐌒	𐌓	𐌔	𐌕	𐌖	𐌗	𐌘	𐌙	𐌚
A	B	C	D	E	F	G	-	H	-	I	K	L	M	N	O	P	-	Q	R	S	T	V	X	-	-	-

for example, sign 48 𐁅 *nwa* had previously been attested in both Cretan Hieroglyphic and Linear B, and it was always reasonable, therefore, to assume that it must also have existed in Linear A,[10] and indeed a recently edited Linear A inscription apparently shows precisely this.[11]

This 72% identity is comparable to the relationship of the Latin alphabet of the end of the 3rd century BC to the Old Italic alphabet out of which it developed (Table 6.1). 20 out of 27 original signs are identical, and Latin has also developed an extra one, giving a sign identity of 74%, a figure quite comparable to what we see between Linear A and Linear B; and if we compare, a few hundred years later on, the local Cretan alphabet to the post-Euclidean alphabet which eventually replaced the autochthonous variety, the figures are again comparable.[12] On the other hand, it is quite clear that some signs were invented within Linear B and specifically on the basis of the Greek language, and this likewise should not surprise us since scripts do evolve. Also, given that no two languages have the same sound system, there may well be a need for additional signs. Likewise, of course, some of the old signs might not be useful in the context of the new language for which the script is adapted (see on this topic Judson, this volume). The best known case clearly is the complex sign 𐁃 *dwo* which is "two *wo*", or in Greek "duo *wo*", in other words, a completely iconic formation by way of doubling the sign for *wo*, 𐀺, a process that is dependent on an element in the Greek language, namely the word for "two" (see Meißner and Steele forthcoming). All in all the correspondence between Linear A and Linear B is substantial, and if gaps still exist we should not be surprised. After all, the amount of text we have written in Linear A is very small; as Younger states: 'There are some 1427 Linear A documents with a total occurrence of 7362–7396 signs (Schoep 2002, 38); if there are 4002 characters (font Times, pitch 12, no spaces) on a 8 1/2 × 11 inch sheet of paper with 1 inch margins, all extant Linear A would take up 1.84 pages.'[13] Schoep's figures now have to be revised upwards slightly; still, all of Linear A would not take up much more than 2 full pages. If the total amount of Latin transmitted to us were similarly limited, it is extremely likely that the very rare sign <K> would not be attested.

[10] Cf. the comment in *Docs*[2] (p. 40): 'Only one Mycenaean syllable, 𐁅, *nwa*, has a close parallel in the "hieroglyphs" [...] but none in Linear A, and even here the omission from A may be due to the accidents of history.'

[11] SY Za 4, see Muhly and Olivier (2008, 207–8 and 216). The drawing of the text is done with confidence while the photograph seems less clear.

[12] See the 'Table of Letters' at the end of Jeffery (1990; not paginated).

[13] Younger, http://www.people.ku.edu/~jyounger/LinearA/#5 under 5. 'Basic Statistics'.

3. The relationship between Cretan and Cypriot scripts

A second argument comes from a much more long-distance comparison. It is evident that Linear A and Linear B are only one part of a writing tradition that was significantly more widespread, and even before the decipherment of Linear B it was clear that the script was related to the syllabic scripts on Cyprus: the undeciphered and unintelligible Cypro-Minoan, mostly in the second millennium BC, and, descended directly from it, the later Cypriot Syllabary that was used to denote the Cypriot dialect of Greek from the beginning of its attestation by the 8th century BC right down to its demise in the 3rd century BC; the latter script was also used to write at least one further language, the so-called Eteocypriot, a language that remains poorly attested and understood (Steele 2011, 2013a, 99–172). The exact details of the relationship between Cypro-Minoan and the Linear scripts from Crete are not clear, and the Cypriot inscriptions show a smaller degree of confirmed correspondence in sign shapes and values than is evident between Linear A and Linear B, pointing towards a script adaptation made in very different circumstances from the creation of Linear B and probably making more radical alterations to the source script (see Steele forthcoming, chapter 1). Nevertheless, it cannot be denied that the Aegean and Cypriot scripts are related, owing to a number of signs in Linear B and in the first millennium Cypriot Syllabary that have clear shared shapes and values (see below). Both of these scripts were adapted to write varieties of the Greek language at different stages.

Cypro-Minoan is first attested in Late Cypriot I, i.e. the first phase of the Late Bronze Age, probably corresponding to the later 16th or beginning of the 15th century BC. This is maybe 100 years, more or less, before the first attestations of Linear B in perhaps Late Minoan IIIA1 at Knossos (the Room of the Chariot Tablets)/Late Helladic IIIA1 at Iklaina near Pylos, which rules out any direct descent from Linear B.[14] It does not necessarily follow that Cypro-Minoan must be a direct descendant of Linear B's ancestor, Linear A, but the timescale must be approximately correct: assuming that the earliest known Cypro-Minoan inscriptions do not date more than 100–200 years after the transmission of writing to Cyprus, the Linear A script is the only well attested candidate for being its direct ancestor.[15] Assumed direct descent from Linear A would leave some unanswered questions, for example why the number of obviously shared signs is quite low (see below), although it is possible that the form of some signs has changed beyond recognition (though see further Valério, this volume), or that the creation of Cypro-Minoan involved the invention of a significant number of new signs alongside the inherited ones, as argued for example by Bombardieri and Jasink (2010).

[14] The basis for the dating of the Room of the Chariot Tablets documents is laid out in Driessen 2000. The Iklaina tablet fragment is published in Shelmerdine 2012.

[15] A link with Cretan Hieroglyphic is not impossible, but there is little positive evidence to support it, either in terms of shared signs or of palaeographic similarities, whereas Linear A shows much more convincing parallels. The relationship between Cretan Hieroglyphic and Linear A is itself far from straightforward: see the papers by Ferrara, Decorte, Tomas and Petrakis in this volume for various aspects of the problem.

An alternative hypothesis is available, namely that Linear A and Cypro-Minoan could be sister scripts, descended from a common ancestor; however, this would require an assumption that they are descended from a script of which no examples have survived, as was long ago suggested by Lejeune (1958a, 328; see also Steele 2014b). This latter hypothesis could potentially be seen to fit in well with the view that there is little in the way of archaeological evidence pointing towards an obvious situation of contact between Crete and Cyprus at the time when the transmission of the script ought to have taken place. However, a non-Cretan origin for Cypro-Minoan (e.g. Sherratt 2013) not only is not any better supported by the archaeological evidence, but also requires an assumption that a related script was widely in use in an area such as Anatolia but has left no traces whatsoever – making it a not very attractive alternative hypothesis. At present, no definite decision can be made between these possibilities.

However Cypro-Minoan is related to Linear A, it is striking that we can identify a certain number of signs that have the same morphology, i.e. shape, in Linear B and the 1st millennium Cypriot Syllabary, as well as sharing the same or a closely related phonetic value. Eleven signs can be identified with a high degree of certainty: *a, i, da* (=*ta* in the Cypriot Syllabary), *na, pa, po, ro* (=*lo* in the Cypriot Syllabary but *ro/lo* in Linear B), *sa, se, ti* and *to* (see Table 6.2). Without quite going as far as Masson (1987), who thought that she could understand exactly a large set of correspondences between the Aegean and Cypriot scripts based mainly on formal resemblance, we can perhaps add others to the list: *si*, for example, is a good contender. Analysis of other possibly related signs in Linear A and Cypro-Minoan, as conducted for example by Valério (this volume), has the potential to reveal further links.

Some of the shared signs raise phonological questions. For example, what can it tell us about Minoan phonology that the sign borrowed into Linear B as *da* /da/

Table 6.2: Shared sign shapes and values across the Aegean and Cypriot scripts

Linear A (form)	*Linear B (form + value)*	*Cypro-Minoan (form)*	*Cypriot Syllabic (form + value)*
𐘇 (AB 08)	𐀀 a	𒿦 (sign 102)	𐠀 a
𐘛 (AB 28)	𐀂 i	𒿨 (sign 104)	𐠂 i
𐘀 (AB 01)	𐀅 da	𒾒 (sign 004)	𐠭 ta
𐘅 (AB 06)	𐀙 na	𒾜 (sign 013)	𐠙 na
𐘂 (AB 03)	𐀞 pa	𒾔 (sign 006)	𐠞 pa
𐘊 (AB 11)	𐀡 po	Not attested?	𐠡 po
𐘁 (AB 02)	𐀫 ro/lo	𒾓 (sign 005)	𐠒 lo
𐘟 (AB 31)	𐀭 sa	𒿔 (sign 082)	𐠨 sa
𐘈 (AB 09)	𐀮 se	𒾲 (sign 044)	𐠩 se
𐘡 (AB 37)	𐀴 ti	𒾠 (sign 021)	𐠯 ti
𐘄 (AB 05)	𐀵 to	𒾖 (sign 008)	𐠰 to

(as opposed to /ta/, /tʰa/) was borrowed into Cypriot Syllabic as *ta* (i.e. /ta/, /tʰa/, /da/), while the signs borrowed into Linear B as *ti* and *to* (i.e. /ti/, /tʰi/ but NOT /di/, etc.) also ended up as part of the Cypriot Syllabic t-series (*ti*, *to* representing /ti/, /tʰi/, /di/, etc.)? Various explanations have been put forward to explain how Linear B *da* and Cypriot Syllabic *ta* are related to each other, including a proposal by Lejeune (1958a, 327) that the Linear B d-series originates from a series representing a Minoan /l/ phoneme of some sort, but none adequately accounts for the mixed affiliations of the Cypriot Syllabic t-series (see Steele 2014b). There is also the perhaps related problem of how Cypriot Syllabic developed two different series for /r/ and /l/ while Linear B developed a single series used for both. The crucial question is whether Linear A or Cypro-Minoan had separate series to represent /r/ and /l/, and there are several possibilities, including: Linear A always had a distinction between /r/ and /l/ but one series was reinterpreted as /d/ in Linear B (cf. Lejeune's suggestion) while the /r/ and /l/ distinction was maintained in Cypro-Minoan; Linear A did not distinguish /r/ and /l/ and passed this lack of distinction on to Linear B as well as to Cypro-Minoan, while Cypriot Syllabic later made the innovation of distinguishing between them; or a situation similar to the last but with the innovation made in Cypro-Minoan and passed on to Cypriot Syllabic. It does not help that we do not know for certain whether Cypro-Minoan is a descendant of or sister to Linear A.

Admittedly the number of definite correspondences across the four scripts is not high, suggesting a complex development process, but it is striking that wherever there is such a correspondence the sound values also correspond very closely (notwithstanding the aforementioned examples). Cypriot Syllabic can only have inherited these values from Cypro-Minoan, and further back from Linear A or the ancestor of both Linear A and Cypro-Minoan, just as Linear B has inherited them directly from Linear A. This suggests that we can be quite confident of the values of these signs in Linear A, a few caveats notwithstanding. The exact phonetic values in Linear A cannot be recovered with precision, as highlighted especially by the more complex cases outlined above, but the shared values are close enough to reconstruct the values approximately. The fact that the obviously shared signs cover several consonant series, as well as the vowel-only signs, gives one further confidence. In other words, despite the fact that both writing traditions went through at least one change of language each (Linear A > Linear B, concomitant with the transition from Minoan to Greek on Crete as the language of administrative documents, and Cypro-Minoan > Cypriot Syllabic representing a change from a completely unknown language to the Cypriot Greek dialect), the sound values attached to the signs are tenacious and remain pretty much constant over a long period of time, even though they are attested in different places and used for various unrelated languages. This means that the much smaller step leading from Linear A to Linear B is even more likely to operate with the same sound values not just in the 11 cases where it is incontestable, but across the board.

4. Shared sign sequences

Next, there is the argument that Hooker (1975) and others started out from. There seems to be a large number of names shared between Linear A and Linear B and if they can indeed be identified as being the same name then this will imply the same or similar sound values for a given sign between Linear A and B. One problem here is word length, and chance graphic identity disguising substantive differences can often not be ruled out entirely. Evidently, the longer a sequence of signs in Linear A and Linear B respectively, the greater, statistically speaking, the likelihood that the identity is real. In this context Duhoux (1989, 69) points out that in a sequence of 3 signs, the likelihood of identity is in the low 80% range, while in the case of a sequence of 4 identical signs, this likelihood rises to 99%.

The list of putative Linear A–Linear B equations between names containing sequences of three identical or sufficiently similar (identity in the consonantal structure with some vocalic alternations) characters is quite considerable (see Table 6.3: personal names unmarked, place names in bold). This is an impressive list, and if we could take it at face value, we would gain 39 signs that have the same sound value between Linear A and Linear B, effectively settling the matter. However, things are not quite so straightforward, for the evidence is of mixed value. Personal names are not a particularly good guide as there usually is no independent confirmation available that two identically or very similarly written forms render the same name; in addition it can be hard, even within Linear B, to tell whether a given form is a personal name or an appellative title, indication of a profession or the like. There must be particular doubt concerning the identification of personal names especially when parallels from Pylos are invoked. Further problems with such identifications can be illustrated by the equation *a-ka-re-u* = *a-ka-ru*. *a-ka-re-u* in the Linear B tablet from Knossos is undoubtedly a man's name, but Linear A *a-ka-ru*, as would appear from its position in the tablet, is a heading and may be a transactional term.[16] Linear A *a-ka-ru* would thus have nothing to do with Linear B *a-ka-re-u*. Likewise, *i-ja-te* in Linear B, attested at Pylos, is probably the entirely Greek word for doctor, ἰατήρ, and has nothing to do with the Linear A term *i-ja-te*. Where, however, the Linear B personal names are limited to Knossos and/or do not have a ready explanation from within Greek, such as *sa-ma-ru* or *qa-qa-ro*, the identification across the two scripts and languages is clearly tempting. It also needs to be pointed out that Duhoux's figures of 81% and 99% likelihood of identity are blind to the relative frequency of the signs in Linear A and Linear B respectively. If we take these into account, even a 3-character sequence like Linear B *qa-*ra_2*-wo* = Linear A *qa-*ra_2*-wa*, containing the sign ra_2, relatively rare in both Linear B and Linear A,[17] reaches a higher likelihood of indicating the same name.

---

[16] See http://www.people.ku.edu/~jyounger/LinearA/lexicon.html.

[17] There are about 68 instances of this sign in Linear B and a maximum of 38 in Linear A (18 of which, however, are found in the name *sa-*ra_2).

Table 6.3: Possible name equations between Linear B and Linear A

Linear B	*Linear A*
a-ka-re-u KN B 416	a-ka-ru HT 2.1, HT 86a.1
a-ra-na-ro KN As 1516.1	a-ra-na-re HT 1.4
a-re-sa-ni-je PY An 724.2	a-re-sa-na THE Zb 2
a-sa-ro KN As 40.4	a-sa-ra_2 HT 89.1
a-si-wi-ja PY Fr 1206	a-su-ja HT 11a.3-4
a-ta-ro PY An 35.5	a-ta-re Za 8.1
da-i-pi-ta KN V 831.4	da-i-pi-ta ZA 8.5, 10a.4-5
da-mi-ni-jo/a KN D and PY A series	da-mi-nu HT 117a.8
di-de-ro KN Dv 1504	di-de-ru HT 86a.3 +
du-pu_2-ra-zo KN Da 1173	du-pu_2-re KO Za 1.b
i-ja-te PY Eq 146.9	i-ja-te PH Zb 4
ka-sa-ro KN C 912b	ka-sa-ru HT 10b.3
ki-da-ro KN E 842.3	ki-da-ro HT47a.4 +
ki-ri-ta KN G 820.1, Ld 785.1	ki-ri-ta HT 114a.1 +
ku-ka-da-ro KN Uf 836.b	ku-ku-da-ra HT 117a.7
ka-*56-no KN Df 1219B	ku-*56-nu HT 1.3-4 +
ku-ru-ka KN Vc 5510	ku-ru-ku HT 87.4
mi-ja-ro KN Ln 1568.1	MI+JA+RU HT 23a.2 +
pa-i-to KN D +	**pa-i-ṭọ HT 97a.3 +**
pa-ja-ro KN As 1519.6	pa-ja-re HT 8b.4
pa-ra-ne KN Vc 7616	pa-ra-ne HT 115a.4 +
qa-qa-ro KN As 604.3	qa-qa-ru HT 93a.4-5 +
qa-ra_2-wo KN Ce 50	qa-ra_2-wa HT 86a.3
sa-ma-ru KN V 655.1	sa-ma-ro HT 88.5-6
se-to-i-ja KN D +	**se-to-i-ja PR Za 1.b**
si-ki-ro KN U 8210.1	si-ki-ra HT 8a.4
su-ki-ri-ta KN D	**su-ki-ri-ta PH Wa 32**
tu-ri-so KN Ce 59.3+	**tu-ru-sa KO Za 1**
wa-du-na KN V 503.3	wa-du-ni-mi HT 6b.1-2 +
cf. also	
di-ka-ta-jo KN Fp 1	**(a-)di-ki-te(-te) PK Za 11**
i-da(-i-jo) KN K 875	**i-da-a KO Za 1**

If we wish to remove the uncertainties connected to the personal names and only accept evidence from place names from Crete (Table 6.4):

> 'we are reduced to much less, and Olivier (1975) and Godart (1984) arrive at 15 or 16 shared signs and sound values, depending or not whether we are prepared to admit a two-character

place name, *i-da*, to be part of this list, which would add the identification of the shared sign ⊦ as *da* to the list.'

Table 6.4: Possible place name equations between Linear B and Linear A

Linear B	*Linear A*
pa-i-to	pa-i-ṭọ
se-to-i-ja	se-to-i-ja
tu-ri-so	tu-ru-sa, a-tu-ṛị-si-ti
di-ka-ta(-jo)	di-ki-te
su-ki-ri-ta	su-ki-ri-ta

If we add the sign values confirmed by the place names to those confirmed through comparison with the Cypriot scripts (section 3 above), then our grid of secure correspondences fills up (Table 6.5). In this way, we arrive at 19 or 20 signs likely to share the same or very similar sound values in Linear A and Linear B, including, crucially, a whole consonantal series (the t-series).

Table 6.5: Confirmed Linear A sound values based on equations between the Cypriot Syllabic script and Linear B, and on place names shared between Linear A and Linear B

	a	*e*	*i*	*o*	*u*
V	a		i		
d	da		di		
j					
k			ki		
m					
n	na				
p	pa			po	
q					
r			ri	ro	
s	sa	se	si?		su
t	ta	te	ti	to	tu
w					
z					

5. Variations in Linear A sign sequences

As well as looking for words that appear in both Linear A and Linear B, we can consider words that recur in Linear A in multiple attestations, sometimes with small variations in the sign sequence usually appearing at the end of the word. Provided that the sequences contain enough shared signs, it is reasonable to assume that these are variations within the same word (as with comparisons across Linear A and B, a four-sign sequence is a very secure indicator, and a three-sign sequence still very likely to indicate the same word). Looking for morphological patterns in this way is important for anyone attempting to identify the language underlying an undeciphered script, putting us in mind of the methods applied to Linear B before its decipherment, especially by Alice Kober (see Kober 1945); but at a basic level it can also give us access to sign values by allowing us to identify signs that share a consonant or vowel (see Duhoux 1989, 66–8). For example, as well as the place name *su-ki-ri-ta* (also attested in Linear B, see above), we find in Linear A *su-ki-ri-te-i-ja*, which looks like the same word with a different suffix (in this case, since *su-ki-ri-ta* is a known place name, we might guess an ethnic adjective suffix describing the content of the jar on which it is found). This confirms that the *ta* and *te* signs share the same consonant and differ in only the vowel, i.e. that *ta* and *te* belong to the same consonant series. Further attested sequences can be considered:[18]

m-series:
*(j)a-sa-sa-ra-**me*** (*ja-sa-sa-ra-me*: IO Za 6; IO Za 12; IO Za 16; PS Za 2.2; TL Za 1b; *a-sa-sa-ra-me*: PK Za 11.b-c; PR Za 1.c)
*ja-sa-sa-ra-**ma**-na* (KN Za 10a-b)

*i-pi-na-**ma*** (IO Za 2.1; KO Za 1c-d; AP Za 2.1)
*i-pi-na-**mi**-na* (PK Za 10; PK Za 11.d)

t-series:
*su-ki-ri-**ta*** (PH Wa 32)
*su-ki-ri-**te**-i-ja* (HT Zb 158b)

*(j)a-di-ki-**te**-te* (*ja-di-ki-te-te*: PK Za 15; *a-di-ki-te-te*: PK Za 11.a-b)
*ja-di-ki-**tu*** (IO Za 2.1)

u and w-series:
? *qe-ra*$_2$-***u*** (HT 1.1-2; HT 95a.4-5, b.4-5)
? *qa-ra*$_2$-***wa*** (HT 86a.3)

*ja-ta-i-*88-**u**-ja* (AP Za 1)
*a-ta-i-*88-**wa**-ja* (IO Za 2.1; IO Za 3; IO Za 7; KO Za 1a; PK Za 12.a; SY Za 1. SU Za 2a; SY Za 3; SY Za 4; SY Za 8; TL Za 1a)

s-series:
? *tu-ru-**sa*** (KO Za 1b-c)
? *a-tu-ri-**si**-ti* (KN Zb 5)

The alternations seen in these pairs, especially the ones that are better attested and share longer sequences of signs, allow us to identify some signs that must belong to the same consonant-series in Linear A.[19] The crucial point to note is that these are

[18] Only certain attestations are listed.

[19] The pair demonstrating an alternation between *u* and *wa* (*ja-ta-i-*88-**u**-ja*, *a-ta-i-*88-**wa**-ja*; the fluctuation between word initial *a-* and *ja-* is attested elsewhere, most notably in *(j)a-sa-sa-ra-me*) gives two signs that do not *sensu stricto* belong to the same series, but they can both be seen as reflexes of a semi-vowel.

Table 6.6: Confirmed Linear A sound values, based on equations between the Cypriot Syllabic script and Linear B, place names shared between Linear A and Linear B, and evidence from internal variations

	a	*e*	*i*	*o*	*u*
V	a		a		
d	da		di		
j					
k			ki		
m	ma	me	mi		mu?
n	na				
p	pa			po	
q					
r			ri	ro	
s	sa	se	si?		su
t	ta	te	ti	to	tu
w					
z					

signs that in Linear B also belong to the same consonant series, making it all the more probable that they were transferred from Linear A to Linear B as whole consonant series – and making it all the less likely that there were random reallocations of signs' values, such as is often suggested based on an assumption that Linear A only had (and only had signs for) three vowels.[20]

As well as ones already identified, this procedure confirms the consonant-value of some signs that were not confirmed by the other methods already discussed, for example three signs in the m-series (*ma*, *me*, *mi*). We could add a fourth sign to the m-series by another, admittedly less certain, method: the sign *mu* doubles as the ideogram for 'cow' in Linear A just as it does in Linear B, perhaps suggesting an onomatopoeic origin for the ideogram. Further slots begin to fill up in the grid of signs with confirmed approximate values (Table 6.6).

[20] See e.g. Younger at http://people.ku.edu/~jyounger/LinearA/, section 7b: 'It is well-known that Linear A uses three main vowels, A, I, U; Linear B adds e- and o-series, and complex phonemes (e.g., dwo, two)'; and Palaima and Sikkenga (1999, 603): 'Linear A has a 3-vowel system, using a, u and i.' Davis (2014, 240–2) accepts that Linear A had three main vowels but argues that the e- and o-vowels attested are the results of monophthongisation of i- and u-diphthongs respectively. Beekes (2014, 8) accepts a five-vowel system: 'Originally, I thought that Pre-Greek had only three vowels: a, i, u... Recently, I have become more inclined to assume a system with the usual five vowels.' A comparative and statistical analysis may well show that, whatever the vocalic system of the underlying Minoan language, Linear A did have full sets of signs for five vowels: see Meißner and Steele (forthcoming).

Table 6.7: The Carian alphabet

A	C	Δ	Ę	F	I	⊕	Γ	N	O	Ϙ	Þ	M	Y	Φ	X	Ψ	ΔΔ	⦶	Ð	□	ᛩ	∇	⫙	╫	↑
a	d	l	ù	r	λ	q	b	m	o	t	š	s	u	ñ	x	n	p	ś	i	e	w	k	ú	í	τ

6. A caution from Caria

But caution is still in order. When some signs have the same or roughly the same sound value, this does not mean that every sign needs to behave in the same way. In this context, it may be salutary to look at the situation from somewhere nearby, Caria, several hundred years later.

The Carians adopted, like many people in the Aegean and Eastern Mediterranean, the alphabet, and given the letter shapes, it is most likely that they adopted it from the Greeks in whose Ionic hinterland they lived. It is attested from about the 7th century BC onwards, and given the apparently higher number of phonemes in their language a few signs were added (Table 6.7). What is highly remarkable is the sound values of the signs.[21] Compared to Greek, only the signs for a, o, s and u are kept with the same sound value. Other signs look as if their sound value was almost deliberately distorted, and in any case they have nothing to do with the Greek *Vorlage*. It is unsurprising, therefore, that Carian for a very long time resisted decipherment, and had it not been for the digraphs of some names and eventually an Greek-Carian bilingual inscription that was found at Kaunos it is almost certain that we would still be in no position to read and understand Carian. The Carian situation may serve as a stark reminder to us that even if some sound values are shared it must not be assumed automatically that this is true for all signs.

Table 6.8: Adaptation of Linear A personal names in -u to Linear B -o

Linear A	*Linear B*
qa-qa-ru	qa-qa-ro
di-de-ru	di-de-ro
ku-*56-nu	ka-*56-no

Table 6.9: Adaptation of Linear A personal names in -o to Linear B -u

Linear A	*Linear B*
sa-ma-ro	sa-ma-ru

Table 6.10: Adaptation of Linear A personal names in -e to Linear B -o

Linear A	*Linear B*
pa-ja-re	pa-ja-ro
a-ta-re	a-ta-ro
a-ra-na-re	a-ra-na-ro

7. Morphological trends

However, there are reasons to think that, in fact, for Linear A we can be more optimistic. For a) it would appear that whole consonantal series are identical between Linear A and Linear B, in particular the impressive s-series and t-series, even if we only accept the place names as evidence; and b) it is encouraging to see certain patterns: personal names ending in -Cu in Linear A tend to end in -Co in Linear B,

[21] For the sound values of the Carian alphabet and how to determine them see, above all, Schürr 1992; Adiego 2010.

an expected adaptation to the morphological structure of Greek where male PNs end in /-os/ much more often than in /-us/ (Table 6.8). But the opposite is, curiously, also attested (Table 6.9). At least it shows precisely the same alternation though it does raise questions as to the phonological status of the o- and u-series in Linear A.[22] Likewise, male PNs in Linear A in -Ce were, unsurprisingly, adapted in Linear B in the same way (Table 6.10).

8. The statistical approach

A completely different type of argument for the legitimacy of applying Linear B sound values to Linear A was provided by Packard (1974), further developed recently by Davis (2014, 246ff.). As is well known, Packard carried out a number of statistical experiments. Particularly impressive are his 'expected frequencies': assuming the sign we read as '*da* were twice as frequent as *di*, one might predict that *ka* should be roughly twice as common as *ki* and that *ma* should be twice as common as *mi*' (Packard 1974, 82), and indeed this relationship is borne out. Packard even constructed 9 random, and therefore in all likelihood false decipherments, where signs of relative similar frequency were randomly distributed, but none of these produced anything like as coherent a result as the application of Ventris's sound values for Linear B did. In other words, this is good statistical confirmation.

This could then be used for the names as well. And indeed Packard was able to show that applying Ventris's sound values to Linear A yields five times as many parallels with Knossian Linear B words as does the average of random, fictitious decipherments. One would not, however, expect the same number of correspondences between names in Linear A and those in Linear B from the mainland, and even this negative correlation is borne out by Packard's study. For there is no significant difference between the results obtained by applying Ventris's values and those obtained by 'random' decipherment.

This does constitute good confirmation of the validity of the application of Ventris's sound values to Linear A from a completely different corner.

9. Ideograms and the acrophonic principle

A further argument comes from within the Minoan language itself. Linear B uses a number of syllabograms and ligatures almost like ideograms. This use is apparently based on the acrophonic principle of representing the first syllable (or, in case of the ligatures, two or three syllables) of a commodity term; the same sign is used both syllabographically and ideographically. Thus, *ni* serves, apart from its syllabic value, as the sign for 'fig' (as also *sa* for 'flax', ra_3 for 'saffron', etc). Linear A also uses the same sign, *ni*, ideographically. It is important to note that those signs that consist

[22] See Davis 2014, 189, fig. 111, and 240ff. and Meißner and Steele forthcoming.

of one syllabogram only never abbreviate a Greek word: the Greek word for 'fig' is σῦκον, and similarly the word for 'flax' is λίνον, i.e. they do not begin with ni and sa, in the same way that the Greek word for saffron, κρόκος (itself not an inherited word), does not begin with rai-/lai-. So one might well wonder where these come from – a Minoan word for fig beginning with ni-? We are helped further here by the much later Greek glossographers. We owe to Günter Neumann (1962) the discovery of the gloss νικύλεον· τὸ σῦκον ἐν ταῖς Κρητικαῖς γλώσσαις (attributed to Hermonax in Athenaeus *Deipnosophistae* 76e). In other words, Hermonax's νικύλεον and the use of *ni* as the ideogram for fig in Linear B very likely are derived from this Minoan word.

An important ligature encountered in the texts is *ma* + *ru*,[23] thus *maru* or *malu*, which designates 'wool' as an ideogram in Linear B and is used in the same way in Linear A – but of course the Greek word for wool is λῆνος. Hesiod has μαλλός for 'fleece' (*Works and Days* 234), and in Hesychius we find a gloss μάλλυκες· τρίχες. If we assume exactly what we already saw in the personal names, namely the substitution of a Minoan u with Greek o so as to integrate the word into the productive o-stem noun class, then we have a very good match indeed. This provides further justification for reading  as *ni* in Linear A,  as *ma* and  as *ru*, and indeed we also have very rare direct evidence for some Minoan words here.

Likewise, the word for the sycamore fig has been identified in Linear A (Neumann 1960). On HT 88.2 the sequence which if we apply Linear B sound values reads as *ki-ki-na* follows the ideogram NI 'fig' and clearly qualifies them. Now, in Hesychius' lexicon there is a gloss κεικύνη· συκάμινος which means sycamore or sycamore fig, a less sweet variety of figs, and Theognostos (*Kanones* 101.7) states that this word is one of the first declension words in -α that are proparoxytona, i.e. accented on the third syllable from the end: τὰ διὰ τοῦ υνα προπαροξύτονα διὰ τοῦ υ ψιλοῦ γράφονται· οἷον χέλυνα, ἄμυνα, εὔθυνα, ἔρυνα, Δίκτυννα, σίγυννα, κίκυνα.

Thus we can add *ni* and *ru* to our grid and confirm some other entries (*ma*, *ki*, *na*) (Table 6.11).

10. The context of adaptation

These considerations lead to the final justification for reading Linear A with Linear B sound values. And for this we do not have to look into the language or even the writing system at all but should rather regard the context of Linear A and Linear B writing. Many of the document types used by Mycenaean scribes are not new inventions: although they differ in some significant ways, they are clearly adopted and adapted from the Minoan administration(s) on Crete. The most obvious continuity is found in the use of clay tablets, which are found inscribed in both Linear A and Linear B, as well as parallels in sealing practices. The most striking similarity here is found in the use of a syllabic

[23] Note that in Linear B this is not a functional ligature any more as it often looks like *ma* + *re* or *ma* + *ro*; see Nosch 2007, 11 and 15–21; Petrakis 2012, 529–31).

Table 6.11: Equations between the Cypriot Syllabic script and Linear B, place names shared between Linear A and Linear B, evidence from internal variations, and evidence from ideographic use of syllabograms

	a	*e*	*i*	*o*	*u*
V	a		a		
d	da		di		
j					
k			ki		
m	ma	me	mi		mu?
n	na			ni	
p	pa			po	
q					
r			ri	ro	ru
s	sa	se	si?		su
t	ta	te	ti	to	tu
w					
z					

script to spell out words alongside the use of ideograms, numerals and other signs to denote commodities and quantities: in both Linear A and Linear B, the whole system of writing, and with it a range of document types, was being used with broadly similar administrative and economic purposes (on the Linear A system see Schoep 2002).

Despite this very important similarity, there were also some major changes made in the size, shape, function and arrangement of documents in the development of the Linear B bureaucratic system. While page-shaped and palm leaf type documents are attested in both administrations, there are a number of differences in their physical form and layout (Tomas 2011), as well as in the arrangement of information and the tidiness with which it is recorded (Tomas 2012a). This, in turn, may well point to differences in administrative practice and the uses to which the tablets were put.

There is also continuity to be found in the use of some types of sealings and nodules, but here again major changes were made as the Linear B administration discontinued some types and made its own innovations (Tomas 2012b).[24] However, in seal use the stylistic continuity is so striking that, as Webb and Weingarten (2012, 97) put it recently, 'if we had only seals to go by, we should never have guessed that the

[24] There are in fact some striking similarities in sealing practices between Linear B and Cretan Hieroglyphic (Hallager 1997/8, and see also the papers by Tomas and Petrakis, this volume).

Mycenaeans took control of Crete in LM II/IIIA', pointing towards other kinds of influence and continuity.

It is not surprising that the Mycenaean administration was not identical to the administrations that preceded it on Crete, necessitating changes to document type, format, arrangement and, eventually, complexity. However, it is obvious from those forms that were continued, even with adaptations, that the early writers of Linear B documents must at least have observed the work of Linear A scribes, and perhaps been trained in their methods before going on to make their own adjustments and improvements. Indeed, it has sometimes been suggested that Linear A scribes were heavily involved in the beginnings of the new administration (e.g. Palaima 2011, 115) and that there may therefore have been real continuity in the personnel writing the documents as well as the techniques used. The adaptations and innovations made in the creation of Linear B were undoubtedly aimed at making the documents better suited to the Mycenaeans' own administrative techniques, and were probably implemented over time as new methods of documentation were tried and tested. Long-term rather than sudden adaptation is also suggested by the early adoption of some document types that are attested only in early Linear B administration and must later have been abandoned, such as the flat-based nodule.[25] The technology of writing and the administrative purposes for which it was used seem to have gone hand-in-hand, which further suggests that the Linear A script did not undergo a sudden and drastic overhaul to create Linear B, just as changes to document type probably did not take place overnight.

All of this means that writing was passed on in a very tightly controlled and finite context. For one thing, the deliberate restriction of Linear B to administrative usage suggests a decisive initial adaptation, followed by later development within a restricted situation. The tightly controlled context of Linear B writing also makes it very likely indeed that reinterpretations on the part of the scribes were kept to a minimum, and there simply was little room for random reallocations of sign values. The Linear A script was borrowed as a whole system.

And it is here where we think the greatest difference with the Carian situation that we saw earlier can be observed. The context in which the Carians adopted the script is unknown but there is absolutely no reason to think that it occurred in the context of a centralised bureaucracy or administration. Much more likely, it was a sort of spill-over which then at some point was worked on and, up to a point, standardised. Up to a point because, in fact, Carian characters typically have a certain variety of morphological shapes which in turn suggests that writing was passed on in a looser, less tightly controlled way and context, and the fact that 90% or so of the documents that we have are graffiti from Egypt would seem to support this.

[25] A small number of flat-based nodules have been found in the early deposit of the RCT at Knossos: see e.g. Driessen 1990, 64.

11. Conclusion

To sum up, therefore, despite the methodological problems mentioned at the beginning there are very strong arguments from a variety of different angles that all point in the same direction. Of course, uncertainties still remain. Given that the sound systems of no two languages are the same, a certain amount of adaptation must have taken place, but the point here is that these are likely to have worked on a principle of phonetic similarity, and to have been done in a relatively systematic fashion. It has often been said that it is likely Linear B had no use for certain Linear A signs, and the fact that some of the signs in Linear B (e.g. **18*, **47*, **49*) are extremely rare, confined (or nearly so) to Knossos and employed here only to write seemingly non-Greek names such as **49-sa-ro* is taken to support this. Here, however, caution is in order. For **18* has no clear Linear A antecedent, and some signs that were thought to be restricted to Knossos are now be attested elsewhere. This is true in particular for **47* for which a doubtful attestation at Mycenae had long been known[26] but which may now also be attested at Ayios Vasileios (HV Oq 18.2). Likewise, Bennet is clearly right in pointing out that Linear B does not appear to have created entire new series of signs,[27] a possible implication being that in theory Linear B could have redeployed Linear A signs to fashion a consonantal series non-existent in Minoan Linear A in a more 'pick and mix' way; i.e. in order to represent consonants not found in Minoan, Greek would have assembled otherwise superfluous 'debris' signs.[28] But it is at least equally possible that Greek at the time of transfer did not possess any phonemes that could not be aligned – for the purposes of script adaptation – with phonemes existing in the Minoan language.

The overall conclusion, then, is clear: there is, quite simply, very little room for a random reallocation of sound values, and positive identifications of sound values in Linear A are so numerous, systematic, and based on a whole number of approaches supporting one another that, on the basis of the evidence so far, in principle the backward projection of sound values from Linear B to Linear A must be regarded as legitimate.

[26] *me-ta-*4̣7̣-wa* at MY Go 610.1; *TITHEMY* read *me-ta-je-wa*.

[27] Bennet 2008, 15: 'The fact that no sign-series in Linear B is entirely new, combined with the probable difference in consonant values, suggest that *some* modification of phonetic values of borrowed signs took place [...]'.

[28] Cf. again Bennet 2008, 15: '[...] meaning that great caution should be exercised in using Linear B-derived values to "read" Linear A inscriptions'.

Chapter 7

Processes of script adaptation and creation in Linear B: The evidence of the 'extra' signs*

Anna P. Judson

The Linear B syllabary can be divided into two main groups of signs. Firstly, the 'core' (or 'basic') signs, each standing for either a vowel or a single consonant plus vowel: these are so-called because they are the only group of signs that is strictly necessary for writing in Linear B according to the usual spelling rules (Figure 7.1).

Secondly, the 'extra' (or 'additional') signs, which can in certain circumstances optionally replace core signs. These extra signs are usually classified according to their orthographic function: 'doublets' replace a single core sign to specify a more precise phonetic value (e.g. the sign a_2 can be used instead of *a* to specify /ha/); 'complex signs' replace a sequence of two core signs (e.g. /dwo/ can be spelt with two signs, *do-wo* or *du-wo*, or with the single complex sign *dwo*).[1] For the purposes of this paper, however, I prefer to divide the extra signs into groups according to their values, as shown in Figure 7.2.[2]

---

* This paper is based on part of my PhD thesis (supported by the UK Arts and Humanities Research Council, grant number AH/J500094/1; the British Federation of Women Graduates' J. Barbara Northend Scholarship, 2015–16; and the Cambridge Faculty of Classics' Graduate Studies Fund), which was submitted to the University of Cambridge in April 2016 (Judson 2016). I would like to thank Pippa Steele for organising the VRBS conference and inviting me to participate; I am also grateful for the support of my PhD supervisor, Torsten Meißner, and for comments from all the attendees of VRBS and of the *III Diálogos Micénicos* (Universidad Autónoma de Madrid, May 2015), at which another version of this paper was presented.

[1] *ra_2* and *ro_2* can, due to a sound change */ry, ly/ > /rr, ll/, replace either the digraphic sequences *ri-ja* and *ri-jo* */rya, lya/, */ryo, lyo/ or the single signs *ra* and *ro* /rra, lla/, /rro, llo/ (Lejeune 1997b, 208–12); they are therefore termed 'pseudo-complex' signs (Duhoux 2008, 247).

[2] I give the most commonly-accepted values for the extra signs, with the exception of *pu_2*: I am unconvinced by the frequent assumption that this represents /bu/ as well as /p^hu/, but discussion of this is beyond the scope of this paper (see, e.g., Melena 1987, 226–30, 2014, 71–3; Lejeune 1972a, 95–6; Thompson 2005, 111–14; Judson 2016). *ra_2* and *ro_2* are generally agreed to represent */rya, lya/ and */ryo, lyo/ and the Mycenaean geminate outcomes of these sequences /rra, lla/ and /rro, llo/, but have been argued to also represent simple /la, lo/ (e.g. Heubeck 1979, 245–54); in the absence of any

a	*e*	*i*	*o*	*u*
da	*de*	*di*	*do*	*du*
ja	*je*		*jo*	
ka	*ke*	*ki*	*ko*	*ku*
ma	*me*	*mi*	*mo*	*mu*
na	*ne*	*ni*	*no*	*nu*
pa	*pe*	*pi*	*po*	*pu*
qa	*qe*	*qi*	*qo*	
ra	*re*	*ri*	*ro*	*ru*
sa	*se*	*si*	*so*	*su*
ta	*te*	*ti*	*to*	*tu*
wa	*we*	*wi*	*wo*	
za	*ze*		*zo*	

Fig. 7.1: The Linear B core syllabary.

Aspirated vowel	a_2 /ha/				
Diphthong	a_3 /ai/	*au*	ra_3 /rai, lai/		
Aspirated stop	pu_2 /p^{h}u/, /bu/?				
Labialised	*dwe*	*dwo*	*nwa*	*twe*	*two*
Palatalised	ra_2 */rya, lya/ > /rra, lla/	ro_2 */ryo, lyo/ > /rro, llo/	ta_2 /tya/	*pte* < **pye*?	

Fig. 7.2: The Linear B extra signs.

The ‘extra’ status of these signs is what makes them of particular interest in discussing processes of script adaptation and creation: given that they are not strictly necessary when writing Linear B, why do they exist in the first place, and why were

unambiguous examples of this, it seems better to assume the smaller range of values. ta_2 has been argued to represent /ta/ (Heubeck 1979, 254–7) or /sta/ (Melena 2014, 78–80) rather than /tya/, based on the fact that original */ty/ had already undergone palatalisation in Mycenaean; however, this sign generally represents secondary /tya/ resulting from resyllabification of /tia/, to which this sound-change would not apply (cf. the similar resyllabification process seen in */ria/ > */rya/ > /rra/, etc.: Lejeune 1997b, 211–12). On *pte*, see pp. 124–6. Most of the undeciphered Linear B signs must also belong to the group of extra signs, since there are few ‘gaps’ in the core syllabary, but as these signs’ values are uncertain they will not be included in this discussion. This issue was addressed in my PhD thesis (Judson 2016).

they used by the Mycenaean scribes? This paper will, firstly, examine the ways in which the extra signs are often used as evidence for the process by which Linear A was adapted to produce Linear B, and thus, by extension, for reconstructing aspects of the Linear A script and the Minoan language;[3] it will then explore how this group of signs can more productively be used to investigate the motivations behind the creation and use of new signs within Linear B itself.

1. Adaptation from Linear A to Linear B

The structures of many of the extra signs, particularly those representing consonant clusters, appear to be anomalous in the context of the Linear B script, compared to the simpler structures (vowel or consonant plus vowel) of the core signs (Figure 7.1). Many of these signs' values appear equally unexpected in a Greek linguistic context: /nwa/, for instance, is not a sequence likely to appear very often in Greek, which does not permit /nw/ as an onset (Meißner 2013, 10) – indeed, apart from the adjective *pe-ru-si-nwa* /perusinwa/ 'last year's', all the terms in which this sign appears are probably of non-Greek origin.[4] It is frequently assumed that such 'odd-looking' features of Linear B must be inherited from Linear A, and, moreover, that such reconstructed Linear A features directly reflect aspects of the Minoan language, enabling a partial reconstruction of Minoan phonology. This assumption applies equally to other features of Linear B which appear ill-suited to representing Greek phonology, such as the lack of distinction between /r/ and /l/ or between voiced, voiceless, and aspirated stops (see, e.g., Lejeune 1958a, 327–8; Packard 1974, 115; Davis 2014, 193–204), but in the context of the extra signs is particularly relevant to the palatalised and labialised signs.[5] These have usually been seen as evidence for a phonemic opposition in Minoan between palatalised, labialised, and plain consonants – a hypothesis first put forward by Palmer (1955, 38, 1963, 38–40), which has often recurred since: for instance, Beekes (2010, xvi–xvii) proposes an essentially identical reconstruction of 'Pre-Greek' phonology (see also Beekes 2014, 4). Stephens and Justeson (1978) and Davis (2014, 193–5 and 236–9) add a further argument, based on the typological 'universal' that writing systems rarely introduce innovations to represent highly-marked sounds if less highly-marked sounds are not already represented: signs representing highly-marked labialised and

[3] For the purposes of this chapter, 'Minoan' refers to the language of the Linear A texts (which are most probably all written in the same language: Duhoux 1978, 103–5, 1989, 92; Davis 2014, 179–81). Other non-Greek languages (whether related to the 'Minoan' of the Linear A inscriptions or not) may well, of course, have existed on Crete during this period: Cretan Hieroglyphic, for instance, is often assumed (though not proven) to represent a different language from Linear A (see, e.g., Olivier 1997, 50; Duhoux 1998, 24–6).

[4] All phonetic interpretations and translations of Mycenaean terms are based on *DMic* and Bartoněk 2003 unless otherwise stated.

[5] Other extra signs have also been used in reconstructions of Minoan, most notably pu_2 – see, e.g., Melena 1987; Davis 2014, 214–20; Judson 2016. For reasons of space, however, this discussion will be restricted to the palatalised and labialised signs, whose impact on the proposed phonological structure of Minoan has been greater.

palatalised stops should not, therefore, have been invented within Linear B, since the script does not systematically represent the less highly-marked Greek phonemic features of aspiration and voice. However, the latter fact is usually accounted for by assuming that aspiration and voicing were non-phonemic in Minoan, so the universal would not be violated if these signs were inherited from Linear A. Thus, out of two (potentially much larger) series of Linear A signs representing Minoan labialised and palatalised consonants, those representing phonemes similar to /d^{w}/, /t^{w}/, /n^{w}/, /r^{y}/, /t^{y}/, and perhaps /p^{y}/ would underlie the Linear B complex signs.[6] In the process of adapting Linear A to write Greek (a language with almost no phonemic labialisation or palatalisation) these signs, originally representing a single consonant plus vowel, would have been reinterpreted as representing consonant clusters (/dw/, /tw/, etc.), giving rise to their apparently anomalous Linear B structures and values. The exception, of course, would be the labiovelars, which were still generally preserved in Mycenaean Greek;[7] the Linear B *q*-series, representing /k^{w}/, /k^{wh}/ and /g^{w}/, would thus be a straightforward continuation of a Linear A series representing labialised velars (*vel sim.*).

Difficulties with this hypothesis arise, however, when the actual palaeographic data is considered, since relatively few of these Linear B signs have known correspondences in Linear A or Cretan Hieroglyphic (Figure 7.3).[8]

Thus, only two palatialised signs, the majority of the *q*-series, and *nwa* are certainly inherited. Of course, the absence from Linear A and/or Cretan Hieroglyphic of an attested correspondence for a given sign could always be due to chance;[9] the fact that a relatively high proportion of Linear B signs in -*o* have no known antecedents in the other Cretan scripts makes the lack of correspondences for *qo* and *ro*$_2$ unproblematic for this hypothesis,[10] whether this situation is due to an actual lack of *o*-series signs in Linear A (in which case *qo* and *ro*$_2$ would be Linear B creations, based on the existing *q*-series and *ra*$_2$) or merely to chances of attestation.[11] The implications of *pte*'s lack

---

[6] The exact phonetic values of such Minoan phonemes may of course have differed from the corresponding Mycenaean Greek consonants; on the reconstruction of Linear A values from Linear B, see Steele and Meißner, this volume.

[7] In all environments except adjacent to /u/: e.g. *qo-u-ko-ro* /g^{w}oukolos/ 'cowherd' < */g^{w}ou-k^{w}ol-os/ (~ βουκόλος) retains the initial but not the medial labiovelar.

[8] Other possible, but not widely accepted, correspondences will be discussed where relevant below.

[9] Cf. the relatively recent discovery of the single known attestation of AB48 (SY Za 4: Muhly and Olivier 2008, 207–8 and 216) – although *nwa*'s Cretan Hieroglyphic equivalent, 006, was already well-attested.

[10] Note that Younger (2003, 10) suggests a possible correspondence for *ro*$_2$ with Cretan Hieroglyphic 040; however, this is much more likely to correspond to AB86 /**86* (*CHIC*, 19).

[11] The absence of known Linear A counterparts to many of the *o*-series has often led to the assumption that Linear A lacked an *o*-series, and that this indicates an absence of this vowel from the Minoan language; this has usually formed part of an argument for a three-vowel system in Minoan, since there are also some Linear B *e*-series signs without Linear A correspondences (e.g. Packard 1974, 112–14; Palaima and Sikkenga 1999, 603–4). However, other explanations have also been put foward, such as that Minoan had *more* than five vowels (Duhoux 1989, 72–3) or that *e*- and *o*-vowels were secondary developments from an original three-vowel system (Davis 2014, 240–1). Most recently, Meißner and Steele (forthcoming)

Linear B	Linear A	Cretan Hieroglyphic
ra$_2$	AB76	069
ro$_2$	–	–
ta$_2$	AB66	–
pte	–	–
dwe	–	–
dwo	–	–
twe	AB87?	–
two	–	–
nwa	AB48	006
qa	AB16	–
qe	AB78	074/075
qi	AB21	–
qo	–	–

Fig. 7.3: Correspondences of labialised and palatalised signs in the Cretan scripts (based on GORILA[5], *xxii and* CHIC, *19).*

of any known correspondence will be discussed below (pp. 124–6). However, for most of the labialised signs, there is some positive evidence to suggest a Linear B creation, beyond simply the lack of any known correspondences.

two

This is found only on PY An 261.2-.5 (Hand 43) in the personal name *o-two-we-o* (/Orthwōwēhos/, genitive of /Orthwōwēs/?). This name is spelt differently by other

argue persuasively that this situation is most likely to be due to chances of attestation, especially given the relative rarity of the *o*-series' attested Linear A correspondences.

Fig. 7.4: twe *(KN So(1) 4430.b: after* COMIK[2]*).*

Fig. 7.5: AB87 (HT 126.b2-3: after GORILA[1]*).*

Pylos hands (genitive *o-to-wo-<we->o*, Un 616 v.4 and An 261 v.7̣, Hand 1; nominative *o-tu-wo-we*, Jn 658.7, Hand 21, and Jn 725.5, Hand 2; dative *o-to-wo-we-i*, Vn 851.9, Hand 12)[12] suggesting that this sign may well have been idiosyncratic to Hand 43 – perhaps even invented in the process of compiling this tablet, in order to write this repeated name more efficiently.

twe

This is found only in the KN So-series in the neuter plural adjective *o-da-twe-ta* (/odat-wenta/ 'fitted with teeth', describing chariot wheels),[13] with five examples in Hand 130 (So(1) 4430.b, 4432, 4436.1, 4440.b, 4441) plus one or two unattributed examples: *o-]ḍạ-twe-ṭạ[*, So 8561; *]ṭwẹ-te*, dual /odat-wente/?, So 8251.a (Figure 7.4). AB87 is a possible correspondence (*GORILA*[5], xxii); however, this Linear A sign is not an exact formal match and moreover is currently attested only as an ideogram on a single tablet, HT 126.b2-3 (Figure 7.5).

While a correspondence between *twe* and AB87 cannot be entirely ruled out, it is thus far from certain, and as both signs have a relatively simple form, an independent development of *twe* is certainly possible. The latter's distribution leads me to regard it as more plausibly a Linear B invention, perhaps by Hand 130 themself, in a similar manner to *two*.[14]

dwo

This sign (found at Knossos, Pylos, and Thebes) has been argued to correspond to AB118 (Figure 7.6), the Linear A syllabogram and metrogram which gave rise to the Linear B metrogram L (Figure 7.7: Consani 1996; Davis 2014, 195, n.1128): *dwo* (Figure 7.8) would therefore represent the continuation of the syllabic use of AB118.

[12] The majority of these probably refer to the same individual (Nakassis 2013, 329–30).

[13] This term is spelt differently by various other scribes: *o-da-tu-we-ta* (KN So 894, -), *o-da-ku-we-ta* (So 4435.B, Hand 128?; L 8̣7̣0̣, Hand 114?), and *o-da-ke-we-ta* (So(2) 4446.1, Hand 131; Sg 1811.5̣.6, -). /odat-wenta/ is the original form, from zero-grade */odn̥t-/ 'tooth' (cf. *o*-grade ὀδούς, ὀδόντος); the alternative form /odak-wenta/ may have arisen through dissimilation (Lejeune 1997a:30-1) and/or reanalysis by comparison with the phonetically and semantically similar root */dak-/, cf. δάκνω 'bite' (T. Meißner, pers. comm.). Although strictly speaking it is therefore possible that *twe* in fact represents /kwe/, the balance of probability is in favour of /twe/: it seems most likely, though not entirely certain, that any scribe wanting to spell /kw/ with a single sign would have used the *q*-series (Melena 2014, 40–41).

[14] Melena (2014, 62, n. 73) mentions A305 as another possible Linear A correspondence, if reversed. Reversed sign-forms do occur in Linear A, and A305 is attested as a syllabogram as well as an ideogram; however, lacking any attestations in the same orientation as *twe*, the same arguments apply to this as to AB87.

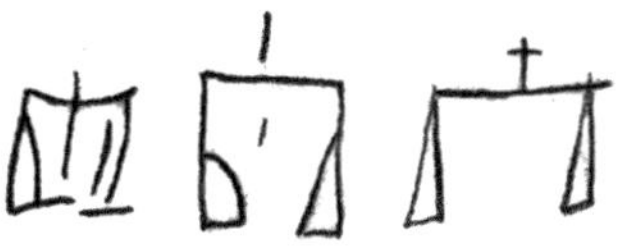

Fig. 7.6: AB118 (HT 13.5, KN 2.2, KN Za 19.2: after GORILA[5]*).*

Fig. 7.7: L *(KN Oa 730: after* COMIK[1]*; PY Ja 749: after a photograph in the Mycenaean Epigraphy Room collection, Faculty of Classics, Cambridge. Not to scale).*

Fig. 7.8: dwo *(KN Fh 360.b: after* COMIK[1]*; PY Ep 539.12: after a photograph in the Mycenaean Epigraphy Room collection, Faculty of Classics, Cambridge. Not to scale).*

This is, however, palaeographically implausible: L and *dwo* are quite clearly distinct signs in Linear B, and there are no other examples of a single inherited sign diverging to this extent in Linear B; moreover, the form of *dwo* is significantly different from that of AB118.

The more widely-accepted view that *dwo* was created within Linear B from mirror-image forms of the sign *wo* is far more probable. This is shown to have taken place in a Greek linguistic context from the fact that two examples of *wo* (which also has no known Linear A antecedent) have been combined to give the sign *dwo*, homophonous with /du̯o/ 'two' (Lejeune 1958b, 261–2, n. 23; see also Meißner and Steele forthcoming).

dwe

This sign (found at Knossos, Pylos and Thebes) is primarily attested in the term *te-mi-dwe* /termid-wents/ 'provided with endings',[15] and most plausibly a Linear B creation by analogy with *dwo*. The sign's 'arms' consist of mirror-image forms of the sign *we*,[16] and it is also possible that the body of the sign was formed in the same way but subsequently simplified (Meißner 2013, 10).

The likelihood is, therefore, that the majority of labialised and some palatalised signs were newly created within Linear B. This appears to be at odds with the typological argument cited above; however, while signs like AB48/*nwa* and AB66/ta_2 may have represented single labialised and palatalised phonemes similar to /n^w/ and /t^y/ in Linear A, in Linear B they and the other complex signs represent *sequences* of two phonemes. The primary motivation for their use is, therefore, not phonemic

[15] This term is the alternative to *o-da-twe-ta* in descriptions of chariot wheels. *te-mi-dwe* (KN So 894.1) is the nominative singular: it is also attested in the dual *te-mi-dwe-te* /termid-wente/ (KN So(1) 4437, So(2) 4433.a) and most commonly in the plural *te-mi-dwe-ta* /termid-wenta/ (PY Sa 791 and 793; KN So-series).]*ṭẹ-mi-we-te* (KN Sg 1811.3) may be another alternative spelling.

[16] This is the most common form of the sign, found in most examples from Knossos (Hands 103, 130, 131, and 135) and the single example from Thebes (TH Wu 99.β). Pylos Hand 26 and the scribe of KN So 894.1.3 use a form with straight horizontal 'arms', but this is plausibly a simplified form.

representation *per se*, but efficiency in writing certain combinations of phonemes – so a typological universal relating to the representation of single phonological features simply does not apply to this particular situation.[17]

It is still likely that Linear A had some signs representing palatalised and labialised consonants, but the evidence of ra_2 (and perhaps ro_2?), ta_2, *nwa*, and the *q*-series seems insufficient to support the reconstruction of a more systematic distinction of labialisation and palatalisation in Linear A and the Minoan language.[18] As Davis (2014, 239) admits, it is not even entirely certain whether these Linear A signs may have represented not single phonemes but sequences of two consonants, as they mostly do in Linear B. Moreover, three of these signs have attested Cretan Hieroglyphic equivalents – which, given that the linguistic relationship between Cretan Hieroglyphic and Linear A is still unclear,[19] makes the question of how far their values reflect aspects of Minoan phonology even more problematic.

In fact, this group of signs is much *less* useful for analysing the processes of adaptation which took place in the formation of Linear B from Linear A, and hence for reconstructing Minoan phonology, than has often been claimed. What it does do is raise an important methodological point, namely that it cannot simply be assumed that any structurally or linguistically unexpected feature of the Linear B script must go back to Linear A, let alone that any such reconstructed feature of Linear A must necessarily be a direct reflection of the Minoan language – and this applies to other assumed Minoan phonological features, such as the lack of distinction between voiced, voiceless, and aspirated stops, or between /r/ and /l/, just as much as to labialisation and palatalisation. This is not to claim that Minoan certainly did not or could not have possessed any or all of these features, only that in attempting to reconstruct Minoan phonology, as in any other discussion of the relationship between Linear A and Linear B, it is just as necessary to examine individual signs in detail as it

[17] The only exception to this is the *q*-series, representing /k^w/ etc. – most of which were indeed inherited from Linear A, as the universal predicts.

[18] Cf. Meißner (2013, 10). The Linear B *z*-series (*za*, *ze*, and *zo*: all inherited from Linear A) have sometimes been argued to represent palatalised velars /k^y, g^y/ (e.g. Petruševski 1979; Risch 1979), but it seems more likely that at the period of the Linear B tablets, at least, these represented affricates (*Docs*², 389; Morpurgo Davies 1985, 79–80 and 105–6; Melena 2014, 53). Possible labialised or palatalised values for undeciphered signs are also frequently cited in support of this reconstruction – e.g. **64* and **82* are often viewed as *swi* and *swa* (e.g. Chadwick 1968, 63–5) or *twi* and *twa* (Melena 1983, 263–6 and forthcoming, 35–6 and 45); for further examples see Melena (2014, 54). However, such decipherment proposals are still uncertain, and not universally accepted; they are, moreover, often founded on the assumption that Linear A and Minoan had whole series of labialised and palatalised consonants and so further such signs ought to exist in Linear B. Using such proposals as evidence for Minoan labialisation and palatalisation is, therefore, both insecure and circular. See Judson 2016.

[19] As remarked above (n.3), it is often assumed (though by no means certain) that the co-existence of Cretan Hieroglyphic and Linear A was because they represented different languages. In addition, it is more likely that both descend from a common ancestor than that Linear A is a direct descendant of Cretan Hieroglyphic (Olivier 1997, 50–1); what language(s) this hypothetical ancestral script would have been used to write is of course unknown.

is to analyse the overall structure of each script – since, as is shown by the labialised and palatalised signs, even signs with similar values may not have been created in the same way or for the same purpose(s). The second half of this paper, therefore, aims to demonstrate the potential wider implications of studying individual signs in this way. I will focus on the extra signs which appear to be new creations, rather than inherited from Linear A, in order to explore the motivations behind their use and the processes of sign creation which took place within the Linear B script.

2. Creation of new signs within Linear B

Nine of the extra signs – *a*$_2$, *a*$_3$, *ra*$_3$, *dwe*, *dwo*, *twe*, *two*, *ro*$_2$, and *pte* – have no certain or probable correspondences in the other Cretan scripts, and we have already seen that there is good evidence for thinking that at least some of these were Linear B creations. The question to be asked, therefore, is why those creations took place – what was the purpose (or purposes) for which these signs were invented?

Examining the corpora of attestations of these nine signs, there are some which immediately appear to have a grammatical or morphological motivation for their use. *a*$_2$ 𐁀 (/ha/), for instance, is used in ca. 25% of its occurrences to denote the nominative/accusative plural ending of neuter *s*-stem nouns and adjectives (e.g. *pa-we-a*$_2$ /p^{h}arweha/ 'cloths', *me-zo-a*$_2$ /meizoha/ 'larger'). In principle such neuter plural endings could equally be spelt with the core sign *-a*, since the marking of aspiration is optional according to the general Linear B spelling rules; in fact, the spelling with *-a*$_2$ is arguably over-marked in phonetic terms, since the lack of a glide being indicated between two non-diphthong-forming vowels would by default represent a hiatus, and could thus function as a means of expressing intervocalic /h/.[20] However, spellings of *s*-stem neuter plurals in *-a* are found almost exclusively at Knossos: there are no more than three examples on the mainland,[21] compared to ca. 40 in *-a*$_2$,[22] demonstrating an overwhelming preference for the more highly-marked spelling in *-a*$_2$ (which is thus very far from being the 'sporadic procedure' described by Melena [2014, 77]). The different situation at Knossos – where spellings in *-a* are by far the more common[23] – is

[20] Cf. the regular use of spellings without a glide following *-i* and *-u* to indicate /h/ (Meißner 2008, 515).

[21] *tu-we-a* /t^{h}uweha/ 'aromatic substances' (PY Un 267.3); *we-]ẹ-ke-a*, probably = *we-je-ke-a*$_2$, an obscure neuter plural adjective (PY Wa 1148.2); *]ko-wo-a*, probably a perfect participle ending (IK X 1: Shelmerdine 2012, 75–6).

[22] *a-ke-a*$_2$ /aggeha/ 'jars' (PY Vn 130.2b); *ke-re-a*$_2$ /skeleha/ 'legs' (PY Ta 641.1a); *no-pe-re-a*$_2$ /nōp^{h}eleha/ 'unusable', *te-tu-ko-wo-a*$_2$ /tetuk^{h}woha/ 'finished', *we-je-ke-a*$_2$, obscure, see n.21 (PY Sa-series); *me-u-jo-a*$_2$ /meiw(i)yoha/ 'less', *me-zo-a*$_2$ /meizoha/ 'larger' (PY Sh-series); *qe-te-a*$_2$ /k^{w}eiteha/ 'to be paid' (PY Un 138.1; TH Wu 51.γ, 65.γ, 96.γ); *pa-we-a*$_2$ /p^{h}arweha/ 'cloths' (MY L 710.2, Oe 127); *tu-we-a*$_2$ = *tu-we-a* (HV X 4.2: Aravantinos and Vasilogamvrou 2012, 53). Perhaps also *ru-de-a*$_2$, obscure, feminine nominative singular or neuter plural (PY Un 853.11) and *]-we-e-a*$_2$ = *we-we-e-a*? see n.23 (PY Ub 1318.3).

[23] Up to c.50 examples: *a-ra-ru-wo-a* /ararwoha/ 'fitted (with), assembled' (Ra(1)-series); *a-te-re-te-a*, obscure (So 894.1); *e-ke-a* /egk^{h}eha/ 'spears' (R 1815); *o-re-ne-a* /ōleneha/ 'with short sleeves'? (L(2) 593.Ab); *pa-we-a* = *pa-we-a*$_2$ (Lc-, Ld(1)-, and L-series); *qe-te-a* = *qe-te-a*$_2$ (Fp(2) 363.1); *te-tu-ko-wo-a* = *te-tu-ko-wo-a*$_2$ (L 871.b); *we-we-e-a* /werwereha/ 'made of wool' (L 178, 870).

likely to be due to linguistic factors, namely the loss of /h/, which seems to have been further advanced at Knossos than at the mainland sites (Meißner 2008, 513). With the exception of texts from the Room of the Chariot Tablets (which may be significantly older than the other Knossos tablets: Driessen 1990 and 2000), the only two terms in which *a*$_2$ certainly appears at this site are *e-ma-a*$_2$ /Hermāhas/ 'Hermes'[24] – which, as a theonym, is perhaps particularly likely to retain a conservative pronunciation and/or spelling – and the neuter plural *pa-we-a*$_2$, used by Hand 114.[25] The fact that this one scribe, at least, uses this conservative spelling for an *s*-stem neuter plural suggests that even in a context where /h/ may have been largely or entirely lost, non-linguistic factors may have similarly encouraged this retention of the more highly-marked spelling, parallel to the clear preference seen on the mainland.

A similar situation can be observed regarding *ra*$_3$ (/rai, lai/), which is attested as a syllabogram only at Pylos (it appears at Knossos as the ideogram CROC 'saffron').[26] This sign appears in *a*-stem nominative plural nouns and adjectives in ca. 50% of its occurrences.[27] The dative singular ending of *a*-stem terms like these would be /-r-āi/ (or /-l-āi/) – homophonous with the nominative plural ending except for the vowel length, which is never distinguished in Linear B. Thus, *ra*$_3$ might also be expected to appear in such dative singular forms; that there are no attested examples of this could be ascribed to chance, but there are at least four probable examples of dative singulars in /-r-āi/ or /-l-āi/ written as *-ra* by scribes who have used *ra*$_3$ in nominative plurals.[28] This may suggest a deliberate choice regarding the use of the more highly-marked spelling with the extra sign, restricting it to just one of the two case-endings it could theoretically represent.[29]

[24] *ẹ-ma-a*$_2$[(X 9669.b); *e-ma-a*$_2$*-o* /Hermāhāho/, genitive (D 411).

[25] KN Ld(2) 787.B; on 786.B and 788.B only]*a*$_2$ is preserved, but the restoration *pa-we-*]*a*$_2$ seems secure from context.

[26] *CHIC*, 19 equates this sign with Cretan Hieroglyphic 023/159bis, which acts as a syllabogram as well as a logogram. However, it is unclear which plant 023 represents; I follow Younger (Cretan Hieroglyphic website, section 'Notes on the Signs') in regarding AB122 = OLIV as a more likely formal correspondence.

[27] *di-pte-ra*$_3$ /dip^{h}t^{h}erai/ 'hides' (PY Ub 1315.1); *ku-te-ra*$_3$ /Kut^{h}errai/ 'women from Kythera'? (Ab 506, 5̣6̣2̣); *o-ka-ra*$_3$, obscure masculine appellative (An 519.4, 654.18, 657.4, Cn 3.3); *pi-je-ra*$_3$ /p^{h}i(y)elai/ 'pots' (Ta 709.1); *ze-pu*$_2$*-ra*$_3$ /Zep^{h}urrai/ 'women from Zephyria = Halicarnassos'? (Aa 61).

[28] *ke-sa-da-ra*, probably /Kessandrāi/, is the recipient of rations on PY Fg 828, Hand 1 (cf. *ku-te-ra*$_3$ Aa 506, *o-ka-ra*$_3$ An 519.14, 654.18, 657.4) and Fg 368, Hand 21 (cf. *ḳụ-te-ra*$_3$, Ab 562); she probably also appears on An 435.2, Hand 1 (the text reads *ḳẹ*[-]*ṣạ-da-ra*) as the supervisor to whom *a-ko-so-ta* /Alksoitās/ is assigning a workforce (Nakassis 2012, 279–281). *au-to-*34-ta-ra* is a recipient on Fn 187.10, Hand 2 (cf. *pi-je-ra*$_3$, Ta 709.1). Since the *a*-stem dative and nominative singular are graphically identical, it cannot be ruled out that the first two examples are nominatives of rubric; however, on Fn 187, all the recipients whose case is identifiable are in the dative, so this is the most plausible case for *au-to-*34-ta-ra*, while the syntax of the heading of An 435 (which begins]*ọ-da-sa-to* , *a-ko-so-ṭạ*[, /hō da(s)sato Alksoitās/ 'thus Alksoitās distributed', requires a dative case for the recipient of the distribution.

[29] Cf. the suggestion of Jiménez Delgado (2008, 85), that the lack of alternations in the spelling of the *o*-stem genitive singular ending *-o-jo* could be due to the scribes' deliberate systematisation of the representation of such endings.

Of course, these grammatical uses are far from being the sole possible reason for using or creating these signs: a_2 is found in a wide variety of Greek and non-Greek personal names, place names, and other terms in addition to neuter plural endings, and the creation of a sign for /ha/ may have also been partly due to the high frequency of /a/ in Greek (and in particular of both /a-/ and /ha-/ word-initially).[30] ra_3 likewise appears in other contexts, including some personal names and appellatives, but most notably the noun *e-ra₃-wo* /elaiwōn/ 'olive oil' (six times in the PY Fr-series) and *pe-ra₃-ko-ra-i-ja* /Per(ā)-aigalaia/,[31] the 'Further Province' – thus, ra_3 can also be seen to have a lexical function in enabling the more efficient representation of two important terms at Pylos. However, the prominence of plural forms, even at the expense of other case-forms, is noticeable in both instances, and this has a further parallel in the spelling conventions governing the representation of *-i* diphthongs. Although in word-medial position *-a-i-* may represent either /-ai-/ or /-ahi-/ (that is, either a diphthong or a hiatus between vowels),[32] final *-a-i* is restricted to sequences of the latter type, with final /-ai/ being represented by *-a* only; the same applies to final *-e*/*-e-i* (/-ei, -ehi/) and *-o*/*-o-i* (/-oi, -o(i)hi/). The practical outcome of this concerning, for instance, the *a*-stem declension is that the dative singular /-āi/ and nominative plural /-ai/ are each spelt only as *-a* (as, for that matter, are the nominative, accusative, and feminine genitive singular and accusative plural), while the dative plural /-a(i)hi/, spelt *-a-i*, is one of the few graphically distinct case-forms in the whole declension. As in the case of ra_3, there is no linguistic or orthographic reason why both /-ai/ and /-a(i)hi/ should not be spelt *-a-i*; rather, it seems a deliberate convention to enable the distinction of at least one of these cases, namely the dative plural.

What emerges from these three examples, then, is a balancing act between two opposing concerns: one for accuracy and clarity in the distinction of certain linguistic forms, the other to avoid the complications that would arise from any major structural changes to the script. It should also be noted that the choice to distinguish particular forms appears not to be aimed at accurate linguistic representation *per se*, whether phonemic or morphological, but rather to maximise the distinctiveness of categories considered particularly important by the scribes. As we have already seen, there is in principle no reason why ra_3 should not be used for dative singulars, nor is the use

[30] Melena (2014, 74) argues that the high frequency of a_2's appearances word-initially or at compound boundaries indicates that it may originally have had a 'demarcative' function restricted to these positions, and subsequently acquired the value of /ha/ due to the higher frequency of /a/ compared to the other Greek vowels. However, this sign actually appears in these positions much *less* frequently than the signs for diphthongs (ca. 25% of occurrences, compared to 100% of certain occurrences of both a_3 and *au*). The suggestion of Pierini (2014, 131–5) that this sign originally denoted */s/ plus a short vowel and, after the merger of intervocalic */s/ and */y/ > /h/, came to represent the outcome of the latter as well, does not explain what the origin of such a sign would have been, nor why it should have undergone the change of */s/ > /h/ while the *s*-series did not.

[31] PY Ng 332.1 and Wa 114.2; this is also spelt *pe-ra-ko-ra-i-ja* (Pa 398.a), and the corresponding ethnic adjective as *pe-ra-a-ko-ra-i-jo* (On 300.8).

[32] E.g. *pa-i-to* /P^{h}aistos/; *o-pi-ra-i-ja* (also a place-name) probably /Opilāhiā/, from */lāh-/ 'stone' ~ λᾶας.

of a_2 to mark neuter plurals strictly necessary according to the conventions of the script; and the usage of the spellings *-a* and *-a-i* are not compatible with a principal goal of either linguistic accuracy or orthographic consistency. The apparent focus of a_2 and ra_3 on plural forms can, perhaps, be ascribed to the practical needs of the Linear B administrative documents. As is amply demonstrated by the frequency of nominatives of rubric in the Linear B texts, distinguishing the case of a particular entry is not always of the greatest importance – whether a certain person is the donor or recipient of the listed items, for instance, could generally be worked out from context, whether specified in the text or simply known by the scribe – whereas ambiguity in the number of people or items recorded is potentially both less easy to resolve from context and more likely to lead to problematic accounting errors. In the case of spellings in *-a-i*, the fact that the dative plural is the single case-form distinguished is not necessarily significant, since once the choice has been made to restrict the use of this spelling, this is the only way to ensure the distinctiveness of at least one case-form. However, the point is that here, as in the use of a_2 and ra_3, we can see what appears to be a deliberate adaptation of the writing system – here understood in a broad sense as including spelling rules and conventions as well as the syllabary itself – for the purpose of making clear distinctions in areas of particular importance within the context of the Linear B documents. There would have been no special need to ensure that the spelling *-a-i* was restricted to dative plurals had these not been a frequently-occurring category in the records.

Grammatical or morphological usefulness is, naturally, neither confined solely to motivating the creation of new Linear B signs, nor the only possible motivating factor for such creations. ra_2, for instance, has clear correspondences in AB76 and 069, but its usefulness in representing the relatively common Mycenaean Greek *a*-stem nominal and adjectival ending /-r-ia/ may well have been an important factor in its being retained and used in Linear B;[33] cf. the parallel sign ro_2, whose ability to represent the *o*-stem equivalent /-r-ios/ may well have contributed to its use, whether this sign was a Linear B creation or a continuation of a (currently unattested) Linear A sign (see p. 114).[34] a_3, on the other hand, is probably a Linear B creation,[35] but since

[33] ca. 25–30% of ra_2's attestations are in appellatives referring to female work-groups, such as *me-re-ti-ra*$_2$ */meletriai/ > /meletirrai/ 'flour-grinders' (on the phonetic interpretation of such terms, see Lejeune 1997b, 211–12); these are found throughout the PY Aa-, Ab-, and Ad-series and on TH Of 36.1.2.

[34] ca. 30% of ro_2's attestations are in nouns such as *tu-ro*$_2$ */turyos/ > /turros/ 'cheese' (and the monogram *TU+RO*$_2$: PY Un-series), *qe-ro*$_2$ /skʷellos/ 'armband'? (KN K(1) 740.3.ẹ, Sk-series), and *ku-pa-ro*$_2$ */kuparyos/ > /kuparros/ 'cyperus' (PY Un-series), as well as the adjective *po-pu-ro*$_2$ */porpʰuryō/ > /porpʰurrō/ 'purple' (feminine nominative dual: KN L 758.a); it is also frequent in masculine personal names in */-r-ios/ or */-r-iōn/, e.g. *u-ro*$_2$ /Hullos/ < */Hulyos/? (KN Db 5367).

[35] Palaima (2003) identifies a sign on a cauldron from Mycenae (Karo 1930-1933 no.576, pl. CLIX lower right; classed as 'MY Zf 2' in Younger [Linear A website, section 'Other Texts']) as a Linear A antecedent to a_3, (A)B43. While morphologically this sign does appear closer to a_3 than any other Linear A or B sign, other identifications are still possible – for example, Linear B *i* or *no*, cf. AB28 and Cretan Hieroglyphic 008 (Grumach 1962; Packard 1974, 110) – and the identification of this sign with A306

it is used only in word-initial position clearly cannot have a morphological function. Instead, its primary usefulness is in enabling the unambiguous representation of initial /ai-/, which may be lexically important, enabling distinction of otherwise homographic names or words; the pre-existence of *au*, inherited from Linear A, may well have also been a strong motivating or enabling factor in creating a parallel sign for /ai/.

Even a single sign can show a mixture of possible different motivations, any or all of which may have contributed to its original creation and subsequent continued use – a point which is well-illustrated by the group of labialised signs. *twe* and *dwe* both appear solely or primarily in adjectives containing the highly productive Mycenaean suffix /-went-/: *twe* in *o-da-twe-ta* and *dwe* in *te-mi-dwe*.[36] *dwo* similarly appears in two terms which probably contain the equally productive suffix /-wos-/ (> /-woh-/ before a vowel): *e-re-dwo-e*, plausibly a masculine nominative plural perfect participle in /-woh-es/, though the verb represented by *e-re-d-* is uncertain;[37] and *wi-dwo-i-jo*, a personal name, probably /Widwohios/ < */Wid-wos-ios/, based on the perfect participle of the root */wid-/ 'see' (PY Ep 539.12; TH Uq 434.13).[38] This morphological importance – representing heteromorphemic sequences in which a root ending in a dental is followed by one of these highly productive suffixes – seems, however, unlikely to have been the primary motivation behind the creation of these signs (as is argued by Palaima and Sikkenga [1999, 605]), though it may have contributed to their continued use in some cases.[39] *o-da-twe-ta* and *te-mi-dwe* are both repeated frequently by particular scribes throughout the same series of tablets recording chariot wheels (KN So-series, Hands 130 and 131; PY Sa-series, Hand 26): as suggested above in the case of *two* (pp. 115–16), a desire to represent these key repeated terms more efficiently may well have been the original motivation (and the prior invention of one could then have influenced the subsequent creation of the other). *dwo*, on the other hand, appears three times on its own representing the numeral 'two' /du̯o/ (PY Eb 338.B, Eo 278, Ub 1315.3b) – the only instance in Linear B of a single sign being used to write a word, which the Mycenaean scribes seem generally to have avoided (Melena 2014, 125) – as well as in the related name *dwo-jo* /Dwoios/ (literally 'double': KN V(3) 492.1, X 8126) and a second (unrelated) name *ma-si-dwo* (KN Fh 360.b). Given that the sign *dwo* itself was apparently created on the basis of the word /du̯o/, the possibility of using this to represent the

and the suggestion that this may have the value A_2 or AI (Packard 1974, 108–9; Younger [Linear A website, section 'Introduction: Language']) are both highly doubtful. More importantly, the sign's context – an isolated sign on a vessel – makes its function as an inscription and its relationship to any existing writing systems questionable. I therefore do not regard a_3 as currently having a secure Linear A correspondence.

[36] See pp. 116–18.

[37] A possible interpretation would be /ēreidwohes/, meaning 'set to work' (Melena 2014, 60), cf. ἐρείδω (*LSJ q.v.* II.2); this is plausible from context, since *e-re-dwo-e* appears in the headings of two personnel tablets (KN As(1) 604.1, V(3) 655.1).

[38] This is also spelt *wi-do-wo-i-jo* (PY Ae 344, An 5.2) and *wi-du-wo-i-jo* (PY Jn 415.3).

[39] Although *twe* is found only in the KN So-series, *dwe* and *dwo* are more widely attested. *dwe* also appears in a possible personal name]*ṃị-dwe* (KN As 5605.2); a personal name or adjective]*mi-dwe* (KN Ga(1) 680 lat.inf.); and the obscure term *a-dwe-ẹ* (TH Wu 99.β). On *dwo*, see below.

numeral may well have been a strong motivation for this creation; its morphological usefulness in representing the /-wos-/ suffix was perhaps a contributing factor to its wider use, but still secondary to a concern for efficient lexical representation similar to that seen in the cases of *dwe* and *twe*.

Finally, the sign *pte* remains to be examined. This sign (which has no known Linear A or Cretan Hieroglyphic equivalent),[40] is unusual even amongst the extra signs in representing a sequence of two stops, rather than a stop plus a glide. It is generally assumed (following Lejeune 1997b, 204–5), that its original value would have been **pye*, making it in origin one of the palatalised signs; this value would have become *pte* by the regular Greek sound change of */py/ > /pt/ (the results of which are seen in Classical Greek in, e.g., verbs such as κλέπτω 'steal' < */klep-yō/: Lejeune 1972b, 79). Although this hypothesis makes *pte* fit in with the apparent structure of the Linear B script according to the evidence of the other extra signs, it does not take account of the actual contexts in which the sign is attested. A remarkably high proportion of these consists of Greek vocabulary items, which account for at least 54% of lexemes in which *pte* appears and over 90% of its total attestations; moreover, this includes some terms which incorporate the highly productive agent suffix /-tēr/.[41] Considering that the majority of the Linear B corpus as a whole consists of personal names and place names,[42] not to mention terms of non-Greek or obscure origin, *pte*'s extremely low proportion of attestations in such terms is highly noticeable.[43] (For comparison, of the certain attestations of a_2, whose use is strongly motivated by Greek phonological and morphological factors, only ca. 50% are in Greek vocabulary words, and even this is a relatively high proportion in the context of the Linear B corpus.) Moreover, in *none* of these Greek terms does the /-pt-/ sequence originate from */py/. This is not in

[40] Two Cretan Hieroglyphic signs, 034 and 036, bear some resemblance to *pte*, but neither is close enough to make identification more than a slight possibility; neither is given as a correspondence to this sign by either *CHIC* or Younger (Cretan Hieroglyphic website, section 'Notes on the Signs'). Younger tentatively suggests 022 as a possible correspondence; since this sign is a hapax identified as an ideogram and requires turning through 180° to resemble *pte* even slightly, I do not find this a convincing suggestion.

[41] Terms including /-tēr/: *ra-pte*(*-re*) /raptēr(es)/ 'leather worker(s)/saddler(s)' (PY An- and Ea-series; KN Fh 1056, V(2) 159.5), *ra-pte-ri-ja* /raptēriai/, feminine plural adjective formed from *ra-pte* (PY Ub 1315.2). Other terms: *di-pte-ra*$_{(3)}$ /dip^{h}t^{h}era(i)/ 'hide(s)' (PY Ub-series; TI Uh 12.2̣), *DI-PTE* 'hide(s)' monogram (KN U 8210.2, X 9̣7̣4̣0̣), *di-pte-ra-po-ro* /dip^{h}t^{h}erap^{h}oros/ or /dip^{h}t^{h}erapōlos/ 'carrier/seller of hides' (PY Fn 50.6, Un 219.6); *pte-no* /*pternō*/ 'footrest?' of a chariot (KN Sd-series); *pte-re-wa* /ptelewās/ 'elm', genitive (KN Se- and So-series); *tu-ru-pte-ri-ja* /struptēriās/ 'alum', genitive (PY An 35.5, Un 443.1; TI X 6.ḅ).

[42] According to the figures given by Bartoněk (2003, 400), 73% of lexemes in the Linear B corpus are onomastic in nature (including names of people, places, gods, animals, and months, as well as patronymic and ethnic adjectives); thus, only 27% are vocabulary terms.

[43] *pte* appears in no more than six proper nouns or uninterpretable words (accounting for up to 46% of lexemes containing this sign, and ca. 7–9% of its total attestations). These include two personal names – *ka-pte*, possibly /Skaptēr/, cf. σκαπτήρ 'digger' (KN Df 1230.B) and *p̣ṭẹ-jo-ḳọ* (PY An 39 v.8) – and four incomplete terms:]*-pte-si*, probably a dative plural noun, perhaps *ra*]*-pte-si* (KN Fh 5432);]*pte-we*, nominative plural noun or dative singular noun/personal name (PY La 623); *pte*[, unknown (KN X 7995), and]*p̣ụ-p̣ṭẹ*[, unknown (PRI Z 1: see Sacconi and Cultraro forthcoming).

itself problematic, since on the completion of the */py/ > /pt/ sound-change a sign **pye* > *pte* could come to be used for any instance of /pte/ regardless of its origin (as remarked by Lejeune [1997b, 205]); however, unless we assume that the absence of any known correspondences to *pte* in the other Cretan scripts is due to chance (which, of course, remains a possibility), the question arises of what the reason(s) might have been for the invention of this sign within Linear B. In fact, why a sign **pye* should have been invented is highly unclear. **pya* and **pyo*, if they existed,[44] could in principle have been used in similar contexts to *ra*$_2$ and *ro*$_2$ (p. 122), but this would not apply to **pye*. Palaima and Sikkenga (1999, 605) argue that this could have been useful in representing linguistic categories such as verbal forms – as seen above, verbs are the main category in Classical Greek where /pt/ < */py/ appears, so that the second or third person of such verbs would be the main context in which the sequence */-pye-/ might potentially occur (e.g. κλέπτεις, -ει 'you steal, he/she steals' < */klep-ye-/). In the context of the Linear B records, however, in which verbal forms of *any* sort are extremely rare, it is difficult to see this as providing a strong motivation for the creation of a new sign within the writing system: why should a scribe (or scribes) invent a sign whose primary use would be in writing a category of words which, although frequent in spoken language, would hardly ever actually be used in the written records?[45] On the other hand, the potential motivation for inventing a sign *pte* seems clear: it is useful in enabling the more efficient writing of various important terms, several of which are frequently repeated by certain scribes throughout particular series of tablets (*pte-no*, three–four times in Knossos Hand 128's Sd-series;[46] *pte-re-wa*, up to 16 times in the Knossos Se- and So-series of Hands 127, 128?, 130, and 131;[47] *ra-pte(-re)*, 18 times in Pylos personnel and landholding tablets;[48] *di-pte-ra*$_{(3)}$, probably nine times on two Pylos Ub-series tablets).[49] The status of *pte* thus seems closely comparable to that of *dwe* and *twe*, which (as discussed above: p. 123), are found repeatedly in the terms *te-mi-dwe* and *o-da-twe-ta*; the parallel is made even closer by the fact that, just as *te-mi-dwe* and *o-da-twe-ta* incorporate an important morphological formation (the adjectival suffix /-went-/), so too does *ra-pte(-re)* (the

[44] Melena (2014, 70) suggests that a sign *pta* (< **pya*) may have been inherited from Linear A and acted as a catalyst for the invention of *pte*; this cannot be ruled out, but note that there is no known case of a Linear B complex sign in *-e* being invented on the basis of a Linear A sign in *-a*.

[45] F. Aurora has pointed out to me that if Linear B was also used to write texts on perishable materials, these could have included a wider range of linguistic categories than the tablets. However, as Bennet (2001, 27–30) has shown, longer-term records on other media appear to be neither required by the Mycenaean administrative system nor suggested by the evidence of the clay tablets themselves.

[46] KN Sd [[4̣4̣0̣1̣]], 4402.a, 4405.a, 4450.b.

[47] KN Se 879.b, [8̣9̣0̣], 891.B, 892, 893, 5̣7̣2̣9̣, [7920] (Hand 127), [9̣3̣0̣7] (-); So(1) 4429.b, 4437, 4440.b, 4448, 4449 (Hand 130); So(2) 4445 (Hand 131), 4431 (Hand 131?). So 4435.A (Hand 128?) reads *pte-re-ẹ*[, perhaps a mistake for *pte-re-wa* (*DMic*).

[48] An 172.1 (Hand 1); An 298.1.2, 424.1.2.2 (Hand 3); An 207.14-.18, Ea 28, 29, [56.a], 325, 460.a, 754.a, 813 (Hand 43).

[49] Ub 1315.1 (Hand 31), 1318.1.1̣.1̣.2.3̣.3̣.4.7 (Hand 32).

agent suffix /-tēr/). I suggest, therefore, that it may not be necessary to reconstruct a process by which an original *pye became *pte*, but that the sign may in fact have been created as *pte*.[50] Clearly, it remains a possibility that a Linear A antecedent of *pte* did exist, and that future discoveries could necessitate a revision of this argument; but in any case, what I aim to stress is not so much the details relating to *pte* or to any other individual sign, but, as in the first part of this paper, the methodological points they raise – namely the importance of considering the circumstances of use of individual signs, rather than simply drawing conclusions on the basis of what we perceive to be the structure or 'system' of Linear B (or Linear A, or any other script) as a whole.

3. Conclusions

Just as discussions of the creation of Linear B tend to focus (quite naturally) on the single point of its adaptation from Linear A, discussions of the extra signs tend to focus on their potential to act as evidence for the structure and values of the Linear A script and the phonology of the Minoan language. The first part of this paper demonstrated that their use in this way is much less well-founded than is normally assumed, and that the palaeographic evidence is insufficient to support the systematic reconstruction of Minoan phonology for which it has often been used. However, as the second part of this paper has shown, a detailed analysis of the extra signs can give a very different view of the processes by which Linear B was created. Rather than focusing on the single point of its adaptation from Linear A, the process of creation can be seen as an ongoing one, involving a period of significant further development after this initial point;[51] rather than viewing apparently anomalous features of Linear B as symptomatic of a 'failure' to adapt Linear A to a Greek context, the process can be seen as a less passive and more creative one on the part of the adaptors and subsequent users of Linear B. A complex set of possible motivations has been identified for their creation and use of new signs, whether relating to phonemic and/or morphological representation, efficiency in writing, or a combination of these factors; but, crucially, these are generally rooted in the practical needs of the Mycenaean scribes in writing administrative documents. It is these kinds of potential motivations within the context of a writing system's use, and the possible interplay between them, which need to be taken into account in any analysis of processes of script development and the relationships between scripts.

[50] I am aware of two previous arguments for *pte* being the original value of this sign. Ruijgh (1967, 53, n. 35) suggests that *pte* originally denoted a Minoan phoneme /p^t/, traces of which survive in doublets such as πτόλεμος/πόλεμος and πτόλις/πόλις; however, even aside from *pte*'s apparent absence from Linear A and its infrequent use in words of non-Greek origin, the fact that both πτόλεμος/πόλεμος and πτόλις/πόλις have probable Indo-European etymologies (*CDE s.v.* πτ-) means there is no evidence to support this. The argument of Neumann (1996, 96–8) is based on an acrophonic derivation from πτέρυξ 'bird' or πτερόν 'wing', with the sign representing a bird's wings; I regard this as neither a plausible explanation for the shape of *pte* nor a secure basis on which to reconstruct its original value.

[51] Cf. Palaima (1988a, 341), who argues for a gradual development process post-adaptation of various aspects of the writing system such as the creation of additional ideograms, text formatting, etc.

Chapter 8

Script comparison in the investigation of Cypro-Minoan*

Miguel Valério

1. Investigating Cypro-Minoan

Cypro-Minoan refers to a group of undeciphered syllabic inscriptions dated roughly to the 16th or 15th through the 11th or 10th centuries BC and found mostly in Cyprus, with small numbers of documents from coastal Syria and Tiryns (Peloponnese). Despite their common chronological and geographical background, these inscriptions show 'limited overall epigraphic coherence' (Steele 2013a, 241) and this circumstance hinders our understanding of the writing system(s) they employ. It has been underlined that a decipherment of Cypro-Minoan is impossible *tout court* (see e.g. Steele 2013a, 13) owing to two factors. On one hand, the corpus is relatively small, at present comprising around 250 inscriptions (Steele 2014a, 129, n. 1; Valério 2014b) containing less than 4,000 attested signs; on the other hand, the script is essentially phonographic and lacks a set of logograms for commodities comparable to that of Linear A and B that might provide us with semantic clues on the contents of the texts. The latter is indeed a disadvantage, but regarding the former one must note how difficult it is to come up with a universal amount of epigraphical material after which the decipherment of any given script becomes possible. As Chadwick (1970, 26) once put it, '[h]ow much is needed depends upon the nature of the problem to be solved, the character of

* The research contained in this chapter was conducted thanks to a Doctoral Degree Grant (no. SFRH/BD / 77529 / 2011) from the Fundação para a Ciência e Tecnologia of Portugal, granted in support of my dissertation project 'Investigating the Signs and Sounds of Cypro-Minoan' at the University of Barcelona (Valério 2016). I would like to thank Philippa Steele for having invited me to the conference from which this volume arises, as well as Silvia Ferrara for her comments and suggestions.

the material, and so forth.' In this regard, Cypro-Minoan does present a number of advantages:

- It has obvious affinities with two deciphered syllabaries (Linear B and Cypro-Greek[1]) and another that is readable to some extent, albeit remaining undeciphered (Linear A). This allows for comparisons between their signs, with the aim of suggesting hypothetical phonetic values.
- It includes four tablets/tablet fragments from Enkomi (ENKO Atab 002, 002bis, 003 and 004 = ##207–209) which have astonishing similarities in terms of script and technique of writing, shape and layout. The fact that they yield between 1,300 and 1,500 legible syllabograms[2] means that this subcorpus, conventionally dubbed 'CM 2', certainly deploys most, if not all, of the signs of the script it uses. This in turn, gives us some insight into what the signary (or one of the signaries) of Cypro-Minoan looked like.
- It shows meagre yet encouraging traces of inflection, which may suggest phonetic relations between some syllabograms on an abstract level (i.e. independently from any comparisons with other scripts).
- It contains a small number of sign-sequences repeated in objects that are typologically and functionally diverse, therefore providing semantic clues on their content.
- It includes RASH Atab 004 (##215), a complete clay tablet found at Ugarit (Syria) whose text is relatively long and has a transparent list structure. Because of its Syrian background and the likelihood that it contains a list of persons (Schaeffer, *apud* O. Masson 1969, 392, n. 22) there is a chance this document contains onomastics or other elements from the local languages, particularly Ugaritic, Akkadian and Hurrian, that we might recognise from external (cuneiform) sources.

A decipherment is not on the horizon, but a fresh study that follows a methodology adjusted to these circumstances can provide new insights and substantiate or challenge old claims about the values of Cypro-Minoan signs. Elsewhere (Valério 2016), I undertake a study of the script by means of three successive analytical steps. The first two steps are *script comparison* (see detailed description in section 3) and *internal analysis* (which covers a series of approaches, including analysis of distribution and possible interactions of signs that reflect morphological phenomena and reveal abstract phonetic links between some syllabograms), and their goal is to suggest, independently, hypothetical phonetic values for the signs of Cypro-Minoan. The

[1] I follow Egetmeyer (2010a, 1) in using 'Cypro-Greek' for the writing system that is traditionally termed 'Cypriot Syllabary'. The traditional term is vague and inconsistent with the obvious existence of more than a syllabary from Cyprus, whereas 'Cypro-Greek' is accurately descriptive (Greek is the language of the vast majority of this script's inscriptions and probably the one for which it was created).

[2] Each scholar has their own understanding of the degree of certainty with each sign has been read, hence there are different counts: Palaima (1989, 157) estimates 'some 1310 signs' and Olivier (2013, 11, 13–14) ca. 1,500; Duhoux (2013, 31) calculates 1,369.

aim of the third step is to *test these hypothetical values* by using them to transliterate certain Cypro-Minoan texts and finding out whether they produce readings such as place or personal names that can be recognised from external sources and agree with the function of the objects they were inscribed on (as inferred from their physical characteristics). At present, the abovementioned tablet RASH Atab 004 is the most promising inscription for this testing procedure. Given the scope of the conference from which this volume arises, the following contribution focuses on the role of script comparison in an investigation of this kind.

The possibilities presented by the Cypro-Minoan corpus have been discussed on multiple occasions and I wish to make clear that the methodology I have just described is far from new.[3] What remains a *desideratum* in the field is a painstaking study of the Cypro-Minoan signary that maps the full palaeographical variation of each sign and distinguishes them from mere variants (as much as possible in the pre-decipherment stages). In section 2, I argue that this task must come before any enquiry into the sign values is conducted since our sign individualisations affect our perceptions of the script (Valério 2016). Another central argument – but one that is the means, not the end – of this contribution is that Linear A can and should be used in comparative analyses of Cypro-Minoan; to substantiate this claim, in section 3 I put forward palaeographical evidence that the two writing systems are directly related. Finally, section 4 presents an example of how comparisons with Linear A and Cypro-Greek, aided by palaeography, can be used to investigate the values of Cypro-Minoan signs.

2. Problems of signary

A key question in Cypro-Minoan studies is whether the inscriptions represent *one* or *multiple* script systems. The latter view is materialised in the tripartite classification of the bulk of inscriptions into three sub-scripts, CM 1, 2, and 3, inaugurated by É. Masson (1974, 11–16 and figs 1–4):

- CM 1: The main Late Bronze Age script in Cyprus, used by the indigenous population throughout the island; it comprises the majority of the documents (more than 200), making up a heterogeneous body of inscriptions (many of them very short) executed on typologically-mixed materials.
- CM 2: It is restricted as to place (Enkomi) and consists of only four clay tablets/ fragments of tablet (see above) that contain relatively long texts in a very homogeneous script. É. Masson saw it as being restricted in time (late 13th

[3] Nahm (1981) was the first *comprehensive* attempt to decipher the values of Cypro-Minoan signs by combining comparative and internal analyses, and then confirming the readings by identifying Semitic and Hurrian names in tablet RASH Atab 004 from Ugarit. A similar multidimensional approach, combining 'homography-based readability', 'statistical analysis' and 'onomastic material in CM documents' has recently been advocated by Facchetti *et al.* (2013).

and early 12th centuries BC) as well, but the chronology of the inscriptions is problematic.

- CM 3: In É. Masson's original formulation, it denotes a script restricted to four inscriptions from coastal Syria (RASH Atab 001, 004 and Mvas 001, and SYRI Psce 001 = ##212, 215–217) and developed for a local language, presumably Ugaritic, with new signs added for sounds foreign to the language of CM1. Following Hiller (1985, 72–3), Olivier (2013, 11 and n. 12) has revised CM 3 to include all inscriptions from Syria and be strictly geographical, while acknowledging that such construction cannot reflect a script proper (*HoChyMin*, 21). See also Duhoux (this volume).
- Alongside these categories, É. Masson theorized an 'archaic' stage (late 16th and 15th century BC) of Cypro-Minoan, which she defined as a different script system, previous to CM 1–3 and closer to a Linear A model. This has been revised in *HoChyMin*, as will be discussed below.

At present, this classification can be considered widely accepted, on occasion uncritically. However, criticisms regarding the criteria for its construction have been issued, first by Palaima (1989) and, more recently, by different authors (Davis 2011; *CM I* and Ferrara 2013), including myself (Valério 2013, 2014b).[4] In short, most palaeographical differences might be due to variations in chronology, geography, inscribed media and inscribing techniques, scribal idiosyncrasies and even textual genre.[5] Personally, I think if there is anything that might constitute a distinct system, then that is CM 2, but even some of the peculiar signs of this subcorpus[6] may turn out to be not so peculiar, as will be argued below.

The dividing of Cypro-Minoan has at the same time roots in, and implications for, the handling of its signary. Recently, Olivier and Ferrara published two independent and different compilations of Cypro-Minoan inscriptions, *HoChyMin* (2007) and *CM I* and *II* (2012, 2013), the first of their kind. Both include sign-lists. Olivier's (Figure 8.1) represents a reduction and *normalisation* of É. Masson's 1974 signary, and therefore follows the categorisation of Cypro-Minoan into three subscripts. The author merges as individual signs a number of forms he thinks are allographs, thus narrowing É. Masson's CM 1–3 list of 114 sign shapes down to 96 'syllabograms', and although he mostly maintains Masson's drawings, in his general grid he provides only one example of each sign shape per subcorpus. Ferrara (*CM* I, 255 and table 5.10) surveys Cypro-Minoan sign variations and presents as its result a 'tentative rationalized signary' that

[4] For reasons of space, I can only mention briefly the issues involved. The criteria for defining CM 1 as a separate script are at the very least dubious: as duly noted by Steele (2013a, 47), 'CM 1' is a 'catch-all' term for any Cypro-Minoan inscription from Cyprus or doubtful provenance that does not meet É. Masson's (more specific) criteria for separating the other two (alleged) scripts. As noted above, CM 3 has been separated based exclusively on geographical criteria and even Olivier admits it is not a writing system 'proper' (*HoChyMin*, 21).

[5] See Duhoux (this volume) for a different view regarding CM 3.

[6] Since I consider the unitary and multiple script theories both unproved at this point in the investigation, instead of '(sub)script' I use the more neutral term 'subcorpus' to refer to CM 1, 2 and 3.

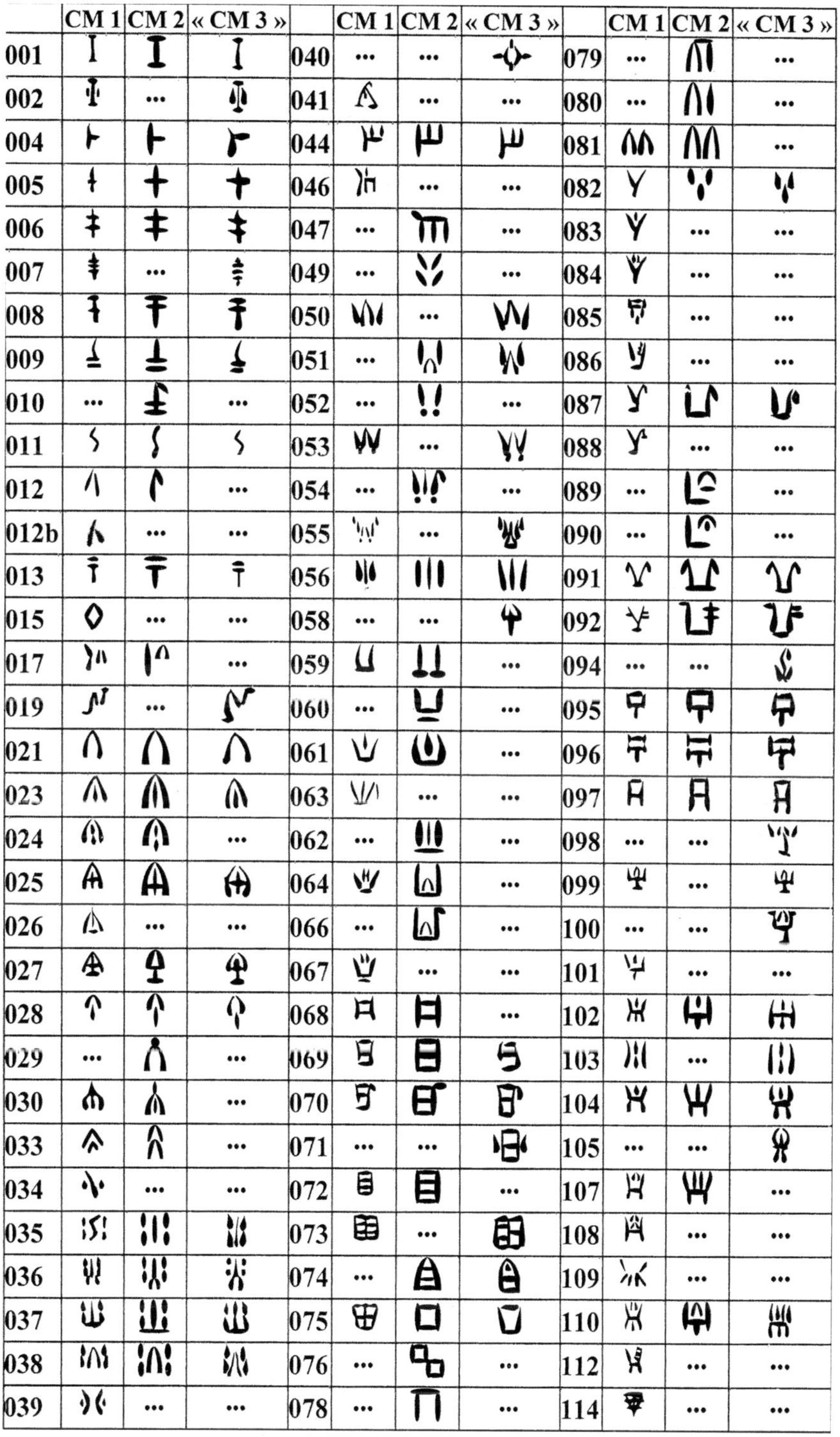

Fig. 8.1: Olivier's general table of CM 1–3 syllabograms (HoChyMin, *413*).

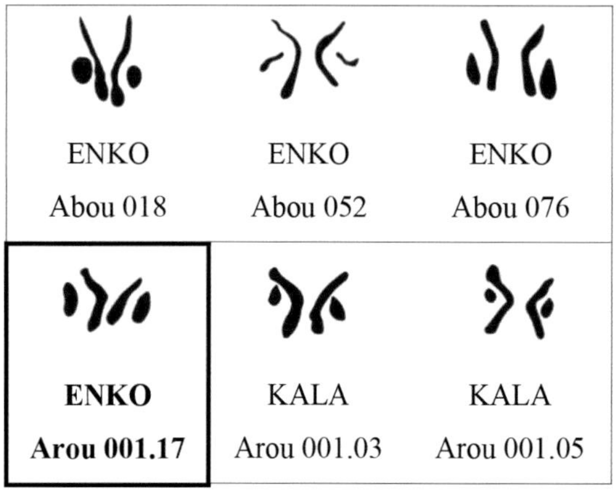

Fig. 8.2: Attestations of form CM1 39 (drawings based on the photographs in HoChyMin*).*

further condenses the repertoires of É. Masson and Olivier to 74 signs, although she also resorts to normalised forms.

Although the sign-list in *HoChyMin* is becoming the main reference for citing Cypro-Minoan signs, no existing repertoire has achieved consensus as an accurate representation of the actual signary (or signaries) of the script(s).[7] This stems from the fact that neither collection of inscriptions is accompanied by charts mapping the range of palaeographical variation for each sign (such as those provided by Olivier and Godart in *GORILA* for Linear A). As a consequence, as things stand it is very hard to distinguish between individual signs (*graphemes*) and formal variants (*allographs*), which not only hinders chances of decipherment but should also make anyone wary of using peculiar sign *forms* as arguments for isolating different Cypro-Minoan scripts.

Following is an example that showcases how the shortcomings of the existing sign-lists affect any investigation of sign values. It is drawn from an extensive investigation of the Cypro-Minoan signary (Valério 2016) which (1) takes as starting point signaries employed in the lengthier inscriptions or homogeneous subsets of inscriptions and (2) studies the ductus and palaeographical variation of the signs *as seen on the inscriptions.* To be considered here is the possible relationship between form CM 39 ( ), supposedly exclusive to CM 1, and CM 49 ( ), supposedly peculiar to CM 2. At first sight, we are led into interpreting them as distinct graphemes because the drawings of É. Masson, closely followed by Olivier (see Figure 8.1), capture very different shapes. Yet when we consider their ductus and variation in different inscriptions (Figures 8.2 and 8.3), they no longer look so distinct. Particularly, the instance of CM 39 in the Enkomi cylinder (ENKO Arou 001 = ##097) seems *identical* to CM 49.

This may not be a coincidence: if CM 39/49 (, ,) were a single grapheme, we would expect similar ductus under similar epigraphical conditions, and indeed both

[7] For a critique of some of the choices in *HoChyMin*, see Del Freo (2010, 310) and Valério (2013); for some considerations on Ferrara's survey and list, see Valério (2014a, 713–14).

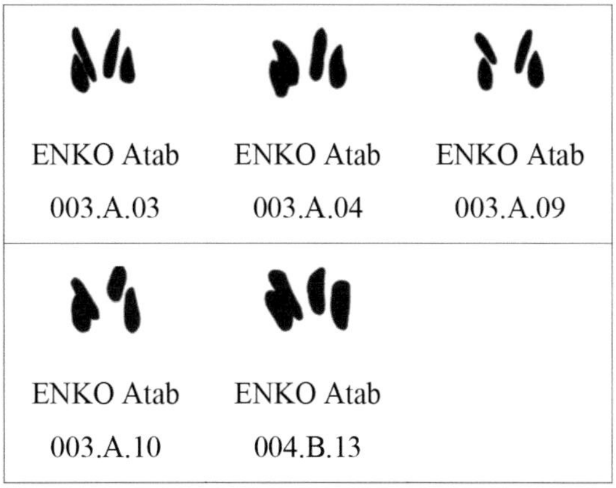

Fig. 8.3: Attestations of form CM2 49 (drawings based on the photographs in HoChyMin*).*

ENKO Arou 001 and the CM 2 tablets employ signs of very small size, hence more schematic. Other types of evidence do not (at least) contradict palaeography: CM 39 and 49 are never attested together in the same inscription and both fail to appear in sequence-final position (even if, given the infrequency of these shapes, both facts could be the product of chance). If we accept the merger we go from having two signs supposedly peculiar to different Cypro-Minoan subcorpora to having one sign used both in CM 1 and 2.

Cases like this (for a different example, see Valério 2013) do not just show that our sign lists and individualisations need revising, they also highlight the need to do so *prior* to any investigation of the sound values of the signs. Based on the drawings of É. Masson, some authors have ventured reading CM 39 () as *mu* (Faucounau 1977, 379; É. Masson 1987, 375) and CM 49 () as *pi* (Saporetti 1976, 91; Faucounau 1977, 379; Facchetti *et al.* 2013, 65), apparently due to similarities with Cypro-Greek (CGk) *mu* () and *pi* (), respectively. Yet, if CM 39/49 (, ,) represent one grapheme, its greatest similarity is with CGk *mu* () alone. The less accurately we can discern individual signs from allographs, the less accurate the comparisons will be; the undesirable implications extend also to any sort of statistical analysis.[8] However, I wish to emphasise that one can, and perhaps should, remain agnostic about whether Cypro-Minoan embodies one or multiple scripts while investigating its signs.

3. Preliminaries to a comparative analysis of Cypro-Minoan

3.1. The method

By script comparison I mean the well-known procedure of investigating the sign values of an undeciphered writing system by finding similar sign *shapes* in closely related scripts and comparing their *phonetic values.* The results are sounder if there is more

[8] The history of the decipherment of Linear B well demonstrates this point (see Palaima 2011, 54).

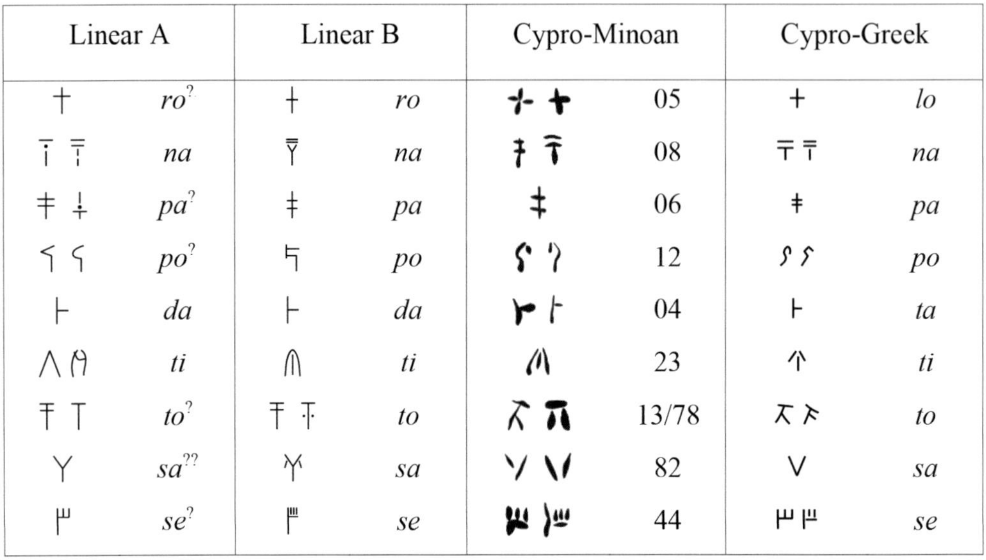

Fig. 8.4: Homomorphous and homophonous signs of simple design in the Aegean-Cypriot scripts.

than one direct 'relative', including the model and at least one derivative script. If a sign of the undeciphered system has *formal counterparts* in more than one relative, and the comparanda present a *similar or identical phonetic value*, then that value is assigned to the undeciphered sign as a *working hypothesis*. In other words, the compared signs should at the same time be *homomorphous* and *homophonous*, or nearly. These criteria help to avoid matching 'false friends', i.e. graphemes formally similar but phonetically different (cf. the classical example of Greek Ρ /r/ vs. Latin P /p/).

Deciphered as they are Cypro-Greek and Linear B betray a certain *continuity* in the history of this family of syllabaries (Steele and Meißner, this volume). Scripts of both Cyprus and the Aegean feature a number of syllabograms that preserved with little change their basic form *and* value, usually signs with simpler designs involving fewer strokes. Figure 8.4 lists nine of the most compelling cases of syllabograms that changed little or nothing across four scripts – Linear A and B, Cypro-Minoan and Cypro-Greek (CGk) – and which scholars routinely acknowledge in the literature (on the legibility of Linear A, see the next section and Steele and Meißner, this volume).[9]

From the 1950s onwards, this continuity motivated more or less extensive comparative approaches (sometimes articulated with other methods) by a number of scholars who hypothesised phonetic readings for many more than nine Cypro-Minoan syllabograms. However, in recent works (with the exception of Facchetti *et al.* 2013, 65) authors like Duhoux (2009b, 42, fn. 15), Olivier (2013, 8) and Steele (2013a,

[9] All of these are also contemplated in Olivier (2013, 8) in a list that also includes comparisons between less schematic signs.

Sign	Value	Agreement	Sign	Value	Agreement
01	*we*	Near-consensual	23	*ti*	Consensual
04	*t/da*	Consensual	25	*k/ga*	Near-consensual
05	*l/ro*	Consensual	44	*se*	Near-consensual
06	*p/ba*	Consensual	87	*l/ra*	Near-consensual
08	*na*	Near-consensual	102	*a*	Consensual

Fig. 8.5: Consensual or near-consensual hypothetical values of Cypro-Minoan syllabograms from comparative approaches (1956–2013).

50–60) have been more cautious about attempting to ascertain the sign values of Cypro-Minoan and only highlight the small number of syllabograms that show clear homomorphy and homophony (fourteen according to Duhoux and Olivier, ten as per Steele). Figure 8.5 shows ten sign values on which most researchers have nonetheless agreed as tentative readings (see also Steele and Meißner, this volume).[10]

Of the several possible hypotheses as to why we do not have a larger number of *obvious* LA-CM-CGk cognates (cf. Steele 2013a, 50), I think the most likely is a combination of two: (1) that many of the remaining Cypro-Minoan signs have undergone formal adaptations and palaeographical developments throughout the life of the script, and (2) the adaptive processes that saw the remodelling of Linear A as Cypro-Minoan and of the latter as Cypro-Greek each brought about a number of structural changes that deleted, added, or changed the value of, some signs. Whatever the case may be, an upheaval of the Aegean template seems unlikely: even the few syllabograms that have gained consensus as clear cognates imply values representing various vowels (*a*, *e*, *i*, *o*) and consonants (*d*/*t*, *k*/*g*, *n*, *p*/*b*, *r*/*l*, *s*, *t*, *w*) (Figure 8.5), so the essential phonographic matrix must have been preserved throughout.

Inter-script comparisons are practicable only when two conditions are satisfied: (1) the writing systems to be compared have a well-established and direct relationship; (2) they are deciphered or at least their signs are legible to a significant extent (regardless

[10] To be brief, the nine works on which this table is based are: Sittig (1956, 41); É. Masson (1973, 1974, fig. 26); Saporetti (1976, fig. 41); Faucounau (1977, 1980, 1994); Nahm (1981, Abb. 1–3; 1984, Abb. 2–3); Duhoux (2009b, 42, n. 15, 2013, 42); Facchetti *et al.* (2013, 65); Olivier (2013, table 1.1); Steele (2013a, 55–60). Like Sittig, Mann (1960, 41) and Ephron (1961, fig. 3) also produced 'decipherments' of Cypro-Minoan as a Mycenaean Greek dialect, but they are not contemplated here because these authors assigned phonetic values to the signs in a way that was too arbitrary. Terminology: *near-consensual*: six/seven out of nine authors; *consensual*: eight/nine out of nine authors. In the cases of stop signs, the value is to be taken generically as 'unmarked': for instance, *p/ba* might represent not only the voiceless bilabial stop /p/, but also its voiced counterpart /b/ or any other marked version of the sound.

of whether the underlying languages are understood).[11] The Cypro-Greek syllabary fulfils these two requirements,[12] but the situation with Linear A is more intricate: on one hand, the majority view that it was the model of Cypro-Minoan (or an early form thereof) still attracts some reservations; on the other hand, it is only partially deciphered. These two issues are addressed in the next section.

3.2. Linear A as valid comparandum

Although its *language* still defies interpretation, the Linear A *script* is far from being impenetrable (see Steele and Meißner, this volume). Based on formal proximity with the syllabograms of Linear B, the signs of Linear A have long been assigned, in a conditional fashion, the same phonetic values of the Mycenaean script. Naturally, we cannot expect *all* values to be *exact* matches as Linear B is the product of the adaptation of Linear A to another language, Mycenaean Greek, with its own sound inventory. Nonetheless, scholarship has succeeded in corroborating a good number of analogous Linear A–B readings. Initial efforts (Packard 1974; Hooker 1975; Godart 1984) have been confirmed by Duhoux (1989), who resorted to multiple validating tests, namely: 1) the examination of the positional frequency of the suspected vowel syllabograms; 2) orthographic alternations in Linear A; and 3) the listing of close correspondences between Linear A sequences and Linear B words (mostly personal and place names). Duhoux was very cautious about the results, considering different levels of certainty for each of the values depending on how many tests supported them. The grid of Linear A phonetic values in Figure 8.6 summarises his conclusions, as revised by Davis (2014), by means of a system of question marks (the fewer question marks on a reading, the more secure it is).

The caveat that most Linear A sound values are unconfirmed needs to be taken into account, but I would argue that including the script in comparative analyses is less hazardous than overlooking it. By doing so, we can identify direct LA-CM-CGk *formal* matches even if some Linear A *phonetic* values are uncertain or yield inexact matches. Conversely, some authors (É. Masson 1974, 1987; Steele 2013a) prefer to use Linear B as term of comparison because we are certain of its signs' *readings*, but in this way the *forms* of Linear A counterparts, which tend to be more akin to Cypro-Minoan characters, are disregarded. The implication is that potential LA-CM-CGk correspondences can be overlooked. A case in point is that of LA 11/$\mathit{po}^{?}$ > CM 12 > CGk *po*. All syllabograms concerned are identical in *form and value* (see Figure 8.4),[13] yet, unlike other signs that fulfil the same conditions, they are not

[11] Concerning the Aegean-Cypriot scripts, a similar formulation is first found in Evans (1895, 83), who reinforced it after the discovery of Cypro-Minoan (*SMI*, 72).

[12] For instance, this seems to be the consensus amongst the contributors to Steele (2013b).

[13] Figure 8.4 does not cover more than a few variants of each sign and, to be sure, the shape of CM 12 in the CM 2 subcorpus is slightly different (), but this may well be due to epigraphical constraints. The fact remains that in the Enkomi clay balls CM 12 has shapes identical to LA 11/$\mathit{po}^{?}$ even as regards their alternation between leftward and rightward orientations (see *HoChyMin*).

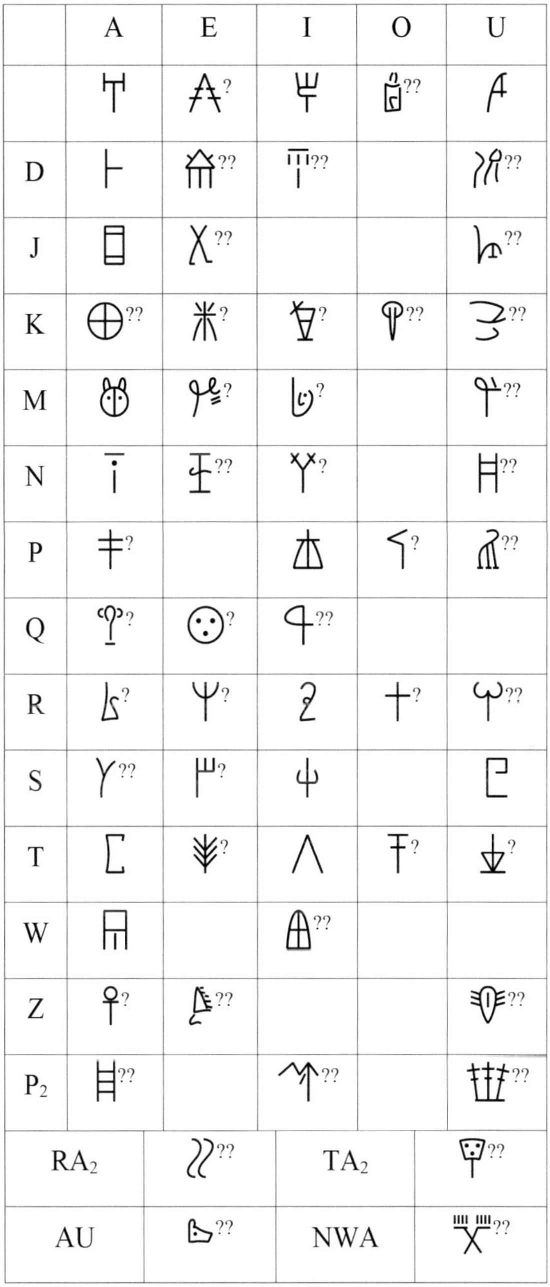

Fig. 8.6: Phonetic values of Linear A syllabograms (adapted from Duhoux 1989 and Davis 2014, fig. 111).

recognised as clear cognates in recent scholarship (with the exception of Olivier 2013, 8).

In the literature it has been widely accepted that Linear A provided the template for Cypro-Minoan,[14] but objections are still issued by some scholars. These can be narrowed down to three points: (1) anxiety over the apparent Cypriot choice for an Aegean model that was more distant to Cyprus than other East Mediterranean writing systems; (2) the lack of a clear historical-archaeological setting in which Cretan writing could have been introduced to the island; (3) alleged palaeographical divergences. One problem with the first two objections is that they focus on the external circumstances[15] when the *main* factor for establishing a script's structural affinities should be its internal features.[16]

At the epicentre of the debate is the Cypro-Minoan clay tablet ENKO Atab 001 (##001), which in *HoChyMin* becomes the sole member of a new 'CM 0' category that replaces É. Masson's 'Archaic' CM. Two circumstances make it crucial. The first is chronology: the tablet's find-spot tells us it is no later than the LC IB period (1525–1425 BC) (Dikaios 1963, 43–7; Duhoux 2009a, 6–7, n. 10), which is also the date before which no other Cypro-Minoan inscription can be placed with certainty. The second circumstance is its signary, which is more similar to Linear A syllabograms than that (or those) of later Cypro-Minoan texts.[17]

A full physical description of ENKO Atab 001 is available in the new collections (*HoChyMin*, 60; *CM II*, 13–14 and 127) and there is also a recent in-depth study by Duhoux (2009a), so here I describe only the features relevant for our purposes. The object is a fragment of tablet preserving three inscribed lines with ruling (Figure 8.7) and has close morphological parallels in Neopalatial Crete, as it fits the Aegean type

[14] Among others, see É. Masson (1973, 32–3), Palaima (1989, 140) and Olivier (2013, 7–8).

[15] Very recently, Sherratt (2013) expresses both types of preoccupations, but see also Baurain (1980, 568, citing Godart and Sacconi 1979, 133) on the lack of archaeological evidence for contacts between Crete and Cyprus in the period around the emergence of Cypro-Minoan. The subject deserves more attention than I can devote here, but I would like to point out that for the ancient Mediterranean the notion of scripts 'travelling' great lengths is not shocking. Nor is it normal for us to be able to pinpoint the exact time and place where the transmission of a script took place. For example, while there is still a great debate as to where and when the Greek alphabet was created, not many doubt that its creation was based on a Phoenician model.

[16] To solve the supposed problem of distance and the apparent palaeographical and phonetic divergences between signs of the Aegean and Cypriot syllabaries, some scholars (Sherratt 2013; Steele 2014a) ponder a version of Lejeune's (1958a) hypothesis that Linear A and Cypro-Minoan are different offshoots of a third, wholly unattested writing system, 'Linear X'. In light of the evidence presented here, I find this account uneconomical and unnecessary.

[17] The second earliest document is ENKO Apes 001 (##095). In theory, since it has been dated to the LC IA-B (*CM II*, 51), it could be earlier than ENKO Atab 001, but this is no more than a possibility. In any case, it contains only signs that are attested in Cypro-Minoan, including sign shapes CM 11 ([illegible]), 64 (or 37?) ([illegible]), 97 ([illegible]) and 108 ([illegible]), which have no formal counterparts in Linear A and are diagnostic. There is little doubt the system used in this inscription is Cypro-Minoan proper.

Fig. 8.7: Photograph of ENKO Atab 001 (courtesy of S. Ferrara).

of 'page-shaped' tablets (É. Masson 1969, 66; Palaima 1989, 136).[18] The text comprises 23 signs inscribed in *scriptio continua*. The first two on the right edge of the first line are repeated, in the same order, at the right side of the tablet, suggesting they functioned as a sort of heading or label, perhaps for archiving purposes (see Duhoux 2009a, 10). This repeated sequence and the orientation of certain sign shapes imply that the inscription is written in *boustrophedon* (Ventris 1956; Janko 1987), although Duhoux (2009a, 22–5) maintains the opposite view.[19]

The most substantial issue with the edition of ENKO Atab 001 concerns the interpretation of signs no. 10 and 11 (line 02), whose great similarity makes it hard to decide whether they are the same grapheme or two different ones (É. Masson 1969, 66, 68; Palaima 1989, 138). Duhoux (2009a) has shown prudence in his analysis and ponders both possibilities. I will take his stance as a starting point, but see below for a hypothesis that they represent distinct signs. Thus, the twenty-three signs of ENKO Atab 001 make up a signary of twenty *or* twenty-one individual graphemes (see Figure 8.8).

[18] Parallels include the following Linear A tablets: PH 8 (Phaistos) – chronology: MM II; ruling: yes; edge inscribed: no); PK 1 (Palaikastro) – chronology: probably LM I; ruling: yes; edge inscribed: yes (one sign); and TY 3 (Tylisos) – chronology: LM IB; ruling: yes; edge inscribed: no (see *GORILA*).

[19] Each line has signs suggesting a *boustrophedon* reading. The first sign in l. 01 ([sign]) resembles LA 60/*ra*? and CM 87 ([sign]) but is oriented leftwards; such orientation is rare in the Linear A counterpart ([sign]) and unseen in CM 87. A sinistrorse reading direction can also be surmised for l. 03, where sign CM0 18 again matches both LA 01/*da* (⊢) and CM 04 ([sign]), but with an unusual leftwards orientation (⊣). Conversely, in l. 02, sign CM0 14 ([sign]), equal to LA 09/*se*? ([sign]) and CM 44 ([sign]), appears to be oriented rightwards (Ventris 1956, 41).

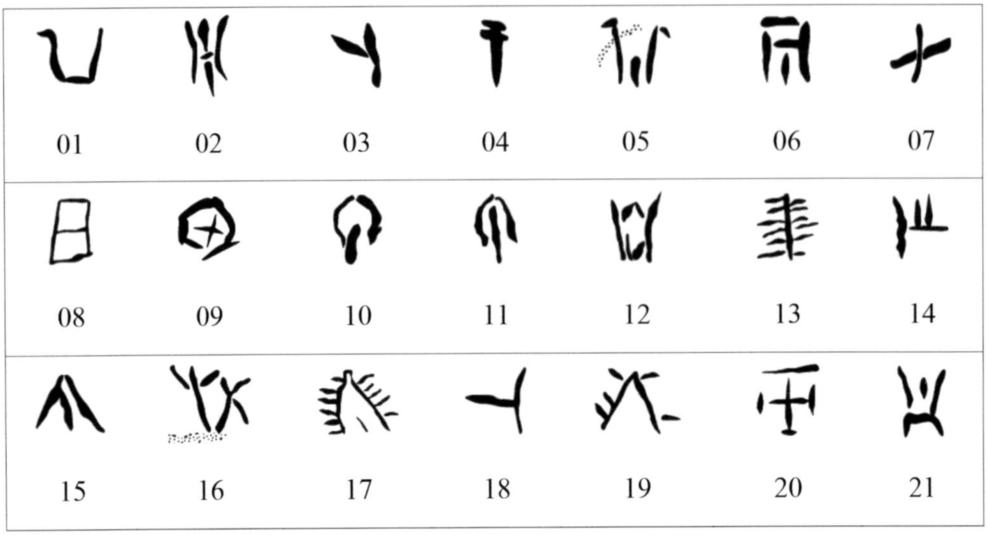

Fig. 8.8: The signary of ENKO Atab 001 (drawings by the author, based on the photographs in HoChyMin *and* CM II; *not to scale).*

Scholars have different views on what the signary of ENKO Atab 001 represents. We have already seen that É. Masson saw it as an example of the first indigenous Cypriot writing, one very similar to Linear A. Olivier, who made the tablet the single member of a CM 0 subcorpus, claims that its script cannot be the ancestor of the later Cypro-Minoan *ones* and must be a 'dead branch' in the evolution of Aegean writing in Cyprus (*HoChyMin*, 21; Olivier 2013, 9). Duhoux (2009a, 31, 2013, 30) has expressed on different occasions the view that significant amounts of the 20(-1) signs of CM 0 differ from Linear A and CM 1. Godart and Sacconi (1979, 131–2) judge only three signs to be surely identical to Linear A ones. At the opposite end of the spectrum, Palaima (1989, 136–8) argues that for '17 of the 20 potentially distinctive signs, one can propose parallel signs in Linear A', and underlines that this number is 'convincingly high for so brief a text'.

However, the debate has never been accompanied with, or founded on, an actual assessment of the formal affinity between the signs of our tablet and those of Linear A and remaining Cypro-Minoan by means of a systematic comparative-palaeographical analysis.[20] This was understandable when comprehensive collections of Linear A and Cypro-Minoan inscriptions were not available, but now we are in the position to fill this lacuna. Below, I present a sign by sign analysis of ENKO Atab 001, following Palaima's (1989, 138) plea for comparing signs as they appear on the inscriptions, not standardised forms. For Linear A syllabograms, I resort to the drawings from *GORILA*;

[20] In her original study of ENKO Atab 001, É. Masson (1969) did compare the tablet's signs to those of the two scripts abovementioned, but either Linear A signs were cited generically or the reader was referred to the tables of Brice (1961). At the time the palaeographical charts of *GORILA* were not available.

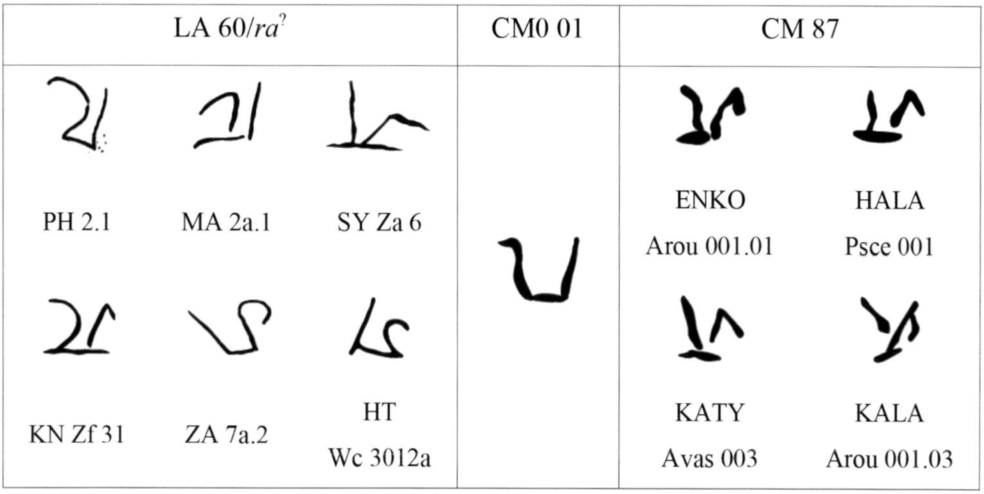

Fig. 8.9: Comparison of LA 60/ra?, CM0 01, and CM 87.

for Cypro-Minoan ones, I produced new drawings based on published photographs. Since the earliest Cypro-Minoan inscriptions are likely to contain the forms that are closest to those of the model script, I attempt to use the oldest known examples of each parallel. Finally, and although I have doubts about its usefulness, I use the label 'CM 0' to refer to the signs of ENKO Atab 001 for the sake of simplicity: thus, 'CM0 01' means the first sign of the tablet, and so on.

CM0 01 (Figure 8.9) matches closely LA 60/*ra*? and CM 87. It is oriented leftwards, which never happens with CM 87 but occurs twice with LA 60, namely in tablets from Phaistos and Malia (PH 2 and MA 2). This may have to do with ENKO Atab 001 being written in *boustrophedon* instead of being a trait common to one or the other script. Probably due to epigraphical constraints, on some occasions Cypro-Minoan allows for a 'stemmed' version of 87 (e.g. KALA Arou 001 = ##098 and KATY Avas 003 = ##129), which for LA 60/*ra*? is very rare (but see SY Za 6).

CM0 02 (Figure 8.10) is comparable to LA 08/*a* and CM 102. In Cypro-Minoan, the CM 2 version of 102 is very close to CM0 02, but later variants such as those in the clay balls are perhaps even more alike. This may owe to similar epigraphical constraints (e.g. the use of thin styli on clay) and warns us that we should not always expect perfect matches for the signs of ENKO Atab 001. In fact, there are Linear A and later Cypro-Minoan forms much more similar to each other (e.g. LA 08 in KN Zb 5 and Zc 6 contrasted with CM 102 in KATY Avas 002 = ##128) than to CM0 02. This may be interpreted as an indication that the signs of ENKO Atab 001 represent a divergent branch of an Aegean script (Olivier's proposal), but it is as likely that they had their own range of palaeographical variation, depending on epigraphical factors, and that, should we have more documents from this period, we would possibly find examples of CM0 02 resembling closer both scripts.

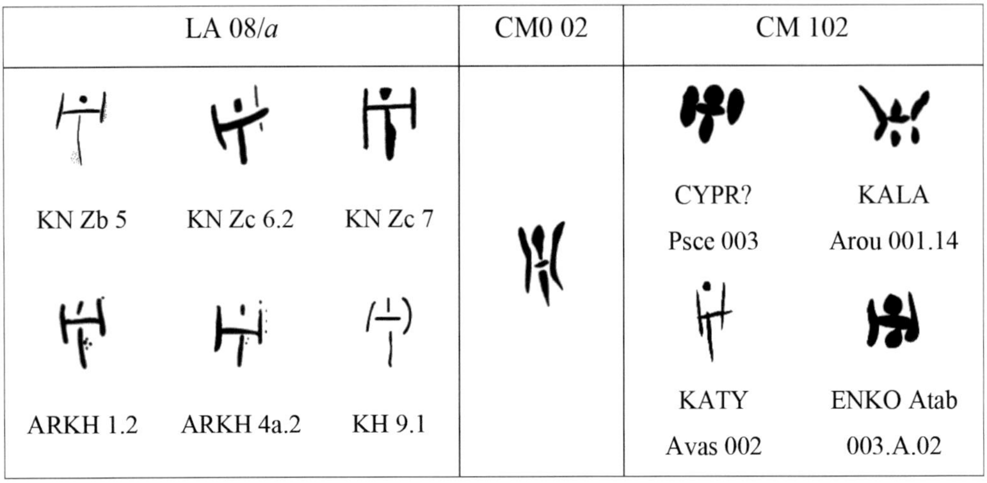

Fig. 8.10: Comparison of LA 08/a, CM0 02, and CM 102.

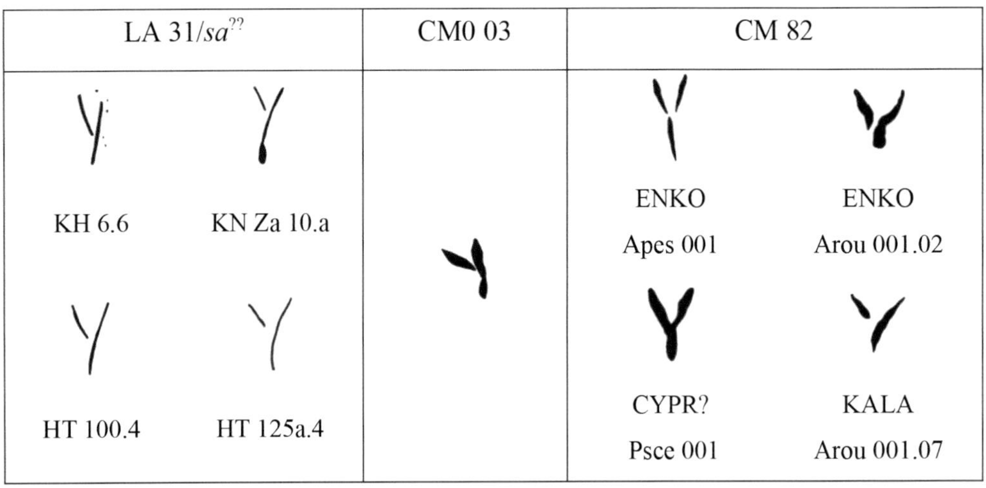

Fig. 8.11: Comparison of LA 31/sa??, CM0 03, and CM 82.

Although we cannot entirely rule out equating CM0 03 (Figure 8.11) with CM0 18, it appears sufficiently distinct (cf. Figure 8.8). The best comparanda are LA 31/*sa* and CM 82, but these signs' very simple shapes make it difficult to be more precise.

In theory, LA 05/*to*? and 06/*na* can both match CM0 04 (Figure 8.12), but in Cyprus, later, only CM 08 provides a suitable match. The most promising of the two Aegean candidates is a priori LA 05/*to*? because its vertical stroke always connects with both horizontal strokes (like CM0 04) on the upper part, and is never split. However, CM 08 exhibits a wider range of variation and uses optionally traits that in Linear A are diagnostic of one or the other sign. For this reason, and because CM0 04 is a very schematic shape, we cannot decide which comparandum is the closest.

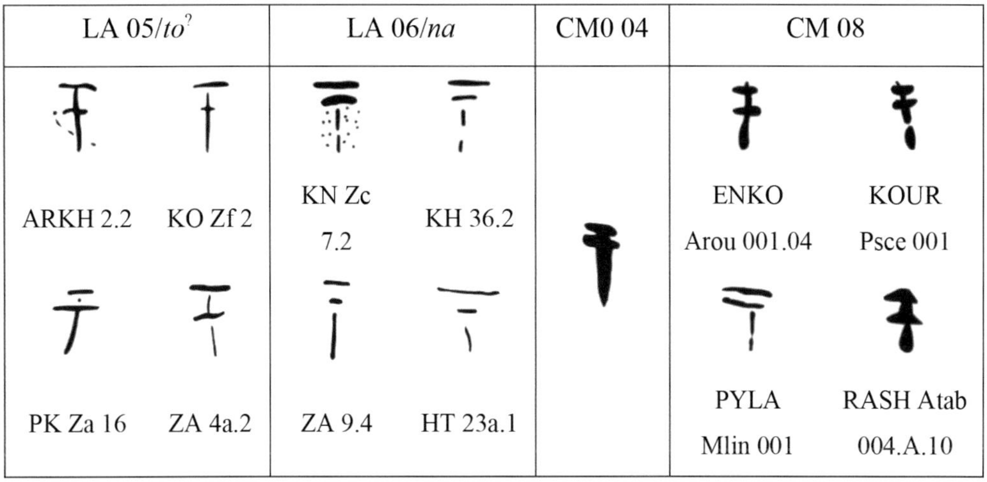

*Fig. 8.12: Comparison of LA 05/*to*? and 06/*na*, CM0 04, and CM 08.*

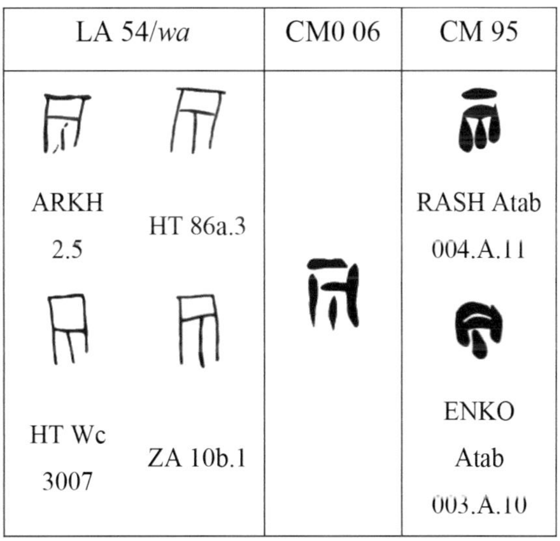

*Fig. 8.13: Comparison between LA 54/*wa*, CM0 06, and CM 95.*

For CM0 05 (see Figure 8.8) there is no obvious cognate in Linear A and possible comparisons, e.g. with CM 55 ( ) or 91 ( ), would be very conjectural.

CM0 06 (Figure 8.13) matches closely LA 54/*wa* (also used logographically for 'cloth' and transcribed as TELA) and CM 95. The Linear A sign consists of a rectangular shape from whose lower side three or more vertical strokes can descend, but CM0 06 and CM 95 match the three-legged variant that is attested in LM IB inscriptions from different Cretan sites. CM0 06 is therefore the expected 'midway' between the Linear A and Cypro-Minoan forms.

LA 02/*ro*?	CM0 07	CM 05
 HT 9a.6		 ENKO Apes 001
 ZA 15b.2		 ENKO Atab 003.A.10

Fig. 8.14: Comparison between LA 02/ro?, CM0 07 and CM 05.

CM0 08	CM 69
	 ENKO Arou 001.01
	 PARA Psce 001

Fig. 8.15: Comparison between CM0 08 and CM 69.

Sign	Regular form	Variant with optional traits
56/$pa_3^{??}$	 HT 8a.1	 AP Za 2.1
57/*ja*	 HT 7a.2	 IO Za 3

Fig. 8.16: Diagnostic and optional traits of LA 56/$pa_2^{??}$ and 57/ja.

CM0 07 (Figure 8.14) matches LA 02/*ro*? and CM 05, but given its schematic design it cannot be said to be closer to any of the two.

CM0 08 (Figure 8.15) fully matches later CM 69, but has no direct equivalent in Linear A.

Still, there are two Linear A syllabograms that bear some resemblance to it: LA 56/$pa_3^{??}$ and 57/*ja* (Figure 8.16). LA 56/$pa_3^{??}$ is drawn as a rectangle split in two halves by a central horizontal stroke, like CM 69, except that it is shaped like a ladder (the lateral strokes are extended beyond its upper and lower edges). 57/*ja* is a plain rectangle divided into three parts, although in at least one instance (IO Za 3) its lateral strokes have been prolonged as well. Since the shape of LA 56/$pa_3^{??}$ is also divided into three

<table>
<tr><th colspan="2">LA 77/ka??</th><th>CM0 09</th><th colspan="2">CM 25</th></tr>
<tr><td></td><td></td><td rowspan="4"></td><td></td><td></td></tr>
<tr><td>HT 49b.4</td><td>HT Wa 1028.γ</td><td>CYPR? Psce 001</td><td>ENKO Arou 001.14</td></tr>
<tr><td></td><td></td><td></td><td></td></tr>
<tr><td>HT Wa 1349</td><td>HT Wa 1368</td><td>KALA Arou 004.02</td><td>RASH Atab 004.A.04</td></tr>
</table>

*Fig. 8.17: Comparison between LA 77/*ka??*, CM0 09 and CM 25.*

portions least once, we can deduce that what distinguished it from 57/*ja* was the ladder-like shape, regardless of the number of horizontal strokes. This suggests that CM0 08 and CM 69 derive from LA 57/*ja*, which is simply a divided rectangle.[21]

CM0 09 (Figure 8.17) matches closely CM 25 and some variants of LA 77/*ka*??. The latter usually looks like a circle divided into four similar parts (i.e. a four-spoke wheel), but the ductus of some instances from LM IB Agia Triada, particularly on nodules, tends to leave the circle unclosed at the lower edge of the sign. It can be suggested that this was the form borrowed into Cyprus and that, judging from CM0 09 and CM 25, from then on there was an increasing propensity to open the sign at its lower edge. From this perspective, CM0 09 is a plausible intermediate form.

CM0 10 and 11 (Figures 8.18 and 8.19) are very similar: the upper part of both comprises two parallel curved strokes placed on the top of a vertical one. Their ductus has two main differences: 1) the upper strokes of CM0 10 are much more curved and have a sub-circular form, while those of CM0 11 are more open and make the sign look like an arrow; 2) in CM0 10 the vertical stroke barely enters the sub-circular structure and is mostly limited to the lower portion of the sign, but in CM0 11 it almost touches the two arching strokes at the top. But are these differences intentional?

If we assume for the sake of argument that these are diagnostic traits and that CM0 10 and 11 are separate graphemes, then we can compare each with different

[21] Although I cannot dwell on this topic here, the question of which Linear A sign best compares to CM0 08 and CM 69 is further complicated by the unclear relation between forms CM 69 () and 72 (). At the outset it would seem like they are distinct graphemes, at least in CM 2, where they co-exist in the same text (ENKO Atab 003). Yet in other subcorpora they are never attested together and the fact is that the positional frequency and distribution of form CM1 72 (, ,) is more consistent with CM1/2 69 () than the *very rare* CM2 72 () (cf. *HoChyMin* and *CM I*, appex 5–6).

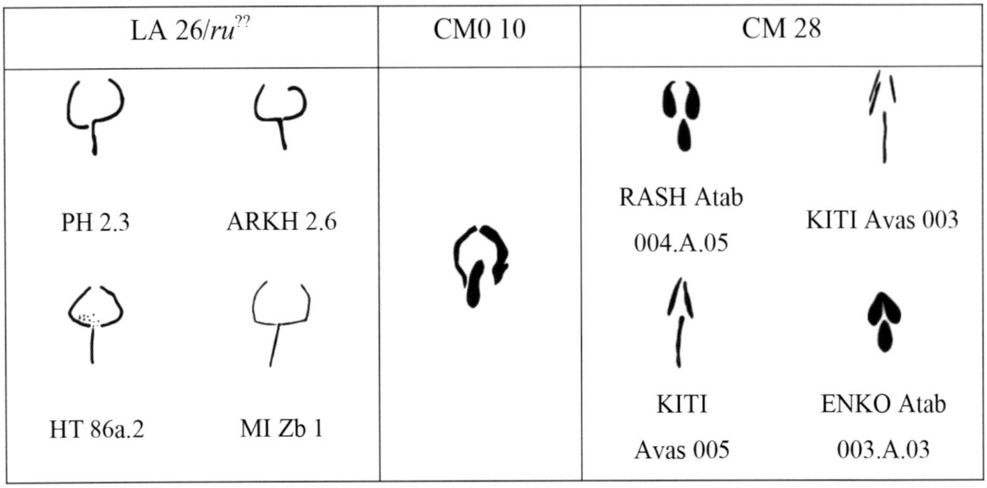

*Fig. 8.18: Comparison between LA 26/*ru??*, CM0 10 and CM 28.*

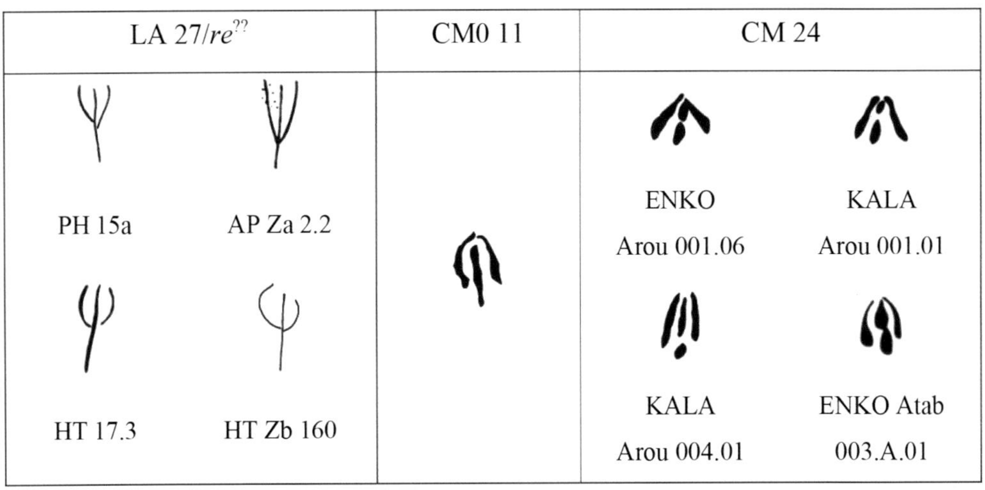

*Fig. 8.19: Comparison between LA 27/*re??*, CM0 11, and CM 24.*

Linear A and Cypro-Minoan signs. CM0 10 resembles the variants of LA 26/*ru*?? in which the upper curved strokes are more closed and could be the antecedent of CM 28, reflecting the progressive closing of its upper portion (Figure 8.20). It is true that most examples of CM 28 look like an arrow, but the early example (if not the earliest) in RASH Atab 004 is still somewhat open, and since the sign is fairly rare, its palaeographic variation may not be well represented.

In theory, CM0 11 looks enough like an arrow to be comparable to CM 28 as well. However, since its vertical stroke reaches almost the top of the shape, we can rather

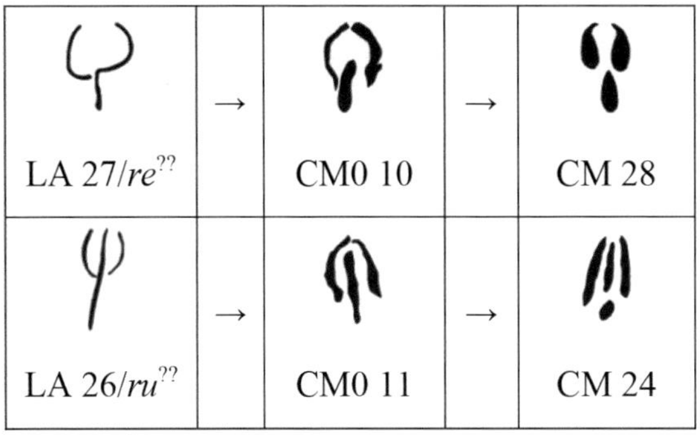

*Fig. 8.20: Hypothesised developments LA 27/*re*?? > CM 28 and LA 26/*ru*?? > CM 24 in parallel.*

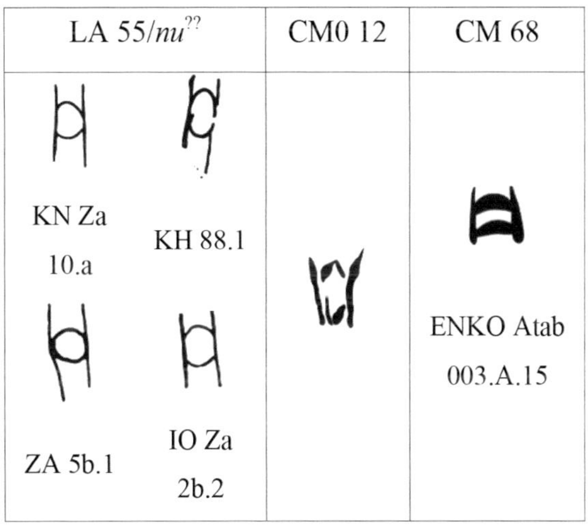

*Fig. 8.21: Comparison between LA 55/*nu*??, CM0 12, and CM 68.*

compare it to LA 27/*re*?? (Ψ), which, as a rule, has its vertical stroke extended to its upper portion and curved strokes that are less slightly less curved. Assuming, then, that CM0 11 is not related to CM 28 (< CM0 10?), what other Cypro-Minoan sign is there for comparison? Taking into account its variants in KALA Arou 001 and ENKO Atab 003 (Figure 8.19), I propose as a working hypothesis that CM 24 (⁂) is derived from LA 27/*re*?? (Ψ) with CM0 11 as the intermediate form.

Notice that CM 24 as it is has no recognizable equivalent in Linear A. Although it possesses two vertical strokes (⁂), not just one, my suggestion is that this may have been a modification prompted by a need to distinguish ⁂ from ⁂ (see Figure 8.20), as well as from the arrow-like CM0 15 (⁂). See section 4 for a further discussion of this hypothesis.

CM0 12 (Figure 8.21) is comparable to LA 55/*nu*?? and CM 68. However, it resembles most the variants of LA 55 in which the two central horizontal strokes are curved;

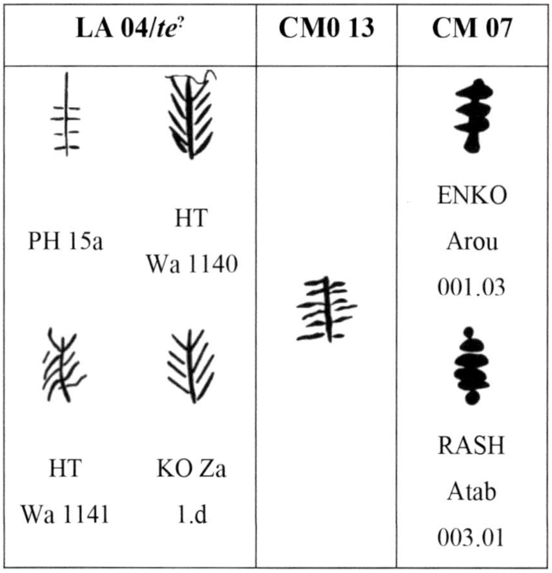

*Fig. 8.22: Comparison between LA 04/*te?*, CM0 13, and CM 07.*

the corresponding strokes in CM 68 are less curving and therefore closer to other variants of the Linear A sign. Once more, I underline the possibility that the script of ENKO Atab 001 had a higher palaeographical variation than we can see, whereby CM0 12 had less curving variants matching CM 68 closer.

CM0 13 (Figure 8.22) matches closely LA 04/*te*? and CM 07. However, with LA 04 the number of horizontal strokes on each side of the vertical line is normally three or four, which is also the number of horizontal strokes in the rare attestations of CM 07. Differently, CM0 13 has a series of six horizontal lines on each side of the vertical stroke, making its closest match one instance of LA 04 in HT Wa 1140 (LM IB), which has five such strokes. This is yet another case where the CM0 form shows divergence regarding both comparanda, leaving us with two possibilities: its script is either a dead branch with no continuation in Cypro-Minoan, or it displayed much more palaeographic variation than we are given to see.

CM0 14 (Figure 8.23) matches in equal measure both LA 09/*se*? and CM 44.

CM0 15 (Figure 8.24) equates with LA 37/*ti* and CM 23.

CM0 16 (Figure 8.25[22]) is close to the rare CM 67 and even closer to the 'stemless' variants of LA 30/*ni*? (also used as the logogram FIC or 'figs'). LA 30 is normally structured from a Y-shape, with strokes (usually two) crossing each of the upper stripes in an X-like manner (). However, CM0 16 resembles much more the 'stemless' version, based on a V-like shape. It is unsurprising that the most similar parallel

[22] For CYPR? Psce 004, which is in a private collection, we have only the drawing of O. Masson (1957, fig. 5), which I reproduce here.

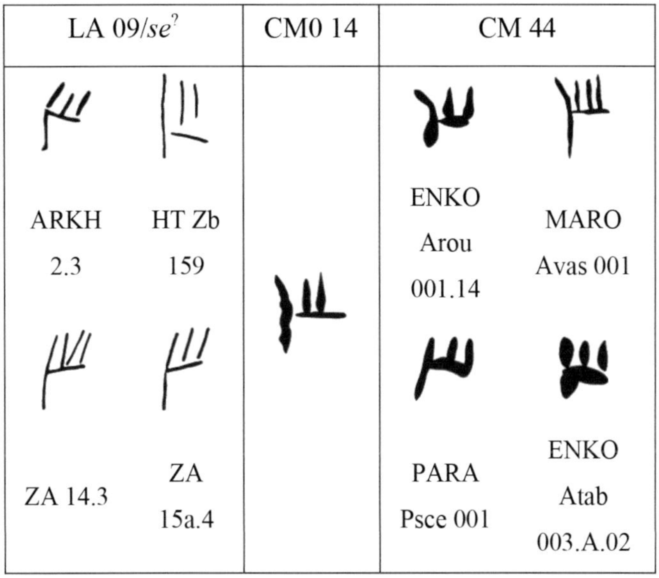

*Fig. 8.23: Comparison between LA 09/*se*?, CM0 14, and CM 44.*

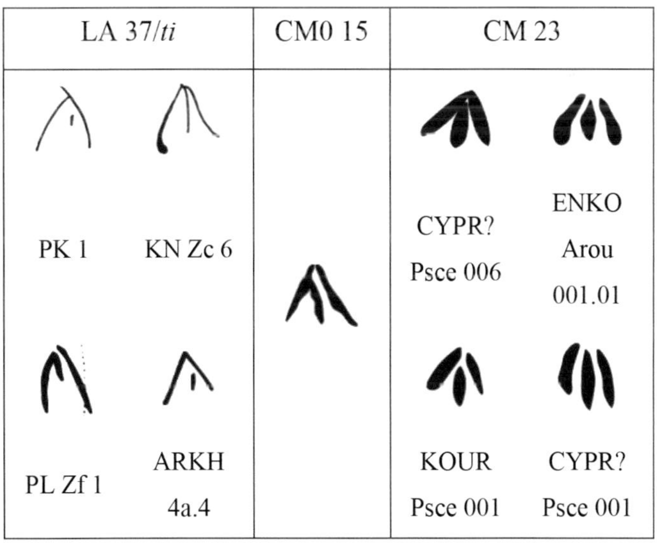

*Fig. 8.24: Comparison between LA 37/*ti*, CM0 15, and CM 23.*

in Cypro-Minoan is one early instance of CM 67 on CYPR? Psce 004, a cylinder seal dated to 1400-1325 BC. This also squares well with the *possibility* that the ductus of CM0 16 = CM 67 evolved throughout the lifetime of the script and took different forms that É. Masson and Olivier list as separate signs (e.g. CM 65 = [sign] or 99 = [sign]).

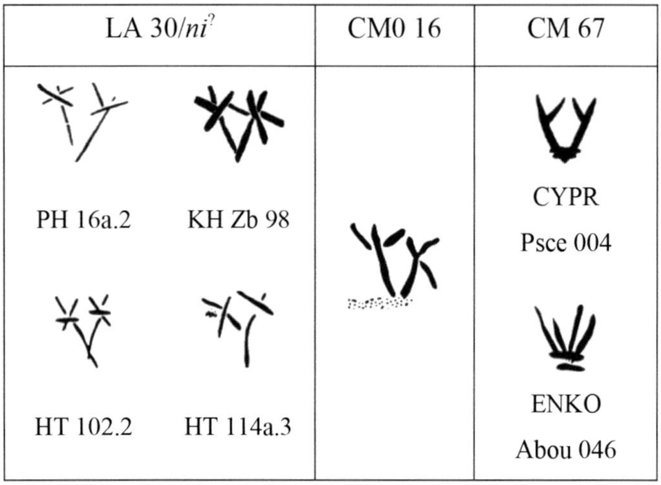

*Fig. 8.25: Comparison between LA 30/*ni?*, CM0 16, and CM 67.*

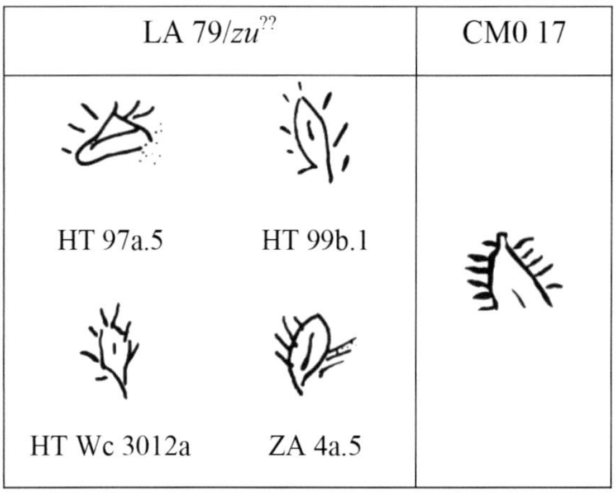

*Fig. 8.26: Comparison between LA 79/*zu??* and CM0 17.*

CM0 17 (Figure 8.26) is similar to some variants of LA 79/*zu*?? but has no obvious counterpart in later Cypro-Minoan. Often, the Linear A character resembles an Egyptian *ankh* glyph with inner and lateral strokes added to the oval segment, but the older variants seem to be the eye-shaped ones without the 'leg'. Of these, those found in LM IB texts from different Cretan sites (Arkhanes, Agia Triada and Zakros) are very similar to CM0 17 (see Palaima 1989, 136 for a similar view), especially the example in HT 99.

CM0 18 (Figure 8.27) fully equates LA 01/*da* and CM 04, but it is one of those schematic shapes that cannot be said to be closer to any. The fact that it is oriented leftwards, unlike its equivalents in Linear A and Cypro-Minoan, is most probably due to the orientation of the inscription.

LA 01/*da*	CM0 18	CM 04	
 HT 95a.2		 ENKO Arou 001.10	 PARA Psce 001
 ZA 5a.3		 CYPR Psce 003	 RASH Atab 004.A.05

*Fig. 8.27: Comparison between LA 01/*da*, CM0 18, and CM 04.*

LA 38/*e*$^?$		CM0 19	CM 38	
 KE Zb 4	 HT 23b.3		 KATY Avas 001	 ENKO Arou 001.01
 HT 91.4	 ZA 11b.1		 MARO Avas 001	 RASH Atab 004.A.06

Fig. 8.28: Comparison between LA 38/e$^?$, CM0 19, and CM 38.

CM0 19 (Figure 8.28) matches closely LA 38/*e*$^?$ and CM 38. LA 38 shows some variance and is not always similar to CM0 19 and CM 38, but very close counterparts occur in the Agia Triada texts (LM IB), and outside Crete in the island of Kea (KE Zb 4, dated to the MM III). They consist of an inverted V-shape crossed by two oblique (but nearly horizontal) strokes on each 'arm'. Similarly, CM 38 is normally an inverted V-shape with two oblique strokes or two dots to each of its sides. It is unclear whether the third stroke on the left side of CM0 19 is part of the sign or accidental, but in any case this does not seem enough to divorce it from its comparanda.

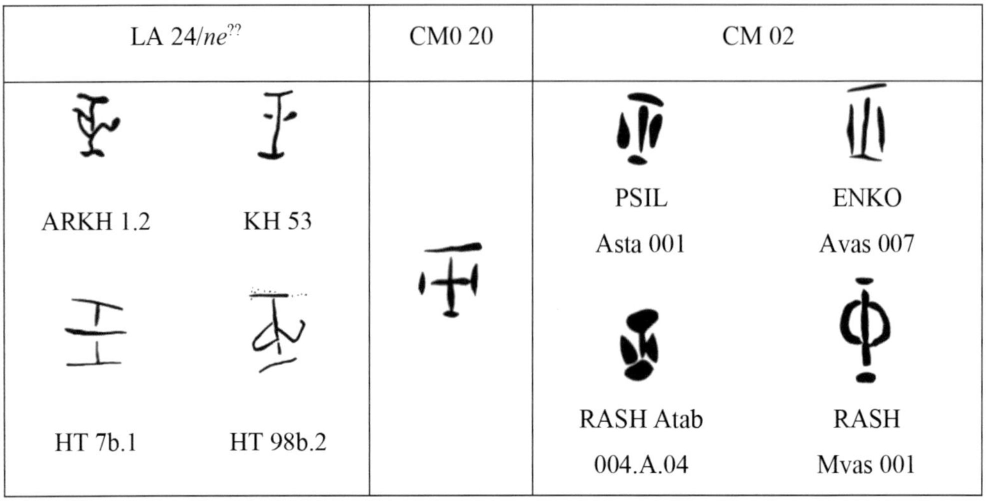

*Fig. 8.29: Comparison between LA 24/*ne??*, CM0 20, and CM 02.*

CM0 20 (Figure 8.29) bears some resemblance to LA 24/*ne*?? and CM 02. However, the three forms differ from one another as per the tips of their horizontal strokes ('arms'). LA 24 shows significant variation, as it ranges from specimens fairly pictorial, resembling a handled pitcher, to variants much more schematic. CM0 20 possibly derives from a Minoan variant somewhere in the middle of this spectrum, since its two 'arms' end with short vertical strokes at their tips, i.e. they are T-shaped. On the other hand, it might well be the antecedant of CM 02, but if this is so then the 'arms' were simplified to lateral vertical strokes disconnected from the central vertical line in Cypro-Minoan. If these comparisons are correct, then CM0 20 is as an intermediate form.

CM0 21 (Figure 8.30) closely matches LA 28/*i* and CM 104. LA 28 normally looks like an open hand, but some variants have two vertical strokes instead of just one in the inferior part. The latter would appear to be the antecedents of CM0 21 and CM 104.

It is now time to take stock. Seventeen or eighteen out of twenty or twenty-one signs of ENKO Atab 001 (depending on the interpretation of CM0 10 and 11) can be described as intermediate forms, as they either have exact or near-exact matches in both Linear A and Cypro-Minoan, or shapes that diverge slightly from both, but could be interpreted as the early Cypro-Minoan steps towards the later forms. This larger group is important on its own: irrespective of the affiliation of ENKO Atab 001, it reflects a very close relationship between Linear A and Cypro-Minoan. As regards the remaining three signs, one has a counterpart in Cypro-Minoan only, one has parallels in Linear A only, and one does not have obvious parallels in either (Figure 8.31).

The intermediate forms are evidently ambiguous, while the form with a counterpart only in Linear A (CM0 17) and the form without parallels (CM0 05) do not prove that the script of ENKO Atab 001 is not Cypro-Minoan, as implied by Olivier's interpretation. To the best of my knowledge, no long-lived writing system has ever had a stable and

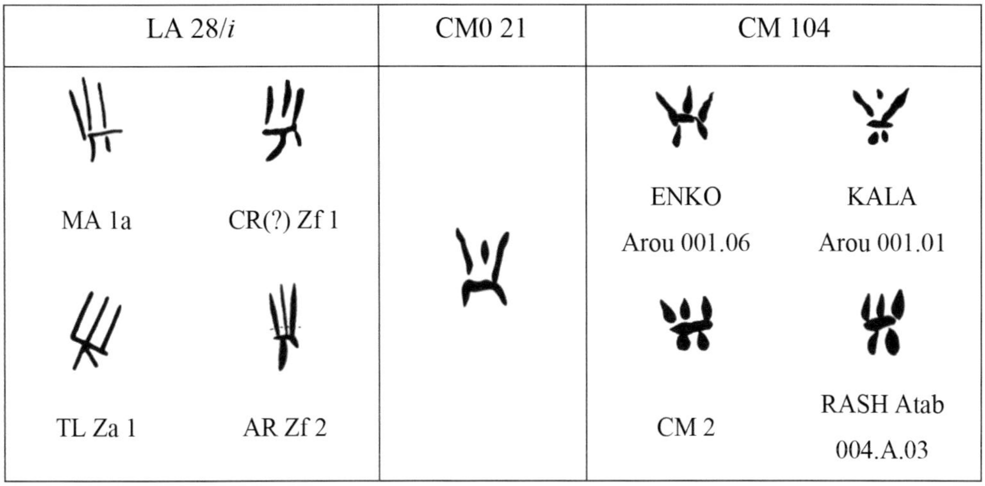

Fig. 8.30: Comparison between LA 28/i, CM0 21, and CM 104.

Types of form in terms of comparanda	*Amount*
Intermediate	17 (18)
Cypro-Minoan counterpart only	1
Linear A counterpart only	1
Without obvious parallels	1
Total	20 (21)

Fig. 8.31. Assessment of ENKO Atab 001 sign forms in comparative terms.

monolithic history: signs can be dropped, modified or added during the lifetime of a script, without the system ceasing to be the same. In addition, we must keep in mind the limitations of the Cypro Minoan corpus: later counterparts of CM0 05 and CM0 17 may be lacking only because of accidents of preservation. It is much more telling that the tablet uses CM0 08 (), whose shape matches CM 69 (). Even if this sign were ultimately derived from LA 57/*ja* (), its form is already fully Cypriot. To sum up, the script of ENKO Atab 001 is closely related to Linear A, but contains a sign that is characteristic (we might say 'diagnostic') of Cypro-Minoan and had a continuation in it. In light of the current evidence, it cannot be considered a 'dead-end'.

From a cautionary standpoint, ENKO Atab 001 neither demonstrates nor impedes the simplest scenario: that Linear A is the direct ancestor of Cypro-Minoan and the tablet represents just a brief, isolated snapshot of the earliest stages of the Bronze Age Cypriot script. I refer to this as the 'simplest scenario' because it does not require theorizing extra writing systems that are otherwise unattested. On the contrary, the opposing view – that it employs a distinct system, not Linear A anymore, but not Cypro-Minoan proper either – remains possible, but quite dangerous when more texts analogous to ENKO Atab 001 are lacking. As a consequence, I hope this survey demonstrates that, as long as we remain cautious about the results, we are justified in comparing Cypro-Minoan to Linear A.

4. Example of script comparison: the 'liquid' series

With the above in mind, the purpose of this section is to illustrate how a comparative-palaeographical approach that includes Linear A and Cypro-Greek can be used in investigating Cypro-Minoan sign values.[23] The case selected is that of signs suspected of being part of two distinct Cypro-Minoan 'liquid' series: CM 05 (+), 09 ( ), 24 (,), 33 ( ), 28 ( ), 87 ( ), 75 ( ) and 97 ( ). I wish to emphasize that the majority of the *hypothetical* sign values that will be proposed as a result of this example have previously been suggested by other scholars, as will become apparent below. Beyond the hypotheses defended here, my aim is to argue that the methodology outlined is valid.

Let us start with the comparative evidence for three straightforward developments. We have seen above that LA 60/*ra*? > CM 87 (Figure 8.9), but CM 87 is also the model for CGk *la* (Figure 8.32). Likewise: LA 60/*ri* > CM 09 > CGk *li* (Figure 8.33), and LA 02/*ro*? > CM 05 > CGk *lo* (see Figures 8.14 and 8.34).

These three developments imply strongly that LA *r*, whose underlying sound is uncertain (see below), was the basis for a liquid series in Cypro-Minoan, which in turn was the source for CGk *l*.

Beyond the wide recognition that CM 24 is the formal prototype of Paphian CGk *le* (Figures 8.35 and 8.40), which occurs already in the Opheltas' spit (PPAP Mins 001 = ##170), in the study of ENKO Atab 001 above I proposed as a working hypothesis that LA 27/*re*?? > CM 24 (see Figures 8.19 and 8.20). The three developments that point to LA *r* > CM > CGk *l* make it less difficult to accept the evolution of LA 27/*re*?? > CM 24 > CGk *le*. We would, in this case, have four Cypro-Minoan signs with a similar trajectory, one in which they were part of the same series. While there is no indisputable indication that Cypro-Minoan had a five-vowel grid like Linear B and Cypro-Greek, we may investigate the possibility that this hypothetical series had a fifth syllabogram. Again, hand in hand with the proposal that LA 27/*re*?? > CM 24, I hypothesized that LA 26/*ru*?? > CM 28 (Figures 8.18 and 8.20).[24] CM 28 ( ) has no obvious continuation in Cypro-Greek, but it is not wholly inconceivable that CGk *lu* ( ) derived from it, even if we need to assume a palaeographical change to its lower portion. Notice that CM 23/*ti*?? ( ) > CGk *ti* ( ), so the shape may have been intentionally modified to in early Cypro-Greek to avoid ambiguity.

For the sake of argument, let us consider these two more tentative proposals alongside the three more straightforward ones above. One of the peculiarities of

[23] For Cypro-Greek, I use the earliest examples available to me of each sign and cite the inscriptions mainly according to Egetmeyer (2010a). The drawings given (Figures 8.32–8) are mine and based on the published photographs, except when photographic material was not at hand, in which case I reproduce the illustrations provided in the respective publications.

[24] Notice that the developments hypothesized for these signs can hold even if the interpretation of forms CM0 10 and 11 as distinct graphemes (see section 3.2) is incorrect.

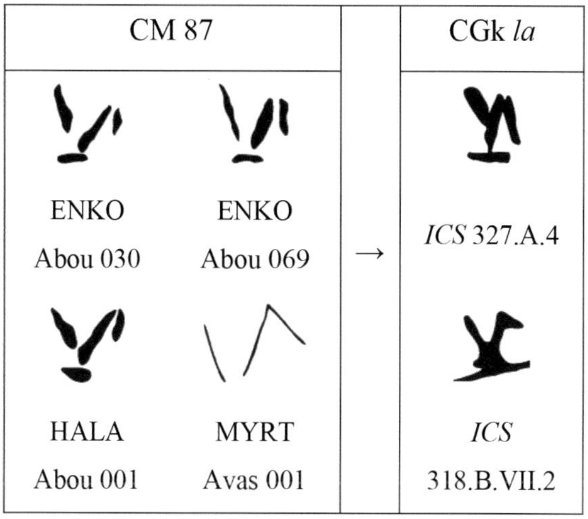

Fig. 8.32: Comparison between CM 87 and CGk la.

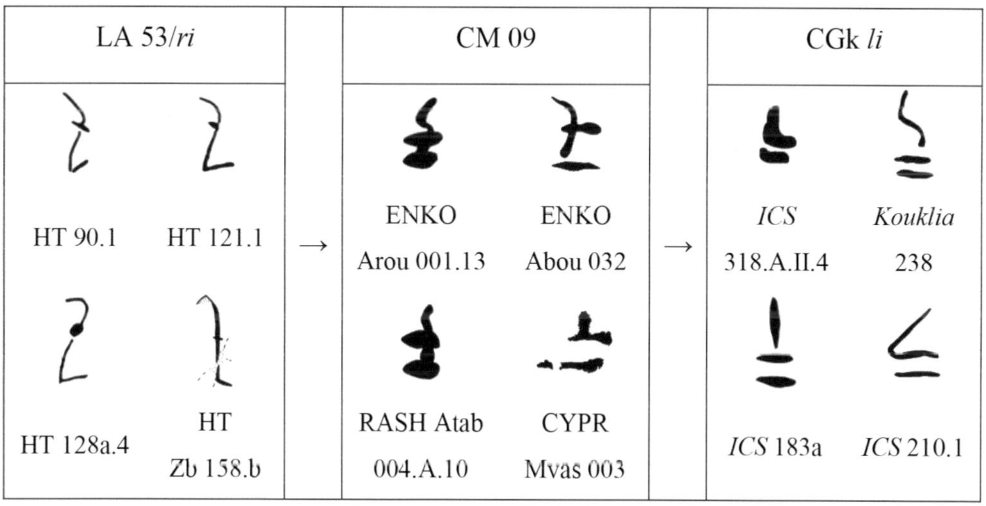

*Fig. 8.33: Comparison between LA 53/*ri*, CM 09, and CGk* li.

Linear B is its use of a single syllabographic series, transliterated *r* by convention, for denoting the phonemes /l/ and /r/. This situation, unideal from the Greek point of view, appears to be inherited from Linear A, but we do not know exactly what type of sound(s) *r* represented in the Minoan script, or whether it actually transcribed more than one phoneme, as in Linear B. Cypro-Greek presents different circumstances, this time ideal from a Greek perspective: it has separate liquid series, *l* for /l/ and *r* for /r/. This suggests that at some point in the evolution from Linear A to Cypro-Greek there was a structural modification. Evidence indicates that this

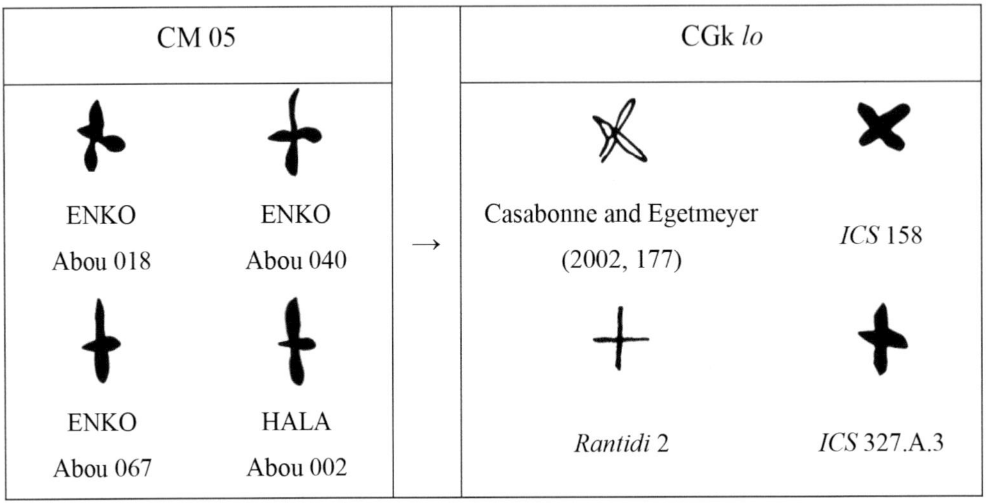

Fig. 8.34: Comparison between CM 05 and CGk lo.

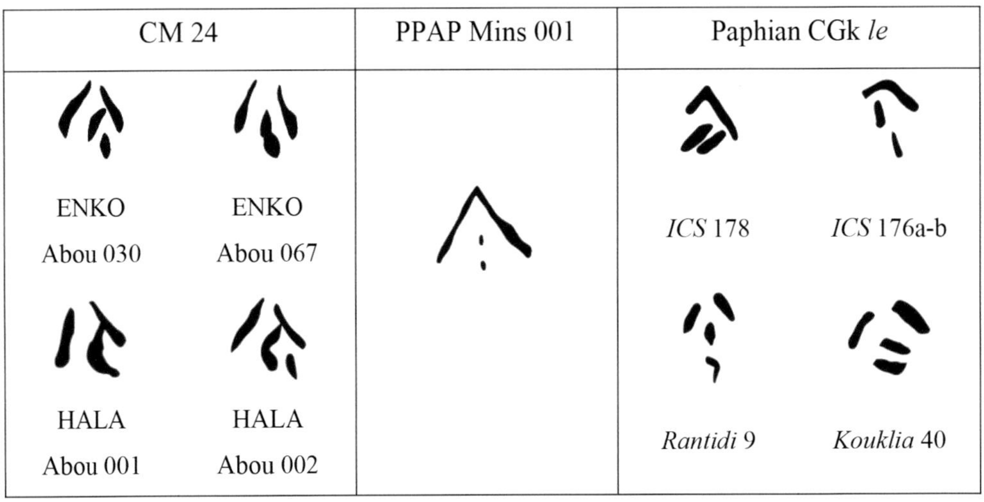

Fig. 8.35: Comparison between CM 24 and Paphian CGk le.

took place in Cypro-Minoan. CGk *ra*, *re*, and *ro* have obvious formal predecessors in Cypro-Minoan: CM 75 > CGk *ra*, CM 33 > CGk *re* and CM 97 > CGk *ro* (Figures 8.36[25],

[25] The development CM 75 > CGk *ra* features a change from a four-stroke quadrangular shape to a three-stroke subtriangular shape on the top of a horizontal line. This makes sense if we assume some cursivisation in late Cypro-Minoan, early Cypro-Greek, or both, especially if in the period between ca. 1100 and 700 BC writing was predominantly done with ink, on perishable materials. Cf. perhaps a *painted* potmark from Erimi-*Kafkalla* (Hirschfeld 2012, 291 and 298, fig. 5), which could correspond to CM 75 but is formally reminiscent of CGk *ra*.

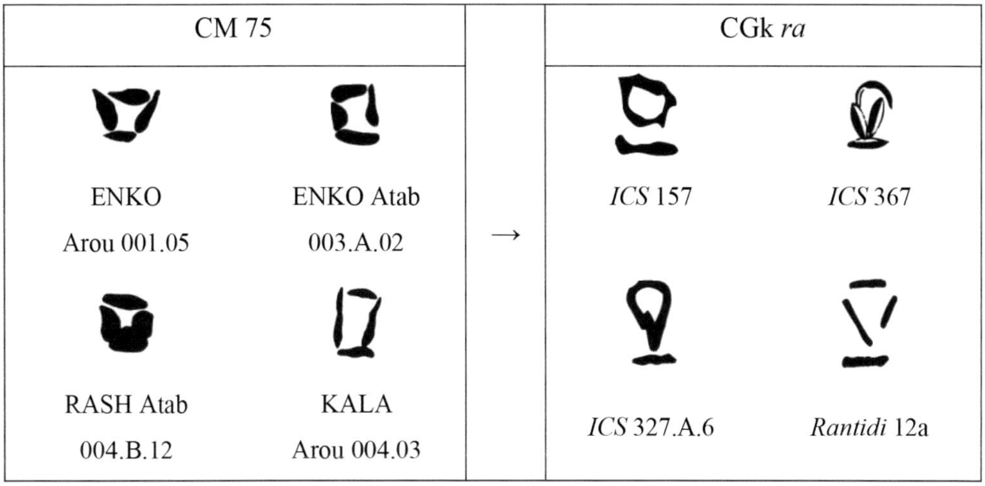

Fig. 8.36: Comparison between CM 75 and CGk ra.

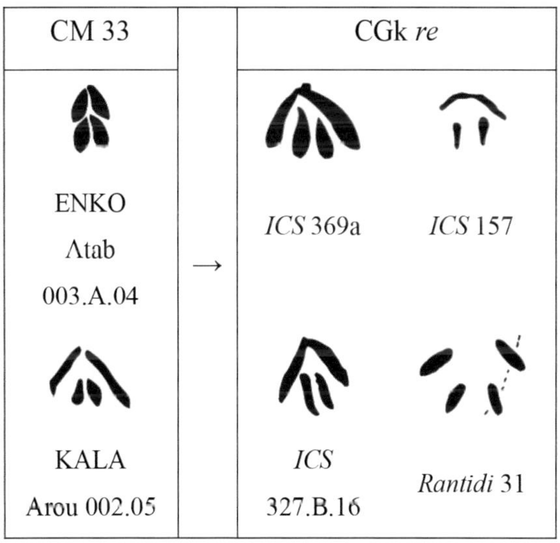

Fig. 8.37: Comparison between CM 33 and CGk re.

8.37, 8.38[26]), but no antecedents whatsoever in Linear A, thus hinting strongly at a Cypro-Minoan innovation.

[26] Drawings not by the author: ENKO Avas 002 (##109): from É. Masson (1979, 560, fig. 2, apud *HoChyMin*, 176); *ICS* 158: from *ICS*^{2}, fig. 43. The sign from PPAP Mins 003 (##172), dated to the Cypro-Geometric I (1050–950 BCE), is here included as an intermediate form. However, this inscription presents problems of classification because, as Olivier duly notes (*HoChyMin*, 245), it is doubtful as writing proper. Yet its status as Cypro-Minoan would be debatable even if it were *bona fide* because it comes from the same tomb as PPAP Mins 001, which I agree is Cypro-Greek (see Duhoux 2012b).

CM 97		PPAP Mins 003	CGk *ro*	
 ENKO Abou 048	 CYPR Mvas 002		 *ICS* 18c	 *ICS* 176a-b
 KITI Avas 001	 KITI Ipla 001*v*		 *ICS* 158	 *Rantidi* 30

Fig. 8.38: Comparison between CM 97 and CGk ro.

Conversely, the two variants of CGk *ri* (Paphian ᛘ and 'Common' ⋎) and CGk *ru* (›‹) have no straightforward formal matches even in Cypro-Minoan. The hapax CM 83 (Ɣ), suggested by É. Masson (1987, 372) as the model for Paphian CGk *ri*, is not promising because it is more likely a variant of another sign (*HoChyMin*, 99). This does not necessarily mean that CGk *ri* and *ru* lack predecessors in Cypro-Minoan, only that we cannot detect them easily relying on form alone. Still, the absence of a Cypro-Minoan precursor for CGk *ru* may be real, possibly to be compared with the lack of Bronze Age prototypes for CGk *nu* (ʔ¦) and *tu* (ㅠ); the latter rather appear to be innovations in the Cypro-Greek syllabary, perhaps based on the shapes of CGk *no* (ʔᒋ) and *to* (ㅈ, ⊧), respectively.[27]

A clear picture emerges from this survey (see Figure 8.39). We do not know what type of liquid(s) LA *r* transcribed, namely whether it was a *lateral*, a *rhotic*,[28] or both, but its ultimate fate in Cyprus was to be used for Greek /l/. Conversely, a set of Cypro-Minoan signs with no Aegean background was recycled in Cypro-Greek, as a second liquid series, to transcribe /r/. This strongly implies that LA *r* was *maintained* or

[27] We find the sign ʔ¦ in PPAP Pblo 001 (##171), but this occurrence is in line with the hypothesis that the syllabic inscriptions found in Tomb 49 of Palaepaphos-*Skales*, including the latter and the Opheltas' spit (for which see Duhoux 2012b), are written already in the Cypriot Greek syllabary and not Cypro-Minoan.

[28] *Lateral*: a type of sound 'in which the tongue is contracted in such a way as to narrow its profile from side to side so that a greater volume of air flows around one or both sides than over the center of the tongue' (following the definition of Ladefoged and Maddieson 1996, 182). The most common phoneme of this type is the voiced lateral approximant [l]. *Rhotic* or 'r-sound': a type of sound 'in which there is a single or repeated brief contact between the tongue and a point on the upper surface of the vocal tract, i.e. principally apical trills, taps and flaps' (*ibid.*), i.e. [r], [ɾ], etc. Other definitions of rhotics may include the uvular trill [ʀ].

Linear A		Cypro-Minoan			Cypro-Greek	
Sign	Value	No.	Sign	Value	Sign	Value
	ra	87		*la*$^{??}$		*la*
	re	24		*le*$^{??}$	(P)	*le*
	ri	09		*li*$^{??}$		*li*
+	*ro*	05	+	*lo*$^{??}$	+	*lo*
	ru	28		*lu*$^{??}$		*lu*
—	—	75		*ra*$^{??}$		*ra*
—	—	33		*re*$^{??}$		*re*
—	—	?	?	?	(P) (C)	*ri*
		97		*ro*$^{??}$		*ro*
—	—	?	?	?		*ru*

Fig. 8.39: Summary of the correspondences proposed for the liquid series of Linear A, Cypro-Minoan and Cypro-Greek (P = Paphian; C = Common).

specialised (depending on its value) as *l*$^{??}$ in Cypro-Minoan, while a new series, which we can transliterate tentatively as *r*$^{??}$,[29] was introduced for distinguishing one or more rhotic sounds.[30] This explanation accounts for all facts with the least assumptions.

Figure 8.40 shows the values that previous authors assigned more or less tentatively to the signs examined here, and compares them with the results offered here. For the major part, these are not novel. Similar readings were first offered by Saporetti (1976, fig. 41), leading to one of the earliest suggestions of distinct CM *l* and *r* series,[31] while Nahm (1981) hypothesised the same phonetic values proposed here in all cases

[29] For the transliterations of Cypro-Minoan signs proposed here I employ a system of question marks representing different degrees of safety: – Two question marks (*ra*$^{??}$): value suggested by one method (comparative or internal); – One question mark (*ra*$^{?}$): value suggested by two methods (comparative and internal); – No question mark (*ra*): value suggested by two methods and validated by readings of sequences corroborated by external sources i.e. a fully deciphered value.

[30] It is worthwhile noting in passing that ENKO Atab 001 contains four signs suspected of being inherited from LA *r* and counterparts to CM *l*$^{??}$ (CM 01 > CM 87/*la*$^{??}$, CM0 07 > CM 05/*lo*$^{??}$, CM0 10 > CM 28/*lu*$^{??}$ and CM0 11 > CM 24/*le*$^{??}$), but none comparable to CM 33/*re*$^{?}$, CM 75/*ra*$^{?}$, CM 96/*ri*$^{?}$ or CM 97/*ro*$^{?}$. Even considering the fragmentary state of the text and the hypothetic nature of the readings, is this a coincidence or a symptom that a new CM *r*$^{??}$ series had not yet been introduced?

[31] Less clearly and involving different signs, É. Masson (1974, 44) had already attempted a grid with distinct *l* and *r* series.

		É. Masson (1973, fig. 8)	Saporetti (1976, fig. 41)	Nahm (1981)	É. Masson (1987)	Duhoux (2009b, 42, fn. 15)	Olivier (2013, 8)	Facchetti *et al.* (2013, 65)	Steele (2013b, 55-60)	Author
87		*tu*	*la*	*la*	*la*	-	*r/la*	*la*	-	*la*$^{??}$
24		-	-	*le*	*le*	*le*$^{??}$	-	-	-	*le*$^{??}$
09		*li(e)*	*li*	*li*	*li*	-	-	*li*	-	*li*$^{??}$
05		-	*lo*	*lo*	*lo*	*l/ro*$^{?}$	*r/lo*	*lo*	*l/ro*$^{?}$	*lo*$^{??}$
28		*nu*	*ni*	*ru*	*nu*	-	-	-	-	*lu*$^{??}$
75		*r*V	*ra*	*ra*	*re*	-	-	*ra*	-	*ra*$^{??}$
33		-	*re*	*re*	*re*	*re*$^{??}$	-	*re*	-	*re*$^{??}$
97		-	*ro*	*ro*	*ri/ro*	-	-	*ro*	-	*ro*$^{??}$

Fig. 8.40: Hypothetical values assigned to signs discussed in §4 by previous scholarship (1973–2013) vis-à-vis *the author's suggestions.*

except that of sign CM 28.[32] What is new is the corroboration of these proposals by broader palaeographical evidence.

As mentioned in section 1, I advocate a step-by-step methodology where script comparison functions as one of two independent methods, the other being the internal one, to suggest hypothetical sign values to be considered validated only if in a third stage they produce readings that can be confirmed by external evidence. It would be beyond the scope of this contribution to extend the example discussed here to these additional procedures, but it is worthwhile mentioning in passing that É. Masson (1970, 93–4, fig. 15; 1978, fig. 9) and Saporetti (1976, 99) have long ago presented *internal* evidence from CM 2 supporting the notion that signs CM 33, 75 and 97, as well as 96 (), possess the same consonantal value.

5. Palaeography meets comparison

The above discussion adds to earlier pleas for multidimensional approaches to the sign values of Cypro-Minoan, but calls for and puts weight on palaeography as

[32] At least regarding the signs in question, Faucounau (1980, 379 and 382, 1994, 94–6) makes suggestions very similar to those of Saporetti (1976). However, among other incongruences he makes the hazardous proposal that some syllabograms had different values in different subcorpora.

groundwork for investigating this group of inscriptions. So far, the rule in the field has been the appeal to single, or a few, normalised sign shapes, which are suitable for in-text explications, but hazardous if used as the building blocks of interpretations of Cypro-Minoan and its relations. Conversely, a deeper and broader examination of sign shapes shows that (1) some signs of Cypro-Minoan have been prematurely individualised (see above and Valério 2013); (2) ENKO Atab 001 (*terminus ante quem* 1525–1425 BC) features more and closer formal counterparts to Linear A signs than most authors have recognised, but as many as seen by Palaima (1989); and (3) evident LA-CM-CGk cognates on the formal and phonetic level have more recently been discounted (Figure 8.40) without motive. Thus, in the framework of the methodology endorsed, the first task that should concern us is the revision of the Cypro-Minoan signary with the goal of addressing problematic grapheme individualisations; only afterwards can we embark on the sort of comparative investigation advocated here.

To illustrate the potential of palaeographically-grounded script comparison as a method to investigate Cypro-Minoan sign values, I consciously chose a set of signs that are unproblematic as regards their individualisation and which were widely interpreted in the 1970s and 1980s as members of distinct CM $l^{??}$ and $r^{??}$ series, but whose external correspondences and tentative values have largely been dismissed in more recent scholarship as overly premature. The approach adopted here linked the selected signs to counterparts in Linear A and Cypro-Greek and did so by looking systematically at various actual instances of the characters of the three scripts as they appear on the inscriptions. The conclusion is that palaeography adds depth to previous superficial comparisons and, when value is considered alongside shape, legitimates some of the phonetic values they suggested for Cypro-Minoan signs of $l^{??}$ and $r^{??}$ series (especially Nahm 1981) as working hypotheses or allows for new propositions. Their validity is to be proven and should not be taken for granted, but whichever the exact readings of Cypro-Minoan signs, the illustrative comparisons in section 4 (discounting the admittedly more tentative cases of LA 27 > CM 24 and LA 26 > CM 28 > CGk *lu*) showcase compelling shape/value connections with syllabograms of Linear A and Cypro-Greek. That this is the general situation within a sample of eight signs, along with the close affinities between Linear A and Cypro Minoan signs revealed as a by-product of the analysis of ENKO Atab 001, constitute reasonable evidence to assume that a comparative-palaeographical study of the entire Cypro-Minoan corpus would establish well beyond a dozen clear LA-CM-CGk cognates, therefore casting serious doubt on the view of Cypro-Minoan as a disruptive adaptation, if not a parallel branch (Sherratt 2013, 98), of Aegean writing.

Chapter 9

Is there anything like a Cypro-Minoan 3 script?

Yves Duhoux

1. Introduction

A writing system may be characterised by several features. For example:

- Signs: number of the different signs; forms; variability; value of each sign (phonetic, if phonogram; semantic, if ideogram).[1]
- Typology: is the script's main constituent ideographic or phonetic? Are the phonograms alphabetic, syllabic, or alphabeto-syllabic? If syllabic, what kind of syllables do the syllabograms render: open, closed or both?
- Graphic features: direction(s) of writing; layout of the texts; reading aids; characteristics of handwritings.
- Writing tools.
- Inscribed media: materials; variety of objects.
- Contextual data: geographical; archaeological; historical; sociological.
- Language(s) rendered.
- Etc.

Not all these criteria are useful for characterising an undeciphered script. For instance, we should never consider the language(s) possibly rendered by such a writing. The reasons are simple. First, if the script is really undeciphered, we completely ignore the language(s) that it renders. Second, there is no necessary link between any language and any writing system. For instance, the so-called 'Classical

[1] I call 'ideogram' any sign having an intrinsic meaning (for instance, in English script, the signs *1* or the comma [,], which express in themselves respectively the 'unit one' or 'a separation of parts in a sentence or items in a list'). I conventionally consider that 'ideogram' and 'logogram' are synonymous. A 'phonogram' has no intrinsic meaning but expresses a meaningless sound. Phonograms may render either phonemes (or the like; these signs are called 'letters', like the English signs *b* or *y*) or syllables (these signs are called 'syllabograms', like the 'Classical Cyprus Syllabary' signs ⚹ and ☿, that we transliterate respectively as *e* and *ro*).

Cyprus Syllabary'[2] (below: 'CCS') is used to write both Greek (Cypriot) and a non-Greek language, conventionally called Eteocypriot. Conversely, a single language may be recorded in different scripts. Again in Cyprus, Cypriot Greek appears both in 'CCS' and in Greek alphabet. Let us then exclude any linguistic consideration when we attempt to identify an undeciphered writing.[3]

I shall try here to see if the undeciphered script generally called Cypro-Minoan 3 (below: CM 3) has a real specificity and how it could be designated. These questions are nowadays in doubt: there is no agreement about the inscriptions that could be labelled as CM 3, nor about the very existence of this writing system (section 2).

Since this paper will concentrate on the CM 3 script itself and more specifically on its signs, almost no attention will be paid to the data provided by the contexts or the contents of the inscriptions: I believe that it is appropriate to devote distinct studies to these important questions.

2. Characteristics of the CM 3 texts

There are a few characteristics of the CM 3 texts that are unquestionable.

(a) Most of them undoubtedly belong to the Cypro-Minoan class (below: CM).
(b) They offer a geographic unity. Indeed, they were discovered in the modern Syria, and more precisely in or near the ancient town of Ugarit (at present Ras Shamra). Nine of the edited texts labelled as CM 3 come from Ugarit itself; one cylinder seal is said to come from Lattakia, very near Ugarit.
(c) When a date is available, they belong to the period between the last quarter of the 14th and the 12th centuries (ca. 1320–1190 and ca. 1320–1100).[4]
(d) Their script is still undeciphered despite several unsuccessful attempts.

Here is the list of the currently published texts.[5] In the count of their signs, the obviously ideographic ones (dividers, etc.) have been conventionally excluded as well as the reconstructed or unidentified signs.

[2] I conventionally adopt this denomination, though it is not the best one – I prefer the admittedly complicated 'non-Cypro-Minoan Cypriot syllabary' – see Duhoux (2013, 47).

[3] Of course, the language is crucial whenever one attempts to decipher an undeciphered script.

[4] I adopt the absolute chronology of Åström and Åström reproduced by Ferrara (*CM* I, 8).

[5] See Olivier (*HoChyMin* 385–409); Ferrara (*CM* II, 108–13), whose find-places I reproduce. The text (9) has been published by Valério (2014b, 117–18, 122); its context and chronology are not reported. Ferrara (*CM* II, 126) gives the description (but not the text) of an inscription of five signs on a pottery-pithos rim. The edition of Olivier (*HoChyMin*) provides no photographs, excepted that of text (1). Its facsimiles are almost always those of E. Masson (1974). Ferrara (*CM* II, 254–64, pls xxxv–xlv) gives excellent black-and-white photographs of every published item, new facsimiles (made by Dimitris Tsouris), plus colour pictures of texts (3)–(7). Some of her photographs and facsimiles are not satisfactory, however. Text (3): the line A.1 is incomplete; the photographs and facsimile of side B are upside down. Text (6): the extreme right of the lines A.9-11 is incomplete; most of the line B.1 is incomplete – see Ferrara (*CM* II, 255–6, pls xxxvi–xxxvii; 258–9, pl. xli; correct also her caption 214, bottom of p. 257: RS 17.06 should become RS19.02).

(1) = ## 210; RASH Aéti 001 (RS 94.2328): clay label (2 non-obviously-ideographic signs); Ugarit, residence of Urtenu in the filling of a tomb
(2) = ## 211; RASH Aéti 002 (RS 99.2014): clay label (3 non-obviously-ideographic signs); Ugarit, residence of Urtenu
(3) = ## 212; RASH Atab 001 (RS 17.06): clay tablet (58 non-obviously-ideographic signs); Ugarit, residence of Rasapabu
(4) = ## 213; RASH Atab 002 (RS 19.01): clay tablet (4 non-obviously-ideographic signs); Ugarit, residence of Yabninu, room 203
(5) = ## 214; RASH Atab 003 (RS 19.02): clay tablet (20 non-obviously-ideographic signs); Ugarit, residence of Yabninu, room 203
(6) = ## 215; RASH Atab 004 (RS 20.25): clay tablet (161 non-obviously-ideographic signs); Ugarit, residence of Rapanu
(7) = ## 216; RASH Mvas 001 (RS 3.389): silver bowl (3 non-obviously-ideographic signs); Ugarit, building close to the Library of the High Priest
(8) = ## 217; SYRI Psce 001 (YaleMusUniv 358): hematite cylinder seal (4 non-obviously-ideographic signs); Lattakia (?)
(9) = ## 251; RASH Avas 002 (RS 23.119): handle of a clay vessel (2 non-obviously-ideographic signs); Ugarit.

Total of the non-obviously-ideographic signs of this corpus: 257.

It is Olivier Masson who submitted that a specific CM script was used in (3), the first Cypro-Minoan tablet unearthed in Ugarit in 1953.[6] In the next years, CM in Ugarit became an intricate question, however. After the discovery of several new texts, O. Masson described them in 1968 as constituting a small group of different CM-like scripts.[7] In 1969, he added that each of them was relatively independent but that at least the script of tablet (6) was closely linked to that of (3).[8] A few years later, Olivier Masson's wife Emilia offered a survey of almost the whole corpus[9] and christened it

[6] O. Masson (1955, 178) stated that 'il est clair que l'on doit admettre désormais l'existence d'un nouveau chypro-minoen, celui de Ras Shamra, pour le XIVe ou le XIIIe siècles'. O. Masson (1956, 245) concluded that 'en raison des divergences nombreuses qui existent entre le répertoire des signes de notre tablette [i.e. my (3): YD] et les autres syllabaires chypro-minoens, il semble nécessaire d'admettre l'existence d'un syllabaire inédit, révélé en partie par la tablette de Ras Shamra [i.e. my (3): YD] : je proposerai de le nommer "chypro-minoen d'Ugarit"'.

[7] 'Un petit groupe d'écritures d'aspect chypro-minoen': O. Masson (1968a, 422).

[8] 'Chaque écriture est relativement indépendante ... L'écriture de la nouvelle tablette, RS 1956 [i.e. my (6): YD], certainement apparentée à celle de RS 1953 [i.e. my (3): YD] – et peut-être plus encore à celle des fragments RS 1955, (I) et (II) [i.e. my (5) and (4): YD], pour lesquels la comparaison est malaisée – apparaît donc comme une variété de l'écriture que j'ai proposé de nommer "chypro-minoen d'Ugarit"': O. Masson (1969, 390, 392).

[9] E. Masson (1974). She studied all the texts available in 1974, but the two clay labels (1) and (2).

as CM 3,[10] with the exception of the tablets (4) and (5) that she considered as not written in CM 3 but in CM 1.[11]

J.-P. Olivier (2013, 11, 15) seemed tempted to endorse this exclusion, though he believed that to 'distinguish between CM 1 and CM 3 on the Syrian coast ... turns out to be almost impossible'. He further classified as CM 3 *stricto sensu* the tablets (3) and (6), and expressed some doubts about the CM 3 identification of the labels (1) and (2), the silver bowl (7) and the cylinder seal (8).

Philippa Steele (2013a, 40–1) considered that: (a) the two labels (1) and (2) are nearer to the Cypro-Minoan script of Cyprus than to the other examples of Cypro-Minoan found in Ugarit; (b) the silver bowl (7) is alien to Cypro-Minoan; (c) the cylinder-seal (8) 'is difficult to judge'; (d) all the tablets 'appear to belong to the same writing tradition'. Valério (2014b, 122) believes that the text (9) has 'nothing ... that makes its two signs different from their Cypriot counterparts' and adds that 'CM 3 as it is conceived today is an artificial construct'.

This last view had been anticipated by Palaima (1989) and Ferrara (*CM* I-II). Tom Palaima (1989) questioned the very existence of an autonomous CM 3. He accepted E. Masson's view about the CM 1 character of the tablets (4) and (5), but added that the same could be true for: the clay tablets (3) and (6); the silver bowl (7); the cylinder seal (8). Palaima also suggested that CM 2 would simply be a form of CM 1. He concluded that the current classification of Cypro-Minoan should be completely reassessed. This is what Silvia Ferrara (*CM* I-II) has recently tried to do, with the conclusion that we should abandon the current division of the Cypro-Minoan script family in several groups and recognize that there exists only one unique CM writing.

3. The existence and identity of CM 3

What, then, about the very existence and identity of CM 3, if there is any? It is true that none of its published inscriptions has escaped criticism. We should therefore be prepared to reorganise and even suppress the whole CM 3 category. I will provisionally do so in this paper. I shall tentatively suppose that the CM 3 script does not exist at all and that it should be included in the other CM writing(s). Of course, this is only a hypothesis and we must test it. The only possible way is to start from the texts mentioned above. This is what I shall do, but with a severe limitation.

[10] First in E. Masson (1973); already alluded to in E. Masson (1972, 99), but without any specific name, then fully in E. Masson (1974).

[11] E. Masson (1974, 20–23); E. Masson (1973, 35) observed 'une très nette ressemblance entre l'écriture des deux fragments trouvés en 1955 [i.e. my (4) and (5): YD] dans les archives du Petit Palais et le CM I. Les mêmes groupes de signes qui figurent sur ces pièces et aussi sur certaines inscriptions de Chypre rédigées en CM 1 semblent indiquer la présence ici d'une seule et même langue'.

I will restrict myself to only two inscriptions, the tablets (3)[12] and (6)[13] – see section 4 for their transnumerated texts. Both have a conspicuous distinctive appearance. Palaima (1989, 159–60) recognises 'the Near Eastern aspect of the tablet [my (3): YD] itself', and tells us that (6) exhibits 'certain features of text formatting ... that are not attested in the formal CM 1 and CM 2 tablets'. Ferrara is persuaded that 'at least' the tablets (3) and (6) 'were not imported from Cyprus, but were created and written *in situ* at Ugarit. This conclusion is drawn from the epigraphy of the tablets (size and format), their contextual associations, and possible subject matters'.[14] These quotations come from two champions of the inexistence of the CM 3 writing. They show that the texts (3) and (6) have an unquestionable Ugaritic flavour and a real specificity, whatever label we could assign to their script. They will constitute what I shall call our 'Ugaritic CM sample'.[15]

These two inscriptions exhibit 44 different non-obviously-ideographic signs (see section 6.3, Table 9.2) totalling 219 occurrences, plus two different evident ideograms.[16] They provide to date the largest CM texts found in Ugarit. Both were discovered in a high-ranking quarter, in the residence of two prominent officials.[17]

The tablet (3) was discovered in the residence of Rasapabu.[18] It is broken and has seven lines on each side – Emilia Masson estimated that there were nine or ten lines on each face. Five signs are written on the left edge of face B: they are interpreted as a colophon. This document is completely ruled and its 58 non-obviously-ideographic signs are written boustrophedon. It offers no repetition of any sequence of signs and gives the impression of a continuous text, though its real content is disputed.[19] Date: LC IIC (ca. 1320–1190).

The inscription (6) was found in the residence of Rapanu.[20] It is intact and is to date the only Cypro-Minoan tablet in this state. Its recto has 11 lines[21] and its verso 8. It is not ruled and its 161 non-obviously-ideographic signs are written rightwards. It exhibits no less than 11[22] examples of a sequence of two signs almost always written between dividers (*051-028*):[23] this is clearly a key constituent of the text. This inscription has also 19 examples of a supplementary special divider, almost always put at the

---

[12] I.e. ## 212; RASH Atab 001; RS 17.06.

[13] I.e. ## 215; RASH Atab 004; RS 20.25.

[14] Ferrara (*CM* I, 144). She considers also (p. 141) that (6) could have been written by one of the high Ugaritic government officials or one of his assistants.

[15] In Duhoux (2013, 38–40), I had studied all the CM 3 inscriptions as a whole.

[16] Two different dividers (65 occurrences in all).

[17] See Ferrara (*CM* I, 8 and 2, 109–12) for the absolute chronology and the archaeological data given below.

[18] See O. Masson (1956, 239–46) and E. Masson (1974, 24–9) for detailed descriptions and studies of the tablet (3).

[19] See Ferrara (*CM* I, 137–9), who excludes a letter, but is tempted by a list.

[20] See O. Masson (1969) and E. Masson (1974, 29–36) for detailed descriptions and studies of the tablet (6).

[21] Ferrara (*CM* II, 112) counts '12 lines'.

[22] Ferrara (*CM* I, 139, 259) counts 'nine' and 'ten' examples.

[23] See Olivier (*HoChyMin*) for the transnumeration of the CM signs.

end of a line – once (A.9), it comes after the first sequence of a line and just before a normal divider. It is quite likely a 'paragraph' symbol. The tablet (6) looks then like a list of at least 19 entries. Date: LC IIC–LC IIIA (ca. 1320-1100).

The two inscriptions of the 'Ugaritic CM sample' were obviously written by two different hands[24] and the colour of their clay is clearly dissimilar.[25] Their structure is not the same: (6) regularly exhibits the sequence *051-028* and frequently uses a likely 'paragraph' symbol, while (3) has none of these characteristics. They could be but are not necessarily strictly contemporaneous—about two centuries could theoretically separate them.

4. Transnumeration

Here is the transnumerated text of the 'Ugaritic CM sample':[26]

(3) = ## 212; RASH Atab 001; RS 17.06

104-028-092 044-002 005-006-037-102 023-098-023 104-036-⟦023⟧ 006-070 023-094-019 036-008-004 006-025 044-006-100-091 092-044 027[ ] •[ ] •-•[ ] 040 [ ] 036-040[ ] 006-009[ ]008[ ] 094-110-091-023 091-004-023 025-044-040 027[ ] 073-019 •-027-038[ ] 023-105-097 004-091

(6) = ## 215; RASH Atab 004; RS 20.25

102-025-087 051-028 055-009 102-023-051-028 102-074-082-051 104-058-006-009 102-002-100 055-025-051-040 102-004-004-096 051-028 004-071-100 104-071-006-023 051-028 038-105-023-058 051-028 038-035-100 103-035-082-051 051-028 025-051-009 037-004-100 104-009-071-100 037-071-100-040 004-008-100 051-028 104-009-004-055-096 102-002-071-100 051-028 092-028-095-100 019-087-073-096 023-025-006-100-040 021-082-075-051 104-009-055-009-070 051-028 019-091-073-023 102-025-087-051 051-028 055-070 038-001-004-082-009 102-075-051-055-082-021-009 102-074-075-051 027-069 055-070-•-006-096-037 073-092-100 051-028 055-070 082-058-055-009-070 092-011-096 006

5. Procedure

The aim of this research will be to test my basic assumption that the 'Ugaritic CM sample' script is the same as at least one of those used in the CM 1, 2 or 1 + 2 corpora. This will require several counts of the CM 1, CM 2 and the 'Ugaritic CM sample' non-obviously-ideographic signs – in fact, we will see later that all these signs are phonograms, and more precisely syllabograms (section 6.3). These calculations proved to be troublesome. For the CM 1 and CM 2 material, I planned to use the numbers of

---

[24] E. Masson (1974, 30, 34) observes apropos of (6) the 'ductus même de l'écriture, qui est très spécial et n'a guère de parallèle sur d'autres documents chypro-minoens'. She notes that this text 'a dû être rédigé par une « main » peu assurée, pas très familiarisée avec les écritures linéaires'.

[25] See the colour plates of Ferrara (*CM* II, xxxv–xxxvii, xli–xliii).

[26] After Olivier's (*HoChyMin* 387–92, 399–407) edition, but with the suppression of all the dividers and the lines' indication, plus a few corrections. The sequences *036-013-004* and *]013[* of (3) are read as *036-008-004* and *]008[* (on *008* and *013*, see Valério 2013, 113–17). Instead of *022* and *072* in (6), I read respectively *021* and *073*: *021-082-075-051*, *102-075-051-055-082-021-009* and *019-087-073-096*.

Ferrara (*CM* I-II), which is the largest work on the CM topic to date and offers several lists of frequencies. Unfortunately, these data proved unexpectedly to be sometimes incoherent and too frequently different from mine.[27] Even Olivier's book was not always reliable: his indexes (2007, 427–82) and his tables of the CM syllabograms (*HoChyMin* 413–16) need to be carefully checked and corrected. Hence I decided to use my personal counts in this paper. I have thus calculated the frequency of every identified CM 1 and CM 2 phonogram (even if deliberately erased by an ancient writer) as published in the edition of Olivier (*HoChyMin* 63–383). The five phonograms of the Opheltas bronze spit have been excluded, however, because I consider that they are not written in CM, but in 'CCS'– see Duhoux (2012b). All the calculations in the 'Ugaritic CM sample' have naturally also been made by me. Even so, I cannot claim that my numbers are always the right ones: such a goal must be postponed until the edition of a true corpus of the CM inscriptions.

I shall first discuss questions of method: procedure of comparison (section 6.1); the length and problems of the 'Ugaritic CM sample's (section 6.2); script's typology and main constituents (section 6.3). We will then concentrate on the writings themselves: number of different phonograms present in the CM 1, 2 or 1 + 2 collections, but absent in the 'Ugaritic CM sample' (section 7.1); importance of these signs (section 7.2); number of different phonograms of the 'Ugaritic CM sample' that are unknown in the CM 1, 2 or 1 + 2 corpora (section 7.3); importance of these signs (section 7.4); number of the different phonograms in the 'Ugaritic CM sample', the CM 1, 2 and 1 + 2 corpora (section 7.5); length of the CM signaries (section 7.6); conclusions (section 8).

The phonetic readings of the phonograms and the language(s) that they render will not be touched, since Cypro-Minoan is still undeciphered. Similarly, I shall leave aside all the features not directly linked to the signs themselves.

6. Questions of method

6.1. Differences between the corpora

How will we appreciate the differences, if any, between the scripts of the 'Ugaritic CM sample' and the CM 1, 2 or 1 + 2 corpora? The first and most natural way is certainly to follow one's own impression. Is there a contrast? If so, is it marked, or not? This proves to be difficult, however, among other things because the lengths of the CM collections are so dissimilar: 219 ('Ugaritic CM sample') : 1,079 (CM 1) : 1,369 (CM 2) : 2,448 (CM 1 + 2) non-obviously-ideographic signs.[28] Some kind of

[27] For example, here are the numbers for the CM 1 and CM 2 signs. CM 1: Ferrara counts 1,350 signs ('an approximate figure'), while the total of her 'entire CM 1 corpus' calculated by me amounts 740; CM 2: Ferrara counts 1,993 signs, while my total of her 'entire CM 2 corpus' is 1,277: Ferrara (*CM* I, 262, 288–92). My personal count of the CM 1 and CM 2 signs is respectively 1,079 and 1,369 (see section 6.1).
[28] For the length of CM 1 and CM 2, see Duhoux (2013, 27, 31). Reconstructed examples and unidentified ones have not been considered.

yardstick should be supplemented, but which one? I have chosen to compare the CM collections with two samples written in a securely deciphered syllabic script, the 'common' 'CCS'. Such a writing system was selected because the 'Ugaritic CM sample's script is a syllabary too, as we will see soon (section 6.3). Moreover, the scripts of the 'Ugaritic CM sample' and the 'CCS' share an important point: their signaries have a comparable length. Indeed, we do know that the 'CCS' signary has 55 syllabograms whereas the MacKay (1965) formula will establish that the 'Ugaritic CM sample' signary is likely ca. 57 signs long (section 7.6). These numbers are quite close.

The largest 'CCS' comparison sample is the famous syllabic Cypriot inscription of the 1st millennium, the long 'Idalion Bronze' (1,022 syllabograms; 51 different ones[29]). The second, a small composite text made of three inscriptions[30] (219 syllabograms; 42 different ones[31]). Both have exactly or approximately the same length as respectively the CM 1 corpus and the 'Ugaritic CM sample'. When compared one another, they will show how a large and a small collection written in the same script could behave. This picture will then suggest what could happen if the 'Ugaritic CM sample' and the CM 1, 2 or 1 + 2 corpora really shared the same writing.

Our 'CCS' comparison samples and CM collections represent different scripts.[32] Is it then not dangerous to use the former as a tool for appreciating the latter? It would be so if we compared them directly to each other. In fact, we will never do so. We shall consider only the *differences* between the scripts of the large and small samples within, on the one hand, our 'CCS' collections and, on the other hand, the CM ones. This procedure neutralizes most of the risks of bias because it does not concentrate on the collections themselves. Instead, it focuses on the consequences that their different sizes may have on several characteristics of their scripts.

Later on, all our examinations will be subjected to a test to check whether their results are different enough to be considered as statistically significant (section 8.2). This will ensure a more objective appreciation.

6.2. Size of the samples

With its 219 non obviously ideographic signs, our 'Ugaritic CM sample' is extremely short. Does such a small sample allow any study of its writing? In other words, is it representative of its script? Some experiments will help us to decide.

[29] Personal count of *ICS*, 236–7 – see also Egetmeyer (2010a, 2, 631–2). Here are the syllabograms used: *a, e, i, ja, ka, ke, ki, ko, ku, la, le, li, lo, lu, ma, me, mi, na, ne, ni, no, nu, o, pa, pe, pi, po, pu, ra, re, ri, ro, ru, sa, se, si, so, su, ta, te, ti, to, tu, u, wa, we, wi, wo, xe, za*[?], *zo*.

[30] (1) Akanthou, ca. 650–500; 160 syllabograms: *ICS* No. 327; Egetmeyer (2010a, 2, 575–7). (2) Chytroi, 4th century?; 38 syllabograms: *ICS* No. 234; Egetmeyer (2010a, 2, 596). (3) Dhenia, 4th century; the first 21 syllabograms; Egetmeyer (2010a, 2, 603–4).

[31] Syllabograms used in the 'CCS' small composite sample: *a, e, i, jo, ka, ke, ki, ko, ku, la, lo, ma, mi, mo, na, ne, nu, o, pa, pe, pi, po, ra, re, ri, ro, se, si, su, ta, te, ti, to, tu, u, wa, we, wi, wo, xe, za*[?], *zo*.

[32] And presumably languages.

We begin with our two 'CCS' samples (section 6.1). With their 219 and 1,022 syllabograms, they are identical to or quite near the numbers of non-obviously-ideographic signs in the 'Ugaritic CM sample' (219) and the CM 1 corpus (1,079). The MacKay (1965) formula (section 7.6) estimates that the two 'CCS' samples' signaries have likely ca. 52 and ca. 54 syllabograms. These numbers are, first, quite similar and, second, very close to the real length of 55 syllabograms of the 'CCS' signary. Data extracted from a short sample of 219 syllabograms may thus be comparable with those of a 1,022 syllabograms' text in the same script and seem moreover fairly accurate.

The 'CCS' 'Idalion Bronze' will provide another hint on appreciating the representativeness of a 219 signs text. Let us extract from this long document four samples of 219 syllabograms each. Table 9.1 gives the number of their different syllabograms and the estimated length of their signaries.

Table 9.1: Number of the different syllabograms in four samples of 219 'common' 'CCS' syllabograms ('Idalion Bronze') and estimated length of their signaries

	Sample of syllabograms 1–219	*Sample of syllabograms 220–438*	*Sample of syllabograms 439–657*	*Sample of syllabograms 658–876*
Actual number	38	43	45	42
Length of the signaries as estimated by MacKay (1965)	ca. 46	ca. 54	ca. 57	ca. 52

None of these texts exhibits the exact number of 55 different syllabograms of the 'CCS', but they range from 38 to 45, i.e. from 69% to 82% of the theoretical total. This seems not too bad in itself, but the MacKay (1965) formula gives much better results. It suggests that these signaries could have respectively ca. 46, ca. 54, ca. 57 and ca. 52 syllabograms. Since the correct answer is 55, this confirms that texts of 219 syllabograms could be fairly representative of their script.

We may then trust that the short 'Ugaritic CM sample' can offer some reasonable (though limited) insight into its writing system and that the two 'CCS' reference samples could provide a rather faithful tool of comparison.

6.3. Typology

Until now, we have not discussed the nature or typology of the script used in the 'Ugaritic CM sample'. Everybody agrees nowadays that all the Cypro-Minoan texts are written in one or several syllabaries. It may nevertheless be useful to examine the specific case of the 'Ugaritic CM sample'.

All the natural writings offer a mix of phonetic and ideographic constituents, but their proportion may vary widely. For example, a typical English text has dominantly phonetic signs, and more precisely alphabetic, but it may also use ideograms like the figures for the numbers or the punctuation symbols. What we must look for, then, is the main constituent of the scripts. Is it ideographic or phonetic? The answer is rather easy to get: we should just isolate the obvious ideograms such as symbols,

Table 9.2: Facsimiles of the 44 syllabograms in the 'Ugaritic CM sample' (after D. Tsouris and E. Masson).

001	036	087
002	037	091
004	038	092
005	040	094
006	044	095
008	051	096
009	055	097
011	058	098
019	069	100
021	070	102
023	071	103
025	073	104
027	074	105
028	075	110
035	082	

punctuation, numbers, etc. If they outnumber the other signs, the writing system will have an ideographic dominant. If not, it will be mainly phonetic. This may even work with small samples, as illustrated by the short alphabetic English text of Ventris – Chadwick (1953, 85) below (219 signs):

> 'When attempting to decipher texts like these, in which both the language and the script are unknown quantities, it is essential to extract as much data as possible from a purely internal study of the material, before making any assumptions about pronunciation o'

This quotation provides one evident ideogram (a comma: three occurrences) and 23 different other signs (216 occurrences) which must hence be phonograms. This writing system has then a phonetic dominant.

The 'Ugaritic CM sample' has a clear phonetic dominant too, because it uses only two different evident ideograms (section 3) and 44 different non-obviously-ideographic signs (see Table 9.2[33]) that must therefore be phonograms.[34]

Are these phonograms syllabic or alphabetic? Their number provides the answer. Indeed, within the mainly phonetic writings, the syllabaries normally exhibit more different phonograms than the alphabets. The difference is typically at least 40 phonograms vs ca. 20. For instance,

- our 'CCS' composite sample of 219 signs (section 6.1) has 42 different syllabograms;
- the English text of 219 signs quoted above has 23 different alphabetic letters.[35]

With its 44 different phonograms, our 'Ugaritic CM sample' looks like a syllabary – more precisely, an open syllable one, like the 'CCS'. The same conclusion has been reached for CM 1 and CM 2 – see Duhoux (2013, 27–32).

The syllabic dominant of the 'Ugaritic CM sample' script fulfils a first necessary condition towards its identification with the other CM writing(s). It is, however, a too general one and we need more characteristics of detail to clinch the case (section 7).

7. Six comparisons of the scripts

7.1. Comparison 1

Let us check the different syllabograms used in the CM 1, 2 or 1 + 2 corpora but lacking in the 'Ugaritic CM sample'. Before we begin, we shall look at our two 'CCS' reference samples (section 6.1). They will show what could possibly happen if we compare two texts of quite different lengths but written in the same syllabic script.

There are 11 different syllabograms used in the 'Idalion Bronze' that are lacking in the small 'CCS' composite sample.[36]

---

[33] Sources: syllabogram *098*: E. Masson (1974, 26). All the other ones: D. Tsouris in Ferrara (*CM* II, 255–6 [but see n. 5 above], 259–61).

[34] Some 'Ugaritic CM sample' phonograms have been suspected to be variants of other CM signs. Their list varies: for instance, *040, 051, 071, 100, 105*: Palaima (1989, 158–9); *040, 094, 100*: Ferrara (*CM* I, 251–4); *027, 037, 051, 055*: Steele (2013a, 41). Below, I shall conventionally suppose that none of them is a variant of another CM sign and that they are thus unknown in the CM 1, 2 or 1 + 2 corpora.

[35] Its capital has conventionally been considered as a variant of a lowercase letter. The lacking letters are: *j*, *v* and *z*.

[36] Different syllabograms of the 'Idalion Bronze' lacking in the small 'CCS' composite sample: *ja, le, li, lu, me, ni, no, pu, ru, sa, so*. Number of different syllabograms of the 'Idalion Bronze' appearing in the small 'CCS' composite sample: 40.

Table 9.3: Number of different syllabograms used in the CM 1, 2 or 1 + 2 corpora but lacking in the 'Ugaritic CM sample'

CM 1 corpus (1,079 syllabograms)	*CM 2 corpus (1,369 syllabograms)*	*CM 1 + 2 corpora (2,448 syllabograms)*
35[1]	28[2]	49[3]

[1]Different CM 1 syllabograms lacking in the small 'Ugaritic CM sample': *007, 012, 012b, 015, 017, 024, 026, 030, 033, 034, 039, 041, 046, 050, 053, 056, 059, 061, 063, 064, 067, 068, 072, 078, 081, 085, 086, 088, 099, 101, 107, 108, 109, 112, 114* after Olivier (*HoChyMin*, 413); see some corrigenda to his list in Duhoux (2013, 28 n. 5). Number of different CM 1 syllabograms appearing in the small 'Ugaritic CM sample': 36.
[2]Different CM 2 syllabograms lacking in the small 'Ugaritic CM sample': *010, 012, 017, 024, 029, 030, 033, 047, 049, 052, 054, 056, 059, 060, 061, 062, 064, 066, 068, 072, 076, 078, 079, 080, 081, 089, 090, 107* after Olivier (*HoChyMin*, 413). Number of different CM 2 syllabograms appearing in the small 'Ugaritic CM sample': 33.
[3]Different CM 1 + 2 syllabograms lacking in the small 'Ugaritic CM sample': *007, 010, 012, 012b, 015, 017, 024, 026, 029, 030, 033, 034, 039, 041, 046, 047, 049, 050, 052, 053, 054, 056, 059, 060, 061, 062, 063, 064, 066, 067, 068, 072, 076, 078, 079, 080, 081, 085, 086, 088, 089, 090, 099, 101, 107, 108, 109, 112, 114* after Olivier (*HoChyMin*, 413); see some corrigenda to his CM 1 list in Duhoux (2013, 28 n. 5). Number of different CM 1 + 2 syllabograms appearing in the small 'Ugaritic CM sample': 38.

How do the CM collections behave? Table 9.3 gives the results.

The 35, 28 or 49 different CM syllabograms that lack in the 'Ugaritic CM sample' are much more frequent than the 11 'CCS' ones. The CM collections show then a behaviour quite different from texts undoubtedly written in the same script.

7.2. *Comparison 2*

What is the importance of the syllabograms used in CM 1, 2 or 1 + 2 corpora's but lacking in the 'Ugaritic CM sample' (section 7.1)? The count of their occurrences can provide an answer: the highest their total, the more valuable their role.

Once again, we take first a look at our two 'CCS' reference samples. In the 'Idalion Bronze', there are 99 occurrences of the syllabograms that are missing in the small composite sample.[37]

The CM 1, 2 or 1 + 2 collections exhibit much more impressive numbers (Table 9.4). Instead of 99, there are 308, 504 and 812 occurrences of the syllabograms missing in the 'Ugaritic CM sample'. The 'Ugaritic CM sample' and the CM 1, 2 or 1 + 2 behave then quite differently from texts confidently written in the same script.

7.3. *Comparison 3*

It is time to reverse our examination and look for the different syllabograms used in the 'Ugaritic CM sample' but lacking in the CM 1, 2 or 1 + 2 corpora. We shall first compare our two 'CCS' reference samples. In fact, there are almost no syllabograms of

[37] In the 'Idalion Bronze', there are 923 occurrences of the syllabograms that appear in the small 'CCS' composite sample.

Table 9.4: Occurrences of the syllabograms used in CM 1, 2 or 1 + 2 but lacking in the 'Ugaritic CM sample'

CM 1 corpus (1,079 syllabograms)	*CM 2 corpus (1,369 syllabograms)*	*CM 1 + 2 corpora (2,448 syllabograms)*
308[1]	504[2]	812[3]

[1]Total of the frequency of every identified CM 1 phonogram as edited by Olivier (*HoChyMin*, 63–280) – see section 5. My personal count of the frequencies of Ferrara (*CM* I, 288–90) is 209 occurrences. Occurrences of the CM 1 syllabograms that lack in the small 'Ugaritic CM sample': 771.
[2]Total of the frequency of every identified CM 2 phonogram as edited by Olivier (*HoChyMin*, 281–383) – see section 5. My personal count of the frequencies of Ferrara (*CM* I, 291–2) is 451 occurrences. Occurrences of the CM 2 syllabograms that lack in the small 'Ugaritic CM sample': 865.
[3]Occurrences of the CM 1 + 2 syllabograms that lack in the small 'Ugaritic CM sample': 1,636.

the smaller sample that lack in the larger: only two different ones.[38] This could have been foreseen: since both samples are written in the same script, the largest is much more representative than the smaller and should normally exhibit nearly all its syllabograms.

Table 9.5 shows what happens in the CM collections.[39]

Table 9.5: Number of different syllabograms used in the 'Ugaritic CM sample' but lacking in the CM 1, 2 or 1 + 2 corpora

CM 1 corpus (1,079 syllabograms)	*CM 2 corpus (1,369 syllabograms)*	*CM 1 + 2 corpora (2,448 syllabograms)*
9	12	14

If all the CM collections shared the same writing, they should basically behave like the 'CCS' samples. This seems not to be exactly the case: instead of 2, we get 9, 12 or 14 syllabograms missing in the 'Ugaritic CM sample'. The numbers are so small, however, that some doubt may arise upon the validity of the comparison.

7.4. Comparison 4

What is the importance of the syllabograms used in the 'Ugaritic CM sample' but lacking in the CM 1, 2 or 1 + 2 corpora (section 7.3)? In the two 'CCS' reference samples,

[38] Different syllabograms of the small 'CCS' composite sample lacking in the 'Idalion Bronze': *jo*, *mo*. There are 40 different syllabograms of the small 'CCS' composite sample that appear in the 'Idalion Bronze'.

[39] Different syllabograms of the small 'Ugaritic CM sample' lacking in the CM 1 corpus: *040, 051, 058, 071, 074, 094, 098, 100, 105*. Number of different syllabograms of the small 'Ugaritic CM sample' that appear in CM 1: 62.

Different syllabograms of the small 'Ugaritic CM sample' lacking in the CM 2 corpus: *002, 019, 040, 055, 058, 071, 073, 094, 098, 100, 103, 105*. Number of different syllabograms of the small 'Ugaritic CM sample' that appear in CM 2: 49.

Different syllabograms of the small 'Ugaritic CM sample' lacking in the CM 1 + 2 corpora: *002, 019, 040, 051, 055, 058, 071, 073, 074, 075, 094, 098, 100, 103, 105*. Number of different syllabograms of the small 'Ugaritic CM sample' that appear in CM 1+2: 73.

the small composite one has 8 occurrences of syllabograms that are missing in the 'Idalion Bronze'.[40] Table 9.6 shows the numbers for our CM collections.[41]

Table 9.6: Occurrences of the syllabograms used in the 'Ugaritic CM sample' but lacking in the CM 1, 2 or 1 + 2 corpora

CM 1 corpus (1,079 syllabograms)	*CM 2 corpus (1,369 syllabograms)*	*CM 1 + 2 corpora (2,448 syllabograms)*
52	52	104

There is a striking difference between the eight occurrences in the two 'CCS' reference samples vs those of the CM collections.

7.5. *Comparison 5*

Let us now compare globally the number of different syllabograms used in the 'Ugaritic CM sample' vs those used in the CM 1, 2 or 1 + 2 corpora. The two 'CCS' reference samples have 42 vs 51 different syllabograms (section 6.1). If the 'Ugaritic CM sample' used the same script as the CM 1, 2 or 1 + 2 collections, the contrast of their numbers should be presumably comparable. In fact, it is stronger: 44 different syllabograms ('Ugaritic CM sample') vs 72 (CM 1) : 61 (CM 2) : 87 (CM 1 + 2).[42] The 'Ugaritic CM sample' script does thus not behave like texts written in the same script.

7.6. *Comparison 6*

What is the number of different syllabograms in the signary of the 'Ugaritic CM sample'? Such a count is easy when signaries are at hand. Even if there were no real signaries, we could get a fairly good idea of their length provided that the corpora were long enough. For instance, there are no known signaries of the 'common' 'CCS' or Linear B, but their inscriptions are several thousands of syllabograms long. We have then just to count the number of different syllabograms used in their corpora to get a pretty good estimation of their signaries – respectively 55 and 88 different syllabograms.

The difficulty of the 'Ugaritic CM sample' is that it is so small. How could we possibly discover the length of its signary with only 219 syllabograms? Happily, we can use the formula devised by Alan MacKay (1965). Its goal is to provide a reasonable estimation of the length of a signary, even if its writing system is quite badly documented. It needs only two data: the total of the occurrences of signs and the number of the different signs.[43]

[40] In the 'Idalion Bronze', there are 1,014 occurrences of the syllabograms that appear in the small 'CCS' composite sample.

[41] Occurrences of the CM 1 syllabograms that appear in the small 'Ugaritic CM sample': 1,027.
Occurrences of the CM 2 syllabograms that appear in the small 'Ugaritic CM sample': 1,317.
Occurrences of the CM 1 + 2 syllabograms that appear in the small 'Ugaritic CM sample': 2,344.

[42] About CM 1 and 2, see Duhoux (2013, 28, 31).

[43] Here is MacKay's (1965) formula: $(L^2 /(L - M)) - L$. L = total of the occurrences of signs in a corpus; M = number of its different signs.

So far so good, but can we rely on this formula? I propose to test it on a syllabic writing system that we know rather well, the 'Classical Cyprus Syllabary'. I will use our two 'CCS' reference samples (section 6.1): see Table 9.7.

Table 9.7: The small 'CCS' composite sample vs the 'Idalion Bronze': occurrences of the syllabograms; number of different syllabograms; estimated length of the signaries after MacKay (1965); right answer

	Small 'CCS' composite sample	*'Idalion Bronze'*
Occurrences of the syllabograms	219	1,022
Number of different syllabograms	42	51
Estimated length of the signaries after MacKay (1965)	ca. 52	ca. 54
Right answer	55	

Though the MacKay formula does not predict the exact number of syllabograms (55), it gives a excellent estimation of ca. 54 and ca. 52 syllabograms.[44] This comparison also shows that a composite sample and a homogeneous inscription may provide valuable characteristics of their script.

We may then compare the estimated length of our four CM signaries (Table 9.8).

Table 9.8: The 'Ugaritic CM sample' vs the CM 1, 2 or 1 + 2 corpora: occurrences of the syllabograms; number of different syllabograms; estimated length of the signaries after MacKay (1965)

	'Ugaritic CM sample'	*CM 1 corpus*	*CM 2 corpus*	*CM 1 + 2 corpora*
Occurrences of the syllabograms	219	1,079	1,369	2,448
Number of different syllabograms	44	71	61	87
Estimated length of the signaries after MacKay (1965)	ca. 57	ca. 76	ca. 64	ca. 90

If all the CM collections were written in the same script, the length difference of their signaries should presumably resemble that in our two 'CCS' reference samples (ca. 52 vs ca. 54 syllabograms). This prediction is fulfilled for neither CM 1 nor CM 1 + 2, whose estimated signaries seem markedly dissimilar from that of the 'Ugaritic CM sample'. The contrast with CM 2 is less distinctive. This shows that the 'Ugaritic CM sample' script does not have the same behaviour as at least two of the other collections.

8. Conclusions

8.1. Primary conclusion

I began this paper by adopting the idea that the script generally called CM 3 has no individual existence. On the contrary, CM 3 should be considered as a part of CM 1, CM 2 or CM 1 + 2.

This supposition was tested to discover if there were any reasons to accept or reject it. The method adopted tried to avoid every consideration alien to the script

[44] See also section 6.2, Table 9.1 for four other tests.

itself and to be as empirical as possible.[45] I concentrated thus on CM 3, on its signs and on those of the CM 1, 2 or 1 + 2 corpora.

A first difficulty arose from the coherence of the whole CM 3 corpus: were all its inscriptions really written in the same script? This has been questioned, rightly as far as I can see. I decided therefore to focus on what seemed to be the surest possible texts, the two tablets (3) and (6) of my list (sections 2, 4).[46] Both offer a distinct Ugaritic flavour and a clear specificity (section 3). The structure of their texts seems different, but this also happens in the CM 1 and 2 corpora. This 'Ugaritic CM sample' totals 219 non-obviously-ideographic signs and provides to date the largest collection of CM texts found in Ugarit.

The 'Ugaritic CM sample' is very short. Is it not too small for any examination? The answer was provided by a comparison of six 'CCS' syllabic samples: five of them have 219 syllabograms; the sixth one is 1,022 syllabograms long. The short texts proved able to deliver valuable information about their script (section 6.2).

The next study confirmed that the 'Ugaritic CM sample' is written in a syllabary, just like the CM 1, 2 or 1 + 2 corpora (section 6.3). Such a feature is generally admitted and fulfils a prerequisite for considering that all the CM texts are written in a unique script. This condition is necessary, but not sufficient, however, because it is too general. In fact, we need more detailed characteristics. We tried to track them down in further analyses (section 7). These consisted of eighteen examinations of six characteristics of the writing(s) used in the small 'Ugaritic CM sample' vs the larger CM 1, 2 or 1 + 2 corpora. The same inspections were conducted on several texts of other securely deciphered scripts (especially two 'CCS' reference samples: section 6.1): they showed how the syllabograms of a small and a larger sample written in the same syllabary could really be used. If the script of the 'Ugaritic CM sample' and those of CM 1, 2 or 1 + 2 were identical, they should behave in the same way. This method allowed us to concentrate not on the collections themselves, but on the consequences that their different sizes may have on several characteristics of their scripts. We could then check if the *differences* between the CM data were similar to those of the two 'CCS' reference samples.

Let us now summarize our results. Fourteen of the eighteen comparisons suggest that the script of the 'Ugaritic CM sample' does not behave as the CM 1, 2 or 1 + 2 corpora: section 7.1 (3 ex.), 7.2 (3 ex.), 7.4 (3 ex.), 7.5 (3 ex.), 7.6 (2 ex.). Four comparisons seem to have numbers either too small (section 7.3: 3 ex.) or not different enough (section 7.6: 1 ex.). The fourteen differences, then, contradict my basic hypothesis that there is no CM 3 separate writing.

8.2. Testing the conclusion

Can we believe this impression? It would be easier if a less subjective appreciation than a personal pronouncement was available. This is precisely what the calculation of probability offers. It aims at evaluating how likely it is that any observed numerical

[45] Though objectivity is an obvious goal, it is clearly inaccessible, not least because the best possible edition implies subjective, though educated, choices.

[46] I.e. ## 212 (RASH Atab 001; RS 17.06) and ## 215 (RASH Atab 004; RS 20.25).

difference between some samples arose by chance or not – accordingly it will be considered as statistically not significant or significant.

One of these probability techniques is a classic of the comparison of very small-sized sample, Fisher's exact test.[47]

I shall apply the Fisher's exact test to the eighteen comparisons offered above. Here are the results:

- Number of different syllabograms used in the CM 1, 2 or 1 + 2 corpora but lacking in the 'Ugaritic CM sample' (section 7.1): differences extremely statistically significant for CM 1 + 2; very statistically significant for CM 1 and CM 2.[48]
- Occurrences of the CM 1, CM 2 or CM 1 + 2 syllabograms that lack in the 'Ugaritic CM sample' (section 7.2): all the differences are extremely statistically significant.[49]
- Number of the different syllabograms used in 'Ugaritic CM sample' but lacking in the CM 1, 2 or 1 + 2 corpora (section 7.3): difference statistically significant for 'Ugaritic CM sample' vs CM 2. No statistically significant difference for 'Ugaritic CM sample' vs CM 1 or CM 1 + 2.[50]

---

[47] See e.g. Agresti (1990, 60–6, 70). I use QuickCalcs of GraphPad Software (currently free of charge at http://www.graphpad.com/quickcalcs/catMenu/). In the results of this test, the letter P symbolises the probability (expressed in percentage) that the difference between the compared data could be mere coincidence. If this probability is less than 5%, coincidence is conventionally supposed to be excluded. In fact, the result may be considered as: (a) not statistically significant; (b) not quite statistically significant; (c) statistically significant; (d) very statistically significant; (e) extremely statistically significant. It is only if the test detects a significant statistical difference that the contrast may be considered as really meaningful. If not, nothing can be considered as proved: there is just no evidence of significant difference. In this last event, there could be no current statistical difference, but a detectable one could perhaps appear in a further examination (for example in case of increasing the sample size).

[48] 'CCS' data: the 'Idalion Bronze' has 11 vs 40 different 'syllabograms lacking vs appearing in the small 'CCS' composite sample. Comparison with the CM numbers:
(a) CM 1: 35 vs 36 different syllabograms lacking vs appearing in the 'Ugaritic CM sample'. P = 0.23% (very statistically significant);
(b) CM 2: 28 vs 33 different syllabograms lacking vs appearing in the 'Ugaritic CM sample'. P = 0.95% (very statistically significant);
(c) CM 1 + 2: 49 vs 38 different syllabograms lacking vs appearing in the 'Ugaritic CM sample'. P = less than 0.01% (extremely statistically significant).

[49] 'CCS' data: the 'Idalion Bronze' has 99 vs 923 occurrences of syllabograms lacking vs appearing in the small 'CCS' composite sample. Comparison with the CM numbers:
(a) CM 1: 308 vs 771 occurrences of syllabograms lacking vs appearing in the 'Ugaritic CM sample'. P = less than 0.01% (extremely statistically significant);
(b) CM 2: 504 vs 865 occurrences of syllabograms lacking vs appearing in the 'Ugaritic CM sample'. P = less than 0.01% (extremely statistically significant);
(c) CM 1 + 2: 812 vs 1,636 occurrences of syllabograms lacking vs appearing in the 'Ugaritic CM sample'. P = less than 0.01% (extremely statistically significant).

[50] 'CCS' data: 2 vs 40 different syllabograms of the small 'CCS' composite sample lacking vs appearing in the 'Idalion Bronze'. Comparison with the CM numbers:
(a) the 'Ugaritic CM sample' has 9 vs 62 different syllabograms lacking vs appearing in CM 1. P = 20.68% (not statistically significant);
(b) the 'Ugaritic CM sample' has 12 vs 49 different syllabograms lacking vs appearing in CM 2. P = 3.98% (statistically significant);

- Occurrences of the 'Ugaritic CM sample's syllabograms lacking in the CM 1, 2 or 1 + 2 corpora (section 7.4): all the differences are statistically extremely significant.[51]
- Number of different syllabograms in the 'Ugaritic CM sample' vs the CM 1, 2 or 1 + 2 corpora (section 7.5): differences not statistically significant.[52]
- Number of different syllabograms in the signaries of the 'Ugaritic CM sample' vs those of the CM 1, 2 or 1 + 2 corpora as estimated by MacKay (1965) (see section 7.6): differences statistically significant for CM 1 + 2.[53]

Fisher's exact test then shows that 11 out of the 18 differences are statistically significant—seven of them are even 'extremely statistically significant', with the highest level of probability.

Our initial check had already considered that four of these seven not statistically significant comparisons were not different enough (section 7.3: 3 ex.; section 7.6: 1 ex.). The probability test results confirm thus this impression and imply that many of the observed contrasts in sections 7.1–6 are objective ones.

8.3. Final conclusion

All these features suggest that an autonomous CM 3 script exists at least in the 'Ugaritic CM sample', viz the Ugarit tablets (3) and (6). Indeed, this corpus does not behave like the CM 1, CM 2 or CM 1 + 2 ones. Can we consider that the case is proven? Perhaps, and I hope so, but anyway, it makes the opposite view more difficult to support.

(c) the 'Ugaritic CM sample' has 14 vs 73 different syllabograms lacking vs appearing in CM 1 + 2. P = 8.84% (not quite statistically significant).

[51] 'CCS' data: the 'Idalion Bronze' has 8 vs 1,014 occurrences of syllabograms lacking vs appearing in the small 'CCS' composite sample. Comparison with the CM numbers:

(a) CM 1: 52 vs 1,027 occurrences of syllabograms lacking vs appearing in the 'Ugaritic CM sample'. P = less than 0.01% (extremely statistically significant);
(b) CM 2: 52 vs 1,317 occurrences of syllabograms lacking vs appearing in the 'Ugaritic CM sample'. P = less than 0.01% (extremely statistically significant);
(c) CM 1 + 2: 104 vs 2,344 occurrences of syllabograms lacking vs appearing in the 'Ugaritic CM sample'. P = less than 0.01% (extremely statistically significant).

[52] 'CCS' data: the small 'CCS' composite sample has 42 different syllabograms vs 51 in the 'Idalion Bronze'. Comparison with the CM numbers: the 'Ugaritic CM sample' has 44 different syllabograms vs

(a) 71 CM 1. P = 32,55% (not statistically significant);
(b) 61 CM 2. P = 66,86% (not statistically significant);
(c) 87 CM 1 + 2. P = 9.46% (not quite statistically significant).

[53] Signaries as estimated by MacKay (1965). 'CCS' data: the small 'CCS' composite sample is supposed to have ca. 52 different syllabograms vs ca. 54 in the 'Idalion Bronze'. The signary of the 'Ugaritic CM sample' is supposed to have ca. 44 different syllabograms vs:

(a) ca. 76 in CM 1. P = 7,94% (not statistically significant);
(b) ca. 64 in CM 2. P = 27,15% (not statistically significant);
(c) ca. 90 in CM 1 + 2. P = 1,20% (statistically significant).

Chapter 10

Script and language on Cyprus during the Geometric Period: An overview on the occasion of two new inscriptions[1]

Markus Egetmeyer

The Bronze Age is followed by the Iron Age. For Cyprus this means an important change in its population structure due to the settling of Greek and Phoenician peoples. Their languages became the main languages of Cyprus, whereas the former 'Cypriot' language was more and more pushed back, even if not lost. Their script was lost: The Phoenicians arrived with their own script and introduced it notably in the city-kingdom of Kition on the south-eastern coast. The Greeks, however, had abandoned their Linear B script about one, two centuries before and thus arrived on Cyprus without writing. Once there, they started to use the native Cypro-Minoan syllabary (CM) and adapted it to their own needs. The use of the former CM system declined and it finally vanished, the new adapted Cypro-Greek syllabary (CG) replaced it. This happened during the first period of the Iron Age, the Geometric period, but this transition is very badly documented. In relative and absolute chronology the transition concerns the end of the Bronze Age and the first three centuries of the Iron Age, the periods Late Cypriot III (1200–1050 BC), Cypro-Geometric I (1050–950), II (950–850) and III (850–750).

To the main material known since 1983 (Masson and Masson 1983; Szyncer 1983) a new very short Cypro-Greek inscription (Olivier 2015) and in particular a complete Cypro-Minoan inscription can now be added (Egetmeyer 2016). Some remarks on the whole of this documentation, which could not be included in the publication of this last inscription, are presented here. The focus is on the Cypriot syllabic material, but the Semitic material will also be mentioned.

[1] I take the occasion to express my gratitude to the editors Vassos Karageorghis and Philippa Steele for their patience, and to the colleagues Giovanni Boffa, Reinhard Lehmann, Hartmut Matthäus and Benjamin Sass for inspiring exchange on the Geometric period during the recent months.

1. The void in the West

The best documentation for the transition comes from the city of Paphos (Palaepaphos-*Kouklia*) in south-western Cyprus. Moreover, Paphos offers the richest documentation of inscriptions written in the Cypro-Greek syllabary for all periods of its use. The same cannot be said of its documentation for the previous inscriptions written in the Cypro-Minoan syllabary. These inscriptions from Paphos and its greater region, roughly corresponding to the modern district of Paphos, are few, short and late: from Maa-*Palaeokastro*, belonging to the period Late Cypriot (LC) III A (*HoChyMin*, 35), from Paphos itself, only a badly published seal belonging to LC III (*HoChyMin*, 37), the others even later than LC III, and no inscriptions at all from the north-west. Extending the area into the modern district of Limassol of southern Cyprus does not change the situation: few, short and possibly late inscriptions from Kourion (*HoChyMin*, 35: 'indatable', but *CM* II 75–77: LC III), an exception made again by a (cylinder) seal (*HoChyMin*, 37: LC II A), and from Alassa-*Palaeotaverna* (*HoChyMin*, ##104), dating to 1300–1100 (*HoChyMin*, 34). It is only still further to the east, with Kalavasos-*Ayios Dhimitrios* in the district of Larnaca that the situation gets different. Thus, the area of the west and south-west of Cyprus, to the north-east limited by the chain of the Troodos mountains, is almost a void concerning Cypro-Minoan inscriptions. An exception could be the lost iron knife from Limni, east of Marion, for which neither photo nor drawing exist (Egetmeyer 2010a, 690–1; Steele 2013a, 17–18). Astonishingly, for the periods immediately following the end of the Bronze Age, it is only Paphos which gives us some documentation and this not by chance.

2. Bloom in Palaepaphos

All the material from the Geometric period in Palaepaphos comes from cemeteries, from seven different tombs. They were found in the cemetery in Palaepaphos-*Skales*, apart from one inscription (no. 11), found in a tomb near Mount Maokremmos. Including the new inscription, the ten inscriptions thus come from six tombs, among them a surface find belonging to an unknown looted tomb. These tombs are numbers 49, 61, 67, 69, 235 and the unknown one. A cylinder seal from tomb 71 is left aside here; in any case, it probably does not present writing of the Geometric period (Valério 2014b, 120–1; Steele forthcoming, chapter 2). All the other syllabic inscriptions from Palaepaphos-*Skales*, except the new one, are practically combined and presented as drawings on a single page in the *editio princeps* by Masson and Masson (1983, 412, with photos on plates A and B of the same volume), then they were included in Olivier (*HoChyMin*) and Ferrara (*CM* II). According to their editorial rules, these two did not include the simple marks on pottery handles, but they need to be included here (nos 5 and 6). The new inscription is published in Egetmeyer (2016).

Excavations of the cemetery of Palaepaphos-*Skales* started in 1979 and were published in 1983 (Karageorghis 1983), introducing it as an Iron Age cemetery. The excavations of the several necropoleis of Palaeopaphos were recently resumed in

2008 by Efstathios Raptou and have just been published in 2014, for the necropoleis of Plakes, Xylinos and Hadji Abdullah (Karageorghis and Raptou 2014, cf. Matthäus 2016), and in 2016, for the necropolis of Skales (Karageorghis and Raptou 2016). It is Skales again which adds the new inscription; no inscriptions are known from the other cemeteries for the Geometric period. In general, the new excavations come to the result that the use of the Skales cemetery was more extended: concerning the chronology, it was started slightly earlier and thus extends to the final phase of the Bronze Age (tomb 192: Karageorghis and Raptou 2016, 101 and 102–103), and concerning the geography, the area covered by this cemetery was wider than previously known. The use of this cemetery seems now to begin with the period from LC IIIB (1100–1050) and the subsequent Cypro-Geometric periods. This chronology is more founded on the typological classification of the objects than on the stratigraphy (Karageorghis and Raptou 2016, 106–7). All these cemeteries testify to a flourishing aristocratic culture, a transition, certainly, but no 'Dark Age'.

It is important to stress that these tombs could be used and reused for more than one person. This means that not only between different tombs of the same period, but also in the same tomb, material from different decades could be deposited. The situation is further complicated by the fact that these tombs also include heirlooms whose manufacture precedes the lives of the deceased. Thus, epigraphic material, even if deposited in the same period, does not have to represent the same stage of development during this transitional phase from one script to another.

The inscriptions belonging to the Geometric period are the following:

Tomb 49

Five inscribed objects belong to this chamber tomb with dromos: three obeloi, a stone and two handles of the same jug (Karageorghis 1983, I, 59–76 and II, fig. lxxiii-xc).

The obeloi resemble, but are to be distinguished from, typical Cypriot *sigynnae*-spears (Karageorghis 1970). They are still made of bronze, whereas iron obeloi become dominant in the Cypro-Geometric period, both types now also documented in the neighbouring cemetery of Plakes (Matthäus 2016, 631). It might have been 'customary to offer to warriors a pair of fire-dogs and obeloi for roasting their meat in the next life' (Karageorghis 1970, 41). Beside this primary use for roasting meat (Bruns 1970, 20–1 [Mycenaean] and 31–4 [Homeric]), a secondary use of these metal objects as a pre-form of money has been hypothesized (Karageorghis 1983, I, 75; Iacovou 2013, 138–40). This remains uncertain, but the vocabulary denoting other metallic objects used in Cyprus to denote such pre-forms of money allows such a hypothesis (Egetmeyer, forthcoming) as also the history of the word ὀβελός in Greek itself (Plath 1992). However, Charalambous, Kassianidou and Papasavvas (2014, 212-213) are rather sceptical concerning this hypothesis, because of the differences in weight, length and metal composition of these obeloi.

1. Obelos tomb 49:16 = HoChyMin, ##170. PPAP Mins 001. This obelos belongs to the period Cypro-Geometric I (1050–950 BC) according to Karageorghis (1983, I, 61, no. 16), Masson and Masson (1983, 411 [only implicit: '*seconde moitié du 11*e siècle']) and F. Vandenabeele in Olivier (*HoChyMin*, 36, 38 ['*sans aucun doute du CG I (1050–950)*'] and 51; also Duhoux 2012b, 71). Only Ferrara (*CM* II 86) indicates the period Cypro-Geometric II. However, in this tomb '[t]here are no objects which may be attributed with certainty to the CG II period' (Karageorghis 1983, I, 76). One can suppose that Ferrara's indication is just an oversight. More than one person was buried in tomb 49, at least three. This brings us to the main problem of these inscriptions: whereas the two longer and complete inscriptions no. 9 (the new one) and no. 10 (the first certainly, the second possibly, of the same period) are undoubtedly Cypro-Minoan, this one (##170) was first published, and is still considered by some, as an already Cypro-Greek inscription. It must be stressed that this classification was strongly influenced by the Greek language of the inscription, supposing that the presence of Greek language implies the existence of the new Cypro-Greek script. One wonders what would have been the discussion about the script of this inscription, if it had not been in Greek language. Anyway, Jean-Pierre Olivier's decision to consider this linguistically Greek inscription as a graphically still Cypro-Minoan inscription (Olivier 2013, 16–19) has not been unanimously accepted and the problem must be considered as unsettled (Duhoux 2012b; Egetmeyer 2013b, 108–22; *CM* II, 86; Steele 2013a, 90–7, 2016, 11–15; Valério 2014c, 190).

The inscription (Figure 10.1) thus reads

> either as CM — 064-011-024-004-012 or as CG .

In either case, it has to be transliterated as *o-pe-le-ta-u* and to be interpreted as the Greek genitive /*Op*^{h}*eltau*/ of the personal name *Op*^{h}*eltās* (Egetmeyer 2010a, § 311), indicating the owner of the obelos (Karageorghis 1983, I, 75).

2. Obelos tomb 49:17 (Karageorghis 1983, I, 61) = *HoChyMin*, ##171. PPAP Mins 002. This second obelos also belongs to the period Cypro-Geometric I (1050–950 BC), for the

*Fig. 10.1: Palaepaphos Tomb 49:16/*HoChyMin *##170. PPAP Mins 001.*

*Fig. 10.2: Palaepaphos Tomb 49:17 (Karageorghis 1983, I, 61)/*HoChyMin *##171. PPAP Mins 002.*

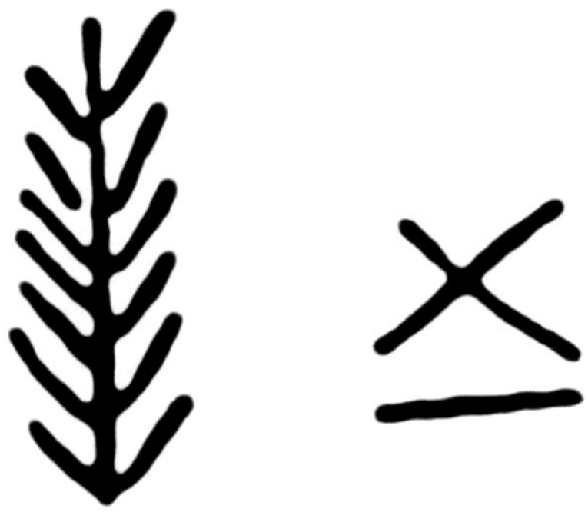

Fig. 10.3: Palapaphos Tomb 49:18 (Karageorghis 1983, I, 61)/HoChyMin *##172. PPAP Mins 003.*

same reasons as indicated above for the first one (add F. Vandenabeele in *HoChyMin*, 36, 38 [‘*sans aucun doute du CG I (1050–950)*’] and 51). Again, Ferrara (*CM* II 87) indicates Cypro-Geometric II (also Hirschfeld 1997, 101).

The inscription (Figure 10.2) is of the well-known, but badly understood type ‘1+1’:

CM ⋔ | ⋔ — 023 | 023.

This can be read with the values of the CG syllabary as *ti* | *ti*. Strangely, Masson and Masson (1983, 413) do not explicitly identify the signs.

3. *Obelos tomb 49:18* (Karageorghis 1983, I, 61) = *HoChyMin*, ##172. PPAP Mins 003. Again, this third obelos belongs to the period Cypro-Geometric I (1050-950) (add F. Vandenabeele *HoChyMin*, 36, 38 [‘*sans aucun doute du CG I (1050–950)*’] and 51; again Cypro-Geometric II according to Hirschfeld 1997, 101 and Ferrara, *CM* II 88).

The inscription is composed of two isolated signs: (a) a herringbone image, perhaps representing a cereal, and (b) a geometric sign ‘| X’. The signs are on different sides of the obelos (*CM* II 88). The position of the first sign on the obelos is better seen on the photo in Ferrara (*CM* II 219), the second one can be seen in Masson and Masson (1983, pl. A, fig. 4). The vertical stroke of the second sign is therefore probably not a divider, but part of this sign. Olivier (*HoChyMin*, 245) equates both marks (Figure 10.3) with script signs:

(a) CM ǂ 007 and (b) Ʀ 097.

If this is true, the presentation of the first sign would be very elaborate, like an image, whereas the second one would be an advanced sign form with ‘H > X’ reduction of the typical basic elements of many Cypro-Minoan signs. However, as the image of the first sign (a) seems clearly oriented to the narrowing part of the obelos, the second one (b) would be oriented in the opposite direction in such a reading. This can neither be seen in Masson and Masson’s presentation alone, where the signs are not presented in the drawing as they appear on the obelos, nor in Olivier’s presentation, where the origin indicated for the photo of the first sign (a) cannot be correct, it is only in the drawing of Ferrara that the orientation of the signs is correct.

4. Stone tomb 49:A (Karageorghis 1983, I, 73) = *HoChyMin*, ##189. PPAP Pblo 001. This inscription can also be attributed to the period Cypro-Geometric I (1050–950) (*HoChyMin*, 36 and [!] *CM* II 96).

The function of the stone is unclear and, like no. 2, the inscription (Figure 10.4) is of the type '1+1':

CM ꟷ | ꟷ (?) — 102 | 017 (?).

Olivier (*HoChyMin*, 262) evokes the possibility to identify the second sign as CM 017 ꟷ. Others prefer to identify this sign with the Paphian variant of the CG signs *e* ꟷ or *nu* ꟷ, of which the second reading would seem preferable (bibliography in Egetmeyer 2013b, 114–15; *CM* II 96). Obviously, this has been used as an argument in favour of the existence of the CG syllabary already in Cypro-Geometric I and thus also in favour of the hypothesis that the *Opheltas* inscription (no. 1) was already written in CG (Valério 2014c, 190). However, CM 017 ꟷ could itself be considered as the precurser of CG *nu* ꟷ and we would again been thrown back to a problem of ductus and not of structure, i.e. a reform by sign addition (Egetmeyer 2010a, 64–5, also Steele forthcoming, chapter 2). As the identification of this second sign remains uncertain and as it is combined with a first sign presenting a typical CM form quite different from the form of the later CG ✳ *a*, the question is left open here.

5. Handles tomb 49:78. These are two script marks on separate handles of the same object (Karageorghis 1983, I, 66) (Figure 10.5). They are not included in Olivier (*HoChyMin*) and Ferrara (*CM* II). The date is again Cypro-Geometric I (1050–950).

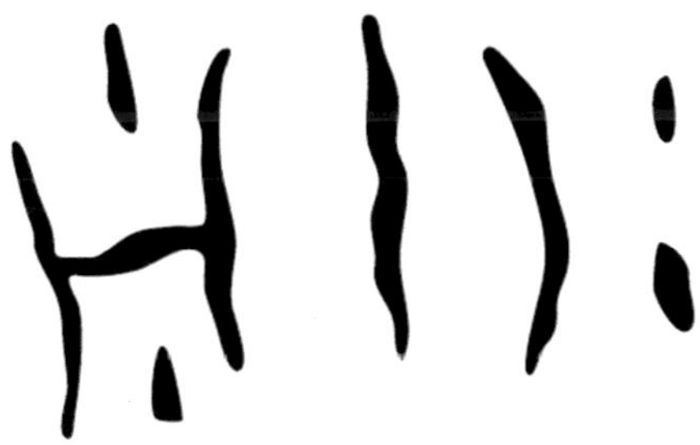

*Fig. 10.4: Palaepaphos Tomb 49:A (Karageorghis 1983, I, 73)/*HoChyMin *##189. PPAP Pblo 001.*

Fig. 10.5: Handles, Palaepaphos Tomb 49:78, (a) and (b).

The first mark corresponds to CM ‡ 006/CG ‡ *pa* (Masson and Masson 1983, 413). The use of this sign as a script mark has good parallels, for example in T323/3 (Hirschfeld 2012, 299, fig. 15). The second one resembles, but does not correspond to, a script sign (Masson and Masson 1983, 413). For a sign with a similar structure one can mention the script mark T128/11 in Hirschfeld (2012, 298, fig. 7).

Fig. 10.6: Handle Palaepaphos Tomb 61:Pyre A.

Tomb 61

It is the pyre outside of this tomb (Karageorghis 1983, I, 130–135) which delivers one inscription.

6. *Handle tomb 61:pyre A* (Karageorghis 1983, I, 130). It is not included in Olivier (*HoChyMin*) and Ferrara (*CM* II). The inscription can be dated to Cypro-Geometric I (1050–950): The pyre is 'located 5 m. southeast of T.61' (Karageorghis 1983, I, 130). Some vases of the Cypro-Geometric I period are found there and thus it is supposed that the whole material belongs to this period (Karageorghis 1983, I, 135).

The script mark (Figure 10.6) corresponds to CM Ұ 112, the later CG ≚ *ke* (Masson and Masson 1983, 413).

It should be mentioned that these handles are from a Canaanite storage jar and incised after firing (Karageorghis 1983, I, 134; Bikai 1983, 396). The presence of this foreign vase type might to be connected with the Semitic inscription from tomb 69, even if this belongs to the following period.

Tomb 67

This tomb (Karageorghis 1983, I, 158–76) delivers one document.

7. *Stone tomb 67:D* (Karageorghis 1983, I, 172) = *HoChyMin*, ##190. PPAP Pblo 002. This inscription is less precisely dated to Cypro-Geometric I–II (1050–850) (Karageorghis 1983, I, 175–6; *HoChyMin*, 37 and *CM* II 97). Comparable to tomb 49, here too at least two burials are present along with ceramic material of the periods Cypro-Geometric I and II. This explains the imprecision of the dating of this simple stone.

This is the third inscription (Figure 10.7) of the type '1+1' and read by Olivier as:

CM ʌ/ (?) | /\ — 109 (?) | 023.

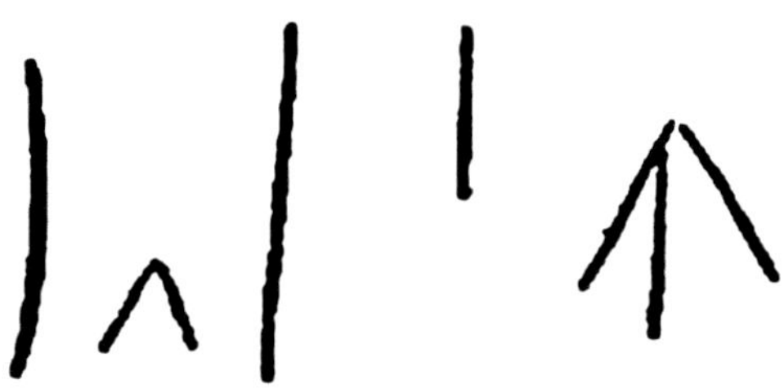

Fig. 10.7: Stone, Palaepaphos Tomb 67:D.

With CG values, this could be read as (⁎) *wa* | (↑) *ti* (Egetmeyer 2013b, 115–16). Masson and Masson (1983, 413), however, read the first sign as CM 51. But this is a CM 2 variant exclusive to Enkomi and absent from CM 1, the variant in use in Paphos. Ferrara (*CM* I 239) proposes to unify this sign with CM 50. In her edition, Ferrara (II 97) admits both possibilities, a CM and a CG reading, but offers no identification of the CM signs, furthermore, a sign CM 109 is missing in her grid (I 255). She also adds (II 97) that it would be a 'problematic factor' to admit an inscription of the type '1+1' written in CG, but there are enough parallels in the later inscriptions from *Rantidi*-Paphos (Mitford and Masson 1983, nos 65–73) and *Kouklia*-Paphos (Masson and Mitford 1986, nos 232, 233 and 236) to exclude this as a problem.

Tomb 69

This tomb (Karageorghis 1983, I, 177–84) delivers a document which is not written in an Aegean syllabary.

8. Jug of Plain White III tomb 69:66 (Karageorghis 1983, 182; Sznycer 1983). This inscription is dated to Cypro-Geometric II–III (950–750 BC), possibly the latest inscription in Skales, in any case not from Cypro-Geometric I. The jug may be attributed to one of the two periods, because there are at least four burials in this tomb dating from the 'middle of CG II to the beginning of CG III' (Karageorghis 1983, I, 184). Transposed in absolute chronology such a precision would mean 900–825 BC, or simply an inscription from the 9th century.

The inscription seems to present an undetermined, but anyhow cursive West-Semitic script. It is inscribed after firing and its twenty-three signs are written sinistroverse without divider. However, the inscription is invisible on the small photo of the jug in Karageorghis (1983, II, fig. cxvii) and although Sznycer (1983) offers a careful presentation and discussion of the signs, he offers no drawing of the inscription presenting its sign sequence on the object. Such a presentation is only added to the object in the show-case of the museum in Nicosia and I owe a photo of this to Benjamin Sass who took autopsy of the inscription.

Karageorghis (1983, I, 182) indicates this inscription in his archaeological record simply as presenting 'signs of the Phoenician alphabet'. Sznycer (1983, 416) is more cautious in his epigraphic commentary and only writes of an undetermined Semitic script of '*allure phénicienne*'. Of course, with Karageorghis, for a non-cuneiform, and not anymore linear Proto-Canaanite, but already cursive Semitic inscription on Cyprus, one spontaneously expects a Phoenician one, but it is not sure whether this is the case here. In the later discussion about the epigraphical material of Cypro-Geometric Palaepaphos-*Skales*, mostly by non-Semitists, this inscription is generally not even mentioned, because it is not written in the Cypriot syllabary. The inscription is not discussed by Steele (2013a, 'The earliest Cypriot Phoenician inscriptions', 175–8) and not even in the clear overview on the West-Semitic alphabetic material by Finkelstein and Sass (2013), who, of course, know the inscription.

As there is no reason to doubt the authenticity of this inscription and as it is the longest inscription in this small group, this inscription seems to be highly important. It shows that also in the domain of West-Semitic epigraphy, there is a lack of documentation for the period of the beginning of the first millenium which not only prevents to read the signs securely, but even from identifying the script. At least to have better documentation, this inscription would be worth a reedition.

Thus, only to give an impression of the inscription, its signs are presented here in their sequence as a drawing (Figure 10.8) and Sznycer's comments on the reading are summarised (Sznycer 1983):

> 1 (*g*? = 13)-2 (*n*)-3-4 (= 9: *m*?)-5 (*k*?)-6-7-8 (*t*)-9 (= 4: *m*?)-10-11 (*b*, = 12)-12 (*b*, = 11)-13 (*g*, = 1)-14-15-16 (= 19)-17 (ʿ)-18 (*d*)-19 (= 16)-20 (*p*)-21 (*s*?)-22 (*y*)-23.

It is remarkable that from 23 signs only four are written twice, which results in 19 different signs. This is a high amount, especially if one considers that the Phoenician alphabet has 22 letters.

Inscription no. 6 which bears only a Cypriot script mark is written on a Canaanite storage jar. Such an object is not isolated among the material from these tombs. On the contrary, there are numerous objects of this kind and Bikai (1983, 404) stresses that '[i]t is a surprise to find such a large group of imports on the western end of Cyprus'. Furthermore, this Levantine material in Cypro-Geometric *Skales* is constituted by two groups, Philistine and Phoenician pottery (Bikai 1983, 405). Also Gilboa (2005, 54) stresses the astonishing great quantity of this material and even admits the possibility of its local production. One can ask whether the unclassified inscription has to be explained in this context. The 9th century, to which the inscription seems to belong, is also generally considered the period of the formal foundation on Cyprus of the Phoenician colony of Kition by the city of Tyre, but the presence of Phoenicians on Cyprus is older (Yon 2004, 35–8).

Semitic cuneiform inscriptions are not totally absent from Cyprus, but the Ugaritic alphabetic tradition precedes the Geometric period (Finkelstein and Sass 2013, 186, n. 166 on these inscriptions outside the Levant) and the Akkadian syllabic cuneiform inscription on the stela of Sargon II in Kition belongs to the following century, probably to its end, 707 BC (Radner 2010, 434). Comparable to the situation of the Cypriot syllabic script, the documentation of West-Semitic alphabetic inscriptions for the period in between is elusive (Finkelstein and Sass 2013, 186–7: 'The elusive Iron I, ca. 1130–900'). Synchronizing Cypriot and Levantine archaeological periods is a problematic matter, but it seems that 'the conventional Aegean chronology, which corresponds to the Low Chronology in the Levant, should be maintained' (Fantalkin *et al.* 2015, 39). Thus, an inscription on Cyprus from certainly Cypro-Geometric II–III (950–750 BC) and probably from 900–825, is contemporaneous to the epigraphical material from the Levant in Late Iron IIA1 (ca. 880–840/830 BC: Finkelstein and Sass 2013, 180 or better slightly higher, ca. 900/880–840 BC: Sass 2016, 199) or even Early Iron IIA (ca. 950–900/880 BC) (Sass 2016, 199). This is a period preceded by important changes or during which important changes

Fig. 10.8: Jug of Plain White III, Palaepaphos Tomb 69:66 (Karageorghis 1983, 182; Sznycer 1983). Drawn by P.M. Steele following Sznycer's interpretation and photographs kindly provided by Benjamin Sass.

in the West-Semitic alphabet took place: 'we place the transition from Proto-Canaanite to the next phase of the alphabet in ca. 940–880 B.C.E. or early Iron IIA' (Finkelstein and Sass 2013, 183 and 215–17: 'The emergence of the cursive ('Post Proto-Canaanite') in the first half of the ninth century BCE') and, improving 'early Iron IIA' to 'late Iron IIA': 'the disappearance of Proto-Canaanite did not occur at the end of early Iron IIA ... but in the course of late Iron IIA. In other words, both script styles coexisted during a ninth-century transitional phase several decades long' (Sass 2016, 219, n. 77). This improvement of the date is linked to the discovery of a new inscription from Megiddo belonging to about 850 BC (Sass 2016, 219, n. 77 and Sass and Finkelstein 2016). During this period there exists a levantine *scriptio franca*, not yet diversified into Phoenician and other 'national' alphabets (Lehmann 2012, 13, 41, 2013, 224; Masetti-Rouault 2016 on Aramaic). Thus, also from a Semitic point of view the inscription from Skales may be a witness of the transitional period which had not yet led to the formation of the later states, neither in the Levant, nor on Cyprus.

Tomb 235

It is the inscription from this tomb which is an important new addition to our knowledge of script and language in Geometric Cyprus (Karageorghis and Raptou 2016, 1, 2, 24 [description of the tomb and plan indicating its objects], 94–8 [catalogue with description of the objects], 149, 153–5 and pls lxviii–lxxi and xcviii–xcix; page xiii: '253/10' to be corrected in '235/10').

9. Bronze bowl tomb 235:10 (Egetmeyer 2016). Cypro-Geometric I: The bowl was found in the intact small tomb 235. It is a chamber tomb with a dromos (Andronikos 1968, 77 and 131). The cremated adult (Karageorghis and Raptou 2016, 144–5, 146, table 4) of the tomb was deposited in its biggest object, an amphora (= object no. 1). The inscribed bronze bowl no. 10 was placed on top of another amphora (no. 6) (Karageorghis and Raptou 2016, 24, 95 and 98 ['Cypro-syllabic' to be corrected to 'Cypro-Minoan'], pls lxviii [no. 6] and lxx [no. 10]). The tomb was not reused and the excavators thus attribute it with all its objects to a single period, Cypro-Geometric I.

This inscription (Figure 10.9) is without doubt written in Cypro-Minoan, because its first sign sequence has older parallels:

 — CM 102-109-004-013-023 '4' 110 | 023.

All the signs have exact matches in the Cypro-Greek syllabary and the inscription could be transliterated as *a-wa-ta-to-ti* 4 *ku* | *ti*.

Fig. 10.9: Bronze bowl, Palaepaphos Tomb 235:10. Drawing by P. M. Steele.

Unknown tomb from Skales

This is a surface find (Karageorghis 1983, I, 370).

10. Bronze bowl = *HoChyMin*, ##186. PPAP Mvas 001. Cypro-Geometric I (F. Vandenabeele in *HoChyMin*, 36): her formulation '*est peut[-]être à dater de 1050–1000*' could render this inscription older than the ones on the three obeloi which are attributed to the larger time span 1050–950. Buchholz and Matthäus (2004, 129), however, are more cautious and speak of an undated surface find.

This inscription (Figure 10.10) reads:

CM Y‡YY'/\ — 082-006-082-088-023.

Again, all the signs have exact matches in the Cypro-Greek syllabary and the inscription could be transliterated as *sa-pa-sa-la-ti* (Egetmeyer 2014, 110).

To these ten inscriptions from the tombs of Skales, south of Palaepaphos-*Kouklia*, one has to add one inscription from a tomb north of it.

*Fig. 10.10: Bronze bowl, Palaepaphos surface find/*HoChyMin *##186. PPAP Mvas 001.*

Unknown tomb near to the mountain peak Maokremmos

The location of this tomb near to the mountain peak Maokremmos (Μαοκρέμμος) is located between Arkhimandrita (Αρχιμανδρίτα) and Phasoula (Φασούλα) (Masson 1968b, 376).

11. Vase of White Painted III (*ICS* 18c/ex 174 and Egetmeyer 2010a, 736–737). Cypro-Geometric III (850–750 BC): pottery period.

This is the latest syllabic inscription from the group and it is also the first one unanimously classified as written in the Cypro-Greek syllabary. It would be written in the Paphian variant, but with the last two sign forms not corresponding to the better known later ones. The inscription (Figure 10.11) is written in non-Greek language and reads dextroverse as:

ᛏXᛏ≚ᐱ *to-ro-to-so-si.*

It is the fourth sign *so* which does not correspond exactly to the known variants. As for the <*o*> in the Opheltas inscription, it seems that we have here in Paphos an archaic form nearer to the common (i.e. outside of Paphos) form ≚ than to the Paphian form ⊥ (Egetmeyer 2010b, 80–5). It is possible to render this inscription in Cypro-Minoan script as ꟻꓤꟻ♆♆ 013-097-013-067-027. At this point, one has to ask what proves that

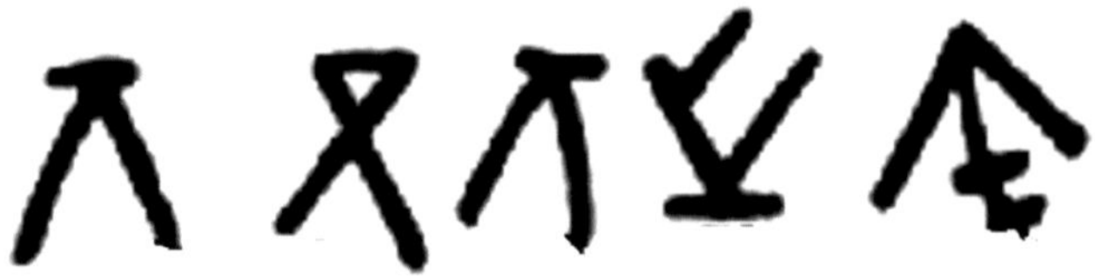

Fig. 10.11: Vase from a tomb near the mountain peak Maokremmos.

*Fig. 10.12: Handle fragment, Kition/*HoChyMin *##147. KITI Avas 018.*

this inscription is a CG one and not a CM one and, inversely, the preceding one (no. 10) a CM one and not a CG one. All the signs belong to both syllabaries and a change in ductus does not make a new script, even more so given that both inscriptions are written in non-Greek language.

3. Kition takes distance

Only few, short or unsecure material can be added from other places than Paphos, mainly from Kition, modern Larnaca.

Kition, area II, courtyard A, on floor I

Archaeological information is given by Ferrara (*CM* II 74).

12. Handle fragment of Plain White Wheelmade = Olivier ##147. KITI Avas 018. Cypro-Geometric I (1050–950): pottery period, date restricted to 1050–1000 by F. Vandenabeele (in *HoChyMin*, 35).

This is the fourth inscription (Figure 10.12) of the type '1+1' and read by Olivier as:

> CM ⩘ | ⵋ — 023 | 107.

With CG values, this could be transliterated as (↑) *ti* | (ⵋ) *ma*, the second sign CM 107 ⵋ being nearer to the more conservative Paphian variant ⵋ than to the common variant ϒ. It must be added that this inscription is indicated as the most recent one of a group of vase inscriptions from Kition (*HoChyMin*, KITI Avas 001-019 and Ferrara *CM* II 67–75), most of them belonging to the preceding period of the end of the Bronze Age, LC III (F. Vandenabeele in *HoChyMin*, 35). Some of these inscriptions are also of the type '1+1' (##135, 137, 138, 139, 142, 143), with the sign CM 023 ⩘

also present as the first one (##135, 136, 137, 138, 139, 141, 142, 143) and one is even identical: ##137. KITI Avas 008 (also *CM* II 74). The forms of the four signs 107 𐠚 (Figure 10.13) are however quite different in inscriptions ##137, ##143, ##147 and ##148 (Egetmeyer 2013b, 118–19), this last one coming from Kition-*Bamboula* like the following inscription.

Kition-Bamboula

The inscription comes from the first millenium sanctuary of Aphrodite-Astarte and Melqart-Heracles.

13. Pottery-sherd of Plain White (Olivier 2015). Cypro-Geometric III (850–750 BC): pottery period.

This is the second new inscription. The inscription is very short, but important, because it is considered by Olivier as belonging to the transitional phase between CM and CG. Furthermore, it is the first inscription (Figure 10.14) of the Cypro-Geometric group for which a sinistroverse reading is proposed:

𐠙𐠒 *ti-ko.*

The language and the meaning of this are unknown. Olivier comments the sign forms and indicates the sign form of *ti* as archaic. One can assume that his reason is that the two outer strokes of the arrow forming this sign reach far down: CM 023 ⩚ differing in this respect from CG 𐠙. For the second sign *ko* he only writes that it is a rare sign form because of its '*barre débordante*' on top. This has, however, an important consequence, because this is a sign where the two variants of the Cypro-Greek syllabary show quite

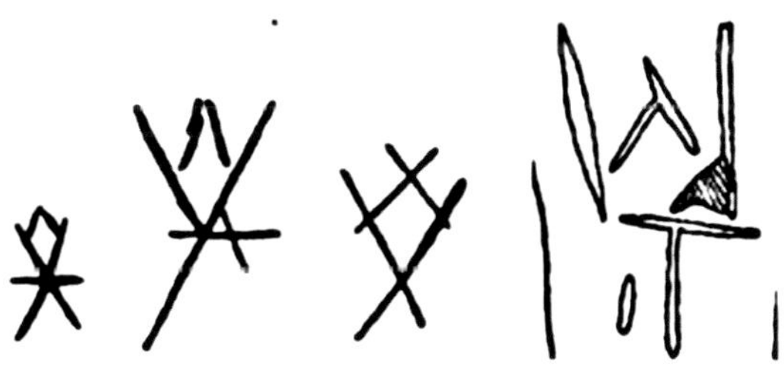

Fig. 10.13: Sign 107 in ##137, ##143, ##147, ##148 and three standardised computer fonts.

*Fig. 10.14: Pottery sherd from the sanctuary at Kition-*Bamboula.

different forms: Paphian ᛟ and common 𐠍. Thus, in Cypro-Geometric III we would have a first example of an inscription in the common variant of the syllabary, thus of the split in the Paphian and the common variant. However, strictly speaking, this could be considered an *argumentum e silentio*, because we have no Paphian parallel from this period (unless no. 15 would deliver one) and no clear match with a Cypro-Minoan sign is known for Cypro-Greek *ko*. If there really is no such match, we would have a first indication of the creation of a new sign and thus of a script reform. Again, difference in ductus, even the split in two different graphic variants alone does not prove the existence of a new script.

Olivier (2015, 347) mentions a later Cypro-Greek inscription identical to this inscription (Palma di Cesnola 1877, pl. 6, no. 33), but the inscription should also be put in the context of the older Cypro-Minoan inscription no. 12 and its group, among which ##148 comes also from Kition-*Bamboula*. The older CM inscriptions are all dextroverse, but the later CG parallel indicated by Olivier should read sinistroverse as usual because of its date and can thus sustain his reading of this no. 13 also as sinistroverse. It would be the oldest one in the corpus of Cypro-Greek inscriptions and it comes as no surprise that it is an inscription from Kition, the later Phoenician city-kingdom whose sinistroverse alphabet was always suspected to be the reason for the change of writing direction in the so-called common syllabary as opposed to the Paphian one which always maintained the inherited Aegean dextroverse direction.

Kition-Kathari

The following inscription comes from the Phoenician sanctuary of Astarte.

14. Bowl of red slip (Yon 2004, 188, no. 1100). Cypro-Geometric III (ca. 800 BC): pottery period (also Yon 2004, 169).

This is a Phoenician dedication to Astarte which can be an import from the Levant. It is treated with some more Phoenician material, supposed to belong to the periods Cypro-Geometric II–III, in Steele (2013a, 175–8, forthcoming, chapter 2). From the periods Cypro-Geometric III/Cypro-Archaic I (8th century BC) on, the Phoenician documentation from the sanctuary at Kition-*Bamboula* also starts (Amadasi Guzzo 2015).

The chronology would demand that we include the inscriptions no. 15 from Kilise Tepe in Cilicia (Egetmeyer and Steele 2011), an incised pottery sherd possibly from the 8th century BC (Cypro-Geometric III or later) and no. 16 from Ashkelon, a painted pottery sherd from the 12th/11th century BC (Cypro-Geometric I or earlier) (Cross and Stager 2006; Egetmeyer 2013a, 149–50; Maeir *et al.* 2016, 323–4). However, regarding the signs, this material is too insecure to be included here. It may just be mentioned that one cannot exclude the presence of a Paphian *ko* ᛟ in the inscription from Kilise Tepe (Egetmeyer and Steele 2011, 128) (Figure 10.15).

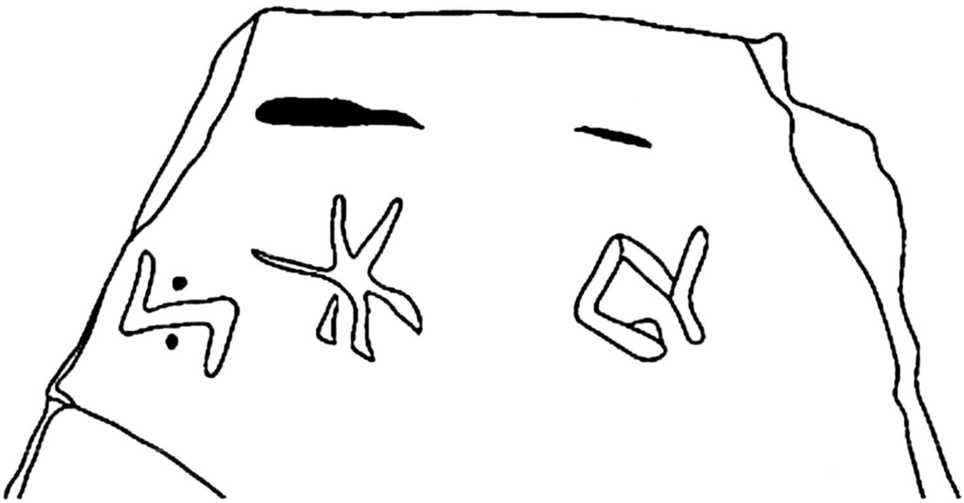

Fig. 10.15: Pottery sherd from Kilise Tepe.

4. Syllabograms and syllabaries

The signs attested in the syllabic inscriptions of the Geometric period are the following, presenting a total of 43 signs, among them 21 different syllabic signs, one number, five dividers and one isolated script mark:

> CM/CG (common, unless otherwise stated) 004 ⊢/⊦ *ta* (2x), 006 ‡/‡ *pa* (2x), 007 ‡/– (1x??), 011 ϟ/ϟ *pe* (1x), 012 ᛍ/⋏ (Paphian) *u* (1x), 013 ꟻ/Ϝ *to* (3x), 017 ⲛ/ᛕ (Paphian) *nu*?? (1x??), 023 ⩚/⍑ *ti* (8x), 024 ⩚/⍑ (Paphian) *le* (1x), 027 ♆/⩡ *si* (1x), 064 ѱ/⩡ *o* (1x), 067 ѱ/≚ *so* (1x), 082 Y/V *sa* (2x), 088 Ꭹ/⩤ *la* (1x), 097 Ꭱ/ꭓ *ro* (1x/2x??), 102 Ж/⁎ *a* (2x), 107 Ħ/⩙ *ma* (1x), 109 ⋋/⋋ *wa* /(1x/2x?), 110 Ж/⩙ *ku* (1x), 112 Ꮙ/ꭓ *ke* (1x). – CG ⋀ *ko* – '4' (1x), divider (5x). – script mark without corresponding syllabic sign (1x).

Nothing absolutely certain can be concluded from this (also Steele forthcoming, chapter 2). The number of different signs is not even half of the signs of the CG syllabary and even less of the CM one, whatever the exact number of signs in this syllabary is. Thus, we could not establish a complete sign list for this period as we can already for the letters of the Greek alphabet. Problems of sign forms have been discussed in Egetmeyer (2013b) and the CM character of the whole material of Skales has been favoured, but this cannot be considered proven. In any case, to single out one inscription (no. 1), because it is written in another language, is not a valid argument. Nevertheless, the three archaeological periods of Cypro-Geometric last all for about a century. The invention of a new script could split the epigraphical material in a before and after at any time during such a period.

There are inscriptions of Early Geometric (I: 1050–950), which come from Palaepaphos-*Skales* tomb 49 (five inscriptions: nos 1–5), tomb 61 (one inscription:

no. 6) and tomb 235 (one inscription: no. 9) and from Kition (one inscription: no. 12). The surface find no. 10 from Skales could, but does not have to belong to this group. The inscription from Palaepaphos-*Skales* tomb 67 (no. 7) belongs also to this period or to the following one. There is no other inscription which belongs to the Middle Geometric period (II: 950–850). Two inscriptions belong to Late Geometric (III: 850–750), no. 11 from Paphos and no. 13 from Kition. The unclassified Semitic inscription (no. 8) belongs to Middle or Late Geometric, while a Phoenician inscription (no. 14) is Late Geometric.

The impression one gets is that from Early Geometric on Greeks start to use the syllabary of the Cypro-Minoans, the form of certain signs evolves, signs are deleted, signs are added, signs may get attributed another sound value. The laboratory seems to have been in Paphos where sign forms were also modified and not adopted anymore elsewhere. In Late Geometric the split into a Paphian and a common variant is apparent.

The presence of CM 064 ᘺ *o* shows that there is no distinction into Paphian ⊥ *o* and common ≚ *o* yet and thus no split in the Early Geometric. The form of sign 109 (⩘/⁎), without and with the upper vertical stroke, could also indicate this. However, the presence of a new grapheme in Kition, the syllabic sign common *ko* ⋀ in Late Geometric would also be the first clear sign of the presence of a new script. The identification of sign 013 ꟸ (not Ŧ) is highly complicated (Egetmeyer 2016, 132–3, with bibliography), the three forms are present in Paphos, the CM ꟸ, the more conservative (later common) form F *to* and the innovative Paphian one ⩞ *to*. The presence of the new Paphian form in Late Geometric strengthens the hypothesis of the split. The most characteristic feature of the differentiated Paphian syllabary is however the creation of a new sign form for *o*: ⊥. The oldest example appears in an inscription on yet another bronze bowl from Paphos which is dated about 700 BC. The inscription reads *pi-le-o-ti* (Egetmeyer 2010a, 782–783). An conserved archaic form of Paphian *le* ⩚ (≠ common 8) preceding the innovated ⊥ *o*, give this inscription a typical Paphian look. Like the others it will be an inscription indicating possession, but the resemblance of the lexical element before the ending *-o-ti* to Greek *P*[h]*ile-* is certainly fortitious: *Pile ...*, *Bile ...* or similar would also give perfect non-Greek names. The presence of a new sign, now in Paphos, shows the split of the local syllabaries. As in linguistics, shared archaisms give less proof than shared innovations.

The new inscription on the bowl no. 10 from tomb 235 is the most secure example of an inscription still written in CM and would prove its use during the Cypro-Geometric I period about 1050–950 BC. Everything is CM, the signs, the sign sequences, the type of inscription. However, it seems that the possibility of an heirloom cannot be excluded, namely with regard to two older bronze bowls with a sign sequence identical to the first one of the bowl, probably a personal name (Egetmeyer 2016, 135; Matthäus 2016, 631). In general, signs which have a continuous graphical evolution from CM into CG are of difficult use, because for these early periods we do not know exactly which sign forms (allographs) can still be CM and which are already CG, which 'advanced' sign forms could still be CM, which forms belong to both and keep CM and CG indistinguishable. What is missing are clear examples of signs (graphemes) which can only belong to CM or to CG, thus deleted from CG by a reform of reduction or invented by a reform of addition. The *Opheltas* inscription remains, however, the only Greek one in this group, the language of the abbreviated inscriptions being unknown. It shows that at least for the signs of this inscription there was no reform by substitution of the phonemic value. The discussion about continued or discontinued CM forms is concentrated on signs 011 (in no. 1) and 017 (in no. 4), but remains unsettled. Sign 007 (in no. 3) seems to be discontinued in CG, but its presence and interpretation are highly speculative.

5. Syllabaries and city-kingdoms

The small amount of epigraphic material from the Geometeric period mostly comes from tombs, only no. 13 (Cypro-Greek) and no. 14 (Phoenician) come from sanctuaries. The 14 objects are three bronze obeloi for roasting meat (nos 1–3), two bronze bowls (nos 9 and 10), seven pottery objects (nos. 5, 6, 8 and 11–14), complete or fragments, and two stones (nos 4 and 7). Three inscriptions indicate possession (no. 1 in Greek language and, probably, nos. 9 [combined with the type '1+1'] and 10 in CM script and language), eight are abbreviations, five are (including the already mentioned no. 9) of the '1+1' type (nos 2, 4, 7, 9 and 12), three are single script marks (nos 3, 5 and 6), three are of unknown type (nos. 8 ['Semitic'], 11 [in CG script and Cypro-Minoan/Eteocypriot language, possession?] and 13 [perhaps to be linked to the '1+1' type]), and one inscription is a dedication in Phoenician (no. 14).

This last inscription left aside, the only inscription we can translate is the one from the Opheltas obelos. Unfortunately for us, the two other obeloi do not present the same type of inscription with a personal name, but only abbreviations, once the type '1+1' and once script marks. Many more obeloi, bronze and iron, are known in the archaeological material, but they present no inscriptions at all (Karageorghis 1970; Matthäus 2016, 631). Thus, the Cypriot inscriptions seem to indicate possession or present abbreviations of unclear function. The bronze bowls are precious objects. Charalambous *et al.* (2014, 210–12 and 2016, 96 and 97 [with quotation]) indicate the higher amount of tin in hemispherical bowls of *Skales* 'in order to produce objects whose colour imitated that of gold'. The indication of possession on these bronze bowls by adding an inscription is a well known practice on Cyprus (Buchholz and Matthäus 2004), independent of the language: it is known for Greek, but also once for a silver bowl with an inscription in the Ugaritic cuneiform alphabet (Yon [and P. Bordreuil] 2004, 365–6) and it can thus also be supposed for Cypro-Minoan/Eteyocypriot inscriptions. It would then be more correct to say that Greeks learned this practice together with the writing itself from Cypriots. The importance of marks may not be underestimated, and they seem also to play a role in the development of the Greek alphabet (Papadopoulos 1994; Verdan *et al.* 2012, 179).

However, there seem to be no votive, curse or poetic inscriptions as we have them among the oldest inscriptions in the Greek alphabet. The only votive inscription is the Phoenician one from a sanctuary. It is important to indicate this, because it is a common hypothesis that the use of the script on Cyprus was 'saved' through the transitional period by people practising writing related to sanctuaries, especially to the important one of the female deity of Paphos. This could thus be the production of texts by people from the sanctuary or votive texts offered by people from outside the sanctuary. However, among the published material from this sanctuary there is very few material from the Late Bronze Age, almost nothing from the Geometric period and it is only with the Archaic period that we get abundant material: '*strenggenommen lassen sich in Alt-Paphos keine figürlichen Weihgeschenke zweifelsfrei den Jahrhunderten der geometrischen Zeit zuordnen*' (Leibundgut and Frey-Asche 2011, 17–18 and 183 [with quotation]). Thus, if this can be generalized, there are no writing activities attested in the sanctuary of the Wanassa/Paphia during the Geometric period. This distinguishes the situation on Cyprus from the one of the sanctuary of Apollo Daphnephoros in Eretria with its alphabetic Greek inscriptions belonging to the very beginning of this writing tradition. Nevertheless, this does not definitely falsify the hypothesis of writing practice related to the sanctuary, because it is probable that the Cypriot Greek vocabulary for writing (the verb, the teacher and the instrument), based on a verb for 'to paint' (ἀλείφω), hint at the existence of painted/written texts on perishable material, perhaps even more abundant than the incised ones almost exclusively known to us. These texts could be written on skin and on folding wood-tablets (Egetmeyer 2010a, § 24, 53 and § 608, 494–5).

The lack in the sanctuary contrasts with the richness of the necropoleis: the (modern) village of Kouklia is surrounded by necropoleis, Plakes (in the west), Xylinos (in the north), Hadji Abdullah (in the east) (Karageorghis and Raptou 2014, also Matthäus 2016), and Skales (in the south) (Karageorghis 1983; Karageorghis and Raptou 2016). The mere existence of these necropoleis indicates the existence of a considerable population namely during the period of Cypro-Geometric I. They are not simple cemeteries, but belong to a culture of rich warrior aristocrats (Karageorghis and Raptou 2016, 101–8). The burial custom of tomb no. 235 with the Cypro-Minoan inscription (no. 9) and of some other tombs was post-Mycenaean 'Homeric' cremation (Andronikos 1968, 21–32: literature and 51 ['*In der Welt der Epen eine Regel ohne Ausnahme*'] –69: archaeology). This distinguishes them from most other tombs which present inhumations, as also tomb 49 with the Greek inscription (no. 1) (Karageorghis 1983, 7–8; Karageorghis and Raptou 2016, 3–5, 105–6). Inhumation was caracteristic of the Aegean Bronze Age, including Cyprus. Archaeologists indicate that cremation was then increasing in the Aegean during post-Mycenaean Late Helladic IIIC/Late Minoan IIIC (~1200– BC) period and became predominant in Submycenaean/Protogeometric period, thus with the beginning of the Iron Age (Ruppenstein 2013, 192, also Deger-Jalkotzy 2013 [Central Greece, 228: linked to population movements]). Cremation in Cyprus is thus considered by archaeologists as an influence from the Aegean and brought in by new people, Greeks (Matthäus 2016, 631, 633). It even seems that there is an astonishing coincidence between dialectal and burial geographies (Luce 2009, 421, 423: 'the Homeric poems (where all funeral scenes are of the Ionian type)' and 2014).

There further seems to be a remarkable parallel concerning archaeology and script and language in nearby Kourion. There are rich tombs on the plateau of Kourion-*Kaloriziki* southeast of the acropolis of Kourion. They belong to the period of LC III B (1100–1050), just preceding the Geometric period. Tomb 40 is outstanding, a very rich tomb by a man buried by the new custom of cremation (Matthäus and Schuhmacher-Matthäus 2013, 2015, 167–8). The tomb contains also a lot of precious heirlooms, objects a hundred to a hundred-fifty years older than the other burial gifts (Matthäus and Schuhmacher-Matthäus 2015, 160, 167–8). This is the reason for the hesitation on the exact stage of script use in Paphian Skales, tomb 235 (no. 9). Kourion does not deliver inscriptions of the Geometric period (however, *HoChyMin*, 35 and *CM* II 75–7, already mentioned p. 181), but it is remarkable that in the archaic period script and language of Kourion seem to be close to those of Paphos, what might mean that there were common developments in the broader region of the south-west of Cyprus already in the preceding period.

The ancient tradition links the arrival of Greeks in this region to Agapenor from Tegea in Arcadia as the founder of the city of Paphos. At least his name would fit very well phonetically in its dialectal form as *Agapānōr* (twice in Akarnania: *LGPN* IIIA, s.u.) and with its old form of the second member of the compound to the later attested Cypriot *Kuprānōr* and *Stāsānōr* (Egetmeyer 2010a, § 366). With the equally 'Achaean' name *Op*^{h}*eltās* we have a first historical person. Karageorghis (1983, 370) wrote on this inscription as being written in the 'Arcadian dialect'. Whether this is exact, we do not know, but he was right to indicate that there was no Cypriot Greek yet.

In any case, one can assume that native Cypriot aristocrats preserved their Cypro-Minoan script to write their 'Cypriot' language and that Greek immigrants started to use and then to adapt the Cypro-Minoan script to their own needs, thus creating the Cypro-Greek script. Paphos can reasonably be assumed to be the place of this adaptation during the Cypro-Geometric period. For comparison, it is useful to read from a Cypriot perspective what Herodotus wrote on the creation of the Greek alphabet, substituting 'Achaeans' for 'Ionians' and 'Cypro-Minoans' for 'Phoenicians': περιοίκεον δὲ σφέας τὰ πολλὰ τῶν χώρων τοῦτον τὸν χρόνον Ἑλλήνων Ἴωνες, οἳ παραλαβόντες διδαχῇ παρὰ τῶν Φοινίκων τὰ γράμματα, μεταρρυθμίσαντες σφέων ὀλίγα ἐχρέωντο, χρεώμενοι δὲ ἐφάτισαν 'Among the Greeks, the Ionians dwelt around them [Phoenicians] in most of the places during this time, who [the Ionians], after having received the letters by instruction of the Phoenicians, after having changed their form [μεταρρυθμίζω] slightly, declared to make use (of them)' (Her. 58, 2; also 58, 1: ῥυθμός '(sign) form' and μετέβαλλον καὶ τὸν ῥυθμὸν τῶν γραμμάτων 'they changed also the form of the letters' (Mavrojannis 2007, 299 and 302 [n. 37 also with a translation]).

However, as for the Greek alphabet and the development of the *polis*, it is only with the establishment of the city-kingdoms that the syllabaries become better visible to us. In fact, in Cypro-Archaic I (750–600 BC) the documentation becomes richer and other places from Cyprus and outside Cyprus can be added. Certain inscriptions from the second half of the 8th century come from Cilicia and Mende (on Pallene, Chalkidike), a colony by Eretria, in mainland Greece (Egetmeyer 2010a, [Cilicia] 845 and [Mende] 841; Karnava 2013, 160–3; also Boffa 2013, 34, n. 13), the first one of a seal-owner *Diweip^{h}ilos* and is one of the oldest post-Mycenaean Greek inscriptions.

From the end of the 8th century we get the first inscriptions of the royal houses of city-kingdoms, of king *Akestōr* of Paphos on a silver bowl (!) (*ICS* 180a; Egetmeyer 2010a, 669), maybe also of king *T^{h}rosydāmos* of Paphos on a bronze bowl, in any case a member of the aristocracy (Egetmeyer 2010a, 781–2), and of a *Diweit^{h}emis* (from Kourion?), again on a silver bowl (*ICS* 178; Egetmeyer 2010a, 668).

The lexical element of the name of the oldest known king *Akestōr* has now an almost contemporaneous parallel in the west-Ionian inscription of *Hakesandros* from Methone and dating to about 720 BC (Μεθώνη 2012, 339–43, esp. 342: 'αυτός που γιατρεύει τους άνδρες', also Janko 2015, 2–3 and Papadopoulos 2016, 1243–1244). The interpretation of these names (Egetmeyer 2010a, 365) has to be corrected taking into account Le Feuvre's distinction between two verbs, ἀκέομαι 'to heal' and *ἀκέω 'to encourage (in combat)' (2015, 255–82, esp. 274–6 on onomastics and 259–60 on initial *h-*). The last one is an *ἀκέω '*piquer*' ('to prick'), derived from the root **h2ek'* – '*scharf sein/werden/machen*' ('be/become/make sharp') (*LIV*, s.u., cf. also *NIL*, 259–62, s.u. **h2ak's* – 'Achse' ('axle'), esp. 261). For the Cypriot king, this gives a perfect agent noun 'instigator' (in combat). Modern German offers also a confirmation for Le Feuvre's distinction with the verb '*scharfmachen*' ('to incite', of a dog for attack).

From a classical Attic viewpoint, a great number of these Cypriot names are thus highly archaic names, including the names of other kings, notably also from 'Eteocypriot' Amathus, where *(W)roikos* and *Epipalos* ruled (Egetmeyer 2010a, 41–5 and § 421 and 353). As in other Greek regions (Woodard 2014, 140–290), poetry was certainly part of the life of this Cypriot aristocracy at any period. Admittedly, poetic inscriptions in the syllabary are very rare (Egetmeyer 2010a, § 724), but the ancient tradition linked to Bronze Age Kinyras (Franklin 2016) and to 'Homeric' Stasinos (West 2013, 32–4) demonstrates that the Greeks were very aware of this.

The adaptation of the Cypro-Minoan script to the Cypro-Greek one is part of a broader cultural evolution which gives the wider western periphery of the Near East access again to script: Greeks and Phrygians adopt the Phoenician alphabet and in the 8th century at the latest inscriptions appear in Euboean context in Lefkandi, Eretria, Methone, Pithecusae, Osteria dell'Osa and in the Phrygian capital Gordion (Boffa 2013, forthcoming; Janko 2015; Papadopoulos 2016; Verdan *et al.* 2012). It seems that the Fayum alphabets even allow to get beyond these inscriptions (Brixhe 2007 and Woodard 2014, 1–139), because they show how Greeks first tried to get along with an alphabet without any addition, not even upsilon. It could have been similar on Cyprus. Greeks adopted the Cypro-Minoan syllabary on the island they then lived on and again it seems that from the 8th century on there is a steady increase in the epigraphical documentation. This new syllabary is as Greek as the new alphabet is Greek. The terminological contortions of modern authors to name the new syllabary are incomprehensible for me. The Greek alphabet did not make the Phoenician alphabet disappear, nor the Phoenician language. On Cyprus the situation was different, the Cypro-Greek syllabary and the Greek language finally replace the Cypro-Minoan syllabary and language. It is imaginable that for a certain time both scripts were in parallel use, especially if speakers of both languages were living in the same place, and that only cultural and political circumstances finally made the Cypro-Minoan script disappear, but not yet its language, then called Eteocypriote by modern scholars. This evolution could be linked to the establishment of the Cypriot city-kingdoms from Cypro-Geometric III on. In any case, Cyprominoans/Eteocypriots finally use the syllabary according to the new Greek writing habits. Their language gets definitely lost only in the Hellenistic period. Also Phrygians had their own alphabet, but they also abandoned it and the late Phrygian inscriptions are written in the standard Greek alphabet. First the native script must cede to the new standard, then the language.

It is encouraging to turn back to what the excavators of the cemeteries of Palaepaphos write, Vassos Karageorghis and Efstathios Raptou. They indicate that still the material of all tombs of Palaepaphos is not published, not even excavated, and among the already known material there are further bronze bowls like the one with the new inscription (Karageorghis and Raptou 2016, xv, 106–7).

Bibliography

Agresti, A. (1990) *Categorical Data Analysis*, New York.

Amadasi Guzzo, M. G. (2015) 'Les inscription phéniciennes' in Caubet, A., Fourrier, S. and Yon, M. (eds) *Kition-Bamboula VI. Le sanctuaire sous la colline*, Lyon, 335–345.

Anastasiadou, M. (2016) 'Drawing the line: Seals, script and regionalism in Protopalatial Crete' *American Journal of Archaeology* 120, 159–193.

Andronikos, M. (1968) *Totenkult*, Göttingen (= Buchholz, H.-G. ed. *Archaeologia homerica. Die Denkmäler und das frühgeschichtliche Epos* III/W).

Aravantinos, V. L. and Vasilogamvrou, A. (2012) 'The first Linear B documents from Ayios Vasileios (Laconia)' in Carlier, P., de Lamberterie, C., Egetmeyer, M., Guilleux, N., Rougemont, F. and Zurbach, J. (eds) *Études Mycéniennes 2010* (Biblioteca di Pasiphae 10), Pisa/Roma, 41–54.

Aruz, J. (2008) *Marks of Distinction. Seals and Cultural Exchange between the Aegean and the Orient.* (*CMS* 7), Mainz am Rhein.

Bagley, R. W. (2004) 'Anyang writing and the origin of the Chinese writing system' in Houston, S. D. (ed.) *The First Writing. Script Invention as History and Process*, Cambridge, 190–249.

Baines, J. (2004) 'The earliest Egyptian writing: development, context, purpose' in Houston, S. D. (ed.) *The First Writing: Script Invention as History and Process*, Cambridge, 150–189.

Baines, J., Bennet, J. and Houston, S. D. (eds) (2008) *The Disappearance of Writing Systems. Perspectives on Literacy and Communication*, London.

Bartoněk, A. (2003) *Handbuch des mykenischen Griechisch. Indogermanische Bibliothek. Erste Reihe*, Heidelberg.

Basso, K. (1974) 'The ethnography of writing' in Bauman, R. and Sherzer, J. (eds) *Explorations in the Ethnography of Speaking*, Cambridge, 425–432.

Bauman, R. and Briggs, C. L. (2003) *Voices of Modernity. Language Ideologies and the Politics of Inequality*, Cambridge.

Baurain, C. (1980) 'Chypre et le monde Égéen', *Bulletin de correspondance hellénique* 104, 566–571.

Beekes, R. S. P. (2010) *Etymological Dictionary of Greek. Leiden Indo-European Etymological Dictionaries 10.1-2*, Leiden/Boston.

Beekes, R. S. P. (2014) *Pre Greek: Phonology, Morphology, Lexicon* (ed. S. Norbruis). Brill Introductions to Indo-European Languages 2, Leiden/Boston.

Begg, I. D. J. (1987) 'Continuity in the West Wing at Knossos', in Hägg, R. and Marinatos, N. (eds) *The Function of the Minoan Palaces*, Stockholm, 179–184.

Bennet, J. (2001) 'Agency and bureaucracy: thoughts on the nature and extent of administration in Bronze Age Pylos' in Voutsaki, S. and Killen, J. T. (eds) *Economy and Politics in the Mycenaean Palace States* (Cambridge Philological Society. Supplementary vol. 27), Cambridge, 25–37.

Bennet, J. (2005) 'Response to Erik Hallager' in D'Agata, A.-L., Moody, J. and E. Williams (eds) *Ariadne's Threads. Connections Between Crete and the Greek Mainland in Late Minoan III (LM IIIA2 to LM IIIC)*, Tripodes 3, Athens, 267–272.

Bennet, J. (2008) 'Now you see it; now you don't!: the disappearance of the Linear A script on Crete' in Baines, J., Bennet, J. and Houston, S. D. (eds) *The Disappearance of Writing Systems*, London, 1–29.

Bennet, J. (2013) 'Epilogue' in Piquette, K. E. and Whitehouse, R. D. (eds.) *Writing as Material Practice: Substance, Surface and Medium*, London, 335–342.

Bennett, E. L. Jr. (1958) 'Some Minoan texts in the Iraklion Museum' in Grumach, E. (ed.) *Minoica. Festschrift zum 80. Geburtstag von Johannes Sundwall.* Deutsche Akademie der Wissenschaften zu Berlin. Schriften der Sektion für Altertumswissenschaften 12. Berlin, 35–49.

Bennett, E. L. (1963) 'Names for Linear B Writing and for its Signs', *Kadmos* 2:2, 98–123.

Bikai, P. M. (1983) 'The imports from the East' in Karageorghis, V. (ed.) *Palaepaphos-Skales. An Iron Age Cemetery in Cyprus*, Constance, I, 396–406.

Boffa, G. (2013) 'Il santuaro di Apollo ad Eretria. Osservazioni sulla documentazione epigrafica di età geometrica' in Giardino, L. and Tagliamonte, G. (eds) *Archeologia dei luoghi e delle pratiche di culto* (colloquium Cavallino/Lecce 2012), Bari, 31–43.

Boffa, G. (forthcoming) 'Il vaso ben levigato. Una proposta di lettura per l'iscrizione più antica dalla necropoli di Osteria dell'Osa', *La Parola del Passato.*

Boltz, W. G. (1986) 'Early Chinese writing', *World Archaeology* 17, 420–436.

Boltz, W. G. (2001) 'The invention of writing in China', *Oriens Extremus* 42, 1–17.

Bombardieri, L. and Jasink, A. M. (2010) 'Decorative repertoire and script signs: a complex "origin" for the writing system in Cyprus?', *Kadmos* 49, 133–157.

Boone, E. H. and Mignolo, W. D. (eds) (1994) *Writing without Words: Alternative Literacies in Mesoamerica and the Andes*, Durham.

Bordreuil, P. and Pardee, D. (2001) 'Textes alphabétiques en ougaritique: 8. Abécédaire' in Yon, M. and Arnaud, D. (eds) *Études ougaritiques I. Trouvaux 1985–1995.* Ras Shamra Ugarit 14, Paris, 341–348.

Bordreuil, P. and Pardee, D. (2009) *A Manual of Ugaritic*, Winona Lake.

Branigan, K. (1965) 'The origin of the Hieroglyphic Sign 18', *Kadmos* 4:2, 81–83.

Branigan, K. (1966) 'The prehistory of Hieroglyphic Signs 12 and 36', *Kadmos* 5:2, 115–117.

Brice, W. C. (1961) *Inscriptions in the Minoan Linear Script of Class A, Edited from the Notes of Sir Arthur Evans and Sir John Myres*, Oxford.

Brice, W. C. (1991) 'Notes on the Cretan Hieroglyphic Script: III. The inscriptions from Mallia Quartier Mu. IV. The clay bar from Knossos. P116', *Kadmos* 30, 93–104.

Bricker, V. R. (1986) *A Grammar of Mayan Hieroglyphs* (Middle American Research Institute, Publication 56), New Orleans.

Bricker, V. R. (2008) 'Mayan' in Woodard, R. D., *The Ancient Languages of Asia and the Americas*, Cambridge, 163–192.

Brixhe, C. (2007) 'Les alphabets du Fayoum', *Kadmos* 46, 15–38.

Broodbank, C. (2004) 'Minoanisation', *Proceedings of the Cambridge Philological Society* 50, 46–91.

Bruns, G. (1970) *Küchenwesen und Mahlzeiten*, Göttingen (- Buchholz, H.-G. ed. *Archaeologia homerica. Die Denkmäler und das frühgeschichtliche Epos* II/Q).

Bryce, T. (2002) *Life and Society in the Hittite World*, Oxford.

Buchholz, H.-G. (2004) 'Zyprische Bronzeschalen der geometrischen und archaischen Periode. Eine Studie zu Typologie, Chronologie, Epigraphik und kultureller Außenwirkung zyprischen Metallhandwerks des frühen ersten Jahrtausends v. Chr.', *Centre d'études chypriotes. Cahier* 33, 99–148.

Cagni, L. (2000) 'I documenti amministrativi mesopotamici del period antico-babilonese: precedenti, tipologie, sigillature' in Perna, M. (ed.) *Administrative Documents in the Aegean and their Near Eastern Counterparts*, Turin, 53–61.

Caplice, R. (2002) *Introduction to Akkadian*, Studia Pohl: Series Maior, Dissertationes Scientificae De Rebus Orientis Antiqui 9, Rome.

Cardona, G. R. (1981) *Antropologia della scrittura*, Turin.

Carrier, D. (1996) 'Gombrich and Danto on defining art', *Journal of Aesthetics and Art Criticism* 54:3, 279–281.

Casabonne, O. and Egetmeyer, M. (2002) 'À propos du sceau de Diweiphilos' (in Borgia, E., Casabonne, O. and Egetmeyer, M. 'Notes ciliciennes'), *Anatolia Antiqua* 10, 177–181.

Catling, H. W. (1979) 'Copper in Cyprus, bronze in Crete: some economic problems' in Karageorghis, V. (ed.) *Acts of the International Archaeological Symposium: 'The Relations between Cyprus and Crete, ca. 2000–500 BC', Nicosia 16 April–22 April 1978*, Nicosia, 69–75.

Chadwick, J. (1968) 'The group *sw* in Mycenaean', *Minos* 9, 62–65.
Chadwick, J. (1970) *The Decipherment of Linear B*, 2nd edition, Cambridge.
Chadwick, J. (1976) 'Who were the Dorians?', *La Parola del Passato* 31, 103–117.
Chapouthier, F. (1930) *Les Écritures Minoennes au Palais de Mallia, Études Crétoises* 2, Paris.
Chapouthier, F. (1951) 'Remarques sur le déchiffrement des hieroglyphs minoens', *Minos* 1, 71–76.
Charalambous, A., Kassianidou, V. and Papasavvas, G. (2014) 'A compositional study of Cypriot bronzes dating to the Early Iron Age using portable X-ray fluorescence spectrometry (pXRF)', *Journal of Archaeological Science* 46, 205–216.
Charalambous, A., Kassianidou, V. and Papasavvas, G. (2016) 'A comparative study of Cypriot bronzes dated to the Late Bronze and the Early Iron Age' in Photos-Jones, E. (ed.) *Proceedings of the 6th Symposium of the Hellenic Society for Archaeometry* (Athens 2013), Oxford, 95–99.
Childe, G. V. (1957) 'Civilizations, cities and towns', *Antiquity* 31, 36–8.
Consani, C. (1996) 'AB 118/DWO tra minoico e miceneo' in Consani, C., Negri, M. and Aspesi, F. (eds) *Κρήτη τις γαῖ' ἔστι: Studi e richerche intorno ai testi minoici. Quaderni Linguistici e Filologici, Università di Macerata, Facoltà di Lettere e Filosofia, Istituto di Glottologia e Linguistica Generale VIII*, Roma, 71–81.
Cooper, J. (2004) 'Babylonian beginnings: the origin of the cuneiform writing system in comparative perspective' in Houston, S. D. (ed.) *The First Writing: Script Invention as History and Process*, Cambridge, 71–99.
Cross, F. M. (1989) 'The invention and development of the alphabet' in Senner, W. E. (ed.) *The Origins of Writing*, Lincoln, 77–90.
Cross, F. M. and Stager, L. E. (2006) 'Cypro-Minoan inscriptions found in Ashkelon', *Israel Exploration Journal* 56, 129–159.
Damerow, P. (1999) *The Origins of Writing as a Problem of Historical Epistemology*, Preprint 114 of the Max Planck Institut für Wissenschaftsgeschichte, Berlin.
Daniels, P. T. (1992) 'The syllabic origin of writing and the segmental origin of the alphabet' in Downing, P. A., Lima, S. D. and Noonan, M. (eds.) *The Linguistics of Literacy*, Amsterdam, 83–110.
Daniels, P. T. (2000) 'On writing syllabaries: three episodes of script transfer', *Studies in Linguistic Sciences* 30, 73–86.
Daniels, P. T. (2003) '(There are) three models of script transfer: the "misunderstanding model"', *American Oriental Society, Abstracts of the Two Hundred and Fourteenth Meeting*, 1–2.
Daniels, P. T. (2006) 'On beyond alphabets', *Written Language and Literacy* 9, 7–24.
Daniels, P. T. (2007) '*Littera ex occidente*: toward a functional history of writing' in Miller, C. L. (ed.) *Studies in Semitic and Afroasiatic Linguistics Presented to Gene B. Gragg*, Chicago, 53–68.
Danto, A. C. (1997) *After the End of Art, Contemporary Art and the Pale of History*, Princeton.
Darnell, J. C. (2003) 'Die früalphabetischen Inschriften im Wadi el-Hôl' in Seipel, W. (ed.) *Der Turmbau zu Babel: Ursprung und Vielfalt von Sprache und Schrift: Eine Ausstellung des Kunsthistorisches Museums Wien für die Europäische Kulturhauptstadt Graz 2003*, Vol. 3A, Vienna, 165–71.
Darnell, J. C., Dobbs-Allsopp, F. W., Lundberg, M. J., McCarter, P. K., Zuckerman, B. (2005) 'Two early alphabetic inscriptions from Wadi el-Hôl', *Annual of the American Schools of Oriental Research* 59, 63–124.
Davis, B. (2011) 'Cypro-Minoan in Philistia?', *Kubaba* 2, 40–74.
Davis, B. (2014) *Minoan Stone Vessels with Linear A Inscriptions (Aegaeum* 36), Leuven/Liège.
Deger-Jalkotzy, S. (2013) 'Cremation burials in the Mycenaean cemetery of Elateia-Alonaki in Central Greece' in Lochner, M. and Ruppenstein, F. (eds.) *Brandbestattungen von der mittleren Donau bis zur Ägäis zwischen 1300 und 750 v. Chr.*, Vienna, 221–229.
Del Freo, M. (2010) 'Review of: Olivier, J.-P. *Édition holistique des textes chypro-minoens*', *Studi Micenei ed Egeo-Anatolici* 52, 305–313.
Dickinson, O. (1994) *The Aegean Bronze Age*, Cambridge.

Dietrich, M. and Loretz, O. (1988) 'Die Alphabettafel aus Bet Semes und die ursprüngliche Heimat der Ugariter' in Mauer, G. und Magen, U. (eds) *Ad bene et fideliter seminandum (Festgabe für K. Deller)*, Neukirchen, 61–87.

Dikaios, P. (1963) 'The context of the Enkomi tablets', *Kadmos* 2, 39–52.

Dikaios, P. (1969–1971) *Enkomi: Excavations, 1948–1958*, Vols I–II, Mainz-am-Rhein.

Dimopoulou, N., Olivier, J.-P. and Réthémiotakis, G. (1993) 'Une statuette en argile avec inscription en linéaire A de Poros Irakliou' *BCH* 117, 501–521.

Diringer, D. (1948) *The Alphabet. A key to the History of Mankind*, London.

Dreyer, G. (1998) *Um11l el-Qaab I: das präidynastische Königsgrab Uj und seine frühen Schrijtzeugnisse*, Mainz.

Driessen, J. (1990) *An Early Destruction in the Mycenaean Palace at Knossos. A New Interpretation of the Excavation Field-Notes of the South-East Area of the West Wing* (Acta Archaeologica Louvaniensia Monographiae 2), Leuven.

Driessen, J. (1997) 'Linear A tablets and political geography', in Hägg, R. (ed.) *The Function of the 'Minoan Villa'*, Stockholm, 216–217.

Driessen, J. (1998–1999) '*Kretes* and *Iawones*. Some observations on the identity of Late Bronze Age Knossians', in Bennet, J. and Driessen, J. (eds), *A-na-qo-ta. Studies Presented to J. T. Killen, Minos* 33–34, Salmanca, 83–105.

Driessen, J. (2000) *The Scribes of the Room of the Chariot Tablets at Knossos. Interdisciplinary Approach to the Study of a Linear B Deposit* (Supplement to *Minos* 15), Salamanca.

Driessen, J. (2011) 'Chronology of the Linear B texts', in Duhoux, Y. and Morpurgo Davies, A. (eds) *A Companion to Linear B. Mycenaean Greek Texts and their World*, vol. 1, Louvain-la-Neuve/Walpole MA, 69–79.

Driessen, J. (2012) 'Excavations at Sissi, 2011: Introduction' in *Excavations at Sissi III: Preliminary Report on the 2011 Campaign*, Aegis 6, Louvain, 17–26.

Driessen, J. and Langohr, C. (2007) 'Rallying round a "Minoan" past: the legitimation of power at Knossos during the Late Bronze Age' in Galaty, M. L. and Parkinson, W. A. (eds) *Rethinking Mycenaean Palaces II* revised and expanded 2nd edition (Cotsen Institute of Archaeology at UCLA Monograph 60), Los Angeles, 178–189.

Driessen, J. and Macdonald, C. F. (1997) *The Troubled Island. Minoan Crete Before and After the Santorini Eruption* (*Aegaeum* 17), Liège/Austin.

Driessen, J. and Schoep, I. (1999) 'The stylus and the sword. The role of scribes and warriors in the conquest of Crete', in Laffineur, R. (ed.), *Polemos. Le Contexte Guerrier en Ègée à l'Âge du Bronze* (*Aegaeum* 19), Liège/Austin, 389–401.

Duhoux, Y. (1978) 'Une analyse linguistique du linéaire A' in Duhoux, Y. (ed.) *Études minoennes I. Le linéaire A.* (Bibliothèque des Cahiers de l›Institut de Linguistique de Louvain 14), Louvain-la-Neuve, 65–129.

Duhoux, Y. (1985) 'Mycénien et écriture grecque', in Morpurgo Davies, A. and Duhoux, Y. (eds), *Linear B: a 1984 Survey*, Louvain-la-Neuve, 7–74.

Duhoux, Y. (1989) 'Le linéaire A: problèmes de déchiffrement' in Duhoux, Y., Palaima, T. G. and Bennet, J. (eds) *Problems in Decipherment* (Bibliothèque des Cahiers de l'Institut de Linguistique de Louvain 49), Louvain-la-Neuve, 59–120.

Duhoux, Y. (1998) 'Pre-Hellenic language(s) of Crete', *Journal of Indo-European Studies* 26, 1–39.

Duhoux, Y. (2008) 'Mycenaean anthology' in Duhoux, Y. and Morpurgo Davies, A. (eds) *A Companion to Linear B: Mycenaean Greek Texts and their World, vol. I.* (Bibliothèque des Cahiers de l'Institut de Linguistique de Louvain 120), Louvain-la-Neuve, 243–393.

Duhoux, Y. (2009a) 'The Cypro-Minoan tablet 1885 (Enkomi): an analysis' *Kadmos* 48, 5–38.

Duhoux, Y. (2009b) 'Eteocypriot and Cypro-Minoan 1–3', *Kadmos* 48, 39–75.

Duhoux, Y. (2012a) 'Les mini-tablettes linéaire B' in Carlier, P., de Lamberterie, C., Egetmeyer, M., Guilleux, N., Rougemont, F. and Zurbach, J. (eds) *Études Mycéniennes 2010* (Biblioteca di Pasiphae 10), Pisa/Roma, 207–225.

Duhoux, Y. (2012b) 'The most ancient Cypriot text written in Greek: The Opheltas' spit', *Kadmos* 51, 71–91.

Duhoux, Y. (2013) 'Non Greek languages of ancient Cyprus and their scripts: Cypro-Minoan 1–3' in Steele, P. M. (ed.) *Syllabic Writing on Cyprus and its Context*, Cambridge, 27–47.

Duhoux, Y., Palaima, T. G. and Bennet, J. (eds.) (1989) *Problems in Decipherment*, Bibliothèque des Cahiers de l'Institut de Linguistique de Louvain 49, Leuven.

Egetmeyer, M. (2010a) *Le dialecte grec ancien de Chypre. Tome I: Grammaire; Tome II: Répertoire des inscriptions en syllabaire chypro-grec*, Berlin/New York.

Egetmeyer, M. (2010b) 'The recent debate on Eteocypriote people and language' (Mycenological colloquium 11, Austin/Texas 2000), *Pasiphae* 3, 69–90.

Egetmeyer, M. (2013a) 'Ougarit et le déchiffrement de ses inscriptions en syllabaire chypro-minoen' in Bordreuil, P., Ernst-Pradal, F., Masetti-Rouault, M. G., Rouillard-Bonraisin and Zink, M. (eds) *Les écritures mises au jour sur le site antique d'Ougarit (Syrie) et leur déchiffrement. 1930–2010. Commémoration du quatre-vingtième anniversaire du déchiffrement de l'alphabet cunéiforme de Ras Shamra-Ougarit* (colloquium Paris 2010), Paris, 133–155.

Egetmeyer, M. (2013b) 'From Cypro-Minoan syllabaries to Cypro-Greek syllabaries: remarks on the phonetic structure of the grids passing from Pre-Greek to Greek' in Steele, P. M. (ed.) *Syllabic Writing on Cyprus and its Context*, Cambridge, 107–131.

Egetmeyer, M. (2014) 'Sur l'état de la recherche en écriture chypro-minoenne' (*Journée des langues rares*, Institut Catholique, Paris 2013), *Res Antiquae* 11, 101–118.

Egetmeyer, M. (2016) 'A bronze bowl from Palaepaphos-*Skales* with a new Cypro-Minoan inscription from the Cypro-Geometric I period' in Karageorghis, V. and Raptou, E. (eds) *Necropoleis at Palaepaphos from the end of the Late Bronze Age to the Cypro-Archaic Period*, Nicosia, 131–136.

Egetmeyer, M. (forthcoming) 'A new bronze weight with a Cypro-Greek inscription', *Report of the Department of Antiquities, Cyprus.*

Egetmeyer, M. and Steele, P. M. (2011) 'A new archaic and possibly Cypriot inscription from Cilicia', *Kadmos* 49, 127–132.

Englund, R. K. (1998) 'Texts from the Late Uruk period' in Bauer, J., Englund, R. and Krebernik, M. (eds) *Mesopotamien: Späturuk-Zeit und Frühdynastische Zeit*, Göttingen, 15–233.

Ephron, H. (1961) 'The Jeson tablet of Enkomi', *Harvard Studies in Classical Philology* 65, 39–107.

Evans, A. J. (1894a) 'A Mycenaean System of Writing in Crete and the Peloponnese', *Athenaeum* 3478, 812–813.

Evans, A. J. (1894b) 'Primitive pictographs and a Prae-Phoenician script, from Crete and the Peloponnese', *Journal of Hellenic Studies* 14, 270–372.

Evans, A. J. (1895) *Cretan Pictographs and Prae-Phoenician Script*, London.

Evans, A. J. (1902–1903) 'The Palace of Knossos. Provisional report for the year 1903', *Annual of the British School at Athens* 9, 1–153.

Evans, A. J. and Bosanquet, R. C. (1923) 'The inscribed objects in stone and clay' in Bosanquet, R. C. and Dawkins, R. M. *The Unpublished Objects from the Palaikastro Excavations 1902–1906*, (BSA Supplementary Paper 1), London, 141–147.

Facchetti, G. M., Negri, M. and Notti, E. (2013) 'Epigraphy and linguistic history of Cyprus: status and perspective', *Pasiphae* 7, 57–66.

Fantalkin, A., Finkelstein, I. and Piasetzky, E. (2015) 'Late Helladic to Middle Geometric Aegean and contemporary Cypriot chronologies: a radiocarbon view from the Levant', *Bulletin of the American Schools of Oriental Research* 373, 25–48.

Faucounau, J. (1977) 'Études chypro-minoennes' (I–III), *Syria* 54, 209–249.

Faucounau, J. (1980) 'Études chypro-minoennes' (IV–V), *Syria* 57.2, 375–410.

Faucounau, J. (1994) 'The Cypro-Minoan scripts: A reappraisal fifty years after John F. Daniel's paper', *Επιστημονικό Περιοδικό Αρχαιολογίας και Ιστορίας της Τέχνης, έκδοση του Συνδέσμου Κυπρίων Αρχαιολόγων* 3, 93–106.

Ferioli, P., Fiandra, E., Fissore, G. G. and Frangipane, M. (1994) (eds) *Archives Before Writing*, Turin.

Ferrara, S. (2013) 'Writing in Cypro-Minoan: one script, too many?' in Steele, P. M. (ed.) *Syllabic Writing on Cyprus and its Context*, Cambridge, 49–76.

Ferrara, S. (2014) 'Desecrating signs: "hieroglyphic" writing systems and secondary script inventions' in Galanakis, Y., Wilkinson, T. and Bennet, J. (eds.) *Critical Essays on the Archaeology of the Eastern Mediterranean in Honour of E. Susan Sherratt*, Oxford, 73–80.

Ferrara S. (2015) 'The royal and the layman. Possible onomastics on Late Bronze Age clay balls' *Studi Micenei ed Egeo-Anatolici* new series 1, 105–115.

Ferrara S. (2016) 'Writing away: Mobility and versatility of scribes at the end of the Bronze Age', *Oxford Journal of Archaeology* 35.3.

Ferrara, S., Weingarten, J. and Cadogan, G. (2016) 'Cretan Hieroglyphic at Myrtos Pyrgos', *Studi micenei ed anatolici* new series 2, 81–99.

Fiandra, E. (1968) 'A che cosa servivano le cretule di Festòs', *Πεπραγμένα του Β' Κρητολογικού Διεθνούς Συνεδρίου/Proceedings of the Second International Cretological Congress,* vol. 1, Athens, 383–397.

Fiandra, E. (1975) 'Ancora a proposito delle cretule di Festòs: connessione tra i sistemi amministrativi centralizzati e l'uso delle cretule nell'età del bronzo', *Bollettino d'Arte* 60, 1–25.

Finkelstein, I. and Sass, B. (2013) 'The west Semitic alphabetic inscriptions, Late Bronze II to Iron IIA: archeological context, distribution and chronology', *Hebrew Bible and Ancient Israel* 2, 149–220.

Firth, R. (1996–1997) 'The find-places of the tablets from the palace of Knossos', *Minos* 31–32, 7–122.

Firth, R. (2000–2001) 'A review of the find-places of the Linear B tablets from Knossos', *Minos* 35–36, 63–290.

Franklin, J. C. (2016) *Kinyras: the divine lyre*, Washington, DC.

Gaur, A. (2000) *Literacy and the Politics of Writing*, Bristol.

Gauss, W. (2007) 'Ägina Kolonna in frühmykenischer Zeit' in Alram-Stern, E. and Nightingale, G. (eds) *Keimelion: Elitenbildung und Elitärer Konsum von der Mykenischen Palastzeit bis zur Homerischen Epoche*, Wien, 163–172.

Gelb, I. J. (1952) *Study of Writing*. Chicago.

Gelb, I. J. (1963) *A Study of Writing*, 2nd edition, Chicago.

Gilboa, A. (2005) 'Sea peoples and Phoenicians along the southern Phoenician coast: a reconciliation: an interpretation of šikila (*SKL*) material culture', *Bulletin of the American Schools of Oriental Research* 337, 47–78.

Godart, L. (1979) 'Le linéaire A et son environnement', *Studi Micenei ed Egeo-Anatolici* 20, 27–42.

Godart, L. (1984) 'Du Linéaire A au Linéaire B' in Nicolet, C. (ed.) *Aux origines de l'hellénisme: La Crète et la Grèce. Hommage à Henri van Effenterre*, Paris, 121–128.

Godart, L. (1999a) 'L'écriture d'Archanès: hiéroglyphique ou linéaire A?' in Betancourt, P. P., Karageorghis, V., Laffineur, R. and Niemeier, W. (eds) *Meletemata. Studies in Aegean Archaeology Presented to Malcolm H. Wiener.* (*Aegaeum* 20), Liège/Austin, 299–302.

Godart, L. (1999b) 'L'inscription en linéaire B de Kafkania – Olympie (OL Zh 1)', in Deger-Jalkotzy, S., Hiller, S., Panagl, O. (eds) *Floreant Studia Mycenaea,* Vienna, 39–43.

Godart, L. (2002) 'L'inscription de Kavkania – Olympie OL Zh 1', in Arapojanni, X., Rambach, J. and Godart, L. *Kavkania. Die Ergebnisse der Ausgrabung von 1994 auf dem Hügel von Agrilitses*, Mainz, 213–240.

Godart, L. and Sacconi, A. (1979) 'La plus ancienne tablette d'Enkomi et le linéaire A' in Karageorghis, V. (ed.) *Acts of the International Archaeological Symposium: 'The Relations between Cyprus and Crete, ca. 2000–500 BC', Nicosia 16 April–22 April 1978*, Nicosia, 128–133.

Godart, L., Kanta, A. and Tzigounaki, A. (2000) 'Les scellés de Monastiraki' in Müller, W. (ed.), *Minoisch-Mykenische Glyptik. Stil, Ikonographie, Funktion*, (*CMS* 6), Berlin, 95–96.

Gombrich, E. H. (1950) *The Story of Art*, London.

Goody, J. and Watt, I. (1963) 'The consequences of literacy', *Comparative Studies in Society and History* 5, 304–345.

Goody, J. (1986) *The Logic of Writing and the Organisation of Society*, Cambridge.

Grube, N. (2010) 'Preposed phonetic complements in Maya hieroglyphic writing' in Carlin, E. B. and van de Kerke, S. *Linguistics and Archaeology in the Americas: The Historization of Language and Society*, Leiden, 27–43.

Grube, N. (2012) 'Maya writing' in Nichols, D. L. and Pool, C. A. (eds), *The Oxford Handbook of Mesoamerican Archaeology*, Oxford, 845–854.

Grumach, E. (1962) 'Mitteilungen: Linear A auf dem Festland', *Kadmos* 1.1, 85–86.

Grumach, E. (1963a) 'Neue hieroglyphische Siegel', *Kadmos* 2.1, 7–13.

Grumach, E. (1963b) 'Nachtrag zu "Zwei hieroglyphische Siegel"', *Kadmos* 2.1, 76–78.

Güterbock, H. G. (1956) 'Notes on Luvian Studies', *Orientalia* 25, 113–40.

Hallager, E. (1990) 'Roundels among sealings in Minoan administration: a comprehensive analysis of function' in Palaima, T. G. (ed.) *Aegean Seals, Sealings and Administration* (*Aegaeum* 5), Liège, 121–147.

Hallager, E. (1996) *The Minoan Roundel and Other Sealed Documents in the Neopalatial Linear A Administration* (*Aegaeum* 14), two volumes, Liège/Austin.

Hallager, E. (2000) 'New evidence for seal use in the pre- and protopalatial periods', in Müller, W. (ed.), *Minoisch-Mykenische Glyptik. Stil, Ikonographie, Funktion*, (*CMS* 6), Berlin, 97–105.

Hallager, E. (2002) 'One Linear A tablet and 45 noduli', *Creta Antica* 3, 105–109.

Hallager, E. (2005a) 'The uniformity in seal use and sealing practice during the LH/LM III period', in D'Agata, A. L. and Moody, J. (eds.) *Ariadne's Threads. Connections between Crete and the Greek Mainland in Late Minoan III (LM IIIA2 to LM IIIC)*, Athens, 243–265.

Hallager, E. (2005b) 'Fold-over nodules' in Perna, M. (ed.) *Studi in Onore di Enrica Fiandra: Contributi di Archeologia Egea e Vicinorientale* (Studi Egei e Vicinorientali 1), Paris, 105–112.

Hallager, E. (2010) 'Development of sealing practices in the Neopalatial period' in Müller, W. (ed.) *Die Bedeutung der minoischen und mykenischen Glyptik* (*CMS* 8), Mainz, 205–212.

Hallager, E. (2011) 'On the origin of Linear B administration', *Πεπραγμένα του Ι' Κρητολογικού Διεθνούς Συνεδρίου/Proceedings of the 10th Cretological Conference, Chania, 1–8 October 2006*, vol. A1, Chania, 317–329.

Hallager, E. (2015) 'Mycenaean administrative sealing practice: a world of its own?' in J. Weilhartner, J. and Ruppenstein, F. (eds) *Tradition and Innovation in the Mycenaean Palatial Polities* (Mykenische Studien 34), Vienna, 141–153.

Harbsmeier, M. (1988) 'Inventions of writing' in Gledhill, J., Bender, B. and Larsen, M. T. (eds) *State and Society: the Emergence and Development of Social Hierarchy and Political Centralisation*, London, 253–276.

Harper, P. O. Klengel-Brandt, E., Aruz, J. and Benzel, K. (1995) *Assyrian Discoveries at Ashur on the Tigris: Antiquities in the Vorderasiatisches Museum, Berlin*, New York.

Harper, R. F. (1904) *The Code Of Hammurabi, King of Babylon About 2250 B.C.*, 2nd edition, Chicago.

Harris, J. F. and Stearns, S. K. (1997), *Understanding Maya Inscriptions: A Hieroglyph Handbook*, 2nd edition, Philadelphia.

Haskell, H. W., Jones, R. E., Day, P. M. and Killen, J. T. (2011) *Transport Stirrup Jars of the Bronze Age Aegean and the East Mediterranean*, Philadelphia.

Havelock, E. A. (1982) *The Literate Revolution in Greece and its Cultural Consequences*, Princeton.

Hawkins, J. D. (1986) 'Writing in Anatolia: Imported and indigenous systems', *World Archaeology* 17.3, 363–376.

Hawkins, J. D. (2003) 'Script and texts' in Melchert, H. C. (ed.) *The Luwians*, Leiden, 128–169.

Hawkins, J. D. (2008) 'The disappearance of writing systems: Hieroglyphic Luwian' in Baines, J., Bennet, J. and Houston, S. D. (eds) *The Disappearance of Writing Systems*, London, 31–43.

Hawley, R. (2008) 'Apprendre à écrire à Ougarit: une typologie des abécédaries' in Roche, C. (ed.) *D'Ougarit à Jérusalem. Recueil d'études épigraphiques et archéologiques offert à Pierre Bordreuil*, Paris, 215–232.

Herder, J. G. (1985) *Schriften zum Alten Testament* ed. R. Smend, Frankfurt.

Heubeck, A. (1979) 'Remarks on the Sign-doublets ro_2, ra_2, ta_2' in Risch, E. and Mühlestein, H. (eds) *Colloquium Mycenaeum*, Neuchâtel-Genève, 239–258.

Heubeck, A. (1982) 'L'origine della lineare B', *Studi Micenei ed Egeo-Anatolici* 23, 195–207.

Hill Boone, E. (2004) 'Beyond writing' in Houston, S. D. (ed.), *The First Writing: Script Invention as History and Process*, Cambridge, 313–348.

Hiller, S. (1985) 'Die kyprominoische Schriftsysteme', *Archiv für Orientforschung* 20, 61–102.

Hirschfeld, N. (1997) *The PASP data base for the use of scripts on Cyprus*, Salamanca.

Hirschfeld, N. (1999) *Potmarks of the Late Bronze Age Eastern Mediterranean*, PhD. Dissertation, University of Texas at Austin.

Hirschfeld, N. (2012) 'Appendix IV: the potmarks' in Karageorghis V. and Violaris, Y. (eds) *Tombs of the Late Bronze Age in the Limassol Area, Cyprus (17th-13th centuries BC)*, Nicosia, 289–299.

Hirschfeld, N. (2014) Book review of P. M. Steele (ed.) *Syllabic Writing on Cyprus and its Context, American Journal of Archaeology* 118.4: http://www.ajaonline.org/online-review-book/1867.

Hooker, J. T. (1975) 'Problems and methods in the decipherment of Linear A', *Journal of the Royal Asiatic Society of Great Britain and Ireland* 2, 164–172.

Hooker, J. T. (1979) *The Origin of the Linear B Script* (Supplement to *Minos* 8), Salamanca.

Hopkins, N. A. (1994) 'Days, kings, and other Semantic classes marked in Maya hieroglyphic writing', unpublished paper presented at the 93rd Annual Meeting of the American Anthropological Association, Atlanta.

Hopkins, N. A. and Josserand, J. K. (1999) 'Issues of glyphic decipherment', unpublished paper presented at the 17th Annual University Museum Maya Weekend, '*Maya Epigraph - Progress and Prospects*', University of Pennsylvania, Philadelphia.

Houston, S. D. (2004a) (ed.) *The First Writing. Script Invention as History and Process*, Cambridge.

Houston, S. D. (2004b) 'Writing in Early Mesoamerica' in Houston, S. D. (ed.) *The First Writing. Script Invention as History and Process*, Cambridge, 274–309.

Houston, S. D. (2004c) 'The archaeology of communication technologies', *Annual Review of Anthropology* 33, 223–250.

Houston, S. D. (2012) (ed.) *The Shape of Script. How and Why Writing Systems Change*, Santa Fe.

Houston, S. D. and Rojas, F. (forthcoming) 'Sourcing novelty. On the "secondary invention" of writing' in Woods, C. and Shaughnessy, E. (eds) *Signs of Writing. The Cultural, Social, and Linguistic Contexts of the World's First Writing Systems*, Chicago.

Iacovou, M. (2013) 'The Cypriot syllabary as a royal signature: the political context of the syllabic script in the Iron Age' in Steele, P. M. (ed.) *Syllabic Writing on Cyprus and its Context*, Cambridge, 133–152.

Iakovidis, S. E, Godart, L. and Sacconi, A. (2012) 'Les inscriptions en linéaire B découvertes dans la "Maison de Petsas" à Mycènes', *Pasiphae* 6, 49–57.

Ilievski, P. H. and Crepajac, L. (eds) (1987) *Tractata Mycenaea*, Skopje.

Jackendoff, R. (2002) *Foundations of Language: Brain, Meaning, Grammar, Evolution*, Oxford.

Janko, R. (1987) 'Linear A and the direction of the earliest Cypro-Minoan writing' in Killen, J. T., Melena, J. L. and Olivier, J.-P. (eds) *Studies in Mycenaean and Classical Greek Presented to John Chadwick* (= *Minos* 20–22), Salamanca, 311–317.

Janko, R. (2015) 'From Gabii and Gordion to Eretria and Methone: the rise of the Greek alphabet', *Bulletin of the Institute of Classical Studies* 58, 1–32.

Jasink, A. M. (2005) 'The so-called klasmatograms on Cretan Hieroglyphic seals', *Kadmos* 44, 23–29.

Jasink, A. M. (2009) *Cretan Hieroglyphic Seals: A New Classification of Symbols and Ornamental/Filling Motifs* (Biblioteca di 'Pasiphae' 13), Pisa/Rome.

Jiménez Delgado, J. M. (2008) 'La situación de *h en griego micénico', *Kadmos* 47.1–2, 73–90.

Judson, A. P. (2016) *The Undeciphered Signs of Linear B*, unpublished PhD Thesis, University of Cambridge.

Judson, A. P. (forthcoming) 'The mystery of the Mycenaean "labyrinth": the value of Linear B pu_2 and related signs', *Studi Micenei ed Egeo-Anatolici* Nuova Serie 3.

Justeson, J. S. and Mathews, P. (1990) 'Evolutionary trends in Mesoamerican hieroglyphic writing', *Visible Language* 24.1, 88–132.

Karageorghis, V. (1970) 'Note on sigynnae and obeloi', *Bulletin de Correspondance Hellénique* 94, 35–44.

Karageorghis, V. (1983) *Palaepaphos-Skales. An Iron Age Cemetry in Cyprus*, Constance.

Karageorghis, V. and Raptou, E. (2014) *Necropoleis at Palaepaphos from the End of the Late Bronze Age to the Cypro-Archaic Period*, Nicosia.

Karageorghis, V. and Raptou, E. (2016) *Palaepaphos-Skales. Tombs of the Late Cypriot IIIB and Cypro-Geometric periods (Excavations of 2008 and 2011)*, Nicosia.

Karetsou, A. (2000) (ed.) *Κρήτη-Αίγυπτος. Πολιτισμικοί Δεσμοί Τριών Χιλιετιών. Κατάλογος*, Athens.

Karnava, A. (1997) 'Review of J.-P. Olivier and L. Godart, 'Corpus Hieroglyphicarum Inscriptionum Cretae' (*CHIC*), *Studi Micenei ed Egeo-Anatolici* 39, 300–304.

Karnava, A. (2000) The Cretan Hieroglyphic Script of the Second Millennium BC: Description, Analysis, Function and Decipherment Perspectives. Unpublished doctoral thesis, Université Libre de Bruxelles.

Karnava, A. (2007) 'Tradition and innovation: the scripts in the Old Palatial period', *BICS* 50.1, 199–200.

Karnava, A. (2013) 'Κύπριοι της 1ης χιλ. π.Χ. στον ελλαδικό χώρο: η μαρτυρία των συλλαβικών επιγραφών' in Michaelides, D. (ed.) *Epigraphy, Numismatics, Prosopography and History of Ancient Cyprus. Papers in Honour of Ino Nicolaou*, Uppsala, 159–169.

Karo, G. (1930–1933) *Die Schachtgräber von Mykenai*, München.

Keller-Cohen, D. (1994) *Literacy: Interdisciplinary Conversations*, Cresskill, NJ.

Kelly, J. D. (2006) 'Writing the state: China, India, and general definitions' in Sanders, S. (ed.) *Margins of Writing, Origins of Culture*, Chicago, 15–32.

Kettunen, H. and Helmke, C. (2014) *Introduction to Maya Hieroglyphs, XIX European Maya Conference Bratislava 2014*, 14th edition, Bratislava.

Killen, J. T. (1964) 'The wool industry of Crete in the Late Bronze Age', *Annual of the British School at Athens* 59, 1–15.

Kober, A. E. (1945) 'Evidence of Inflection in the "Chariot" Tablets from Knossos', *American Journal of Archaeology* 49.2, 143–151.

Krzyszkowska, O. (2005) *Aegean Seals. An Introduction* (*BICS* Supplement 85), London.

Krzyszkowska, O. (2012) 'Seals from the Petras Cemetery: a preliminary overview' in Tsipopoulou, M. (ed.) *Petras, Siteia - 25 years of Excavations and Studies. Acts of a Two-day Conference Held at the Danish Institute at Athens, 9-10 October 2010* (Monographs of the Danish Institute at Athens 16), Athens, 145–160.

Krzyszkowska, O. (2015) 'Why were cats different? Script and imagery in Middle Minoan II glyptic' in Macdonald, C. F., Hatzaki, E. and Andreou, S. (eds) *The Great Islands: Studies of Crete and Cyprus presented to Gerald Cadogan*, Athens, 100–106.

Krzyskowska, O. (forthcoming) 'Seals from Petras Siteia: new insights for MM II hard stone glyptic' in *Proceedings of the Cretological Society, Rethymnon 21-27 October 2011*, unpublished.

Ladefoged, P. and Maddieson, I. (1996) *The Sounds of the World's Languages*, Oxford.

Landenius Enegren, H. (2008) *The People of Knossos. Prosopographical Studies in the Knossos Linear B Archives*, Uppsala.

Laroche, E. (1956) 'Documents hiérogliphiques hittites provenant du palais d'Ugarit' in Schaeffer, C. F. A. (ed.) (*Ugaritica* III), Paris, 97–163.

Larsen, M. T. (1988) 'Introduction: Literacy and social complexity' in Gledhill, J., Bender, B. and Larsen, M. T. (eds) *State and Society: the Emergence and Development of Social Hierarchy and Political Centralisation*, London, 173–191.

Lebessi, A., Muhly, P. and Olivier, J.-P. (1995) 'An inscription in the Hieroglyphic script from the Syme sanctuary, Crete (SY Hf 01)', *Kadmos* 34, 63–77.

Lebessi, A., Olivier, J.-P. and Godart, L. (1974) 'Πινακίδες Γραμμικῆς Α ἐξ Ἀρχανῶν', *ArchEph*, 113–167.

Le Feuvre, C. (2015) Ὅμηρος δύσγνωστος. *Réinterprétations de termes homériques en grec archaïque et classique*, Geneva.

Lehmann, R. G. (2012) '27-30-22-26 – How many letters needs an alphabet?' in de Voogt, A. and Quack, J. F. (eds) *The Idea of Writing. Writing Across Borders*, Leiden, 11–52.
Lehmann, R. G. (2013) 'Ist damit das Nötige gesagt? Zu einem neuen Trend in der althebräischen Epigraphik', *Orientalistische Literatur Zeitung* 108, 221–229 (= review of Rollston, C. A., *Writing and Literacy in the World of Ancient Israel. Epigraphic Evidence from the Iron Age*, Leiden: Brill, 2010).
Leibundgut Wieland, D. and Frey-Asche, L. (2011) *Weihgeschenke aus dem Heiligtum der Aphrodite in Alt-Paphos. Terrakotten, Skulpturen und andere figürliche Kleinvotive*, Darmstadt.
Lejeune, M. (1958a) 'Coup d'oeil sur le système graphique' in Lejeune, M. (ed.) *Mémoires de philologie mycénienne. Première série (1955–1957)*, Paris, 318–330.
Lejeune, M. (1958b) 'Sur les signes notant des syllabes à groupe consonantique initial' in Lejeune, M. (ed.) *Mémoires de philologie mycénienne. Première série (1955–1957)*, Paris, 255–282.
Lejeune, M. (1972a) 'Doublets et complexes' in Lejeune, M. (ed.) *Mémoires de philologie mycénienne. Troisième série (1964–1968)* (Istituto per gli Studi Micenei ed Egeo-Anatolici: Incunabula Graeca 43), Roma, 89–104.
Lejeune, M. (1972b) *Phonétique historique du mycénien et du grec ancien* (Tradition de l'Humanisme ix), Paris.
Lejeune, M. (1997a) 'Les syllabogrammes B et leur translitération' in Lejeune, M. (ed.) *Mémoires de philologie mycénienne. Quatrième série (1969–1996)* (Istituto per gli Studi Micenei ed Egeo-Anatolici: Incunabula Graeca 99), Rome, 25–52.
Lejeune, M. (1997b) 'Pré-mycénien et proto-mycénien' in Lejeune, M. (ed.) *Mémoires de philologie mycénienne. Quatrième série (1969–1996)* (Istituto per gli Studi Micenei ed Egeo-Anatolici: Incunabula Graeca 99), Roma, 197–212.
Levelt, C. (1994) *The Acquisition of Place*, Leiden.
Lévi-Strauss, C. (1955) *Tristes tropiques*, Paris.
Lewis, G. (1999) *The Turkish Script Reform. A Catastrophic Success*, Oxford.
Liberman, I. Y., Shankweiler, D., Fisher, F. W. and Carter, B. (1974) 'Explicit syllable and phoneme segmentation in the young child', *Journal of Experimental Child Psychology* 18, 201–212.
Lomas, K. (2007) 'Writing boundaries: Literacy and identity in the ancient Veneto' in, Lomas, K., Whitehouse, R. D. and Wilkins, J. (eds) *Literacy and the State in the Ancient Mediterranean*, London, 149–169.
Lomas, K. (2008) 'Script obsolescence in ancient Italy: from pre-Roman to Roman writing' in Baines, J., Bennet, J. and Houston, S. D. (eds) *The Disappearance of Writing Systems*, London, 109–138.
Luce, J.-M. (2009) 'Iron Age burial customs in the Peloponnese and their place in the funerary geography of the Greek world' in Cavanagh, H., Cavanagh, W. and Roy, J. (eds) *Honouring the Dead in the Peloponnese* (colloquium Sparta 2009), Nottingham, 415–426 (online: <https://www.nottingham.ac.uk/csps/open-source/hounouring-the-dead.aspx>).
Luce, J.-M. (2014) 'Les modes funéraires et la parole dans la Grèce de l'âge du fer ancien', *Dialogues d'Histoire Ancienne* supplement 10, 37–51.
Luraghi, N. (2010) 'The local scripts from nature to culture', *Classical Antiquity* 29.1, 68–91.
Mackay, A. (1965) 'On the type-fount of the Phaistos disc', *Statistical Methods in Linguistics* 4, 15–25.
Macdonald, C. F. and Knappett, C. (eds) (2007) *Knossos. Protopalatial Deposits in Early Magazine A and the South-West Houses* (British School at Athens Supplement 41), London.
MacNeilage, P. F. and Davis, B. L. (2000) 'Evolution of speech: the relation between ontogeny and phylogeny' in Knight, C., Studdert-Kennedy, M. and Hurford, J. R. (eds) *The Evolutionary Emergence of Language. Social Function and the Origins of Linguistic Form*, Cambridge, 146–160.
Maeir, A. M., Davis, B. and Hitchcock, L. A. 'Philistine names and terms once again. A recent perspective', *Journal of Eastern Mediterranean Archaeology and Heritage Studies* 4, 321–340.
Mander, P. (2000) 'I testi amministrativi e la sigillatura: gli archivi del III millennio' in Perna, M. (ed.) *Administrative Documents in the Aegean and their Near Eastern Counterparts*, Turin, 33–49.
Maniatis, Y., Arapogianni, X. and Godart, L. (2010) 'Kavkania: le mot de la fin', *Pasiphae* 4, 117–134.

Mann, S. E. (1960) 'The decipherment of Cypro-Mycenaean', *Man* 60, 40–42.

Marazzi, M. (1990) *Il Geroglifico Anatolico. Problemi di Analisi e Prospettive di Ricerca*, Rome.

Masetti-Rouault, M. G. (2016) 'Le monde syro-mésopotamien à l'âge du Fer I–II: cultures locales et culture impériale, entre Assyriens et Araméens', *Semitica et Classica* 8, 111–116.

Masson, É. (1969) 'La plus ancienne tablette chypro-minoenne', *Minos* 10, 64–77.

Masson, É. (1972) 'Les répertoires graphiques chyprominoens' in Ruipérez, M. S. (ed.) *Acta Mycenaea* (*Minos* 11, vol. I), Salamanca, 99–109.

Masson, É. (1973) 'La tablette chypro-minoenne 20–25 de Ras Shamra: essai d'interprétation', *Comptes-rendus des séances de l'Académie des inscriptions et belles-lettres* 117.1, 32–60.

Masson, É. (1974) *Cyprominoica: répertoires; documents de Ras Shamra; essais d'interprétation*, Göteborg.

Masson, É. (1979a) 'L'apparition de l'écriture à Chypre: témoignage probable des contacts entre l'île de Crète et l'île de Chypre au cours de la première moitié du deuxième millénaire' in Karageorghis, V. (ed.) *Acts of the International Archaeological Symposium: 'The Relations between Cyprus and Crete, ca. 2000–500 BC', Nicosia 16 April–22 April 1978*, Nicosia, 134–8.

Masson, É. (1979b) 'Quelques inscriptions inédites d'Enkomi', *Ugarit-Forschungen* 11, 559–562.

Masson, É. (1987) 'La part du fond commun égéen dans les écritures chypro-minoennes et son apport possible pour leur déchiffrement' in Killen, J. T., Melena, J. L. and Olivier, J.-P. (eds) *Studies in Mycenaean and Classical Greek Presented to John Chadwick* (= *Minos* 20–22), Salamanca, 367–381.

Masson, É. and Masson. O (1983) 'Appendix 4: Les objets inscrits de Palaepaphos-*Skales*' in Karageorghis, V. (ed.) *Palaepaphos-Skales: An Iron Age Cemetery in Cyprus*, Constanz, 411–415.

Masson, O. (1955) 'La découverte d'une tablette chypro-minoenne à Ras-Shamra (1953)', *Comptes rendus des séances de l'Académie des Inscriptions et Belles-Lettres, 99e année*, N. 2, 174–180.

Masson, O. (1956) 'Documents chypro-minoens de Ras Shamra. I Inscriptions diverses et tablette de 1953; II Fragments de tablettes chypro-minoennes de Ras Shamra (1955)' in Schaeffer, C.F.-A. (ed.) *Ugaritica III. Sceaux et cylindres hittites, épée gravée du cartouche de Mineptah, tablettes chypro-minoennes et autres découvertes nouvelles de Ras Shamra. Mission de Ras Shamra*, Vol. 8, Paris, 233–250.

Masson, O. (1957) 'Cylindres et cachets chypriotes portant des caractères chyprominoens', *Bulletin de correspondance hellénique* 81, 6–37.

Masson, O. (1968a) 'Les écritures chypro-minoennes et les autres écritures chypriotes' in *Atti e Memorie del 1° Congresso internazionale di Micenologia. Roma 27 settembre–3 ottobre 1967*, Rome 1, 417–425.

Masson, O. (1968b) 'Kypriaka' (IV. La plus ancienne inscription paphienne, V. La plus ancienne inscription phénicienne de Chypre, VI. Une inscription étrange de Golgoi, VII. Le sanctuaire d'Apollon à Idalion (fouilles 1868–1869)), *Bulletin de Correspondance Hellénique* 92, 375–409.

Masson, O. (1969) 'Documents chypro-minoens de Ras Shamra' in Schaeffer, C. F. A. (ed.) *Ugaritica VI, publié à l'occasion de la XXXe campagne de fouilles à Ras Shamra (1968) sous la direction de Claude F.-A. Schaeffer. Mission de Ras Shamra* Vol. 17, Paris, 379–392.

Masson, O. and Mitford, T. B. (1986) *Les inscriptions syllabiques de Kouklia-Paphos*, Constance.

Matthäus, H. (2016) Review of Karageorghis and Raptou 2014, *Gnomon* 88, 629–633.

Matthäus, H. and Schuhmacher-Matthäus, G. (2013) 'Social and ethnic change in Cyprus during the 11th century B.C. New evidence from Kourion, Kaloriziki, tomb 40', *Pasiphae* 7, 159–168.

Matthäus, H. and Schuhmacher-Matthäus, G. (2015) 'Kourion-Kaloriziki tomb 40: a republication', in Matthäus, H., Morstadt, B. and Vonhoff, C. (eds.) *PoCA* (Postgraduates on Cypriot Archaeology) (2012), Cambridge, 1–111.

Mavrojannis, T. (2007) 'Herodotus on the introduction of the Phoenician alphabet to the Greeks, the Gephyraeans and the Proto-Geometric building at Toumba in Lefkandi', *Klio* 89, 291–319.

Meißner, T. (2008) 'Notes on Mycenaean Spelling' in Sacconi, A., Del Freo, M., Godart, L. and M. Negri (eds.) *Colloquium Romanum, Pasiphae II*, Pisa/Roma, vol. 2, 507–521.

Meißner, T. (2013) 'Anläßlich von: Beekes, Robert with the assistance of Lucien van Beek: Etymological Dictionary of Greek. Leiden Indo-European Etymological Dictionary Series, 10. Brill Verlag Leiden, 2009', *Kratylos* 58, 1–32.

Meißner, T. and Steele, P. M. (forthcoming) 'Linear A and Linear B: structural and contextual concerns' in Nosch, M.-L.B. and Landenius Enegren, H. (eds) *Aegean Scripts*, Rome.

Melchert, C. H. (1996) 'Anatolian hieroglyphs' in Daniels, P. T. and Bright, W. (eds.) *The World's Writing Systems*, Oxford, 120–124.

Melchert, C. (2004) 'Luvian' in Woodard, R. D. (ed.) *The Cambridge Encyclopedia of the World's Ancient Languages*, Cambridge, 576–584.

Melena, J. L. (1983) 'Notas de filologia micenica III: el silabograma *86', *Emerita* 51, 262–267.

Melena, J. L. (1987) 'On Untransliterated Syllabograms *56 and *22' in Ilievski, P. H. and Crepajac, L. (eds) *Tractata Mycenaea*, Skopje, 203–232.

Melena, J. L. (2000–2001) '24 joins and quasi-joins of fragments in the Linear B tablets from Pylos', *Minos* 35–36, 357–369.

Melena, J. L. (2014) 'Mycenaean writing' in Duhoux, Y. and Morpurgo Davies, A. (eds) *A Companion to Linear B: Mycenaean Greek Texts and their World, vol. 3* (Bibliothèque des Cahiers de l'Institut de Linguistique de Louvain 133), Louvain-la-Neuve, 1–186.

Melena, J. L. (forthcoming) 'On the structure of the Mycenaean Linear B syllabary. I. The untransliterated syllabograms. Preliminary report' in *Proceedings of the 11th International Colloquium on Mycenaean Studies, Austin, Texas, 7th-12th May 2000*, Austin. [https://www.academia.edu/2203598/]

Meriggi, P. (1973a) 'Das Wort "Kind" in den kretischen Hieroglyphen', *Kadmos* 12, 114–133.

Meriggi, P. (1973b) 'Sul geroglifico cretese' in Rizza, G. (ed) *Antichità Cretesi: Studi in Onore di Doro Levi*, vol. 1 (Chronache di Archeologia 12), Roma, 172–181.

Merrillees, R. S. (1993) 'The languages of Cyprus', *Cahiers du centre d'études chypriotes* 20, 3–17.

Messaris, P. and Moriarty, S. (2005) 'Visual literacy theory' in Smith, K., Moriarty, S., Barbatsis, G., and Kenney, K. (eds) *Handbook of Visual Communication*, Mahwah, 481–502.

Michalowski, P. (1990) 'Early Mesopotamian communicative systems: Art, literature and writing' in Gunter, A. C. (ed.) *Investigating Artistic Environments in the Ancient Near East*, Washington DC, 53–69.

Michalowski, P. (1994) 'Writing and literacy in early states: A Mesopotamianist perspective' in Keller-Cohen, D. (ed.) *Literacy: Interdisciplinary Conversations*, Cresskill, 49–70.

Militello, P. (2000) ''L'archivio di cretule' del Vano 25 e un nuovo sigillo da Festòs', in Perna, M. (ed.), *Administrative Documents in the Aegean and their Near Eastern Counterparts*, Turin, 221–249.

Mitford, T. B. and Masson, O. (1983) *The Syllabic Inscriptions of Rantidi-Paphos*, Constance.

Mora, C. (1991) 'Sull'origine della scrittura geroglifica anatolica', *Kadmos* 20.1, 1–28.

Mora-Marín, D. F. (2008) 'Full phonetic complementation, semantic classifiers, and semantic determinatives in ancient Mayan hieroglyphic writing', *Ancient Mesoamerica* 19, 195–213.

Morgan, L. (1985) 'Idea, idiom and iconography' in *Bulletin de correspondance hellénique*, supplement 11, Athens/Paris, 5–19.

Morpurgo Davies, A. (1985) 'Mycenaean and Greek Language' in Morpurgo Davies, A. and Duhoux, Y. (eds.) *Linear B: a 1984 Survey* (Bibliothèque des Cahiers de l'Institut de Linguistique de Louvain 26), Louvain-la-Neuve, 75–126.

Morpurgo Davies, A. (1986) 'Forms of writing in ancient Mediterranean world' in Baumann, G. (ed.) *The Written Word. Literacy in Transition*, Oxford, 55–77.

Morpurgo Davies, A. and Hawkins, J. D. (1978) 'Il sistema grafico del luvio geroglifico', *Annali della Scuola Normale Superiore di Pisa* 8.3, 755–782.

Morpurgo Davies, A. and Olivier, J.-P. (2012) 'Syllabic scripts and languages in the second and first millennia BC' in Cadogan, G., Iacovou, M., Kopaka, K. and Whitley, J. (eds.) *Parallel Lives. Ancient Island Societies in Crete and Cyprus*, London, 105–118.

Muhly, P. and Olivier, J.-P. (2008) 'Linear A inscriptions from the Syme sanctuary, Crete', *ArchEph*, 197–223.

Nahm, W. (1981) 'Studien zur kypro-minoischen Schrift', *Kadmos* 20, 52–63.

Nahm, W. (1984) 'Studien zur kypro-minoischen Schrift II', *Kadmos* 23, 164–179.

Nakassis, D. (2012) 'Labor mobilization in Mycenaean Pylos' in Carlier, P., de Lamberterie, C., Egetmeyer, M., Guilleux, N., Rougemont, F. and Zurbach, J. (eds) *Études Mycéniennes 2010* (Biblioteca di Pasiphae 10), Pisa/Roma, 269–283.

Nakassis, D. (2013) *Individuals and Society in Mycenaean Pylos. Mnemosyne Supplements* (History and Archaeology of Classical Antiquity 358), Leiden/Boston.

Neumann, G. (1960) 'Minoisch kikina "die Sykomorenfeige"', *Glotta* 3/4, 181–186.

Neumann, C. (1992) *System und Ausbau der hethitischen Hieroglyphenschrift*, Göttingen.

Neumann, G. (1996) 'Zur Schaffung der Zeichen *91 *two* und *62 *pte* von Linear B' in De Miro, E., Godart, L. and Sacconi, A. (eds) *Atti e memorie del Secondo Congresso Internazionale di Micenologia* (Incunabula Graeca 98), Roma, 1, 91–99.

Nosch, M.-L. B. (2007) *The Knossos Od Series. An Epigraphical Study*, Vienna.

Nosch, M.-L. B. (2012) 'The textile logograms in the Linear B tablets: *Les idéogrammes archéologiques - des textiles*' in Carlier, P., de Lamberterie, C., Egetmeyer, M., Guilleux, N., Rougemont, F. and Zurbach, J. (eds) *Études Mycéniennes 2010* (Biblioteca di Pasiphae 10), Pisa/Roma, 303–344.

Olivier, J.-P. (1979) 'L'origine de l'écriture linéaire B', *Studi Micenei ed Egeo-Anatolici* 20, 43–52.

Olivier, J-P. (1981) 'Les sceaux avec de signes hiéroglyphique. Que lire? Une question de définition' in Pini, I. (ed.) *Studien zur minoischen und helladischen Glyptik* (*CMS* 1), Berlin, 105–115.

Olivier, J.-P. (1986) 'Cretan writing in the second millennium BC', *World Archaeology* 17.3, 377–389.

Olivier, J-P. (1989) 'The possible methods in deciphering the pictographic Cretan script' in Duhoux, Y., Palaima, T. G. and Bennet, J. (eds) *Problems in Decipherment*, Louvain-la-Neuve, 39–58.

Olivier, J.-P. (1990) 'The relationship between inscriptions on hieroglyphic seals and those written on archival documents' in Palaima, T. G. (ed.) *Aegean Seals, Sealings and Administration* (*Aegaeum* 5), Liège, 11–24.

Olivier, J.-P. (1994–1995) 'Un simili-raccord dans les barres en Hiéroglyphique de Cnossos (*CHIC* #057 ⊕ #058)', *Minos* 29–30, 257–269.

Olivier, J.-P. (1995) 'Les sceaux avec des signes hiéroglyphiques. Que lire? Une question de bon sens' in Müller, W. (ed.) *Sceaux minoens et mycéniens: IVe symposium international, 10–12 septembre 1992, Clermont-Ferrand* (*CMS* 5), Berlin, 169–181.

Olivier, J.-P. (1996) 'Les écritures crétoises: sept points à considérer' in De Miro, E., Godart, L. and Sacconi, A. (eds.) *Atti e Memorie del Secondo Congresso Internazionale di Micenologia, Roma-Napoli, 14–20 ottobre 1991* (Incunabula Graeca 98:1), Roma, 101–113.

Olivier, J.-P. (1997) 'The possible methods in deciphering the pictographic Cretan script' in Duhoux, Y., Palaima, T. G. and Bennett, J. (eds) *Problems in Decipherment* (Bibliothèque des Cahiers de l'Institut de Linguistique de Louvain 49), Louvain-la-Neuve, 39–58.

Olivier, J-P. (2000) 'Les sceaux avec des inscriptions hiéroglyphiques. Comment comprendre?' in Perna, M. (ed.) *Administrative Documents in the Aegean and their Near Eastern Counterparts*, Rome, 141–191.

Olivier, J.-P. (2010) 'Les sceaux et scellés inscrits en "Hiéroglyphique" Crétois, en Linéaire A et en Linéaire B en Crète et en Grèce continentale, en Chypro-Minoen et dans les Syllabaires du Ier millénaire à chypre: un bilan' in Müller, W. (ed.) *Die Bedeutung der Minoischen und Mykenischen Glyptik* (*CMS* 8), Mainz, 287–295.

Olivier, J.-P. (2013) 'The development of Cypriot syllabaries, from Enkomi to Kafizin' in Steele, P. M. (ed.) *Syllabic Writing on Cyprus and its Context*, Cambridge, 7–26.

Olivier, J.-P. (2015) 'Inscription syllabique' in Caubet, A., Fourrier, S. and Yon, M. (eds.) *Kition-Bamboula VI. Le sanctuaire sous la colline*, Lyon, 346–347.

Packard, D. W. (1974) *Minoan Linear A*, Berkeley/Los Angeles/London.

Palaima, T. G. (1982) 'Linear A in the Cyclades: The trade and travel of a script', *Temple University Aegean Symposium* 7, 15–22.

Palaima, T. G. (1988a) 'The development of the Mycenaean writing system', in Olivier, J. P. and Palaima, T. G. (eds) *Texts, Tablets and Scribes. Studies in Mycenaean Epigraphy and Economy Offered to Emmett L. Bennett, Jr* (Supplement to *Minos* 10), Salamanca, 269–342.

Palaima, T. G. (1988b) 'The development of the Mycenaean script and literacy', *Bulletin of the Institute of Classical Studies* 35, 166–167.

Palaima, T. G. (1989) 'Cypro-Minoan scripts: Problems of historical context' in Duhoux, Y., Palaima, T. G. and Bennet, J. (eds.), *Problems in Decipherment*, Louvain-la-Neuve, 121–187.

Palaima, T. G. (1990) 'Origin, development, transition and transformation: the purposes and techniques of administration in Minoan and Mycenaean society' in Palaima, T. G. (ed.) *Aegean Seals, Sealings and Administration* (*Aegaeum* 5), Liège, 83–104.

Palaima, T. G. (1990) (ed.) *Aegean Seals, Sealings and Administration* (*Aegaeum* 5), Liège.

Palaima, T. G. (1994) 'Seal-users and script-users/nodules and tablets at LM IB Hagia Triada', in Ferioli, P., Fiandra, E., Fissore, G. G. and Frangipane, M. (eds), *Archives before Writing*, Rome, 307–337.

Palaima, T. G. (1998) Review of 'Corpus Hieroglyphicarum Inscriptionum Cretae (*CHIC*)', *American Journal of Archaeology* 102, 434–435.

Palaima, T. G. (2002–2003) 'OL Zh 1: *QVOVSQVE TANDEM?*', *Minos* 37–38, 373–385.

Palaima, T. G. (2003) 'The inscribed bronze "kessel" from Shaft Grave IV and Cretan heirlooms of the bronze artist named "Aigeus" *vel sim.* in the Mycenaean Palatial period' in Duhoux, Y. (ed.) *Briciaka. A Tribute to W.C. Brice. Cretan Studies 9*, Amsterdam, 188–201.

Palaima, T. G. (2010) 'Linear B', in E. Cline (ed.), *The Oxford Handbook of the Bronze Age Aegean (ca. 3000–1000 BC)*, Oxford/New York, 356–372.

Palaima, T. G. (2011) 'Scribes, scribal hands and palaeography' in Duhoux, Y. and Morpurgo Davies, A. (eds) *A Companion to Linear B: Mycenaean Greek Texts and their World*, vol. 2, Louvain-la-Neuve/Walpole, 33–136.

Palaima, T. G. and Sikkenga, E. (1999) 'Linear A > Linear B' in Betancourt, P. P., Karageorghis, V. and Laffineur, R. (eds.) *Meletemata. Studies in Aegean Archaeology Presented to Malcolm H. Wiener as He Enters His 65th Year* (*Aegaeum* 20), Liège/Austin, 2, 599–608.

Palaima, T. G. and Wright, J. C. (1985) 'Ins and outs of the Archives Rooms at Pylos: form and function in a Mycenaean palace', *American Journal of Archaeology* 89, 251–262.

Palma di Cesnola, L. (1877) *Cyprus, its ancient cities, tombs and temples. A narrative of researches and excavations during ten years' residence as American consul in that island*, London.

Palmer, L. R. (1955) 'Observations on the Linear "B" tablets from Mycenae', *Bulletin of the Institute of Classical Studies* 2, 36–45.

Palmer, L. R. (1963) *The Interpretation of Mycenaean Greek Texts*, Oxford.

Palmer, L. R. (1980), *The Greek Language*, Bristol.

Palmer, R. (1995) 'Linear A commodities: a comparison of resources', in Laffineur, R. and Niemeier, W.-D. (eds) *Politeia. Society and State in the Aegean Bronze Age* (*Aegaeum* 12), Liège/Austin, 133–155.

Panagiotopoulos, D. (2010) 'A systemic approach to Mycenaean sealing practices' in Müller, W. (ed.) *Die Bedeutung der minoischen und mykenischen Glyptik* (*CMS* 8), Mainz, 297–307.

Panagiotopoulos, D. (2014) *Mykenische Siegelpraxis. Funktion, Kontext und administrative Verwendung mykenischer Tonplomben aus dem griechischen Festland und Kreta* (*Athenaia* 5), Munich.

Papadopoulos, J. K. (1994) 'Early Iron Age potters' marks in the Aegean', *Hesperia* 63, 437–507.

Papadopoulos, J. K. (2016) 'The early history of the Greek alphabet: new evidence from Eretria and Methone', *Antiquity* 90 (353), 1238–1254.

Pardee, D. (1997a) 'Proto-Canaanite' in Meyers, E. M. (ed.) *Oxford Encyclopaedia of Archaeology in the Near East*, Vol. 4, New York/Oxford, 352–54.

Pardee, D. (1997b) 'Proto-Sinaitic' in Meyers, E. M. (ed.) *Oxford Encyclopaedia of Archaeology in the Near East,* Vol. 4, New York/Oxford, 354–355.

Pardee, D. (2007) 'The Ugaritic alphabetic cuneiform writing system in the context of other alphabetic systems' in Miller, C. L. (ed.) *Studies in Semitic and Afroasiatic Linguistics Presented to Gene B. Gragg*, Chicago, 181–200.

Payne, A. (2008) 'Writing systems and identity' in Collins, B. J., Bacharova, M. R. and Rutherford, I. C. (eds) *Anatolian Interfaces. Hittites, Greeks and their Neighbours*, Oxford, 117–122.

Payne, A. (2012) *Iron Age Hieroglyphic Luwian Inscriptions*, Atlanta.

Peirce, C. S. (1931–58) *Collected Writings*, Cambridge, MA.

Pelon, O. (1983) 'L'épée à l'acrobate et la chronologie maliote II', *BCH* 107.1, 679–703.

Perego, E. (2013) 'The other writing: Iconic literacy and situla art in pre-Roman Veneto (Italy)' in Piquette, K. E. and Whitehouse, R. D. (eds) *Writing as Material Practice: Substance, Surface and Medium*, London, 253–270.

Perna, M. (2014) 'The birth of administration and writing in Minoan Crete: some thoughts on hieroglyphics and Linear A' in Nakassis, D., Gulizio, J. and James, S. A. (eds) *KE-RA-ME-JA: Studies Presented to Cynthia W. Shelmerdine,* Philadelphia, 251–259.

Peruzzi, E. (1960) *Le Iscrizioni Minoiche*, Firenze.

Petrakis, V. (2012) 'Reverse phonetisation? From syllabogram to sematogram in Aegean scripts' in Carlier, P., de Lamberterie, C., Egetmeyer, M., Guilleux, N., Rougemont, F. and Zurbach, J. (eds) *Études Mycéniennes 2010* (Biblioteca di Pasiphae 10), Pisa/Roma, 523–536.

Petrakis, V. (2014) 'A tale of system reform: The genesis of the Third Palace Period Aegean literate administrations', *Bulletin of the Institute of Classical Studies* 57.1, 129–130.

Petrakis, V. (forthcoming) 'Figures of speech? Observations on the non-phonographic component in the Linear B writing system' in Landenius-Enegren, H. and Nosch, M.-L. (eds.) *Aegean Scripts. Proceedings of the 14th International Colloquium on Mycenaean Studies, held in Copenhagen, 2–5 September 2015,* Rome.

Petruševski, P. (1979) 'Révision de la transcription des syllabogrammes *17 (*za*), *20 (*zo*), *74 (*ze*) et *79 (*zu*?)' in Risch, E. and Mühlestein, H. (eds) *Colloquium Mycenaeum*, Neuchâtel/Genève, 259–266.

Pierini, R. (2014) 'Ricerche sul segno *25* del sillabario miceneo' in Bernabé, A. and Luján, E. R. (eds) *Donum mycenologicum: Mycenaean studies in honour of Francisco Aura Jorro.* (Bibliothèque des Cahiers de l'Institut de Linguistique de Louvain 131), Louvain-la-Neuve, 105–137.

Pini, I. (1997) *Die Tonplomben aus dem Nestorpalast von Pylos*, Mainz.

Pini, I. (2000) 'Eleven early Cretan scarabs' in Karetsou, A. (ed.) *Kriti-Egyptos. Politismikoi Desmoi Trion Khilietion. Meletes*, Athens, 107–113.

Pini, I. (2002) 'Einleitung', in Gill, M. A. V., Müller, W. and Pini, I. *Corpus der Minoischen und Mykenischen Siegel II.8.1. Iraklion, Archäologisches Museum. Die Siegelabdrücke von Knossos*, Mainz, 1–23.

Pittman, H. (1994) 'Towards an understanding of the role of glyptic imagery in the administrative systems of proto-literate greater Mesopotamia' in Ferioli, P., Fiandra, E., Fissore, G. G. and Frangipane, M. (eds.). *Archives Before Writing*, Turin, 177–210.

Plath, R. (1992) 'Zur Etymologie von homerisch ὀβελός', *Historische Sprachforschung* 105, 243–259.

Pluta, K. M. (2011) Aegean Bronze Age Literacy and its Consequences, unpublished doctoral dissertation, University of Texas at Austin.

Pope, M. (1961–1962) 'The date of Linear B', *Κρητικά Χρονικά. Πεπραγμένα του Α' Κρητολογικού Διεθνούς Συνεδρίου/Proceedings of the First International Cretological Congress, Heraklion 1962*, vol. 1, Heraklion, 310–319.

Pope, M. (1964) *Aegean Writing and Linear A* (Studies in Mediterranean Archaeology monograph 8), Lund.

Pope, M. (1968) 'The First Cretan Palatial Script', *Atti e memorie del primo congresso internazionale di micenologia*, Vol. 1, Rome, 438–447.

Popham, M. (1993) Review of Jan Driessen: *An Early Destruction in the Mycenaean Palace at Knossos*, Leuven, 1990, *Journal of Hellenic Studies* 113, 174–178.

Portugali, Y. and Knapp, A. B. (1985) 'Cyprus and the Aegean: a spatial analysis of interaction in the seventeenth to fourteenth centuries BC' in Knapp, A. B. and Stech, T. (eds) *Prehistoric Production and Exchange in the Aegean and Eastern Mediterranean*, Los Angeles, 44–78.

Postgate, N., Wang, T. and Wilkinson, T. (1995) 'The evidence for early writing: utilitarian or ceremonial?', *Antiquity* 69, 459–480.

Poursat, J. C. (2000) 'Les sceaux hiéroglyphiques dans l'administration minoenne: usage et function' in Perna, M. (ed.) *Administrative Documents in the Aegean and their Near Eastern Counterparts*, Torino, 187–191.

Powell, B. B. (2009) *Writing: Theory and History of the Technology of Civilization*, Oxford.

Preston, L. (2008) 'Late Minoan II to IIIB Crete' in Shelmerdine, C. W. (ed.) *The Cambridge Companion to the Aegean Bronze Age*, Cambridge, 310–326.

Pugliese Carratelli, G. (1945) 'Le iscrizioni preelleniche di Haghia Triada in Creta e della Grecia peninsulare', *Monumenti Antichi dell'Accademia Nazionale dei Lincei* 40, 421–610.

Radner, K. (2010) 'The stele of Sargon II of Assyria at Kition: a focus for an emerging Cypriot identity?' in Rollinger, R. et al. (eds.) *Interkulturalität in der Alten Welt. Vorderasien, Hellas, Ägypten und die vielfältigen Ebenen des Kontakts*, Wiesbaden, 429–449.

Ray, J. D. (1986) 'The emergence of writing in Egypt', *World Archaeology* 17.3, 390–398.

Rehak, P., Younger, J. G. (2000) 'Minoan and Mycenaean administration in the early Late Bronze Age: an overview' in Perna, M. (ed.), *Administrative Documents in the Aegean and their Near Eastern Counterparts*, Turin, 277–307.

Reich, J. J. (1968) 'The rôle of the naturalistic signs in the Minoan hieroglyphic script', *Atti e memorie del primo congresso internazionale di micenologia*, Vol. 1, Rome, 448–461.

Risch, E. (1979) 'Les consonnes palatalisées dans le grec du IIe millénaire et des premiers siècles du Ier millénaire' in Risch, E. and Mühlestein, H. (eds) *Colloquium Mycenaeum*, Neuchâtel/Genève, 267–281.

Ritner, R. K. (1996) 'Egyptian writing', in Daniels, P. D. and Bright, W. (eds) *The World's Writing Systems*, Oxford, 73–87.

Robertson, J. S. (2004) 'The possibility and actuality of writing' In Houston, S. D. (ed.) *The First Writing: Script Invention as History and Process*, Cambridge, 16–38.

Rollston, C. A. (2010) 'The probable inventors of the first alphabet: Semites functioning as rather high status personnel in a component of the Egyptian apparatus', Rollston Epigraphy website: http://www.rollstonepigraphy.com/?p=195.

Rothman, M. S. (1994) 'Seal and sealing findspot, design, audience, and function: Monitoring changes in administrative oversight and structure at Tepe Gawra during the fourth millennium BC' in Ferioli, P., Fiandra, E., Fissore, G. G. and Frangipane, M. (eds.). *Archives Before Writing*, Turin, 97–119.

Ruijgh, C. J. (1967) *Études sur la grammaire et le vocabulaire du grec mycénien*, Amsterdam.

Ruppenstein, F. (2013) 'Cremation burials in Greece from the Late Bronze Age to the Early Iron Age: continuity or change?' in Lochner, M. and Ruppenstein, F. (eds) *Brandbestattungen von der mittleren Donau bis zur Ägäis zwischen 1300 und 750 v. Chr.* (colloquium Vienna 2010), Vienna, 185–196.

Sacconi, A. (1976) 'La scrittura lineare B', *La Parola del Passato* 31, 48–65.

Sacconi, A., and Cultraro, M. (forthcoming) 'Un fragment de vase inscrit de Prinias: PRI Z 1' in Nosch, M.-L.B. and Landenius Enegren, H. (eds) *Aegean Scripts*, Rome.

Sakellarakis, Y. and Sapouna-Sakellaraki, E. (1997) *Archanes. Minoan Crete in New Light*, Athens.

Salomon, R. (2012) 'Some principles and patterns of script change' in Houston, S. D. (ed.) *The Shape of Script. How and Why Writing Systems Change*, Santa Fe, 119–133.

Sampson, G. (1985) *Writing Systems: A Linguistic Introduction*, Stanford.

Sanders, S. L. (2009) *The Invention of Hebrew*, Urbana/Chicago/Springfield.

Saporetti, C. (1976) 'Ipotesi su alcuni segni del sillabario ciprominoico', *Studi Ciprioti e Rapporti di Scavo* 2, 89–108.

Sass, B. (2004–2005) 'The genesis of the alphabet and its development in the second millennium B.C. - Twenty years later', *De Kêmi à Birīt Nāri* 2, 137–156.

Sass, B. (2016) 'Aram and Israel during the 10th–9th centuries BCE, or Iron Age IIA. The alphabet' in Sergi, O., Oeming, M. and de Hulster, I. J. (eds) *In Search for Aram and Israel. Politics, Culture and Identity*, Tübingen.

Sass, B. and Finkelstein, I. (2016) 'The swan-song of proto-Canaanite in the ninth century BCE in light of an alphabetic inscription from Megiddo', *Semitica et Classica* 9.

Schoep, I. (1999) 'The origins of writing and administration on Crete', *Oxford Journal of Archaeology* 18.3, 265–276.

Schoep, I. (2001) 'The role of the Linear A tablets in Minoan administration', *Ktema* 26, 55–62.

Schoep, I. (2002) *The Administration of Neopalatial Crete. A Critical Assessment of the Linear A Tablets and their Role in the Administrative Process* (Supplement to *Minos* 17), Salamanca.

Schoep, I. (2006) 'Looking beyond the First Palaces: Elites and the agency of power in EM III–MM II Crete', *American Journal of Archaeology* 110, 37–64.

Schoep, I. (2007) 'The social and political context of Linear A writing on Crete' in Lomas, K., Whitehouse, R. D. and Wilkins, J. B. (eds) *Literacy and the State in the Ancient Mediterranean* (Accordia Specialist Studies on the Mediterranean 7), London, 53–62.

Shelmerdine, C. W. (2012) 'Iklaina tablet IK X 1' in Carlier, P., de Lamberterie, C., Egetmeyer, M., Guilleux, N., Rougemont, F. and Zurbach, J. (eds) *Études Mycéniennes 2010* (Biblioteca di Pasiphae 10), Pisa/Roma 75–78.

Sherratt, E. S. (2003) 'Visible writing: questions of script and identity in Early Iron Age Greece and Cyprus', *Oxford Journal of Archaeology* 22, 225–42.

Sherratt, E. S. (2013) 'Late Cypriot writing in context' in Steele, P. M. (ed.), *Syllabic Writing on Cyprus and its Context*, Cambridge, 77–105.

Sittig, E. (1956) 'Zur Entzifferung der Minoisch-Kyprischen Tafel von Enkomi', *Minos* 4, 33–44.

Skelton, C. (2009) 'Re-examining the Pylos Megaron tablets', *Kadmos* 48, 107–123.

Smith, A. D. (2013) 'Are writing systems intelligently designed?' in Englehardt, J. (ed.) *Agency in Ancient Writing*, Boulder, 77–93.

Steele, P. M. (2013a) *A Linguistic History of Cyprus: The Non-Greek Languages, and their Relations with Greek, c. 1600–300 BC*, Cambridge.

Steele, P. M. (ed.) (2013b) *Syllabic Writing on Cyprus and its Context*, Cambridge.

Steele, P. M. (2014) 'Distinguishing between Cypriot scripts: Steps towards establishing a methodology', *Kadmos* 53, 129–148.

Steele, P. M. (2016) 'A linguistic approach to population movements to ancient Cyprus' in Maguire, R. and Chick, J. (eds) *Approaching Cyprus* (Proceedings of the post-graduate conference of Cypriot archaeology, University of East Anglia, Norwich, 2013), Cambridge, 2–17.

Steele, P. M. (forthcoming) *Society and Writing in Ancient Cyprus*, Cambridge.

Stephens, L. and Justeson, J. S. (1978) 'Reconstructing "Minoan" phonology: The approach from universals of language and universals of writing systems', *Transactions of the American Philological Association* 108, 271–284.

Stone, A. and Zender, M. (2011) *Reading Maya Art: a Hieroglyphic Guide to Ancient Maya Painting and Sculpture*, London.

Street, B. V. (1984) *Literacy in Theory and Practice*, Cambridge.

Street, B. V. (1993) (ed.). *Cross-Cultural Approaches to Literacy*, Cambridge.

Stuart, D. and Houston, S. (1989) *The Way glyph: Evidence for 'co-essences' among the Classic Maya* (Research Reports on Ancient Maya Writing 30), Washington DC.

Stuart, D. and Houston, S. (1994) *Classic Maya Place Names* (Studies in Pre-Columbian Art and Archaeology 33), Washington DC.

Sznycer, M. (1983) 'Note sur l'inscription gravée sur une cruche de la tombe 69 de Palaepaphos-*Skales*' in Karageorghis, V. (ed.) *Palaepaphos-Skales. An Iron Age cemetry in Cyprus*, Constance, appendix v, 416–417.

Thompson, R. J. E. (2005) 'Two notes on Mycenaean labial stops', *Živa Antika* 55, 107–115.

Thompson, R. J. E. (2012) 'In defence of ideograms' in Carlier, P., de Lamberterie, C., Egetmeyer, M., Guilleux, N., Rougemont, F. and Zurbach, J. (eds) *Études Mycéniennes 2010* (Biblioteca di Pasiphae 10), Pisa/Roma, 545–561.

Tomas, H. (2003) Understanding the Transition between Linear A and Linear B Script, unpublished DPhil Thesis, University of Oxford.

Tomas, H. (2008) 'Comparing Linear A and Linear B administrative systems: the case of the roundel and the elongated tablet' in Sacconi, A., Del Freo, M., Godart, L. and M. Negri (eds) *Colloquium Romanum*, Vol. 2, Pisa/Roma, 767–774.

Tomas, H. (2010) 'Cretan Hieroglyphic and Linear A', in Cline, E. (ed.), *The Oxford Handbook of the Bronze Age Aegean (ca. 3000–1000 BC)*, Oxford/New York, 340–355.

Tomas, H. (2011) 'Linear A tablet ≠ Linear B tablet' in Andreadaki-Vlazaki, M. and Papadopoulou, E. (eds), *Πεπραγμένα του Ι' Κρητολογικού Διεθνούς Συνεδρίου/Proceedings of the 10th Cretological Conference, Chania, 1–8 October 2006*, vol. A1, Chania, 331–343.

Tomas, H. (2012a) 'Linear A scribes and their writing styles' in Kyriakidis, E. (ed.), *The Inner Workings of Mycenaean Bureaucracy* (Pasiphae V/2011), Pisa/Roma, 35–58.

Tomas, H. (2012b), 'The transition from the Linear A to the Linear B sealing system' in Regulski, I, Duistermaat, K., Verkinderen, P. (eds), *Seals and Sealing Practices in the Near East. Developments in Administration and Magic from Prehistory to the Islamic Period.* (*Orientalia Lovaniensia Analecta* 219), Leuven/Paris/Walpole, 33–49.

Tomas, H. (2013) 'Saving on clay: the Linear B practice of cutting tablets' in Piquette, K. E. and Whitehouse, R. D. (eds.), *Writing as Material Practice: Substance, Surface and Medium*, London, 175–191.

Tomas, H. (2014) 'Orality of Linear A, scriptuality of Linear B' in Gordin, S. (ed.), *Visualizing Knowledge and Creating Meaning in Ancient Writing Systems*, Berlin, 101–117.

Tomas, H. (forthcoming) 'From Minoan to Mycenaean elongated tablet' in Landenius-Enegren, H. and Nosch, M.-L. (eds.) *Aegean Scripts. Proceedings of the 14th International Colloquium on Mycenaean Studies, held in Copenhagen, 2–5 September 2015*, Rome.

Topçuoğlu, O. (2010) 'Iconography of protoliterate seals' in Wood, C. (ed.) *Visible Language. Inventions of Writing in the Ancient Middle East and Beyond*, Chicago, 29–32.

Trigger, B. (2004) 'Writing systems. A case study in cultural evolution' in Houston, S. D. (ed.) *The First Writing: Script Invention as History and Process*, Cambridge, 39–68.

Tsipopoulou, M. and Hallager, E. (1996) 'Inscriptions with Hieroglyphs and Linear A from Petras, Siteia', *Studi Micenei ed Egeo-Anatolici* 37, 7–46.

Tsipopoulou, M. and Hallager, E. (2010) *The Hieroglyphic Archive at Petras, Siteia* (Monographs of the Danish Institute at Athens 9), Athens.

Valério, M. (2013) 'Problems of Cypro-Minoan paleography: the case of sign shapes 08, 13 and 78', *Kadmos* 52, 111–134.

Valério, M. (2014a) 'On a new archaeological corpus of Cypro-Minoan inscriptions', *Bibliotheca Orientalis* 71.5–6, 711–716.

Valério, M. (2014b) 'Seven uncollected Cypro-Minoan inscriptions', *Kadmos* 53, 111–127.

Valério, M. (2014c) Review of Steele 2013, *Aula Orientalis* 32, 187–192.

Valério, M. (2016) *Investigating the Signs and Sounds of Cypro-Minoan*, Doctoral Thesis, University of Barcelona. http://diposit.ub.edu/dspace/handle/2445/99521.

Van den Hout, T. (2007) 'Institutions, vernaculars, publics: The case of second-millennium Anatolia' in Sanders, S. L. (ed.) *Margins of Writing, Origins of Culture*, Chicago, 221–262.

Van den Hout, T. (2010) 'The rise and fall of cuneiform script in Hittite Anatolia' in Woods, C. (ed.) *Visible Writing. Inventions of Writing in the Ancient Middle East and Beyond*, Chicago, 99–106.

Vasilogamvrou, A. (forthcoming) 'The West Stoa Archive at Ayios Vasileios: Archaeological context, chronology and preliminary study of the documents' in Landenius-Enegren, H. and Nosch, M.-L.

(eds.) *Aegean Scripts. Proceedings of the 14th International Colloquium on Mycenaean Studies, held in Copenhagen, 2-5 September 2015*, Rome.

Ventris, M. (1956) 'Notes on the Enkomi 1955 tablet' in Dikaios, P. 'A new inscribed clay tablet from Enkomi', *Antiquity* 30(117), 41–42.

Ventris, M. and Chadwick, J. (1953) 'Evidence for Greek dialect in the Mycenaean archives', *Journal of Hellenic Studies* 73, 84–103.

Verdan, S., Kenzelmann Pfyffer, A. and Theurillat, T. (2012) 'Early alphabetic inscriptions from Eretria, Greece. 8th cent. BC graffiti from the sanctuary of Apollo Daphnephoros' in Fuchs, M. E., Sylvestre, R. and Schmidt Heidenreich, C. (eds.) *Inscriptions mineures: nouveautés et réflexions* (colloquium Lausanne 2008), Bern, 179–183.

Warren, P. (1992) 'Knossos revisited' (Review of Jan Driessen: *An Early Destruction in the Mycenaean Palace at Knossos*, Leuven, 1990), *Classical Review* new series 42.1, 137–139.

Webb, J. M. and Weingarten, J. (2012) 'Seals and seal use: Markers of social, political and economic transformations on two islands' in Cadogan, G., Iacovou, M., Kopaka, K. and Whitley, J. (eds.) *Parallel Lives: Ancient Island Societies in Crete and Cyprus* (BSA Studies 20), Athens, 85–104.

Weeden, M. (2014) 'Anatolian hieroglyphs: logogram vs. ideogram' in Gordin, S. (ed.), *Visualizing Knowledge and Creating Meaning in Ancient Writing Systems*, Gladbeck, 81–100.

Weingarten, J. (1986) 'Some unusual Minoan Clay nodules', *Kadmos* 25, 1–21.

Weingarten, J. (1988) 'The sealing structures of Minoan Crete: MM II Phaistos to the destruction of the palace of Knossos. Part II: The evidence from Knossos until the destruction of the palace', *Oxford Journal of Archaeology* 7.1, 1–25.

Weingarten, J. (1990) 'More unusual Minoan clay nodules: Addendum II', *Kadmos* 29, 16–23.

Weingarten, J. (1995) 'Sealing studies in the Middle Bronze Age III: the Minoan hieroglyphic deposits at Mallia and Knossos' in Müller, W. (ed.) *Sceaux minoens et mycéniens* (*CMS* 5), Berlin, 285–311.

Weingarten, J. (2000) 'The transformation of Egyptian Taweret into the Minoan genius' in Karetsou, A. (ed.) *Krete-Aigyptos. Politismikoi desmoi trion chilietion*, Athens, 114–119.

Weingarten, J. (2005) 'How many seals make a heap: Seals and interconnections on Prepalatial Crete' in Laffineur, R. and Greco, E. (eds) *Emporia. Aegeans in the Central and Eastern Mediterranean* (*Aegaeum* 25. II), Liège, 759–766.

West, M. (2013) *The Epic Cycle. A Commentary on the Lost Troy Epics*, Oxford.

Wiener, M. H., Friedrich, W. L. and Manning, S. W. (2009) 'Thera Discussion' in Manning, S. W. and Bruce, M. J. (eds) *Tree-Rings, Kings, and Old World Archaeology and Environment: Papers Presented in Honor of Peter Ian Kuniholm*, Oxford, 316–332.

Wengrow, D. (2008) 'Prehistories of commodity branding', *Current Anthropology* 49, 7–34.

Woodard, R. (2014) *The Textualization of the Greek Alphabet*, Cambridge.

Woods, C. (2010) 'The earliest Mesopotamian writing' in Woods, C. (ed.) *Visible Writing. Inventions of Writing in the Ancient Middle East and Beyond*, Chicago, 33–50.

Yakubovich, I. (2008) 'Hittite-Luvian bilingualism and the development of Anatolian Hieroglyphs' in Kazansky, N. N. (ed.) *Colloquia Classica et Indo-Germanica IV. Studies in Classical Philology and Indo-European Languages*, St Petersburg, 9–36.

Yakubovich, I. (2010) 'Anatolian hieroglyphic writings' in Woods, C. (ed.) *Visible Writing. Inventions of Writing in the Ancient Middle East and Beyond*, Chicago, 203–206.

Yakubovich, I. (2011) 'Luwian and the Luwians' in Steadman, S. R. and McMahon, G. (eds) *The Oxford Handbook of Ancient Anatolia 10,000-323 B.C.E.*, Oxford, 534–537.

Yon, M. (2004) *Kition dans les textes. Kition Bamboula V*, Testimonia *littéraires et épigraphiques et* Corpus *des inscriptions*, Paris.

Younger, J. (1990) 'New observations on hieroglyphic seals', *Studi Micenei ed Egeo-Anatolici* 28, 85–93.

Younger, J. (1998) 'The Cretan Hieroglyphic script: A review article', *Minos* 31–32 (1996–1997), 379–400.

Younger, J. G. (2003) 'Cretan Hieroglyphic transaction terms: "total paid" and "total owed"' in Duhoux, Y. (ed.) *Briciaka. A Tribute to W.C. Brice.* (*Cretan Studies* 9), Amsterdam, 301–316.

Younger, J. (2015) Book review of S. Ferrara *Cypro-Minoan Inscriptions. Vol. 1, Analysis. American Journal of Archaeology* 119.3. http://www.ajaonline.org/online-review-book/2169.

Younger, J. G. (Cretan Hieroglyphic website) The Cretan Hieroglyphic Texts, http://people.ku.edu/~jyounger/Hiero/index.html, accessed July 2015.

Younger, J. G. (Linear A website) Linear A Texts in phonetic transcription & Commentary, http://people.ku.edu/~jyounger/LinearA/, accessed July 2015.

Yule, P. (1980) *Early Cretan Seals: A Study of Chronology*, Mainz.

Zahn, R. (1901) 'Sitzungsberichte Der Archäologische Gesellschaft Zu Berlin: Marz', *Archäologischer Anzeiger*, Berlin, 19–25.